A Biographical Dictionary of World War II

A Biographical Dictionary of World War II

Christopher Tunney

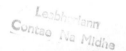

J. M. Dent & Sons Ltd   London

First published 1972

© **Christopher Tunney 1972**

Made in Great Britain
at the
Aldine Press · Letchworth · Herts
for
J. M. DENT & SONS LTD
Aldine House · Bedford Street · London

ISBN 0 460 03868 0

Preface

Most of the people who have entries in this volume made noteworthy contributions to what, in the parlance of the event, was known as 'the prosecution of the war'; their war-time activities—as soldiers, sailors, or airmen, perhaps, or as secret agents, politicians, or propagandists—were essentially warlike. Others played a role that was less obviously military as, for example, entertainers, journalists, or poets. Some others were actively opposed to the war, as conscientious objectors or as determined neutralists. Many were persons of great and lasting distinction; others were heroes or villains of a day. But all helped to create and sustain the miasma and spirit of war time: that electric product of out-of-the-ordinary fears, hopes, and activities.

Though the dictionary is intended primarily as a work of reference, it is also a book to be read or dipped into. Wars throw up interesting characters, and in the compilation of the biographies points of interest were welcomed wherever they did not appear to conflict with accuracy. Throughout, the narrative approach was preferred to the critical, and it is hoped that something of the feeling and flavour of the time can be detected in the interstices of fact.

No inflexible criteria were adopted in deciding who should have entries. Most of the subjects were included because their names occur frequently in the literature of the time, but others were selected precisely because little was known of them while the war was being fought even though their contributions were considerable or particularly interesting. A number of opinions were sought on the entries that should appear; these opinions, useful and greatly appreciated though they were, were distinguished by their lack of unanimity.

In war time, people experience a lifetime within a lifetime; as a general rule the subjects of the biographies have been accorded no existence that extends beyond the end of the war. Thus the entry on Lord Mountbatten is concerned with the exploits of 'Lord Louis' and 'Supremo' and makes no mention of the 'Last Viceroy' or even of 'Earl Mountbatten of Burma'. This restriction is deliberate: to have included post-war material would have made the book less true to its

purpose and would have lessened its value as a record of a definable
period. The lengths of the various biographies are not intended to
reflect the worthiness of their subjects; in many instances the length
of an entry was affected to some extent by the amount of material
available or by its nature, in particular by its interest or lack of
interest.

C. T.

Author's Acknowledgments

Grateful acknowledgment is made of the valuable and pleasant co-operation of the late Commander Robin Bousfield R.N. in the preparation of this volume.

I am also indebted to Dr Irwin Hermann who cheerfully and efficiently shared much of the toil and burden of the day, and to many contributors, researchers and librarians: in particular to Mr S. Adelson, Mr A. Allan, Mr A. M. Barnett, Mr G. C. Best, Miss Honor Biggs, Miss E. Cameron-Kirby, Mrs Patricia Ede, Miss Muriel Grieve, Mr M. D. Freedman, Mr R. MacDonald, Miss Gillian Mather, Mr C. E. T. Moore, Miss C. R. Morrison, Mr Michael Northey, Mrs V. Proctor, Mrs Emma Shackle and Mrs J. Vidal Hall.

To my publishers I owe an especial debt for helpful suggestions and feats of detection in a world of conflicting information.

Abbreviations, Contractions, etc.

A.A.	anti-aircraft	OSS	Office of Strategic Services
A.D.C.	aide-de-camp	'Overlord'	Allied invasion of Normandy, 6 June 1944
A.I.F.	Australian Imperial Force		
Anzac	Australian and New Zealand Army Corps. The word specifically refers to the Australian and New Zealand troops in Gallipoli in World War I, but it was also sometimes used in World War II to refer to Australian and New Zealand troops	Pluto	Pipeline Under the Ocean
		P.O.W.	prisoner-of-war
		R.A.A.F.	Royal Australian Air Force
		R.A.F.	Royal Air Force
		R.A.P.W.I.	Recovery of Allied Prisoners-of-War and Internees
		R.A.S.C.	Royal Army Service Corps
		R.C.A.F.	Royal Canadian Air Force
		R.N.	Royal Navy
A.O.C. (-in-C.)	Air Officer Commanding (-in-Chief)	S.A.	*Sturmabteilungen* (German: Storm Troops)
A.R.P.	Air Raid Precautions	S.A.S.	Special Air Service
A.T.S.	Auxiliary Territorial Service	S.D.	*Sicherheitsdienst* (German: Security Service of the S.S.)
B.B.C.	British Broadcasting Corporation		
		S.E.A.C.	South East Asia Command
B.E.F.	British Expeditionary Force	S.H.A.E.F.	Supreme Headquarters, Allied Expeditionary Force
B.L.A.	British Liberation Army		
C.G.S.	Chief of the General Staff	S.O.E.	Special Operations Executive
C.I.G.S.	Chief of the Imperial General Staff	S.S.	*Schutzstaffel* (German: Guard Detachment)
C.-in-C.	Commander-in-Chief		
D.B.E.	Dame Commander of the Order of the British Empire	T.U.C.	Trade Union Congress
		U.K.	United Kingdom
		U.S.A.	United States of America
D.F.C.	Distinguished Flying Cross	US(A)AF	United States (Army) Air Force
D.F.M.	Distinguished Flying Medal		
D.S.O.	Distinguished Service Order	USN	United States Navy
D-Day	6 June 1944—the Allied landing in Normandy	USS	United States Ship
		V-1	*Vergeltungswaffe 1*—the German flying bomb
E.N.S.A.	Entertainments National Service Association		
		V-2	*Vergeltungswaffe 2*—the German explosive rocket
Gestapo	*Geheimestaatspolizei* (Secret State Police)		
		V.C.	Victoria Cross
G.C.	George Cross	VE-Day	Victory in Europe Day (8 May 1945)
G.O.C. (-in-C.)	General Officer Commanding (-in-Chief)		
		VJ-Day	Victory over Japan Day (2 September 1945)
H.M.S.	His Majesty's Ship		
H.Q.	Headquarters	W.A.A.F.	Women's Auxiliary Air Force
M.C.	Military Cross	W.R.N.S.	Women's Royal Naval Service
M.P.	Member of Parliament	W.V.S.	Women's Voluntary Service
M.T.B.	motor torpedo boat		
Nazi	Term used in relation to the *Nationalsozialistische Deutsche Arbeiterpartei* (National Socialist German Workers' Party), led by Adolf Hitler		

A

ALANBROOKE, Viscount. *See* BROOKE, Sir Alan.

ALEXANDER, Sir Harold, b. 1891.
British general (field marshal, 1944) and one of the most outstanding commanders of the war, who was constantly called upon to 'save the day' and emerged successfully.

Alexander went to France with the B.E.F. as commander of the 1st Division at the beginning of the war. In the withdrawal from Dunkirk he was selected to command the last corps to remain on the beaches when Lord Gort was recalled. He then took over Southern Command in the U.K. and distinguished himself in the urgent training of new armies. When Japan invaded Burma in early 1942 Alexander was sent out to command the retreating British forces. Against superior air power, and an enemy particularly skilled in jungle warfare, he conducted a strategic withdrawal to Assam.

Appointed C.-in-C. Middle East in August of 1942, he directed the great campaigns in North Africa during which Montgomery's 8th Army achieved signal success over Rommel's Afrika Korps. It was agreed at the Casablanca Conference in January 1943 that General Eisenhower should become Supreme Allied Commander in North Africa when the 8th Army entered Tunisia from Tripolitania. Alexander was to be his Deputy and to command 18th Army Group, comprising all the Allied land forces—British, American, and French—in North Africa. He assumed this command in February. By May all the Axis forces had been cleared from North Africa. After that Alexander commanded the forces that invaded Sicily, and in September the invasion of the Italian mainland began. Alexander had a numerically superior enemy, in spite of Italy's surrender in September 1943, and it was easier for the Germans than for the Allies to reinforce when and where necessary. Thus it was the more irksome to have landing craft taken from him for the coming Allied invasion of N.W. Europe, because Italy's coast offered opportunity for flanking operations. The Anzio operation was not an immediate success, but it drew away German forces from N.W. Europe. Rome was taken as D-Day came, in June 1944, and then began the bitter Gothic Line assault.

In December 1944 Alexander succeeded Maitland Wilson as Supreme Allied Commander, Mediterranean Forces. Some of his experienced troops were taken from him for the operations in N.W. Europe and southern France; but Alexander's vigorous offensive in April 1945, from the Po valley northwards, forced the Germans to surrender. By 2 May the battle for Italy was over and Alexander's heterogeneous command—British, Americans, New Zealanders, South Africans, Frenchmen, Indians, Poles, Jews, Brazilians, liberated Italians, and others—was victorious. The campaign on the Italian mainland lasted for twenty months.

Alexander, the 3rd son of the 4th Earl of Caledon, was commissioned in the Irish Guards. He served in World War I, and saw action on the N.W. Frontier of India as a brigadier in the 1930s. He was well known for his imperturbability and charm.

AMERY, Leopold, b. 1873. British politician, who became Secretary of State for India and Burma during the war after Winston Churchill, his friend from schooldays at Harrow, had become Prime Minister. As such, his immediate concern was to satisfy Churchill that India's military manpower was being trained and directed to theatres of war with proper urgency. During the first year very little had been done, and too many trained British troops were being retained in India, although the U.K. was facing invasion. Later, when Japan was proving a threat to India, a special committee was formed in February 1942 to advise Churchill on Indian politics, Amery being the only Conservative member of this committee.

Before the war Amery, realizing that Germany was arming dangerously fast, had backed Churchill in warning ministers and M.P.s of Great Britain's need to arm. In the great Parliamentary debate of 7 May 1940 Amery, addressing Chamberlain from the government benches, quoted Cromwell's words: 'Depart, I say, and let us have done with you. In the name of God, go!'

ANDERSON, Sir John, b. 1882. British Home Secretary and Minister of Home Security at the beginning of the war, whose name became a household word because of the 'Anderson shelter', a simple air-raid shelter which was distributed to families in areas vulnerable to bombing; erected in back gardens, it was made of concrete, corrugated iron, and earth. It saved thousands of lives during air raids.

As Lord President of the Council, 1940–3, Anderson was chairman of the committee which concerted plans of government departments over the whole range of economic policy. This relieved Churchill of economic and home front problems. From the end of 1941 Anderson and Ernest Bevin, Minister of Labour, were responsible for the Manpower Committee which, as Churchill said, 'served us in good stead up to the end of the war, and enabled us to mobilize for war work, at home or in the field, a larger proportion of our men and women than any other country in the world in this or any previous war'.

In February 1942 Anderson served on a Cabinet committee to advise Churchill of significant feelings and movements in India. This was followed by the Cripps mission to India in the following month, and in August he was made responsible to the Cabinet for the supervision of 'Tube Alloys', the British project for developing an atomic bomb. From 1943 to 1945 he was Chancellor of the Exchequer.

ANDERSON, Sir Kenneth, b. 1891. British general who played a leading part in the later operations in North Africa. Anderson went to France with the B.E.F. at the beginning of the war as commander of the 11th Infantry Brigade. Later he commanded the 3rd Division at Dunkirk. In the summer of 1942 the death of General Gott in the Western Desert caused changes in command in that theatre, and Anderson was chosen to command the British 1st Army in the occupation of N.W. Africa, under the overall command of General Eisenhower. The Germans reinforced their strength in Algeria and Tunis and severely tested Anderson's forces. Under him were many untried troops, including American forces having to learn the hard way, and Anderson did not escape criticism from both Churchill

and General Alexander. But, despite setbacks, victory in North Africa was achieved by May 1943, when all German resistance in Tunisia ceased.

From June 1943 to January 1944 Anderson commanded the 2nd Army in the U.K., a post in which he was succeeded by General Dempsey, and for most of 1944 he was G.O.C. Eastern Command, after which he became G.O.C.-in-C. East Africa.

AOSTA, Duke of, b. 1898, a cousin of the King of Italy, Governor-General of Italian East Africa, and Italian Viceroy of Ethiopia when the war began. He was also C.-in-C. of the Italian forces in that area. On 4 August 1940 he invaded British Somaliland and forced the British to evacuate by 19 August. Aosta's fortunes began to decline when in January 1941 the exiled Ethiopian Emperor, Haile Selassie, crossed the frontier of his country at the head of a patriot army. The Emperor was supported by Allied troops, including 'Gideon Force', commanded by Orde Wingate, a force under General Alan Cunningham, directed through Italian Somaliland into southern Ethiopia, and a force under General Platt directed from the Sudan into Eritrea. The Allies achieved a series of spectacular successes, and in April the Emperor's capital, Addis Ababa, was captured. On 16 May Aosta surrendered at Amba Alagi with more than 18,000 troops; but the Ethiopian campaign did not come to an end until November, when Gondar was taken. Aosta died in 1942 while a P.O.W. in Nairobi, Kenya.

Churchill described him thus: 'A chivalrous and cultivated man, partly educated in England and married to a French princess, he was not popular with Mussolini. The Duce regarded him with some justification as lacking in ruthlessness and commanding military ability.'

APPLEYARD, John, b. 1916. British Commando leader. He began the war as an officer in the R.A.S.C. and after the fall of France was among the first to join the Commandos. In amphibious operations he took part in the capture of a large German liner, and in the late summer of 1941 explored Vichy French coastal areas of West Africa to ascertain whether German submarines were operating from there. The

Commando base was a Brixham trawler, *Maid of Honour*.

In 1942 he trained for a small-scale raiding force, making many landings on the coast of France using launches and other small boats. There were many casualties, and he himself was wounded.

In 1943, as a major, he carried out airborne and submarine operations from Malta, including a close reconnaissance of Pantellaria. His information was valuable to General Alexander, who in June took possession of the island.

On the night of 12–13 July 1943 he was in a plane which dropped parachute Commando troops into northern Sicily, but the plane did not return and he was presumed killed.

ARNOLD, Henry H., b. 1886. American air general who commanded the USAAF in all theatres throughout the world. He was a member of the American Joint Chiefs of Staff Committee and of the Combined Chiefs of Staff Committee of the Allies.

A strong opponent of isolationism, Arnold had advocated support for the Allies from the beginning of the conflict in Europe. He believed that the struggle involved American interests, and that the U.S.A. might find itself actively involved. For this reason, from the time of his appointment as head of the air forces in 1938, he worked for increased status for the air arm, since it seemed evident to him that in any future conflict air power must be a deciding factor. In the event, Arnold's dream of equality in the U.S. Services between the air forces, army, and navy was not realized until the war was over, but the amazing power developed by the American air forces in the later stages of the war was in large measure due to his work.

His nickname 'Hap', short for 'Happy', aptly described his nature. His gay and stalwart personality made him extremely popular with his colleagues in many nations, and he had the gift of disguising his formidable knowledge of the technicalities of his profession behind a humorous approach. In 1944 he was promoted to the new rank of general of the army, later altered to general of the air force.

ATTLEE, Clement, b. 1883. British states-man, leader of the Labour party. After having been Churchill's deputy for the greater part of the war, he himself was Prime Minister during the closing stages of the war against Japan.

Churchill found in Attlee a staunch and reliable deputy able to carry the Prime Minister's immense burdens at home while Churchill himself was abroad. There is no question but that Attlee and Ernest Bevin were largely instrumental in keeping the U.K. free from labour troubles during the war.

General Ismay summed up Attlee's war service by saying: 'He was brave, wise, decisive, and completely loyal to Churchill. His integrity was absolute and no thought of personal ambition seemed to enter his mind. His appearance was deceptive: he looked somewhat meek and mild; that he was neither has been proved by his record during two world wars and as Prime Minister from 1945. He was a great servant of his country.'

Inspired by his original dedication to the youth of the East End of London and to his lifelong work for social justice, Attlee's dry and unimpressive manner concealed an astute brain and an ability to see the wood despite the trees. Some of his qualities showed to best advantage in committee, and he has been described as the perfect chairman. Immediately after becoming Prime Minister he had the difficult task of taking over from Churchill at the Potsdam Conference.

AUCHINLECK, Sir Claude, b. 1884. British general who was C.-in-C. Middle East from July 1941 until August 1942, and who was C.-in-C. India in 1941 and again after 1943. Auchinleck, known as 'the Auk', was one of the outstanding generals of the war.

In 1940 he was G.O.C.-in-C. Northern Norway, and then G.O.C. Southern Command; in 1941 he was appointed C.-in-C. India. In May 1941 General Wavell, C.-in-C. Middle East, was hard pressed by the Iraqi army and wanted to negotiate; Churchill would not allow this. Auchinleck sent an Indian division without delay so that the situation was saved and Iraq and Syria prevented from going over to the Axis. On 22 June 1941 Churchill appointed Auchinleck to succeed Wavell. At this period the Germans were advancing deep into Russia, and Rommel was threatening the borders of Egypt. Churchill wanted swift action in the desert, but Auchinleck was more concerned with Syria. He posted a new division of British troops to Cyprus and in fact delayed his attack against Rommel for months. 'Crusader', the desert offensive, began on 18 November 1941 and tremendous tank battles were fought southeast of Tobruk, the garrison of which eventually made contact with the New Zealanders. The German tanks were superior and inflicted great losses, but the British had superior air power. Allied naval and air cover from Malta destroyed numerous ships supplying the Germans and Italians. With the battles not going well enough Auchinleck decided to change the command of the 8th Army, replacing General Cunningham with General Ritchie in November 1941, but finally took over command himself in June of the following year. Meanwhile German submarines had been switched from the Atlantic to the Mediterranean. In November 1941 H.M.S. *Ark Royal* and H.M.S. *Barham* were sunk, and in December H.M.S. *Queen Elizabeth* and H.M.S. *Valiant* were severely damaged in Alexandria harbour.

Tobruk was relieved on 10 December, about the time that a dash eastwards by Rommel threatened the Nile delta; but Rommel was forced back beyond Tobruk. The British took Benghazi on 24 December, and finally Rommel retreated to El Agheila, 60 miles south of Benghazi. Both sides were exhausted, but Rommel had the advantage of the supply line from Tripoli. The British had lost sea and air superiority, and had vastly extended lines of

communication. Rommel allowed no time for remedies and on 21 January 1942 attacked the 8th Army and forced it to retreat. Benghazi fell on 29 January, giving the Germans enormous abandoned supplies and a port close to the new line at Tmimi, 60 miles west of Tobruk. Here the armies stood until May. Churchill, very anxious about Malta, urged Auchinleck to attack, but Auchinleck was convinced that his forces were too weak to attack to the west, as well as hold the Middle East.

On 27 May 1942 Rommel began an offensive with the purpose of taking Tobruk. By mid June the British were in rapid retreat and on 21 June Tobruk surrendered. On 25 June Auchinleck assumed direct command of the 8th Army and by the end of the month he held the corridor of El Alamein between the coast and the Qattara Depression where a sea of sand prevented tank mobility. In the first days of July Rommel tried to break through, and then Auchinleck made a limited counter-attack. Neither side seemed able to exert much force. Churchill visited Cairo for the week of 4–10 August, accompanied by Generals Brooke, Smuts, and Wavell, and the result was the replacement of Auchinleck by General Alexander. The command of the 8th Army went to General Montgomery. General Gott had been appointed to the 8th Army, but had been killed in the air 2 days after Churchill had seen him.

Auchinleck returned to India in 1943, where he provided invaluable support for S.E.A.C. during the campaign against the Japanese.

AVON, Earl of. *See* EDEN, Anthony.

B

BADER, Douglas, b. 1910. British airman who became legendary for his skill, bravery, and triumph over disability during the Battle of Britain and after.

Bader was commissioned into the R.A.F. in 1930. In December 1931 he lost both legs in a flying accident and in 1933 he was invalided out of the R.A.F. in spite of his protests. He mastered his artificial legs with the determination to keep flying. In November 1939 he rejoined and was passed for flying. He was given command of Fighter Squadron 242 in June 1940. By the end of the Battle of Britain his leadership was seen to be so outstanding that he was commanding 5 squadrons (over 60 fighters) in 12 Group Wing. On 30 August 1940 242 Squadron destroyed 12 enemy bombers without loss and on 15 September the 5 squadrons of 12 Group Wing claimed 52 victims with 8 more probables. Similar triumphs were scored on 18 September and 27 September.

Bader constantly complained that because of the deficiency of the warning system he was sent up too late for maximum effect. His particular method was to break up enemy formations by diving into their midst. He also understood his enemy. The Germans always flew from the sun's direction; consequently Bader liked to get into that position first, sometimes ignoring ground control to anticipate the action.

On 9 August 1941 he collided with an enemy aircraft over Béthune and found he had no plane behind the cockpit. He was captured, and escaped from St Omer hospital but was soon recaptured. He was treated with great respect by the Luftwaffe, and the Germans even allowed the R.A.F. to drop a new pair of artifical legs to him by parachute.

BADOGLIO, Pietro, b. 1871. Italian general, Chief of Staff from early in the war until December 1940, when he resigned as a result of Italy's failures in the invasion of Greece.

Badoglio had fought as an artillery officer in the Italo-Ethiopian War of 1896–7, and later in the Italo-Turkish War. A pronounced anti-Fascist, he became Prime Minister of Italy on 25 July 1943 after the fall of Mussolini, an event that he had helped to bring about. In September 1943 Italy surrendered unconditionally to the Allies and on 13 October declared war on Germany. Badoglio signed the 'unconditional surrender' at Malta on 28 September 1943. He had hoped to be spared this, but the Allied commanders who received him insisted that the ceremony was formal and would admit of no discussion. The day ended with a visit to units of the Italian fleet anchored in Malta harbour. Badoglio resigned his office in June 1944.

BALBO, Italo, b. 1896. One of the more colourful and aggressive figures of the Italian Fascist movement. His popularity among the Italians incurred the jealousy of Mussolini, for whom, in turn, Balbo had little respect; he often referred to the Duce in contemptuous terms.

Balbo, who was well known as an aviator and had been Minister of Aviation, was appointed Governor of Libya, Italy's North African colony, in 1936. He disliked and mistrusted the Germans, and openly criticized Mussolini's Axis pact with Hitler. To the end he tried to keep Mussolini from declaring war; in June 1940 Mussolini told him personally that he would not do so. Shortly after Italy entered the war, Balbo was killed when the aeroplane in which he was returning to Libya was shot down, near Tobruk—by mistake, and by the Italians.

BARUCH, Bernard, b. 1870. American government adviser on economics. Although he did good work in a number of public posts, he never held Cabinet rank. He was essentially a man of influence, not of office—the confidant of those in power rather than powerful himself. He was often summoned to Washington for advice and the first members of Roosevelt's brains trust included a number of 'Baruch men'. Although a Democrat, he was con-servatively inclined and disapproved of the more radical experiments of the New Deal. He did, however, share the President's apprehensions of the growing menace of Nazi Germany and conveyed Churchill's views of the European situation to him. The American involvement in World War II seemed to give Baruch the opportunity to repeat his performance in World War I as the mobilizer of American industry. He

5

became special adviser to James F. Byrnes, the Director of Economic Stabilization and later Director of War Mobilization. His counsel was held in great esteem by many people and General Eisenhower wrote: 'If Mr Baruch's recommendations for universal price-fixing and his organizational plans had been completely and promptly adopted in December 1941 this country would have been saved billions in money—possibly much in time, and therefore in lives.' It is a measure of his stature that, at the outbreak of war, he was known as 'Elder Statesman Number One'.

Baruch had tremendous success as a speculator and was one of the few people who liquidated their holdings before the Wall Street crash in 1929. In 1919 he had been at Versailles, where he had met Churchill, who became a close and enduring friend. Churchill's admiration for Baruch can be gauged from the following prediction only partly altered by events: 'War is coming very soon. We will be in it and you (the U.S.A.) will be in it. You (Baruch) will be running the show over there, but I will be on the sidelines over here.'

BASNA, Elias. *See* 'CICERO'.

BEAVERBROOK, Lord (Maxwell Aitken), b. 1879. Canadian-born British newspaper owner and politician who succeeded in greatly increasing the production of aircraft for the R.A.F. in the crucial days of 1940. A strong personality who aroused much disagreement, Beaverbrook was an old friend of Churchill, who appointed him Minister of Aircraft Production in 1940. In August of the same year he joined the War Cabinet. In 1941 he was Minister of State, between 1941 and 1942 Minister of Supply, and from 1943 to 1945 Lord Privy Seal. In 1942 Beaverbrook was also the British Lend-Lease administrator in the U.S.A. and before this had led the Anglo-American mission to Moscow in 1941, which made the agreement for the supply of war materials to Russia.

In the early summer of 1940 Britain urgently needed military aircraft of every kind. To deal with this desperate situation the Air Ministry's Research and Production departments were merged into a single Ministry of Aircraft Production, with Beaverbrook at its head. The

'buccaneering' tactics which some had earlier criticized were now his most valuable asset. The figures speak for themselves: in February 1940 aircraft production lagged far behind schedule; by August it was not merely up to schedule but had overtaken it. In these months total production figures increased from 850 aircraft to more than 2,000. Beaverbrook had the people and the government behind him, but he had the talent to use these advantages to the full. In the long run his methods—reliance on personal initiative and 'hunches', the short cutting of all bureaucratic delays, and meticulous planning—might, as some argued, lead to confusion and loss of production. But in 1940, the hour of need, his methods worked superbly.

BECK, Ludwig, b. 1880. German general, one of the most capable and respected of Germany's military leaders, and a leading member of the 1944 plot to assassinate Hitler. From 1933 to 1938 he was involved in the rebuilding of the German army (forbidden by the Treaty of Versailles after World War I) and made a major contribution towards transforming it once more into a strong fighting force. In 1938 he was appointed Chief of the General Staff, but he resigned the same year in protest against the increasing power of the S.S. in the army, and because he thought that the army was not ready for Hitler's invasion of Czechoslovakia. From then on he was one of Hitler's leading opponents.

Beck's reasons for opposing Hitler are open to question, and have been criticized by some historians of the period. At first, his opposition seems to have been based on his belief that Hitler was pushing Germany towards a war for which her army was not adequate, But he did not oppose war in itself, regarding it, in traditional style, as an extension of politics, to be used when all other means had failed. He was pleased at the rebirth of German military strength and the return to favour of the old military aristocracy—though he was not a Prussian but a Rhinelander. He was an intellectual, and, unlike most of his colleagues, was well aware of the overall state of Europe. He thought Hitler's policy of total war deplorable and dangerous, claiming that it would 'create more bad men than it would eliminate'. More and more, Beck came to regard National Socialism and its founder as a national disaster for Germany, and devoted his strength to resisting what he saw as Hitler's 'un-Prussian' dictatorship. He was convinced that Hitler was unable to foresee the most obvious results of his aggression. In 1942, when Fabian von Schlabrendorff, one of the anti-Hitler plotters, mentioned to him how downcast some of the army leaders were about the progress of the war in Russia, Beck remarked: 'This war was lost before a shot was fired.'

Whatever his reasons, Beck was without question sincere in his opposition to Hitler and tireless in contacting military and civilian opponents of his rule. With Karl Goerdeler, the civilian leader of the Resistance, he organized constructive conservative opposition. Many plots were hatched in the anti-Nazi 'Wednesday club', which Beck joined soon after it was formed.

By 1944 Beck had gained support from many army leaders for the assassination plot. He was accepted as the nominal head of the military side of the plot, but Stauffenberg was the effective leader of the conspirators. The final failure was not caused by any incompetence on Beck's part, but by lack of decisive action in key places when the moment came. The confessions of the captured plotters incriminated Beck and, to avoid certain execution, he took his own life.

BEDFORD, 12th Duke of, b. 1888. His opinions about the causes and nature of war succeeded in making the 12th Duke of Bedford into a notorious public figure, and he was even accused of being pro-Nazi. A month after the outbreak of war he joined a new organization styling itself the British Council for Christian Settlement in Europe, which had John Beckett, a former member of the British Union of Fascists, as secretary. There was a first-class row in Parliament, during which the Home Secretary, Sir John Anderson, made it clear that the new organization was being closely watched and, indeed, some of the people connected with it spent most of the war as detainees in Brixton Prison. One of the duke's most astonishing

exploits was to conduct a private peace offensive with the German Legation in Dublin. He passed on the German terms to Lord Halifax, who described his action as 'rather irregular' but granted permission to him to visit Dublin to see if the terms were genuine. This he did, in February 1940, only to find that the Germans were becoming evasive. When the story reached the press a political storm duly broke over his head. In 1941 he announced his intention of leaving the Church of England because, as a body, it supported the war, and he cut off his stipend to Woburn church. He ran a periodical called *Peace News*, in which as late as 1941 he was still writing of Hitler as 'an untested man whom it is neither necessary, sensible nor right to quarrel with until he has been tested by the one test which to me is worth anything, that of wise, practical and genuine friendliness'. He was in continuous trouble with the War Agricultural Committee about the valuable herds of rare animals in Woburn Park and was accused of diverting quantities of fodder for their upkeep, and of refusing to plough up enough land for productive purposes.

Just before the war Bedford warned of the dangers of an alliance with France and of the inadequacy of the great majority of political leaders to weigh the grave moral and practical issues. During the summer of 1939 he took the step, finally disastrous for his reputation, of becoming chairman and founder member of a new political party called the British People's Party. His attitude and public pronouncements earned him criticism in the press, and he got into further trouble, just before war broke out, by writing letters making disparaging remarks about the Poles.

BELFRAGE, Bruce, b. 1901. B.B.C. announcer, one of the small team of news-readers with whose voices the British public was familiarized as a safeguard against impersonation in the event of invasion. In opening a news broadcast he would say, in what Winston Churchill called 'the fruity port-wine voice of Bruce Belfrage': 'Here is the news, and this is Bruce Belfrage reading it.' This individual manner of introducing the news soon made the announcers national figures.

Belfrage's renown was greatly increased when, on 4 October 1940, a bomb exploded in the upper floors of Broadcasting House while he was reading the nine o'clock news in a basement studio. The explosion was clearly heard by listeners; there was a brief silence and then, after some words of reassurance by another voice, Belfrage continued reading the news, apparently unperturbed.

Belfrage also participated in the propaganda broadcasts which were being put out by the B.B.C. 24 hours a day in 35 languages, and he was one of the newsreaders to whom the Dutch Government later presented plaques expressing gratitude for the 'fortitude and consolation given to the Netherlands in years of oppression'.

In the later years of the war Belfrage spent much time lecturing on Security to R.N. personnel. After D-Day he was lent to the Royal Indian Navy and gave Security lectures throughout India and S.E.A.C.

BELISHA. *See* HORE-BELISHA, Leslie.

BENEŠ, Eduard, b. 1884. Czech patriot, statesman, and President of the war-time Czech government in exile. Under pressure from Hitler, Beneš resigned the Presidency of Czechoslovakia shortly after the Munich agreement in September 1938, and left the country for the West. He played a major part in organizing the Czech National Committee after Hitler's invasion of Czechoslovakia in March 1939, and resumed the office of president in the exiled Czech government set up first in Paris—where it declared war on Germany in October 1939—and later in London. The British government provisionally recognized his government in July 1940, and all the Allied powers had given it full recognition by the end of 1942. As he had done in World War I, Beneš proceeded to build up an army and air force from the ranks of the Czech refugees, and succeeded in establishing a Czechoslovak brigade in the British army. Czech airmen, fighting in national units, played a valued part in the Battle of Britain, thanks largely to his initiative. Beneš also persuaded the British government and de Gaulle's Free French movement to renounce the Munich

settlement, and to pledge that Czechoslovakia's post-war boundaries would not be subject to its concessions.

In 1942 Beneš was assured of Russian support from Molotov, the Soviet Commissar for Foreign Affairs, and a Czechoslovak brigade was formed in the Red army. In 1943 Beneš paid a state visit to Washington, where he addressed both Houses of Congress; this honour was echoed in Canada, where he spoke before Parliament. Later that year he went to Moscow, where he signed a treaty of mutual assistance with Stalin that promised close post-war co-operation. The Russian army reached the borders of Czechoslovakia in 1944, and in April 1945 Beneš established a temporary H.Q. of the restored Czech government in Kosice, Slovakia. He re-entered Prague on 16 May 1945 to a rapturous welcome.

BENNETT, Donald, b. 1910. Australian-born R.A.F. officer who founded the 'Pathfinder Force'—airmen who flew ahead of bombing forces and marked the targets to be attacked. At the outbreak of the war he was a civilian pilot and in this capacity he flew the Polish General Sikorski from occupied France to the U.K. in 1940. Later he went to Canada to supervise the 'Atlantic ferry' of Canadian and American aircraft to the U.K. In 1941 he returned to the U.K. and a post with the Air Navigation School at Eastbourne.

He was then given command of 77 Squadron, Bomber Command. In April 1942, while commanding 10 Squadron, he was shot down over Norway, but escaped to neutral Sweden, where he was temporarily interned.

Bennett had already, in the winter of 1940, suggested to Bomber Command the idea of using pathfinder planes that would pinpoint bombing targets. In night operations it was often difficult for bomber crews to identify accurately the targets they were supposed to attack. The Pathfinder Force was formed in July 1942, under Bennett's command. At this time radar aids were playing a growing part in air navigation. By the end of the war the Pathfinder Force and the Light Night Striking Force of Mosquito bombers, which Bennett also helped to establish, had flown more than 50,000 sorties, playing a vital role in the bomber offensive against Germany between 1943 and 1944, and against the French coast prior to the D-Day landings.

BENNETT, Henry Gordon, b. 1887. Australian general who commanded the Australian forces in Malaya before the Japanese occupation of the country. Subsequently he was criticized for making his escape to Australia after the surrender of Singapore. Although Bennett had never been a regular soldier, in 1939 he was the youngest of the major-generals on the active list of the Australian army. He did not get a command until July 1940, when he was put in charge of the Training Depot, Eastern Command. A month later he was transferred to the A.I.F.'s 8th Division. In 1941 he was appointed G.O.C. of the A.I.F. in Malaya, serving under the supreme command of the British General Percival. He supervised the Australian defence of the southern state of Johore during the Japanese invasion of Malaya. After the surrender of Singapore on 15 February 1942, Bennett managed to escape from the city in a Chinese tongkan, and eventually made his way back to Australia. Shortly after, he was promoted to lieutenant-general as the commander of the 3rd Australian Corps, at that time training in Western Australia. In 1944, after trying in vain to secure another active command, Bennett resigned, and retired to civilian life. After the war Bennett was publicly charged with acting without permission in escaping from Singapore, and a military court of inquiry found that he was 'not justified in handing over his command or in leaving Singapore'. The finding was later upheld by a Royal Commission, but the Commission emphasized that this verdict reflected solely on Bennett's judgment and in no way on his courage or patriotism.

BERNADOTTE, Count Folke, b. 1895. Nephew of King Gustavus V of Sweden, Bernadotte was president of the Swedish Red Cross Association. In this capacity he arranged for the exchange of disabled and sick Allied and German soldiers—at Gothenburg in October 1943 and again in September 1944. His having access to

Swedish ships and other amenities greatly facilitated these transactions. As a consequence of such activities he became acquainted with leading figures in both the Allied and German commands. This made him an obvious mediator for the Nazi leaders to approach when, early in 1945, it was becoming clear that Germany's defeat could not long be postponed. In February 1945 Count Bernadotte travelled to Berlin where he met Himmler, Ribbentrop, Count Schwerin von Krosigk, and Himmler's lieutenants, Kaltenbrunner and Schellenberg. Himmler proposed that the Germans surrender unconditionally to the Anglo-American forces but not to the Soviet forces. Bernadotte saw Himmler for the last time at Flensburg on 27 April to tell him that his proposal had been rejected. Bernadotte's book, *The Fall of the Curtain*, published in 1945, describes this incident and provides a fascinating insight into the characters and motives of those involved. He was assassinated in Palestine in 1948.

Bernadotte's upbringing and background destined him for a military career, and he served as an officer for a number of years. But other interests soon gained the ascendancy, and his involvement with the Boy Scout movement and the Red Cross dated from World War I. In spite of his long association with the Red Cross, he lived in comparative obscurity until the events of World War II drew him dramatically into the limelight.

BERNHARD, Prince of the Netherlands, b. 1911. German-born husband of Princess Juliana, the heiress to the Dutch throne, Bernhard was a leader of the Resistance to the German occupation of the Netherlands.

After the German invasion of the Netherlands in 1940 Bernhard and his family fled to London. His family moved to Canada, but he himself stayed in Britain, where he became a pilot in the R.A.F. He was given the job of liaison officer between the British and the many Dutch people now escaping from occupied Holland to Britain. Using the information they brought, Bernhard completely reorganized the Dutch Intelligence Service, and made it the most efficient in any German-occupied country. During this time he secretly visited the Dutch East Indies (then occupied by the Japanese), and also went to Canada and the United States.

In 1944 Bernhard became C.-in-C. of the Dutch armed forces. He secretly returned to the Netherlands, where he integrated the different Resistance groups which were to be used in driving the Germans out of the country.

Born Prince Bernhard of Lippe-Biesterfeld, he grew up in Germany during the period in which Hitler rose to power. He opposed the Nazis from the start and, as soon as he could, he went into voluntary exile in Paris. He married Princess Juliana in 1937.

BEURLING, George, b. 1922. Canadian pilot in the R.A.F., known as 'Screwball' Beurling, who in 14 days of fighting over Malta in 1942 shot down 27 German and Italian aircraft in combat—with 3 more listed as 'probables'—and damaged 8 others. For his exploits he was awarded the D.S.O., the D.F C., and the D.F.M. and Bar. Ironically, he had the greatest difficulty in persuading the R.A.F. to accept him; before joining he was forced to journey from England to his home in Canada and back just to collect his birth certificate. After 12 months' initial training, Beurling had his first taste of aerial combat with 11 Group, a Spitfire unit, in late 1941. In 1942 he destroyed his first 2 enemy planes while flying as fighter escort on bombing missions over occupied Europe. In June 1942 Beurling was sent to Malta, at a time when German and Italian bombers were attacking the island almost round the clock. Assigned to 249 Squadron, he quickly became a celebrity among the Spitfire pilots of the island as a result of his uncanny marksmanship, which generally enabled him to bring down an enemy plane with a single short burst of fire. In 7 flying days between 6 July and 29 July, he accounted for 15 enemy aircraft and damaged 5 more. On 30 July, he shed his sergeant's stripes for the ring of a pilot-officer. His 4 decorations were gained in successive months between July and October 1942. Beurling was eventually shot down, in October of that year, baling out safely into the Mediterranean with a cannon-shell wound in his heel.

BEVAN, Aneurin, b. 1897. British politician, a Welshman, and a leading member of the Labour party, who, in the course of the war, frequently set up a lone opposition to Churchill. One instance of this was his attack on the Prime Minister's conduct of affairs in Greece, when he attempted to mount a vote of censure on Churchill. He was not afraid to fight for his principles even when these were unpopular.

Churchill, much tried and abused by Bevan, once called him a 'merchant of discourtesy' and 'a squalid nuisance'. But Bevan was a man of considerable courage, and a witty and able adversary in debate.

Bevan was active in the Trade Union movement, but up to and including the war he held no political office. He was well known as a skilful—and at times passionate and controversial—orator.

BEVERIDGE, Sir William, b. 1879. British economist, chairman of the committee that produced the 'Beveridge Report' in 1942. This document, officially called *The Report on Social Insurance and Allied Services*, proposed a scheme of social insurance that would provide a definite minimum of financial security for every member of the community. Beveridge himself said that its aim was to ensure that there should be 'bread and health for all before cake and comfort for anybody'. It was prepared at the government's request, and Beveridge's colleagues on the committee were experts from several government departments. The report reflected war-time desires and hopes for a future of greater social justice, and in fact many of the committee's ideas were put into effect in post-war legislation—for example, in the establishment of the National Health Service and in schemes for children's allowances and for assistance for the poorer sections of the community.

Beveridge's talents in social research and his special knowledge of the organization of manpower were also utilized in directions more specific to the prosecution of the war: his *Report on Skilled Men in the Services* led to the creation of the Corps of Royal Electrical and Mechanical Engineers (R.E.M.E.) and to the introduction of general recruiting for the army; he worked on plans for the recruitment of workers for the armaments industry, and he prepared an *Outline Scheme of Domestic Fuel Rationing*—this particular aspect of war-time rationing being considered as possibly the most difficult of all.

Although he had decided on a legal career, in 1903 Beveridge became sub-warden at Toynbee Hall, and, as a result of what he saw there, determined to find a solution to poverty through economics. Later he worked at the Board of Trade on unemployment insurance, published a remarkable report, *Unemployment: A Problem of Industry* (1909), and became Director of Labour Exchanges. During World War I he worked with Sir Stephen Tallents at the Ministry of Food on food rationing. From 1937 to 1945 he was Master of University College, Oxford; he was a Liberal M.P. 1944–5.

BEVIN, Ernest, b. 1881. British Labour politician, Minister of Labour and National Service in Churchill's war-time Coalition government. Bevin was responsible for the mobilization of Britain's manpower in the war, a complex task which he completed by 1943. As Minister of Labour he saw to it that the country's entire industrial resources were placed at the service of the war effort. To do this, he presented the Emergency Powers (Defence) Bill to Parliament a mere 9 days after taking office in 1940. This Bill gave the government absolute power over all industry and all labour, and put 33,000,000 men and women directly under Bevin's authority. In 1941 he introduced conscription for women. By a series of Essential Works Orders, affecting key industries, he made it illegal for workers to leave their jobs and for employers to dismiss workers without the agreement of specially appointed National Service Officers. In this way he eventually reduced the time lost by industrial stoppages to something less than one hour per worker per year. Surprisingly, he rarely needed to use the emergency powers vested in the government to enforce obedience, but managed to secure the voluntary co-operation of both trade unions and employers. Bevin became a full member of the War Cabinet in October

1940. Three years later he drafted the plans for post-war demobilization, working out the formula that was successfully applied when the time came in 1945. His ability to win popular support for his measures undoubtedly played a major part in the Labour electoral victory of 1945.

Bevin had practically no formal education, but he trained himself to hold his own, and his determination usually won the day. He was a patriot and could be a formidable and unyielding antagonist. When one of his opponents was referred to as 'his own worst enemy', Bevin replied: 'Not while I'm alive, he ain't.'

BIDDLE, Francis, b. 1886. American lawyer, Solicitor General, and, from 1941, Attorney General. In 1939 Biddle accepted the appointment of Judge of the U.S. Court of Appeals in Philadelphia and in January 1940 became Solicitor General, where his chief function was to represent the Federal government in arguments before the Supreme Court. Part of his job was to carry out the transfer of the Immigration and Nationalization Service from the Department of Labor to the Department of Justice, and to operate the Alien Registration Act of June 1940. At that time there were already $3\frac{1}{2}$ million aliens in the U.S.A., and more were crowding in from Nazi-conquered Europe. Biddle had the double task of protecting law-abiding aliens from public panic and of protecting the country from those subversively inclined. He was at all times a convinced defender of civil liberties and his treatment of aliens was wise and moderate. He protested in vain against the evacuation of U.S. citizens of Japanese origin from the west coast areas: it was largely due to his efforts that Italians were eventually removed from the category of enemy aliens.

In August 1941 he became Attorney General. In that office he forbade prosecutions for sedition without his personal authority. After Roosevelt's death in 1945 President Truman asked for his resignation, but subsequently appointed him U.S. member of the International Military Tribunal which tried the major war criminals at Nuremberg. The Russians nominated him for president of the tribunal, but he stood down in favour of

Lord Justice Lawrence of Britain. In the disputes that inevitably arose among the members of the tribunal his magnanimity and tenacity of purpose helped to steer the members towards agreement. In his autobiography, *In Brief Authority*, he writes in detail of the issues which constantly threatened to divide the tribunal. His words: 'I do not believe in dissents, any more than resignations, simply to make one's position clear', were typical of his attitude.

BLACKETT, Patrick M. S., b. 1897. British physicist, a leading exponent of the importance of the scientific approach to military planning. From 1935 he served as a member of the Tizard Committee, the purpose of which was to study how scientific advances could be used in improving defence against air attack. By the time the war began it was clear to all concerned with A.A. defence that in detecting and pinpointing aircraft some defensive weapon more sophisticated than the searchlight was urgently needed. Fortunately such a weapon was already in being in the form of radar, and Blackett was given the task of fostering the executive co-operation between scientist and serviceman necessary to make radar defence effective.

In early 1941 he became scientific adviser to Coastal Command H.Q., and in the following year he was asked to advise on and supervise a department of operational research at the Admiralty. At this time success in the war against the U-Boats had still to be won—and success was essential to the U.K.'s survival. Blackett's unrelenting and systematic analysis of the facts of the Battle of the Atlantic was a major factor in the eventual defeat of the U-Boats.

In 1943 he published *The Methodology of Operation Research*, and he advocated and promoted the statistical approach whenever he could in any department of the British war effort. In a statement of his aims that became celebrated he observed that 'Scientists can encourage numerical thinking on operational matters and so help to avoid running the war on gusts of emotion'. Blackett's contribution to planning resided not only in the scientific resources he brought to bear, but also in

the contribution he made to inculcating an attitude of objectivity in many war leaders.

BLAKESLEE, Donald, b. 1915. American fighter 'ace'. Shortly after the outbreak of war he joined the R.C.A.F. and trained in Canada. In May 1941 he arrived in the U.K., was posted to 401 'Ram' Squadron at Digby, had considerable success in a number of aerial fights, and was decorated. After an operational tour of 200 hours he was told that he would have to rest up as an instructor. However, he managed to retain combat status by joining 133 'Eagle' Squadron at Biggin Hill in Kent—a squadron of American volunteers formed in 1941—where he served briefly as a flight commander. In August 1942 he shot down an FW 190, and at least one more while operating over the Dieppe landings. In the following month 133 Squadron was amalgamated with 71 and 121 'Eagle' Squadrons to form the USAAF 4th Fighter Group, of which Blakeslee later became commander. The group destroyed a total of 1,016 enemy aircraft, and Blakeslee himself had a confirmed score of 15 enemy aircraft shot down and 2 more destroyed on the ground.

A handsome six-footer of partly Finnish blood, Blakeslee was one of the most famous of the USAAF aces. He was an outstanding leader and a man of great stamina. He once led his group from England to Russia, and once returned from a mission with 71 cannon holes in his Thunderbolt plane. In one attack on Berlin he was chosen to direct all the fighter planes of the 8th Air Force—some 800 planes in all. He became something of a legend during the war, and was said to be able 'to fly all day and sing all night'. He declared that 'fighting is a grand sport', but unlike many aces he painted no swastikas on his aircraft or any name other than that of his squadron.

BLAMEY, Sir Thomas, b. 1884. Australian general who became C.-in-C. Allied Land Forces in the S.W. Pacific, receiving the Japanese surrender in 1945. On the outbreak of war, Blamey was the chairman of the Australian Manpower Committee. His chief task had been to survey his country's human resources in anticipation of war. In rapid succession he held the posts of G.O.C. of the Australian Special Force; of the 1st Australian Corps; and of the A.I.F., Middle East. In 1941 he arrived in Greece to command the Anzac Corps that had been sent in to oppose the imminent German invasion. He directed much of the fighting there and supervised the initial stages of the Allied evacuation. He was recalled to Alexandria before Greece fell, and was appointed deputy C.-in-C. Middle East. The appointment, which was merely a conciliatory gesture towards the Dominion forces, carried little real power, and a rift soon developed between Blamey and Auchinleck, the C.-in-C., mainly over the diversion of A.I.F. troops to non-Australian commands.

After Pearl Harbor, in 1941, 2 of the 3 divisions composing the A.I.F. were recalled to Australia to face the threat of a Japanese invasion. Blamey soon followed them, at the behest of the Australian government, arriving there late in March 1942. On the establishment of the S.W. Pacific Command, he was appointed C.-in-C. of the Australian military forces and commander of the Allied Land Forces, under the supreme command of General MacArthur.

Blamey met the threat to his own country with perhaps his greatest military work. Convinced that attack is the best means of defence, he started with the repulse of the Japanese forces on the Kokoda trail in New Guinea, and his final triumph was the recapture of Papua. He exercised personal command in the field between September 1942 and January 1943, supervising the recapture of Buna and the blocking of the Japanese thrust towards the Australian mainland. From 1943 onwards he played a less prominent part in the war against Japan, as the fighting shifted northwards and the number of Australian troops engaged was gradually reduced. He retained the position of C.-in-C. Allied Land Forces, S.W. Pacific Area, until the end of the war.

BLASKOWITZ, Johannes von, b. 1884. German general who commanded the German forces in the Netherlands during the Allied operations in N.W. Europe in 1945. He commanded an army in the invasion of Poland, and in Russia in 1942 and 1943. He was there looked upon as an able but unspectacular commander, and was said to have been disturbed at the treatment by the S.S. of civilians. Later he was given an army group in the West. In May 1945 he surrendered to the Canadians and the Netherlands forces under Prince Bernhard. Blaskowitz was put on trial before a war crimes court at Nuremberg, but committed suicide.

BLEICHER, Hugo ('Colonel Henri'), b. 1899. German counter-intelligence agent, also known by the alias 'Monsieur Jean'. Although, in Ian Colvin's words, 'between the years 1942 and 1944 he may well have done more harm to the Allied cause on the intelligence front than any other one man', Bleicher became a counter-intelligence operator almost by mistake. A businessman in Hamburg in 1939, he answered a circular that advertised for men and women possessing a knowledge of foreign languages, for censorship work. The real aim of the circular was the recruitment of field police for work in the occupied countries of Europe, and in 1940 Bleicher was posted first to The Hague and then to France. As a result of his efficiency, he was put to work on the case of 'Interallié', the first major Resistance network established in France after the German occupation. He succeeded in his task and personally arrested the Circle's leader, Major Roman Czerniawski. This led to Bleicher's transfer to the Abwehr, the German military counter-intelligence organization. His work there was often hampered by the antagonism of the S.D.

Bleicher's single most important case was the infiltration of a Franco-British Resistance network controlled from London. Bleicher personally arrested two of its British leaders, Captain Peter Churchill and the celebrated Odette Sansom. He became acquainted with the French Resistance organizer Major Henri Frager, who was later arrested, in 1944, at an address that he had previously passed on to 'Colonel Henri' as a refuge where he could hide in case of an Allied invasion. Bleicher also played a major part in creating the 'Lisiana', a Resistance group based on Lisieux in Normandy that was penetrated by German agents right from

the start. Curiously he never rose above
the rank of sergeant, in spite of his
invaluable services to the German cause.
Bleicher was eventually arrested by the
Dutch police in Amsterdam in 1945. He
was later imprisoned by an Allied court,
after writing his war memoirs under orders
from his captors.

BLUM, Léon, b. 1872. French Socialist
statesman, arrested on the orders of the
Vichy régime in 1940, and gaoled in France
and Germany until 1945. Blum was a Jew,
a Socialist, and an intellectual, so he was
a ready-made target for the collabora-
tionists. The social reforms that his Popular
Front government introduced in 1936 had
alienated French right-wing opinion.
Though he had given support, with reser-
vations, to the Munich settlement, Blum
was unyielding in his opposition to any
compromise with the Germans after the
invasion of France in 1940, breaking with
the pacifist element of the Socialist party
on this issue. He refused to be drawn in
public during the surrender debates, but
scorned the opportunity to escape from
France, and travelled to Vichy in a final
attempt to rally the Socialist party against
Laval. Arrested and imprisoned in France
in 1940, he was sent to the prison camp at
Buchenwald in Germany in 1943, where he
spent the remainder of the war.

When put on trial with other political
leaders of the Third Republic at Riom
(February–April 1942) by the Vichy
government, Blum scored a personal
triumph. He defended his own record so
ably that his accusers were discredited.
The Vichy government was embarrassed,
and the Germans—angry that the
defendants had been charged, not with
declaring war, but with leading France
into war without adequate preparation—
insisted on the trial being stopped.

Though constantly expecting to be
executed, Blum spent his time in prison
thinking and writing, finishing *À l'Echelle
Humaine* in 1941 and working on his
Memoirs. He also wrote a number of
letters and memoranda in support of de
Gaulle's Free French movement. These he
attempted to smuggle out of the country.
On his return to France in 1945 Blum was
warmly welcomed and resumed an active
political life.

BOISSON, Pierre, b. 1898. Governor
General of France's colonies in N.W.
Africa. On the fall of France, Boisson, like
other colonial governors, urged that the
war against Germany should be continued
from the African colonies, where much of
the French army and navy was based. But
after Marshal Pétain's order that the
armistice applied to France's colonies as
well as France, Boisson remained loyal to
the Vichy administration and resisted all
Free French efforts to gain control in
Africa. For this, de Gaulle never forgave
him.

When Germany violated the armistice
(11 November 1942), Boisson realized that
his arguments in favour of collaboration
no longer held water, and that loyalty to
Vichy was now pointless. He supported
Admiral Darlan's attempts to reach an
agreement with the Allies in N.W. Africa.
But, with typical lack of logic, he still
opposed any Allied or Free French landings in Africa pending Darlan's order of a
cease-fire. However, he did persuade the
leaders of French colonial armed forces to
back Darlan and to put their forces at the
disposal of the Allies. Boisson backed
General Giraud's appointment as head of
the combined French armies in North
Africa. But de Gaulle fiercely opposed
Giraud's appointment of Boisson as a
member of the 'Imperial Council'. When
de Gaulle became head of the provisional
French National Committee, Boisson was
promptly sacked from the Council and
from the governorship of N.W. Africa.
Boisson was then tried as a collaborator,
and in December 1943 he was imprisoned
for the duration of the war.

BONHOEFFER, Dietrich, b. 1906. German Lutheran pastor and theologian,
executed for his part in the resistance to
Hitler. Although he had been forbidden by
the Nazis to publish, to lecture at universities, or to address public meetings,
Bonhoeffer succeeded in obtaining employ-
ment in 1940 in the Abwehr (the Intelligence department of the Armed Forces
High Command), at that time headed
by the anti-Nazi Admiral Canaris. Until
1943 Bonhoeffer was involved with church
duties, writing, and work for the Resistance
movement aiming at the assassination of
Hitler. To this end he several times

travelled outside Germany in 1941 and 1942—trips that were sponsored by the Abwehr. His most interesting encounter was with Bishop Bell of Chichester in Stockholm (30 May–21 June 1942), when he transmitted to the bishop the anti-Nazi conspirators' proposals for peace terms should there be a successful *coup d'état* in Germany. The Nazis arrested Bonhoeffer, and in April 1943 he was held in Tegel prison and charged 5 months later with 'destruction of fighting power'. The failure of the bomb plot against Hitler in July 1944, and the discovery of documents implicating the Abwehr in the plot, left him seriously exposed. In October he was sent to the Gestapo prison in Berlin. On 8 April 1945 he was court-martialled at Flossenburg prison camp, sentenced to death, and hanged the following day. Two weeks later his brother and two brothers-in-law were killed in Berlin. An English officer who spoke to him shortly before his execution quoted him as saying, as the Gestapo officials came for him: 'This is the end; for me, the beginning of life.'

Bonhoeffer wrote a number of books dealing with the challenge facing the Christian Church in the twentieth century. His teachings have significantly influenced the thinking of modern and progressive churchmen.

BORGHESE, Prince Valerio, b. 1912. Italian naval commander in charge of the 10th Light Flotilla, an Italian assault craft force that carried out some of the boldest and most successful naval raids of the war. A submarine commander when the war started, Borghese learned about assault craft when his submarine was selected to carry 2-man 'human torpedoes' (the prototype for the British 'Chariot') in their first full exercise. In September 1940 Borghese's submarine ferried these human torpedoes into Algeciras Bay in order to attack shipping in Gibraltar harbour. This was the start of a series of engagements between the assault craft and the harbour defences that continued intermittently until the armistice with Italy. They cost the 10th Light Flotilla only 3 men dead and 3 captured; the Allies suffered a total of 73,000 tons of shipping sunk or damaged.

In 1941 Borghese was put in command of the under-water division of the assault

craft force, and was awarded the gold medal, the highest military decoration, for his services. His most successful operation was the daring attack on Alexandria harbour in December 1941. A squad of human torpedoes led by Borghese entered the harbour while the boom defences were open to admit British ships, and attached delayed-action mines to the hulls of H.M.S. *Queen Elizabeth* and H.M.S. *Valiant*. Both warships were seriously damaged and Admiral Cunningham was deprived of the battle squadron potential whose mere presence in the Mediterranean had for so long kept the more powerful Italian fleet inactive. In May 1943 Borghese was given command of the entire flotilla, which also included explosive assault boats, midget submarines, and assault swimmers. He coolly continued operations against Gibraltar from the hull of an Italian merchantman that was being repaired in Algeciras harbour. Just before the armistice was announced he was planning an attack upon New York. *Sea Devils*, Borghese's own account of his flotilla's operations, was published in English in 1952.

BORIS III, b. 1894. King of Bulgaria, who, after struggling to prevent his country becoming involved in the war, finally joined on the side of the Axis. On the outbreak of war the Balkan rulers became increasingly uneasy in their precarious neutrality. Both France and Britain were concerned to preserve Bulgarian neutrality, and in September 1939 King George VI wrote to Boris personally on the matter. Hitler was impressed by Boris's character, and said: 'Under the rod of the old fox [Ferdinand I], son Boris himself became a young fox.' In 1940 Nazi pressure was turned upon Bulgaria, but Boris managed to put up a long resistance to Hitler's demands. Summoned to meet Hitler at Berchtesgaden in November 1940, he returned to Bulgaria without having committed himself. But by the spring of 1941 the pressure was too great to resist and Boris was forced to align his country with the Axis. In view of subsequent events, it seems that the value placed on the Balkans by both sides was excessive. Bismarck had much earlier expressed this view: 'They are not worth the bones of a Pomeranian or any other sort of grenadier.'

Boris was not sympathetic to the Nazi cause but, witnessing the successive defeats by the Nazis of neighbouring states, considered it advantageous to adhere to them rather than submit to the occupation of his own country. The result was that a German-Bulgarian alliance was signed that allowed German troops free access to Bulgaria, while preserving Bulgarian autonomy. Then, in December 1941, Boris allowed his government to declare war on the Allies—a decision he later regarded as his worst mistake. But he did respect pro-Russian feeling in Bulgaria and did not declare war on the Soviet Union, in the misguided hope that Bulgaria might benefit from this if Russia turned out to be the victor.

Boris's manner of death remains shrouded in mystery. It happened after an interview with Hitler on 28 August 1943, in which he opposed the increasing Nazi demands on Bulgaria. He was either assassinated or simply died of a heart attack. He was succeeded by his young son Simeon II.

BORMANN, Martin, b. 1900. German Nazi leader, and confidant of Hitler. He joined the party early, and rose from Reichsleiter (national organizer) of the party to Reichsminister—chief of all party affairs and second only to Hitler himself. Bormann reached this position in 1941 after Rudolf Hess's flight to Britain. He exploited it to the full, remaining close to Hitler to the time of his death, and reinforcing the Führer's refusal to face defeat and surrender. After Germany's final surrender Bormann could not be found and was presumed dead. It is possible that he died during the breakout of Hitler's staff from the Chancellery in May 1945, but no body was found. Bormann was tried in his absence as a war criminal at Nuremberg and condemned to death.

In 1918 Bormann, along with Goering, Hess and others, was a member of the Freikorps, a group devoted to the crushing of Germany's internal disorders after the 1918 armistice. After joining the Nazi party Bormann rose rapidly in it, and, on becoming Reichsminister, made himself indispensable to the Führer by always being in attendance on him. He became highly skilled at dealing with

Hitler's unpredictable and frequently violent moods. He often used this skill to steer Hitler into approving his own schemes. In the later part of the war Bormann soothed the Führer's frayed nerves, and, by reducing complex situations to simple, easily comprehensible formulas, managed to guide Hitler's decisions. Bormann took away much of the strain of Hitler's life and the latter rewarded him with his confidence. Bormann, fearing attempts to supplant him, guarded Hitler so closely that it was practically impossible, even for top Nazis such as Goering, to approach Hitler except through him. He used his powerful position not only to protect Hitler from anxiety but also to conceal from him any of the more sensible or conciliatory proposals put forward by others in the party. According to Himmler, Bormann was responsible for many of Hitler's more mistaken decisions; '. . . in fact he has not only confirmed his [Hitler's] uncompromising attitude, he has stiffened it'.

In 1945, well aware of Germany's disastrous position, Bormann made a determined but abortive attempt to come to an understanding with Russia. There had always been Nazis who favoured making an alliance of convenience with the Russians. But this attempt came to nothing, as it was bound to. Bormann was in the Führerbunker of the Chancellery in Berlin when Hitler committed suicide there. He had begged to be allowed to die with his Führer. But in his political testament Hitler ordered Bormann 'to put the interests of the nation before his own feelings' and to save himself. What Bormann then did, no one knows for sure. But, as late as 1964, there were reports that he was secretly living in South America.

BOSE, Subhas Chandra, b. 1897. India's only revolutionary Nationalist leader, whose activities came to a head during the war when he escaped to Berlin in 1941 to organize a campaign of Indian opposition to Britain and her Allies.

Before the war Bose had joined Pandit Nehru's left-wing group and had led the younger members of the National Congress, advocating Socialist ideals. He was President of Congress in 1938, but became extreme on the outbreak of war, seeing it as India's great opportunity to win freedom. He believed that this freedom must be fought for and would not be achieved by supporting the British. Bose was imprisoned in July 1940 for his propaganda activities and tried fasting as a means of forcing his captors to release him: then in January 1941 he made a spectacular escape into Afghanistan, and thence went to Berlin, where he formed the nucleus of an Indian National Army, advocating a government of Free India to work in Europe with the Axis powers. He broadcast from a radio station in Afghanistan, encouraging sabotage.

These activities were worrying for the British, especially when in August 1942 the attitude of Congress hardened with the 'Quit India' resolution, and passive non-co-operation began. This for Bose was too tame and in 1943 he threw in his lot with the Japanese, went to Tokyo and from there organized the Indian National Army from among Indian P.O.W.s. With these he planned to be in the vanguard of the Japanese invasion of India. This was not to be, and in 1945 Bose was killed in an air crash in Formosa.

Whatever view is taken of his activities Bose may be admired for his courage in the struggle for Indian independence. He at first worked through legitimate channels of opposition, but dissatisfaction with lack of genuine progress drove him to extremes. Many of his ideals for India were modelled on the aspirations and achievements of the Young Turks; he greatly admired the methods of Kemal Atatürk in building his new Turkey.

BRACKEN, Brendan, b. 1901. British politician, one of Churchill's closest wartime associates. In the 1930s he had been a newspaper publisher connected mainly with the *Financial Times* and *The Economist.* From 1940 to 1941 he was parliamentary private secretary to Churchill. In July 1941 he succeeded Duff Cooper as Minister of Information, a job for which his pre-war experience well suited him, and held this post for the rest of the war. In September 1944 he became a member of the Emergency Housing Committee, which was concerned with producing houses for demobilized Servicemen. In the Caretaker government of 1945 Bracken was First Lord of the Admiralty.

Before the war, Bracken was one of the few who realized the danger to Europe from Nazi Germany. He backed Churchill in his warnings about Hitler, and tried to persuade Russia to agree to an alliance with Britain. As Churchill's Minister of Information in the war, Bracken was in charge of all information and propaganda—broadcasting, film, newspaper reports—and did this job efficiently with a far greater respect for the truth than was shown by the German Propaganda Ministry under Goebbels.

BRADLEY, Omar, b. 1893. American general, who in 1944 led the invading American armies through France into the heart of Germany. He also played a major part in the North African and Sicilian campaigns of 1943. During the war years he quickly rose from comparative obscurity to international fame. In 1941, after being commandant of the Fort Benning Infantry School, he was given command of the 82nd Infantry Division, later transferring to the 28th Division. General Marshall and General Eisenhower, who had graduated with Bradley from West Point in 1915, chose him for service in Tunisia. At first Bradley acted as Eisenhower's 'eyes and ears' at the front, informing him of the battle performances of the U.S. troops. But it was not long before General Patton appointed him deputy commander of the 2nd Corps, and he later was given command of this force, the entire American ground force engaged in the fighting. Troops under his command captured Bizerta on 7 May 1943 and took more than 40,000 prisoners. The 2nd Corps, still under his command, was included in the U.S. 7th Army for the invasion of Sicily, where his troops landed at Gela and Scogliti. After driving northwards across the island, they turned east, encountering heavy German resistance, and reached Messina 38 days after the landings.

Bradley's greatest contribution to the Allied victory was the part he played in Operation 'Overlord', the invasion of France. On the strength of his superb combat record, he was chosen by General Eisenhower to command the American landings in Normandy on D-Day, 6 June

1944. Bradley's 1st Army established itself on Omaha and Utah beachheads and then stormed inland to capture St.-Lô and Cherbourg. He was responsible for a major breakthrough when he raced his army through the gap between Mortain and Avranches into the heart of France. On 1 August Bradley was given command of the newly formed U.S. 12th Army Group, and had under his control more than 1,300,000 ground troops, the largest army ever assembled under the command of a single American general. His men liberated Paris, and bore the brunt of the Battle of the Bulge, the shock counter-offensive in the Ardennes, in which Bradley's outflanking tactics produced a decisive Allied victory. After breaching the Siegfried Line along Germany's western frontier, his troops established a bridge-head across the Rhine at the Remagen bridge in March 1945, crossing so swiftly that 335,000 encircled German troops in the Ruhr area surrendered. Battling their way across Germany to the Elbe, forces of the 12th Army Group met the Russian army smashing in from the east on 25 April 1945. Thirteen days later Germany surrendered unconditionally.

Bradley was unquestionably one of the most consistently successful Allied commanders of the war. His success was based on his sure grasp of tactics, the respect he always showed for his troops, and his 'unflappability' and quiet confidence under stress. *A Soldier's Story*, his war memoirs, was published in 1951.

BRAUN, Eva, b. 1912. Hitler's companion from 1932, and, for the last few hours of his life, his wife. Of middle-class Bavarian origin, she met Hitler in 1930 in Heinrich Hoffman's photographer's shop, where she was an assistant. After the death of Geli Raubal, Hitler's niece, she became his mistress, living at his flat in Munich. In 1936 she moved to Hitler's house at Berchtesgaden, where she was his hostess. In April 1945 she joined Hitler in the Führerbunker as the Russians closed in on Berlin. On 29 April 1945 they were married; next day she committed suicide by taking poison shortly before Hitler shot himself. On Hitler's orders, both bodies were cremated with petrol in the Chancellery Garden above the bunker and

buried. The Russians discovered the charred corpses and carried out autopsies, but published the results only in 1968.

Eva seems to have taken the lead in seeking Hitler's acquaintance and went to great trouble to secure the relationship she wanted. In other ways, though, she was no schemer. She took no part in the intrigues amongst those who surrounded Hitler, and never tried to influence him politically. A 'pretty, empty-headed blonde', without intellectual gifts, she occupied herself with romantic films, sport, animals, her own appearance, clothes, and sex. She read little except cheap novelettes. Her pleasure in dancing, drinking, and smoking incurred Hitler's disapproval, and the price she paid for her position as his mistress was to endure domestic tyranny.

Eva was essentially a typical German *hausfrau*, who provided Hitler with a secure domestic background to which he could retreat for peace and quiet. Hitler kept her very much part of his private life, and they rarely appeared in public together. Even the Führer's closest associates did not know exactly what their relationship was. At least one over-curious journalist ended up in Dachau concentration camp.

In the last days of the Third Reich Eva claimed that she was the only person still loyal to Hitler, and was still convinced of his importance to Germany. 'Poor, poor Adolf,' she would repeat endlessly, 'deserted by everyone, betrayed by all. Better that ten thousand others die than he be lost to Germany.' Though she was once called 'the great enigma of the Third Reich', Speer's remark that 'For all writers of history, Eva Braun is going to be a disappointment' seems much closer to the truth.

BRAUN, Wernher von, b. 1912. German rocket engineer who developed the V-2 rocket, one of Hitler's 'secret weapons', which brought London and other cities in Britain under heavy bombardment in the later months of the war. The V-2 rocket was able to carry almost a ton of explosives over distances of up to 190 miles.

At the age of 25 von Braun became Technical Director of the German army's immense rocket research centre at Peenemunde on the Baltic. His priority orders were to produce 'a field weapon capable of carrying a large warhead over a range much beyond that of artillery'. By 1938 von Braun had already developed the prototype of the V-2—the A-4 rocket, a self-propelled and self-steering apparatus with a maximum range of 11 miles. But from 1940 onwards his research was seriously slowed down when Hitler shifted priorities in men and materials from guided missile research to the Luftwaffe. In the summer of 1941 von Braun pleaded in vain with Hitler for improved research facilities and his project was not finally given the full go-ahead until 1943, when Hitler demanded mass production of the *Vergeltungswaffe* (retaliatory weapon) 2. After foiling an attempt by Himmler to take control of the project, von Braun was arrested and imprisoned by the Gestapo. He was accused of planning to fly to Britain with secret documents. However, Hitler himself ordered his release. The first V-2 was eventually launched against England on 8 September 1944. A total of about 3,600 were fired against English cities until The Hague, from which most of the rockets were launched, was captured by Allied forces 7 months later.

In March 1945 von Braun decided it was time to leave Peenemunde when Russian forces reached a point within 100 miles of the station. With about 400 of his colleagues, he hid from the S.S. until he was able to give himself up to Allied troops. A star prize of the American search for former technical experts, he was sent to London for interrogation, and later released to continue his research in the United States.

BRERETON, Lewis, b. 1890. American general who commanded the 9th Air Force during the war in Europe, and who assumed command of the 1st Allied Air-borne Army in 1944 Promoted major-general in 1941, Brereton was commander of the American Far East Air Force, which suffered heavily in that year. Describing in November 1941 the state of preparation for war in Manila Brereton wrote: 'The idea of an imminent war seemed far removed from the minds of most. . . . There was a comprehensive project on paper for the construction of additional airfields, but unfortunately

little money had been provided prior to my arrival.' In 1942 he held an air command in India, and then was transferred to command the newly established U.S. Middle East Air Force. In an early venture in Allied co-operation, Brereton's units in the Western Desert were integrated with the British squadrons under Air Vice Marshal Coningham.

In the U.K., from October 1943, Brereton gradually built up the U.S. 9th Air Force into the world's most formidable tactical air unit. The force was of major importance in the prelude to 'Overlord', particularly in its offensive against German transport communications before D-Day. The attack on the bridges over the rivers Seine, Oise, and Meuse, in which the 9th Air Force used fighters as dive-bombers, was outstandingly successful.

In the spring of 1944 Brereton produced an explicit and accurate report on Rommel's anti-invasion preparations. In August of that year he was put in command of the newly formed 1st Allied Airborne Army, and it was troops of this command that fought the bitter Nijmegen-Arnhem battle of the following month.

'BRITTON, Colonel'. *See* RITCHIE, Douglas.

BROOKE, Sir Alan, b. 1883. British general (field marshal, 1944) who played a major part in the strategic direction of the war.

At the beginning of the war Brooke commanded the 2nd Corps of the B.E.F. in France. He showed great skill in covering the withdrawal to Dunkirk in May–June 1940. Later in that year as C.-in-C. Home Foces he had to reorganize the army almost from scratch to resist invasion and prepare for operations overseas. At the end of 1941 he succeeded Sir John Dill as C.I.G.S. with a seat on the Chiefs of Staff Committee, becoming chairman in June 1942 and remaining in this position until the end of the war. This three-man committee was responsible for the government for the day-to-day running of the war as well as its future conduct.

Of all the British war leaders Brooke was the master of strategy, recognized as such by the Americans as well as the other

Allies until the 1944 landings in Normandy. It was a disappointment to him not to be made the supreme commander for 'Overlord' and the campaign in Europe.

Churchill respected him and his outspoken arguments; with the other chiefs of staff behind him, he was listened to when he disagreed with the Prime Minister's often grandiose schemes. In dealing with politicians Brooke was on the whole patient, and confined himself to military considerations. He had a clear and rapid mind and did not suffer fools gladly.

At the Teheran Conference in 1943 Stalin complained that Brooke was brusque and unfriendly towards the Russians, but later Stalin changed his mind. In shaking hands with Brooke, he said warmly: 'The best friendships are those founded on misunderstandings.' Roosevelt was highly appreciative of Brooke's qualities.

Brooke served in the artillery from 1902 and in World War I with Indian and Canadian troops. From 1929 to 1936 he was Commandant of the School of Artillery, then Director of Military Training at the War Office, C.-in-C. Anti-Aircraft Command, and G.O.C. Southern Command. He was an expert ornithologist. His war diaries, *The Turn of the Tide* and *Triumph in the West,* were edited by Sir Arthur Bryant.

BROOKE-POPHAM, Sir Robert, b. 1878. British air marshal in charge of the defence of British territories in the Far East at the time of Japan's early victories. In 1940 the British government was anxious not to endanger British possessions in Asia whilst the country's energies were fully engaged in Europe. Brooke-Popham's orders were to avoid war with Japan at all costs, even to the extent—as eventually happened—of allowing the Japanese to gain the initiative and themselves open hostilities.

The defence of Britain's Asian possessions rested mainly on air power. But, as Brooke-Popham reported at the outset, Britain had not nearly enough planes in the East for the job. Brooke-Popham did everything he could to remedy the shortcomings of his air strength and, also, to establish co-operation between the Services, which until then had been almost

non-existent. But in neither respect could he succeed with the limited means at his disposal. Despite his pleas to the Chiefs of Staff in London, urgently needed supplies were not forthcoming. The result of all this was that Brooke-Popham was powerless to stop the Japanese invasion of Malaya and Singapore. At the end of 1941, with British forces fighting a losing battle on land and in the air, Brooke-Popham was relieved of his command. But most of the blame for the disaster in the East rested on those responsible for the failure to make necessary preparations—a failure that Brooke-Popham himself had castigated, to no avail.

BROSSOLETTE, Pierre, b. 1903. French teacher and left-wing journalist, who was one of the earliest leaders of the French Resistance. After France fell in 1940, he refused to write for the Vichy press, and opened a small bookshop in Paris. In April 1942 he came to England, where he became a political adviser to de Gaulle and a deputy to 'Colonel Passy' (André de Wavrin), the chief of the Central Bureau of Intelligence and Action (B.C.R.A.). This Free French organization was concerned (unlike the British S.O.E.) not only with active resistance but also with espionage. Brossolette worked closely with S.O.E. and was secretly parachuted into France several times. On some of these missions the British agent Yeo-Thomas accompanied him. While on a mission in France in 1944, Brossolette was given away and was arrested by the Germans. In fear of betraying his colleagues while under torture, he threw himself to his death from the fifth floor of a block of flats in Paris which was a Gestapo H.Q.

Brossolette's job as mediator between the many separate Resistance groups in France and between them and the Free French in London and the British was a hard one. There was much rivalry between the groups and they had a rather equivocal attitude towards the Free French. Nevertheless his dedication and force of character enabled him to impress them all with the vital necessity for close co-operation with the Allies in the 1944 Normandy landings.

BROWNING, Frederick, b. 1896. British general, a pioneer of the use of airborne troops. In early 1940 Churchill had requested the War Office to form a corps of at least 5,000 parachute troops. Browning was transferred from the Guards armoured training group in 1941 and ordered to raise an airborne division composed of parachute and glider troops. In the face of considerable difficulties, not the least of which was that he had to start a completely new project that in any case aroused much opposition from the Air Ministry, Browning was remarkably successful in building the new parachute brigades and other airborne forces into a strong and aggressive force that eventually became an important part of the Allied war effort. Under his command the airborne formation had by 1943 expanded to comprise 3 parachute brigades and an air landing brigade; the Parachute Regiment eventually comprised 17 battalions. 'Boy' Browning was extremely popular with the personnel of the new units, but was known not to be tolerant of inefficiency. General Brooke said of him: 'If it had not been for this difficult pioneer work of Browning we should certainly not have had our Airborne Division ready in time.' In 1942 the parachute troops were given their famous emblem, the red beret. Nicknamed the 'Red Devils', they came to be a force much respected by the enemy.

In April 1943 Browning was appointed major-general, Airborne Forces; later in the same year he was promoted lieutenant-general. In the Arnhem operation of September 1944 Browning (who was deputy to General Brereton) commanded the 1st Airborne Corps; the 1st Airborne Division, which was in the van of the airborne forces, fought one of the most gallant actions of the war. The division suffered considerable losses—only 3,400 men succeeded in withdrawing to safety— but its conduct was an inspiration to all the troops in action in N.W. Europe. Hilary St George Saunders paid Browning this tribute in his book *The Red Beret*: 'To this tall guardsman and fine soldier the Parachute Regiment owes much . . . he was intimately concerned with its creation and expansion, and later on with its exploits in the field. The spirit of the Brigade of Guards was strong in him, and the Parachute Regiment will always be grateful to him for all that he did to link

it with a splendid tradition. . . .' Browning became Chief of Staff to the Supreme Allied Commander, S.E. Asia, in the latter part of the war against the Japanese in 1945. He was the husband of Daphne du Maurier the novelist.

BRUCE, Stanley (Viscount Bruce), b. 1883. Australian High Commissioner in London throughout the war who, in spite of frequent differences of opinion with Churchill, always supported the U.K.'s role in the war. A former Prime Minister of Australia (1923–9), he was from 1942 to 1945 Australia's representative in the British War Cabinet. He was also adviser to the Dutch government in exile.

Bruce's early conviction that the war would be won by superior air power led to his founding the Dominions training scheme for pilots. The result of his foresight was that from the Battle of Britain onwards Australian and Canadian air squadrons gave valuable support to the R.A.F.

Though a convinced Conservative, Bruce espoused ideas that seemed radical to many of his colleagues. He constantly advocated the need for a post-war world far different from that envisaged, for instance, by Churchill. He strongly disagreed with Churchill over the treatment of Germany, in the event of an Allied victory. His knowledge of pre-war conditions in Germany (as a former president of the Council of the League of Nations) had convinced him that the victorious Allies in World War I had imposed too harsh a peace settlement in the Treaty of Versailles, and that this mistake should not be repeated.

BUCKMASTER, Maurice, b. 1910. British officer who was head of the French Section of S.O.E., the purpose of which was, in Churchill's words, 'to set Europe ablaze'. S.O.E. had to start virtually from nothing: collecting information about conditions, events, and possibilities in the enemy-occupied countries and then building up Resistance organizations that would form effective military forces for use against the Germans and their allies. Buckmaster's French Section was independent of de Gaulle, though many Frenchmen served in it. The Free French had a similar and parallel organization in the 'action militaire' section of the Bureau Centrale de Renseignments et d'Action commanded by Colonel André de Wavrin ('Colonel Passy'). Buckmaster reported to the French Section as Information Officer in March 1941 at its office at 64 Baker Street, London. Since it seemed that a main purpose of the Section was sabotage, he decided to begin by making a page-by-page analysis of a French industrial and commercial directory, drawing also on his personal knowledge of factories in France. He learnt, too, that a number of S.O.E. agents were in training to be sent to France. Soon, it was hoped, information would be coming in by radio from them. From these small beginnings, Buckmaster—who was appointed head of the Section in September 1941—built up a force that eventually numbered several hundred agents in its *réseaux* in France, carried out innumerable acts of sabotage against the Germans, and organized, trained, and armed groups of *Maquisards* who, in the event, supplied a valuable military function when the Allied armies landed in France in June 1944. Some Maquis groups even succeeded in bringing whole German armoured divisions—including the Hermann Goering Division—to an untidy halt before they could reach the battle front where they were urgently needed.

The cost of so much ingenuity, determination, hardship, and heroism was inevitably heavy. The Germans made every effort to counter the work of the French Section and the Section had its failures as well as its successes. Its agents worked under conditions of great difficulty, security was hard to attain, and mistakes and treachery were hard to detect until they led to disaster. Many agents were captured and tortured or killed. But the Section was able to make an immense contribution not only to the defeat of Germany but also to fostering the pride and hope of hundreds of thousands of people in German-occupied France.

BUCKNER, Simon Bolivar, b. 1886. American general who commanded the 10th Army in one of the last battles of the war—the Battle of Okinawa against the Japanese in spring 1945. Buckner had spent most of the war—'straining to get

into the saddle', as he put it—in command of the defence forces in Alaska. His appointment to the 10th Army gave him his first taste of action, apart from a few months in the Pacific. In the bloody struggle against the tenacious Japanese defenders of the Ryukyu Islands, Buckner gained himself a reputation as a commander of great force and aggressiveness, and as an able tactician. He was killed in action in June 1945 on Okinawa.

BUDENNY, Semyon, b. 1883. Russian marshal who commanded the Soviet armies on the S.W. front in 1941 when they suffered their most devastating defeats. Possibly the most flamboyant of the Russian generals—with a yearning for the cavalry charge—he appeared to have little real aptitude for high command.

After Hitler's invasion of Russia in June 1941, the Soviet State Committee for Defence appointed Budenny C.-in-C. of the armies in the Ukraine and Bessarabia. Stalin wanted Kiev held at all costs and ordered that priority should be given to the southern sector of the front in the allocation of men and materials. This meant that Budenny had an overwhelming numerical superiority over the German forces. But the superior generalship of Rundstedt and Kleist more than made up for this, and by 10 July they had severed the Russian north-to-south communications between Budenny's two major concentrations of forces at Kiev and Uman. Budenny completely failed to grasp the seriousness of the situation. He was too late redeploying his forces, with disastrous consequences. By 3 August the Germans had managed to move their forces to surround the Uman concentration. Budenny withdrew across the Dnieper and, as he went, complied with Stalin's order to 'scorch the earth' about to be occupied by the invader. Budenny and his commissar, Khruschev, charged with the evacuation of industry, ordered the smashing of the famous Dnieper dam at Zaporozhe. This effectively paralysed industry in the eastern Ukraine. When the Germans marched into Kiev on 19 September they found that it, too, had been systematically destroyed. By rushing vast numbers of men to the S.W. front Stalin had hoped to hold the Germans back at all costs in order to give him a breathing space at least until the spring of 1942 in which to reorganize. Budenny's incompetence let him down, and Kiev had to be abandoned. In one of the most catastrophic land battles in history Budenny lost more than one and a half million soldiers—which at that time was more than half the active strength of the Red army—in the two concentrations at Kiev and Uman. He was relieved of command and given the job of training recruits for the Red Army. There is no record of his taking any further part in the strategic planning or prosecution of the war.

A spectacular figure with his handlebar moustaches and mahogany-butt revolvers, Budenny had Patton's showy glamour with none of his ability. Eisenhower, who met Budenny at the time of the Japanese surrender, was astonished at the Russian's reaction to the end of the war; Budenny said he was glad that the war was over but 'we should have kept going until we had killed a lot more of those insolent Japanese'. As Eisenhower remarked: 'The Marshal seemed to be a most congenial, humane, and hospitable type, but at the same time he seemed to have no concern that even one day's continuance of war meant death or wounds for additional hundreds of Russian citizens.'

BURKE, Arleigh, b. 1901. American admiral, one of the ablest naval commanders of the war. He gained recognition during 1943 and 1944 in operations in the South Pacific, where his skilful handling of destroyers earned him the nickname '31-knot Burke'. His force, Destroyer Squadron 23, known as the 'Little Beavers', covered the American landing on Bougainville, one of the last Japanese strongholds in the Solomon Islands. Altogether Burke's squadron fought in more than 20 separate engagements against the Japanese. Later he served as Chief of Staff to the commander of the Fast Carrier Task Force 58. In 1945 he became head of the Research and Development Division of the Ordnance Bureau in Washington.

BUSH, Vannevar, b. 1890. American scientist and engineer who guided much of the U.S. weapons research. Bush served in many government administrative posts dealing with research and innovation, and his wide experience and high reputation in this field led to his being appointed director of the Office of Scientific Research and Development in 1941, a position he held for the rest of the war. Within six months of becoming involved in the war, the U.S.A. had evolved a Joint Committee on New Weapons and Equipment under Bush's chairmanship—a fact that, as Professor A. V. Hill pointed out, contrasted favourably with the position in Britain where the government had no central technical advisory body. As early as 1940 Bush was made responsible for co-ordinating research on the scientific aspects of the atom bomb project. Throughout the war he was also president of the Carnegie Institute in Washington.

BYRNES, James, b. 1879. American lawyer and politician who directed the mobilization of the U.S.A. from 1943 and who became Secretary of State in the last weeks of the war. Byrnes had an amiable personality, was an expert on budgetary matters, and was a clever and determined negotiator. As a Democratic senator and a member of the Senate Foreign Relations Committee in 1939, Byrnes fought for the 'cash and carry' Arms Act, and ably helped to steer through the controversial Selective Service and Lend-Lease Acts. In 1941 he resigned from the Senate to take up a commission to the Supreme Court as an Associate Justice; but after Pearl Harbor President Roosevelt offered him a job as Director of the newly formed Office of Economic Stabilization. His task was to halt inflation and at the same time encourage full war-time production. Byrnes issued an edict freezing all wages and salaries in the U.S.A. and imposed a $25,000 ceiling on salaries. In May 1945 he was made Director of War Mobilization, a post that Roosevelt himself called 'Assistant President on the Home Front'. In that capacity he became a useful link between the President and Congress.

He failed in his attempt to get the Vice-Presidential nomination at the 1944 Democratic convention, but travelled to the Yalta Conference as the President's adviser on shipping, Lend-Lease, and Home Front affairs. Four days before

Roosevelt died he resigned his position as Director of War Mobilization, but soon returned to Washington at President Truman's invitation. In July 1945 Byrnes was sworn in as Secretary of State. He played a major part in the Potsdam Conference and, after the war, at the London Conference of Foreign Ministers and the Paris peace conference of 1946. Byrnes was one of the 'hard liners' who urged the dropping of the atomic bomb on Japan and who refused to countenance anything less than unconditional surrender by that country.

C

CALLAGHAN, Daniel, b. 1892. American admiral, Chief of Staff to the commander of U.S. naval forces in the South Pacific. In November 1942 he took part in one of the most intrepid naval engagements of the war. He was in command of the cruiser *San Francisco* when a large Japanese force moved in, under cover of night, on American positions in the Solomon Islands. The spearhead of the force sent to intercept them was under Callaghan's direction. The *San Francisco* sailed right into, and through, the whole enemy fleet with her guns blazing. She disabled 3 enemy vessels, sinking 1 of them. At point-blank range she engaged an enemy battleship, heavily her superior in size and fire-power, silenced the battleship's big guns and so crippled her that she was later sunk by torpedoes from American destroyers and aircraft. The *San Francisco* herself was hit many times and 30 of her crew were killed when a burning Japanese aeroplane fell onto her deck. Callaghan lost his life in this action, but the *San Francisco* was brought safely back to port by a lieutenant-commander and was the first of the USN's vessels to be decorated for outstanding service.

Callaghan was naval aide to President Roosevelt from 1938 to 1941 and became a close personal friend of the President. He was in command of the *San Francisco* at Pearl Harbor, where she was undergoing repairs at the time of the Japanese attack in December 1941.

CALVERT, Michael, b. 1913. British soldier nicknamed 'Mad Mike', a leader of the Chindits in Burma. After service in the Norwegian campaign of 1940, Calvert returned to the U.K. to help in training Commandos. From 1940 to 1941 he accompanied a mission to Australia and New Zealand, where he trained Commando-type units for combat in the South Pacific. At the end of 1941 he took charge of a jungle warfare school in Burma.

Calvert took a leading part in Wingate's special force to operate behind enemy lines, commanding a column of Chindits (as the long-range penetration groups were nicknamed) in their first campaign of

1943. When the Chindits were expanded, Calvert was promoted brigadier (at the age of 30) and given command of 77 Brigade. In the second Burma campaign Calvert's brigade distinguished itself in combat behind the Japanese lines.

In late 1944 Calvert returned to Britain to lecture on the war in Burma. He was then posted to the S.A.S., which he led through Belgium and Holland and across the Rhine, later taking part in the liberation of Norway.

CAMERON, Donald. *See* PLACE, Godfrey.

CAMPBELL, John ('Jock'), V.C., b. 1894. British soldier renowned during the Desert War in North Africa for his personal dash and unorthodox tactics. At the time of the Italian advance into Egypt in September 1940 Campbell was in command of 4th Regiment, Royal Horse Artillery, which took part in a number of rearguard engagements and became known for its skill and tenacity. Campbell conceived the idea of forming mobile columns, each including a few guns, to harass the Italian lines of communication. These units, which came to be known as 'Jock columns', had considerable success, and were later used against the Germans.

Campbell's most celebrated feat occurred at Sidi Rezegh on 21 and 22 November 1941 when he was a brigadier commanding 7th Support Group. The group was outgunned and almost surrounded, but Campbell provided an unexcelled demonstration of the power of determined and spirited leadership. He personally guided attacks by his armour on the enemy, directing the tanks from his famous cut-away staff car by waving a coloured handkerchief, and he even took part in servicing the guns. He was wounded in the action, but could not be persuaded to be evacuated for medical attention. For his gallantry in this incident, Campbell was awarded the V.C.

In February 1942 he was appointed to command the 7th Armoured Division, the 'Desert Rats'. But on 26 February he was killed when his staff car skidded and overturned on a clay road near Halfaya Pass.

Canaris   Carré

CANARIS, Wilhelm, b. 1888. German
admiral, who headed the Abwehr, the
Intelligence department of the Armed
Forces High Command. He was a somewhat remote personality, of mystical ten-
dencies, who despised the crudities of the
Nazi régime, and who pursued an equivocal course that eventually led him to the
gallows as one of the July plotters against
Hitler. Canaris was one of the first to
perceive that the aggressive policies of the
Nazis could end only in disaster for Germany. When he heard that the order to
attack Poland had actually been given, he
exclaimed, in a voice filled with emotion:
'This means the end of Germany.' Although
his advice was received by the conspirators
against Hitler with a great deal of respect,
he never could bring himself to play an
active and decisive role in the conspiracy.
His co-operation, however, was invaluable.
Under his aegis some more active plotters
used the formidable and widespread
apparatus of the Abwehr to organize and
strengthen the Resistance movement. The
fact that many officers in the Abwehr were
anti-Nazi by inclination and tradition has
led some to suggest that the department
was working for the Allies. This suggestion is unjustified, for although Canaris
and his staff may have been inefficient,
they were most assuredly German
patriots. Canaris was sincere in both his
professional and his Resistance activities,
but he was efficient at neither. If he gave
aid to the enemies of the Reich, as he did
in warning Denmark, Norway, Belgium,
and the Netherlands of impending Nazi
aggression, it was to prevent, not to
encourage, German defeat and humiliation. That the Abwehr was hampered in
its Intelligence activities by its 'negative'
attitude to Nazism is probable; that it
tried, and failed, to provide adequate
information for Germany's fighting forces
is incontestable.

As an example of this, Kesselring's
Chief of Staff recorded that in January
1944 Canaris, pressed for intelligence
regarding the Allied intentions, was unable
to provide any regarding the assault
forces, prior to the Anzio landings. In
1944 the defection of some Abwehr
agents to the British resulted in a scandal
which Himmler used to destroy Canaris,
whom he saw as a rival. On 18 February

1944 Hitler signed a decree unifying the
German Intelligence services under the
control of Kaltenbrunner, the head of the
S.D. Canaris was removed and the powers
of the Abwehr were severely restricted.
Although Canaris was not publicly dis-
honoured, Himmler made it quite clear in
private that he knew of 'the little
admiral's' intrigues. From this point
onwards it was obvious that Canaris's
only hope of survival lay with the success
of the plot against Hitler. After the failure
of the assassination plot on 20 July 1944
he was arrested, and was executed in
Flossenburg concentration camp on 9
April 1945 along with Bonhoeffer and
others.

The son of a Westphalian industrialist
of Italian ancestry, Canaris commanded
U-Boats in World War I and rose to
command the battleship *Schlesien*. In the
late 1930s he was sent to Spain to persuade Franco to enter the war on Germany's side. In fact he advised Franco
against doing so, a warning which the
Spanish leader took to heart.

CARLSON, Evans, b. 1896. American
soldier, commander of a marine battalion
using Commando tactics that became
known as 'Carlson's Raiders'. Carlson had
already gained considerable experience in
irregular military tactics before World
War II began: he had served as an
observer with the forces of Chiang Kai-
shek and had spent some time with
guerrilla troops operating behind the
Japanese lines. He was thus familiar both
with guerrilla methods and with Japanese
methods of warfare. The exploits of
'Carlson's Raiders' included an incursion
into the Japanese positions on Guadalcanal in November 1942, during which they
spent a month causing as much disruption
as possible and spreading alarm.

CARRÉ, Mathilde ('The Cat'), b. 1910.
French spy, at first a valued agent of the
Allies, and later an agent for the Germans.
After a short spell as a nurse on the
French eastern front during the 'phoney
war', she went to Toulouse where she met
a young Polish airman, Major Roman
Czerniawski—an encounter which changed
the course of her life. He was in touch
with a Polish organization in Marseilles

26

which was in contact with London, and on this foundation they formed the first great Intelligence network of the war, 'Inter-allié'. Their messages always began: 'To room 55a, War Office, London: The Cat reports . . .' and that which the Cat reported through the spring, summer and autumn of 1941 was both accurate and, without question, of great service to the Allied cause. The Cat herself was both impudent and daring—she had once remarked that 'there is almost a sensual pleasure in real danger'. She would deliberately seek out personal encounters with German officers, chatting to them pleasantly in the Métro, in restaurants, and in cafés—then going home to add to 'Armand's' (Czerniawski's) military reports some new detail she had thus acquired. In the winter of 1941, Inter-allié's H.Q. in the Rue Villa Leandre were raided by the Abwehr and she was arrested by Sergeant Bleicher ('Colonel Henri'), who persuaded her to save her own life by working for the Germans. Within a few weeks of the beginning of the Cat's co-operation with Bleicher, there were not far short of a hundred former members of Interallié, from both Paris and the provinces, under arrest. Using her old code name 'Victoire', she now began to send less reliable reports to the British. Pierre de Vomecourt ('Lucas'), a member of the French Section of the S.O.E. of the War Office, discovered her association with the Germans and she was forced to play a hazardous double role. In 1942 she went to Britain, where the War Office finally decided to put her out of circulation and interned her in Holloway Prison. After the liberation of France she was sent back to be tried for treason, her sentence of death being later commuted to imprisonment. Her maiden name was Mathilde Belard. She obtained her Law diploma in the 1920s and married M. Carré, a quiet, scholarly Frenchman living in Oran, in 1933.

CARTON DE WIART, Adrian, b. 1880. British general, a holder of the V.C., and, with his black eye-patch, a legendary warrior. Originally in the 4th Dragoon Guards, he was chief of the British Military Mission to the Polish army at the outbreak of war and was the only British officer to experience the 'Blitzkrieg' on Poland. Escaping from Poland via Romania he was then called upon to command the central Norwegian Expeditionary Force, which operated near Namsos in the Narvik campaign. In the spring of 1941 he went on a mission to Yugoslavia, crash landed, and was taken prisoner by the Italians. He escaped and was recaptured. He accompanied the Italian General Zanussi to Lisbon to discuss peace terms in August 1943; these broke down but he was released by the Italians, having volunteered to return to Italy as a P.O.W.

Carton de Wiart then became Churchill's personal representative with Chiang Kai-shek. Wounded four times in his career, he had lost an eye and hand. He was a flamboyant man, who chafed when denied action. He once said, 'Politics and soldiering are like port and champagne—they don't mix.'

CASEY, Richard, b. 1890. Australian politician, the British government's chief adviser in the Middle East during the most difficult period of the war in that region. In November 1939 he had gone as representative Australian Cabinet minister to London to confer on the war situation and, with Anthony Eden, had toured the Maginot Line. He had come away with strong impressions of the inadequacy of the preparations made. In 1940 he was sent to Washington as Australian Minister to the U.S.A.—an important post as the threat from Japan drew Australia and the U.S.A. closer together.

In March 1942 he succeeded Oliver Lyttelton as Minister of State in the Middle East, taking up his duties in Cairo in May. He was made a member of the British War Cabinet. The C.-in-C. in the Middle East considered Casey's post vital to the war in that area, since it dealt with political, economic, and propaganda problems, and the minister was able to advise on military policy from these points of view. The post became even more important as difficulties within the Arab world and relations between British and Americans in North Africa began to pose problems not basically military at all. In July 1942 Casey's advice was sought by Churchill on military reorganization: in August General Alexander was made C.-in-C. Middle East, and General Montgomery took over command of the 8th Army.

From 1943 onwards Casey became more involved with the Arab-Jewish question, and with the role of the French in Syria and the Lebanon. As a result of a memorandum on Anglo-American relations in the Middle East (which called for greater understanding of the interests of both sides) fruitful consultations were held in London in April 1944. As for the problem of Palestine, he was against repudiating British promises to the Arabs, and he was very conscious of the threat of growing Russian influence in the Arab world. Another problem that he and Harold Macmillan had to handle was the potentially dangerous relationship between the French and the anti-French Lebanese. In all these issues Casey showed unusual diplomatic and political skill, and the British government owed much to his ability to foster smooth relations with the many interested groups at a time of real war danger. In December 1943 the post of Minister of State in the Middle East was abolished when the North African and Middle Eastern commands were amalgamated. In the following year Casey became Governor of Bengal, a post he held until 1946.

'CAT, The'. *See* CARRÉ, Mathilde.

CAVALLERO, Count Ugo, b. 1880. Marshal of Italy and Chief of the Italian General Staff from 1940 until 1943. In 1940 the disastrous Italian campaign in Greece led to the resignation of Badoglio as Chief of Staff and his replacement by Cavallero in December. Cavallero's appointment was regarded in Berlin as an encouraging sign of future improvement in the Italian conduct of the war and of closer co-operation between the two allies. Cavallero imposed, in a fashion hitherto unknown in the Italian armed forces, a strong military leadership, and in particular he forced the navy—in spite of its opposition—to take action in supplying Libya. With his experience of industry he also made his influence felt in the chaotic sector of Italian war production. Despite his brilliant administrative gifts, he was

considered excessively subservient to the Germans and his fortunes thus depended to a great extent on German influence. Curiously enough, he was a convinced partisan of collaboration with the French, although he had no friendly feelings towards them.

By the beginning of 1942 his position had weakened, since things were going badly for the Italians in the Mediterranean and the Duce was rapidly losing confidence in him. Moreover, Cavallero suspected the existence of a Fascist plot to take over the army and police, which were separate from the party, and to depose the King. The actions which he took to counter this threat caused the circulation of rumours in Rome that he was almost openly preparing to succeed Mussolini. In January 1943 Mussolini informed the King that he had appointed General Ambrosio to replace Cavallero as Chief of Staff, and in August of that year Cavallero was arrested for an alleged plot with the former party secretary, Muti. He was released soon afterwards but committed suicide when he realized that the truth about his intrigues would soon be discovered.

After World War I Cavallero had abandoned his military career to work for the Pirelli Rubber Co., but was appointed by Mussolini to the position of Under Secretary of War in 1925. Three years later he returned to business life as a director of the giant Ansoldo shipbuilding yards. Cavallero was a great admirer of the efficiency of German war production and military structure, and on his return to active service as C.-in-C. in East Africa he became identified with the pro-Axis party in Italy.

CHADWICK, Roy, b. 1893. British aircraft designer who designed about 40 planes in his lifetime. His 'Anson' was widely used by the R.A.F. for training during the war. After 1935 he concentrated all his energies on military design, and produced the 'Manchester' twin-engined heavy bomber. This was a great advance in its day, but Chadwick nearly had to stop work on the project because he could not find enough power in the engines. However, he persisted and created the 'Lancaster' which could carry a 10-ton bomb. This plane made many night raids over Germany. It was his greatest success; he produced in addition the war-time 'York' and 'Lincoln' planes.

Chadwick was a friendly man, always restlessly experimenting to improve techniques. His work had a sound mixture of visionary insight and a very detailed and practical grasp of design.

CHAMBERLAIN, Neville, b. 1869. Prime Minister of the U.K. from May 1937. Chamberlain will long remain a controversial figure in British history. In trying to prevent war he set out to appease the dictators, while rearming at home. Yet the Munich agreement of 1938 was a Pyrrhic victory; he did not understand Hitler's mentality of ruthless aggression. Once he had been pushed into declaring war with Germany, on 3 September 1939, his moral courage and fortitude never deserted him, even though the year of war through which he lived was personally heart-breaking.

Chamberlain resigned as Prime Minister on 10 May 1940, and Churchill formed a National government of all three parties. Perhaps he should have resigned in September 1939, when his policy had failed to preserve the peace he longed for. He was not prepared or equipped for conducting a long war, believing as he did in the effectiveness of the blockade, in German economic difficulties, in the growing unpopularity of the war in Germany, and in the sympathy of neutral states. It was only after the fall of Poland, followed by the fall of Norway, Denmark, and the Low Countries, that he realized that the war was total. He rejected peace moves in late 1939, rightly seeing in them a false hope, and determined to create national unity at home.

In the House of Commons neither Labour nor Liberals would work with him. Various groups met to discuss how best to change the machinery of war, and to co-ordinate government, industry, and the armed forces. Chamberlain's Cabinet was unimaginative and, apart from Churchill and Eden, all were associated with his peace-time policies. Chamberlain's authority had been shaken by the inadequate support given to the Finns, and by their collapse; it was further shaken by the vacillating policy in Norway. As feeling in

the House grew, it became obvious that a National coalition was inevitable and essential, and that Churchill was the minister best fitted for the direction of this war.

Under Churchill, Chamberlain remained as Lord President, with a seat in the War Cabinet, and also as leader of the Conservative party. But in July 1940 he fell ill, never fully to recover from a serious operation; on 30 September he resigned from the Cabinet and on 9 October ceased to be leader of the Conservative party. He died on 9 November 1940.

CHANDOS, Viscount. *See* LYTTELTON, Oliver.

CHANDRA BOSE. *See* BOSE, Subhas Chandra.

CHENNAULT, Claire, b. 1898. American air force officer who led one of the most celebrated formations of the war, the 'Flying Tigers'. He was himself a pilot of unusual versatility and precision and had formerly been a member of an exhibition team. In 1942, before the U.S.A. entered the war, he organized the 'Flying Tigers', from a group of American volunteer pilots, to fight for the Chinese in their war against Japan. In July 1942 the group was incorporated into the USAAF in China. Although they never numbered more than 250, they destroyed nearly 300 Japanese aircraft in 6 months' fighting over Burma, Indo-China, and China, and succeeded in blunting the Japanese offensive in Chekiang and Kiang of July 1942. In 1943 Chennault was promoted major-general and became commanding officer of the 14th US (Volunteer) AAF in China. In May 1943 Chennault attended the Washington Conference on Far Eastern strategy.

By July 1943 Chennault's force had driven the Japanese from the skies of China, despite shortage of planes and equipment. His next task was to support the Chinese armies pushing the Japanese ground forces eastwards. However, in July 1945 he resigned his command, following his refusal to disband the Chinese-American joint wing of the Chinese air force.

CHERWELL, Lord (Frederick Lindemann), b. 1886. British physicist, of half Alsatian origin, a close personal friend of Churchill and the Prime Minister's chief scientific adviser during the war. He advised Churchill, too, on a variety of general problems of policy and administration; for example, by supplying him with analyses of supply requirements and bombing effectiveness. At first he had no official government post, but from 1942 to 1945 he was Paymaster-General, and was the only scientist in the Cabinet. In the words of his biographer, Lord Birkenhead, he had power greater than 'any scientist in history'. Churchill called him 'the Prof.'.

Cherwell undoubtedly made many and important contributions to the success of the British war effort, not least by his backing for original research. But some of the advice he gave the Prime Minister proved highly controversial. In March 1942 he wrote a minute to Churchill in which he estimated that aerial bombing could shatter German morale by rendering one-third of the German people homeless. In spite of the more sober opinions of Sir Henry Tizard and P. M. S. Blackett, and the dangerous diversion of planes from the Atlantic battle of 1942–3, bombing of civilians became official policy. Of course Cherwell's minute was not solely instrumental in the decision being reached. Blackett claimed that the bombing policy lengthened the war by up to 12 months; Cherwell's estimate, in the event, proved to be wildly optimistic.

Another matter on which Cherwell's judgment was impugned was the question of whether or not to use the anti-radar device 'Window'. The device was relatively simple: it involved the disturbance of enemy radar by dropping pieces of tinfoil. Cherwell had at first favoured the development of 'Window', but he later considered that the danger of the Germans borrowing the idea and using it against the Allies was too great: the Allies stood to lose more. 'Window' was not used until July 1943, and it has been strongly argued that its earlier use would have saved substantial plane losses.

Cherwell was too influential and had too vigorous a faith in the correctness of his own opinions to be universally popular.

Some associates accused him of vindictiveness. He himself felt unliked, but once he had accepted a man as a friend he never failed him, and many of his war-time colleagues remembered him with affection. A strict vegetarian, he was a man of passionate feelings who hated Hitler and his works. Loyal to Churchill through the thirties and often of one mind with him, Cherwell saw the danger of Hitler by 1933 and gathered together some of the best refugee scientists from Germany at his Clarendon Laboratory in Oxford. He returned there to his Chair in 1945.

CHESHIRE, Leonard, b. 1917. British air force officer, a holder of the V.C., and one of the war's most outstanding bomber pilots.

It was while in command of 617 Squadron, R.A.F.—the precision bombers —that Cheshire had his greatest success. The air battles of 1942 had spurred on aeronautical invention, especially in the field of radar, and now effective night bombing seemed possible. Cheshire was constantly on the look-out for new techniques and ways of using the latest devices, and on 8 February 1944 he achieved a spectacular success with the very accurate use of the target indicator bomb in the destruction of an aero-engine factory at Limoges. He concentrated on precision marking, and 617 Squadron, within a year of its formation, became the spearhead of the main bombing offensive, widening R.A.F. operations from simple area bombing to target bombing. In this, Cheshire, with Wing-Commander Gibson, V.C., and Squadron-Leader Martin, was the driving force and inspiration. They flew in first, low over the target, in Mosquitoes and dropped visual markers, thus enabling the following Lancaster bombers to concentrate on a precise target. Cheshire commanded 617 Squadron until July 1944. Considering the sheer number of missions he flew, and his position in battle with 5 Group, it is incredible that he survived this phase of the war.

In 1944 he went to H.Q. Eastern Air Command, S.E. Asia, and in 1945 to the British Joint Staff Mission in Washington. While he was there the U.S. authorities gave permission for Cheshire and the atomic scientist William Penney to accompany the A-bomb team to the island of Tinian in June 1945. An A-bomb was dropped on the Japanese city of Hiroshima on 6 August, and when the Japanese still did not surrender Nagasaki was bombed on 9 August. Cheshire was in the camera plane, as official British observer, and reached the target 10 minutes after the explosion. In discussing the morality of the operation, Cheshire later said that, along with the operations over Germany, it was so impersonal and seemed so necessary for victory that it appeared to him as regrettable but never as morally wrong: isolated in his cockpit, he found it difficult to conceive realistically the sufferings of the populations involved, who to him might not have existed at the moment of attack.

CHIANG KAI-SHEK, b. 1887. Chinese revolutionary generalissimo, leader of the Kuomintang party and one of the most prominent personages of the war. To the Allies he was the symbol of China's long defiance of the Japanese, and he was the Allied Supreme Commander in the China theatre of operations. His country had been at war with Japan since 1937, and after the devastation of Shanghai and Nanking, Chiang had retreated with his government to Chungking, a centre selected for its remote and defensible position in the heart of the country. In 1939 he became chairman of the National Defence Council and in 1943 Chief of State.

With the Japanese attack on the U.S. Pacific Fleet at Pearl Harbor at the end of 1941, Chiang's defiance of the Japanese was rewarded by American help and a new lease of life for his ideology. But by the beginning of 1943 the Americans were apprehensive of internal collapse in China through the growing strength of the Communists unless Chiang were given more positive support by the Allies. With Roosevelt and Churchill, he attended the Cairo Conference in November 1943. In Roosevelt's words, it was 'Chiang's conference'.

Chiang was not entirely popular with all the Allied leaders. General Stilwell, the tough and uncompromising American commander of Chinese and American

troops in the China-Burma-India theatre, sometimes showed considerable hostility to the generalissimo. The years 1942 and 1943 marked the climax of Chiang's power and prestige. Even before the Cairo Conference, U.S. policy had changed and the emphasis was not on the development of the Chinese army but on American air power in China. Chiang would not allow the unification of Chinese forces under American command; eventually the trouble generated led to the recall of Stilwell in November 1944.

Chiang's prestige with the Allies lay in his stubborn resistance to Japanese aggression. The accepted belief in American circles was that Chiang would be the head of the fourth Great Power in the world after victory had been achieved; but these views had to be cast aside when he was defeated by the Communists in his own country after the war ended.

CHIFLEY, Joseph, b. 1885. Australian statesman, Prime Minister of the country in the last weeks of the war. He was an old backbench colleague of the previous Prime Minister, John Curtin, and became Commonwealth Treasurer in Curtin's administration in 1940. He proved himself an extremely able and resourceful minister. Inspired by the Beveridge Report in the U.K., he went a long way towards introducing a comprehensive scheme of social insurance in Australia. In 1942 he was given the additional portfolio of Minister for Post-War Reconstruction, but he surrendered this office in the subsequent reorganization of the government. Although not an eloquent speaker, his supreme parliamentary skill and quiet sense of humour made him liked and respected on both sides of the House.

Although at the time of Curtin's death, in July 1945, Chifley had no ambition for the leadership of the party, he would have been Curtin's own choice, and this fact, together with his strong sense of duty and his conscientiousness as an administrator, marked him out for succession. He was acting Prime Minister from 30 April 1945, and when he became Prime Minister he promptly announced his intention of following in Curtin's footsteps and, in the event, showed himself capable of exerting a similar unifying influence within the Labor party.

CHURCHILL, Peter, b. 1909. A British agent in France of the S.O.E., which promoted Resistance in enemy-occupied countries. Calm in the presence of danger and a skilled navigator, his first missions were concerned with conducting various parties of agents to and from submarines off the Riviera coast. In January 1942 he landed by submarine at Miramar, bearing instructions for operatives at Lyons and under orders to find out the nature of a Resistance organization called 'Carte'. After some eventful weeks he made his way back to England by way of Perpignan, the Pyrenees, Madrid, and Gibraltar. In August of the same year he returned by parachute to France, this time to act as principal liaison officer between 'Carte' and London. In addition, under the code name of 'Raoul', he took charge of the 'Spindle' circuit.

Thus all of Churchill's time was devoted to the complex tasks of liaison and organization, which he did exceedingly well, leaving him no opportunity to engage in actual sabotage work—a fact which much annoyed some of his colleagues on the Riviera. Moreover he had a tendency to handle his contacts and subordinates with panache rather than tact, a circumstance that did not endear him to everybody. In April 1943, Churchill was arrested by the Germans, who had been keeping a watch on his courier, Odette Sansom. The Abwehr agent Hugo Bleicher ('Colonel Henri') was responsible for his apprehension, and Odette Sansom was arrested at the same time. Sent to prison and concentration camp, he was lucky to survive the German policy of executing captured agents.

Educated at Malvern and Caius College, Cambridge, Churchill was an ice-hockey Blue. Before the war he had travelled a good deal in Western Europe as a freelance journalist and writer.

CHURCHILL, Winston Spencer, b. 1874. British statesman, war-time Prime Minister and Minister of Defence. To the people of the British Commonwealth, especially in the dark early years of the war, Churchill seemed a living pledge of ultimate victory:

his solid figure, his dogged and humorous expression, and his rich but blunt oratory expressed an impregnability beyond argument or temporary reverses. His personal habits—his love of good living, his eternal cigar, his 'V for Victory' sign, his siren suit, his witticisms, his desire to see action at first hand—captured the imagination of his countrymen and millions of others among the Allies and gave rise to countless anecdotes about him. Had Churchill died during the war, his death would undoubtedly have lowered the morale of the people of Britain more than any military defeat.

Churchill succeeded Neville Chamberlain as Prime Minister on 11 May 1940, and formed a National government, with himself as Minister of Defence. He at once won the confidence of Parliament with his speech: 'What is our policy? I will say it is to wage war by land, sea and air with all our might and with all the strength that God can give us . . . Victory at all costs, Victory in spite of all terror, Victory however long and hard the road may be.' On 22 May Parliament passed legislation placing 'all persons, their services and their property at the disposal of His Majesty'.

Churchill made several visits to the French government before the evacuation of the British army from Dunkirk (27 May–4 June) and on 16 June 1940 suggested an Anglo-French union with common citizenship. This idea was rejected, and in fact could have been little more than a rhetorical statement of goodwill. Britain now faced invasion with a navy intact and a skeleton air force to protect an otherwise almost defenceless country. Churchill's inspiring and stubborn oratory provided a substitute for this unpreparedness. During the agonizing Battle of Britain in the summer of 1940 he made his most famous speech: 'Let us therefore brace ourselves to our duties and so bear ourselves that if the British Empire and its Commonwealth last for a thousand years men will say "This was their finest hour".' His bold and solid presence, whether inspecting defences, broadcasting, or giving his 'V' sign to those bombed out, epitomized the spirit of the nation. His friendship with the President of the U.S.A. resulted in the conception of Lend-Lease or mutual aid. In August 1941 a meeting with the President—the Argentia Conference, in Newfoundland—produced the Atlantic Charter, the seminal statement of the democratic ideals which were to be embodied in the United Nations Charter.

One of Churchill's early acts as Minister of Defence was to set up a Directorate of Combined Operations. This, at first treated with doubt and suspicion in some quarters, grew until the fruits of its experience produced the successful invasion of the European mainland four long years later.

During the whole of the war Churchill maintained close relations with his Chiefs of Staff, and had the wholehearted support of his Cabinet. General Ismay remarked that in military matters he was prone to count chickens before they were hatched, but another member of the Chiefs of Staff Committee said about him: 'His whole mind was concentrated on winning the war whatever happened, and in many ways his thinking was far ahead of the military machine. People are apt to believe that he thought up some of his famous sayings after the event which occasioned them, but this is not so. They were made up on the spur of the moment and he had the effect of keeping everyone up to the mark and at the same time cheering them up.' The Prime Minister's method of working, with brief concise minutes sent for 'Action this Day' to all civilian as well as military heads, certainly created the impression that Churchill's eye was on every aspect of the war effort.

One of his most notable broadcasts was made on 22 June 1941 when German armies invaded Russia. Without retracting his anti-Communism he promised every possible help to the Russian people. After the Japanese attack on the American Pacific Fleet at Pearl Harbor on 7 December 1941 he set to work to bring the Grand Alliance to fruition. This entailed Britain and America sharing military and economic resources under the Combined Chiefs of Staff, and the agreement that the defeat of Germany should take priority over the defeat of Japan. This last decision, however, caused criticism at home after the fall of Singapore (February 1942). In 1942 Churchill ratified

the 20-year treaty of friendship between the U.K. and Russia. But at the 'turn of the tide' for the Allies' fortunes in August 1942 he resisted strong pressure from Russia and the U.S.A. to establish a 'Second Front' that year.

On 1 July 1942 Churchill faced a motion of censure in the Commons for his conduct of the war, but defeated this by an overwhelming majority. He guided much post-war planning: proposing early in 1943 a 4-year reconstruction plan; and, later, a Health Service and co-operation between state and private enterprise.

After the Allied landings in North Africa in November 1942, Churchill and Roosevelt met at the Casablanca Conference (January 1943), and agreed on plans for further operations in the Mediterranean. In Cairo in November priorities were settled for the worldwide effort. Meanwhile in August at Quebec the strategy for the invasion of the European mainland was discussed. At the same time a new war theatre was established in S.E. Asia. At the conference in Teheran which followed Cairo, Roosevelt and Churchill were outmanœuvred by Stalin in the latter's determination to keep Anglo-American forces out of the Balkans.

On 6 June 1944 the long-awaited 'Second Front' was opened in Europe. The Anglo-American landings in Normandy were successful, and shortly afterwards Churchill experienced one of the most emotional moments of his leadership when he visited the beach-head in France. The Allied landing was one of the great milestones of the war, ranking with the forging of the Grand Alliance after Pearl Harbor and the German defeat at Stalingrad. It commenced the phase that culminated in victory in Europe on 8 May 1945.

But the war in the East had still to be won. In June 1944 the Japanese defeat at Imphal cleared the way for the liberation of Burma and Malaya. But the Americans were interested primarily in the Pacific. Churchill took the initiative, meeting Roosevelt at Quebec on 12–16 September 1944 and succeeding in including the British navy in the final plans for the Pacific war. However, Roosevelt, believing himself to be on intimate terms with Stalin, refused to be drawn on the question of relations with the Soviet Union, and was suspicious of Churchill's anti-Communism. In October Churchill met Stalin in Moscow in an attempt to resolve the Polish question and to divide the Balkans into spheres of influence. To prevent a Communist take-over in Greece, Churchill organized British intervention there.

In February 1945 Churchill and Roosevelt met Stalin at Yalta. Roosevelt wanted to end the war as soon as possible in Europe and the East. Russia had much aid to offer; Britain, exhausted, had very little; and Roosevelt subordinated every other aim to that of securing Russian co-operation. Churchill tried to intervene over the Polish question, but British power was declining and he made little headway.

In July 1945 the Allied leaders held their last meeting at Potsdam, but in the middle of this the Conservative party was defeated in the general election in Britain. Churchill's place as Prime Minister was taken by Clement Attlee.

CIANO, Galeazzo, b. 1903. Mussolini's son-in-law and Italian Foreign Minister from 1936 to 1943. In August 1939 Ciano had met Hitler and Ribbentrop at Berchtesgaden, and realized that they meant to start a European war that year by attacking Poland. He returned to Rome alarmed and disillusioned. He had already shown his distrust of Germany by his reluctance to sign the 'Pact of Steel', but now his suspicions were strengthened by Hitler's obvious indifference to his nominal ally's unreadiness for war, and his determination to act without consultation. During the first 9 months of the war Ciano tried to wean Mussolini from German influence and to establish a policy of non-belligerence. For his pains he earned Ribbentrop's hatred—an honour in Ciano's opinion—but he failed to overcome Mussolini's dreams of martial glory and his reluctance to ally himself with the democracies. With the fall of France, Mussolini's fear of being deprived of the fruits of victory was added to these two motives.

Ciano had commanded a bomber squadron in the Ethiopian campaigns, and when Italy entered World War II he again did so, taking part in occasional active missions. He remained Foreign Minister,

but Italian military weakness severely limited his scope for initiative in foreign affairs and he maintained an ambivalent attitude to Italy's part in the war.

On 5 February 1943 Mussolini dismissed Ciano from his position as Foreign Minister and appointed him ambassador to the Holy See. On 25 July, at the crucial meeting of the Fascist Grand Council, which led to Mussolini's deposition, Ciano opposed Mussolini, presented the evidence of German bad faith that he had collected during his years in office, and recommended a separate peace. But after the overthrow of Mussolini, he was charged with peculation and left Rome. He was later captured by the 'base trickery' of the Germans, who made him promises of transport to Spain and alarmed him with veiled threats about the fate of his children. He was held at Verona and after a mock trial was executed in January 1944, on Mussolini's instructions.

Ciano's career had been greatly advanced by his marriage to Mussolini's daughter Edda. His contribution to history is his *Diary*, which gives an intimate account of Mussolini and his close associates. His enthusiasm for imperialist adventure (such as the invasion of Albania) suggests that the cause of his rupture with Ribbentrop stemmed from rivalry rather than from principle.

'CICERO' was the code name given by the Germans to one of the most pedestrian, successful, and ill-rewarded spies in the history of espionage. On the evening of 26 October 1943 a man giving no name called at the German Embassy in Ankara and asked to see the First Secretary, who was Ribbentrop's brother-in-law. He was, instead, interviewed by an Intelligence attaché, L. C. Moyzisch, to whom he offered photographs of secret British documents in return for a payment of £20,000. He claimed to be the valet of the British ambassador to Turkey, Sir Hughe Knatchbull-Hugessen. The Germans, sceptical at first, were astonished to discover that the man was in fact as good as his word: over the next six months he supplied them with 400 photographs of documents from the British Embassy, many of them of the highest secrecy. Some of these documents contained information about Allied war plans that should have been of vital importance to the German leaders; they were forwarded from Ankara to Berlin and, there, virtually ignored. 'Cicero' received in payment £300,000 in sterling banknotes—the currency he had asked for.

The story given by 'Cicero' to the Germans was true in its essentials. He was, as he said, the British ambassador's valet and he obtained access to the embassy's most secret papers by borrowing the ambassador's keys when opportunity offered. His real name was Elias Basna and he was Albanian by birth. 'Cicero's' dream was to build and run an hotel in a favoured resort in his home country. After the war he succeeded in building his hotel, using the money he had earned from the Germans. But before the building was put into use, 'Cicero's' dream world collapsed: he was accused of issuing forged banknotes. It then transpired that nearly all the notes the Germans had given to him in return for his photographs were counterfeit.

CLARK, Mark Wayne, b. 1896. American general, one of the most forceful and successful field commanders of the war. A West Point graduate, Clark became a major-general in 1942, and commanded American ground forces in Europe as Eisenhower's second-in-command. He made a daring trip by H.M. submarine *Seraph* to North Africa in October 1942 for a secret meeting with French officers near Algiers to co-ordinate details for the planned invasion—unfortunately Clark gave an impression of not trusting the French completely, for the invasion date had already been set.

After the Allies landed in Algeria in November 1942, Clark negotiated with Admiral Darlan. He placed Darlan under protective custody and arranged a cease-fire with him. Clark at once told Eisenhower in Gibraltar, 'I now have two grand-daddies on my hands'—referring to Giraud and Darlan. Eventually Eisenhower and Clark accepted Darlan as French 'Head of State' in French North Africa.

Clark became a lieutenant-general in November 1942, and in the following January was put in command of the U.S. 5th Army. In early September 1943 he was

responsible for the Salerno landings. The troops were nearly pushed back into the sea at first, but succeeded in establishing a bridgehead. The 5th Army then forced the mountain passes to the north, onto the plain, and entered Naples on 1 October 1943. By winter it had crossed the River Volturno. Clark's troops then took Anzio, 50 miles behind the German lines. But they were not able to consolidate by a break to the Alban hills. The Germans pushed the Anzio troops back, but by February 1944 the position was stabilized. The British 8th Army, which had been pushing up the east coast, now came alongside. Clark next reluctantly asked and received permission from General Alexander, supreme commander in Italy, to bomb the monastery at Cassino, believed to be of advantage to the Germans. Eventually in May combined British, American, Polish, and French troops under Alexander and Clark defeated the Germans at Cassino, after bitter fighting. On 4 June the 5th Army entered Rome.

After some advances up the west coast, the 5th Army was checked before Bologna when the left flank gave way under attack. In December Alexander succeeded Maitland Wilson as Supreme Allied Commander of the Mediterranean theatre, and Clark became commander of the Allied armies in Italy, commanding the 15th Army Group. This appointment was Churchill's suggestion.

Clark gained a decisive victory in the next 6 months. In early April the 8th Army led across the Senio, followed 5 days later by the 5th. After a week's hard fighting, the German front broke. It was then a matter of time. The 8th raced up the eastern plain, the Americans took the centre, meeting the French at Genoa. The Germans surrendered to Alexander on 2 May.

Clark was extremely successful in commanding troops of mixed nationalities. Churchill was impressed at their first meeting, and nicknamed Clark 'the American Eagle'.

CLAY, Lucius, b. 1897. American general, from 1945 deputy chief (to Eisenhower) of the U.S. military government in Germany. In 1942 he was placed in charge of the Army Procurement programme. After brief assignments as base section commander in Normandy, where he performed invaluable services in the logistics system, and as Deputy Director of the Office of War Mobilization and Reconversion, he returned to Europe in April 1945 to act as Eisenhower's deputy for the government of Germany.

From the beginning he was convinced that a civil agency of government should take over the control of Germany, and his whole organization was definitely separated from the military staff. In this way he was prepared to turn over military government to the State Department with no necessity for complete reorganization. It was his ardent belief that Germany should be reconstructed and not castigated and that the rehabilitation of the Ruhr was vital to American and world economic interests. Eisenhower stated that: 'More than any other two individuals, Clay and Wickersham deserve credit for the initial establishment of American military government in Germany—a performance that, in view of the frustration, obstacles, divided counsels and responsibilities, and difficulties in post-war Allied co-operation, must be classed as brilliant.'

After graduating from West Point in 1918 he became an instructor in an officers' training camp. Between the wars he gained much experience as an engineer and was in charge of the construction of the Denison Dam, Texas, at the time of the outbreak of war.

COCKCROFT, John, b. 1897. British scientist, a nuclear physicist, who directed research into defence against aerial attack. In 1939 he became assistant director of research at the Ministry of Supply, and from 1941 to 1944 he was chief superintendent, Air Defence Research and Development. Cockcroft served in World War I at a very early age, and afterwards entered Metro-Vickers as an apprentice and read electrical engineering at Manchester University. In 1932 he produced with Ernest Walton the first 'atom-smashing' machine, discovering how to accelerate protons artificially to energies high enough to break open atomic nuclei. For this he and Walton shared a Nobel Prize in 1951.

Cockcroft played an important part in the installation of the radar early warning system of stations round the coast of Britain. The potentialities of radar detection were demonstrated in August 1942 during the Dieppe Raid when Cockcroft from a spot in the Isle of Wight was able to chart the progress of the miniature invasion fleet more than 100 miles away.

As Sir Henry Tizard's second-in-command on his visit to the U.S.A. in 1940, he helped to involve American scientists in defence research. For two years from 1944 he directed the Atomic Energy Division of the National Research Council of Canada.

COHEN, Morris ('Two Gun Cohen'), b. 1889. An Englishman who became a Chinese Republican general and a legend in Chinese revolutionary history.

In 1941 the Chinese government sent him to Hong Kong on two delicate assignments: the first was to start talks with General Grasset, the garrison commander, about Chinese military co-operation to deal with the imminent threat of Japanese invasion, the other was to help Admiral Chan Chak to keep track of the 'fifth column' of Chinese inside the colony. He found his work frustrating, being hampered by the British government's policy of non-provocation of the Japanese and strict neutrality in the Sino-Japanese War. On Boxing Day 1941 his assignments were abruptly cut short by the surrender of Hong Kong to the Japanese. Despite his exceptional bravery, he admitted to experiencing a great deal of trepidation as he sat in the lounge of the Hong Kong hotel waiting to be arrested by the victorious Japanese. 'I thought of all the things the Japs might have against me. I began to feel more frightened than I'd ever been in my life.' He was interrogated at length, severely beaten up and threatened with decapitation. Although he had been a successful entrepreneur in the half-world of illicit arms traffic, he was a man of uncompromising integrity, and he refused to collaborate with the Japanese in return for his freedom. His refusal landed him in Stanley prison camp where he spent eighteen months in squalid and inhuman conditions.

The eldest son of an immigrant Jewish couple, he was brought up in the East End of London, where he soon learned to fend for himself. At the age of 16 he emigrated

to Canada and spent some time selling
real estate. There he met and befriended an
old Chinese, Mah Sam, who encouraged
him to join the Tsing Chung-hui (Chinese
revolutionary party), whose leader was
Sun Yat-sen, whom he accompanied on his
tour of Canada and the U.S.A. as a bodyguard. In 1922, after the successful revolution in China, he left Canada to become
Sun Yat-sen's A.D.C. He soon proved
himself an indispensable and loyal servant
of the Republican cause and was made a
general in the Chinese army. Until the
Manchurian Incident in 1931 he had dealt
in arms mainly for gain and only half-
heartedly to help rearm the Cantonese
armies against their potential enemies in
the north.

COLLINS, Joseph ('Lightning Joe'), b.
1896. American general, a brilliant infantry
commander. In 1941 Collins was Chief of
Staff, 7th Army Corps, and then Chief of
Staff, Hawaiian Department. He commanded the 25th Infantry Division in the
bitterly contested campaign which drove
the Japanese from Guadalcanal early in
1943. After his experience in jungle and
coconut grove the *bocage* of Normandy
seemed almost spacious when he came to
command the 7th Army Corps in the
invasion of France in 1944.

Collins was quite used to operating
without benefit of roads and tanks, and
had come to expect his troops to advance
through thick country relying almost
entirely on the fire-power of the weapons
they could carry themselves. His corps
landed on 'Utah' beach, captured Cherbourg 20 days after the landing, led the
break-out from Normandy, pierced the
Siegfried Line, captured Aachen and
Cologne, enveloped the Ruhr from the
south and east, and then continued eastwards to a meeting with the Russians on
the Elbe at Dessau. He drove his commanders and men hard and had no com-
punction about removing those who failed
him. Yet his enthusiasm and frankness
earned him the label of 'the G.I.'s General'.
His policy was to hit hard and keep the
enemy on the run, but he was no 'smash
and grab' commander. Thorough in
planning and flexible in direction, he was
always ready to adapt his tactics to the
special needs of the occasion.

He graduated from West Point in 1917,
and was later sent overseas to take command of a battalion of the 18th Infantry
at Coblenz. Between the wars he gained
expertise as a student and later instructor
on various infantry and artillery courses.

CONINGHAM, Arthur, b. 1895. British
air marshal who commanded the air
forces supporting the invading troops of
the 'Second Front'. As an air commodore
in 1939, Coningham commanded No. 4
Group of long-range bombers based in
Yorkshire. He spent the next few years in
the North Africa campaign, where his
various air forces gave cover to the Allies
on their westward advance. In 1941 he
was in command of the Desert Air Force
supporting the 8th Army. In January 1943
Tripoli was captured, and Coningham
travelled west to Algeria, commanding the
1st Allied (North African) Tactical Air
Force. This meant that he controlled the
British and American air forces covering
their armies in the Tunisian campaign.
After Tunis was taken Coningham commanded the air forces used in the capture
of Pantellaria and Sicily. They moved
across to southern Italy and gave air cover
to the Allied armies.

In January 1944 he was back in England
commanding the 2nd Tactical Air Force.
He went with the force to Normandy in
July. For the last year of the war he had
forces of about 1,800 front-line planes and
100,000 men, ranging across Europe from
Copenhagen to Marseilles. These included
parts of the air forces of seven nations.

Coningham had a distinguished military
career from 1914 onwards. From earlier
service with New Zealanders he gained
the nickname 'Maori', inevitably changed
to 'Mary'. He always knew how far to
stretch those under his command. He was
dynamic and young in outlook, passing on
his excitement to his men. A ruthlessly
efficient and hard-working man, he was
always clear in his objectives.

COOPER, Alfred Duff, b. 1890. British
minister, a determined worker for Anglo-
French understanding and alliance. Before
the outbreak of war Duff Cooper had
been a member of Stanley Baldwin's
Cabinet, first as Secretary of State for
War, 1935–7, then as First Lord of the

Admiralty, 1937–8. After a dramatic resignation over Chamberlain's Munich policy he sat on the back benches, a member of the Churchill-Eden group, opposed to the government's policy of appeasement.

After war was declared Cooper remained on the back benches until Churchill became Prime Minister. During that time he made a lecture tour of the U.S.A. and gained a valuable insight into opinion there, which was then hostile to the idea of involvement in a European war. This knowledge was useful to him as Minister of Information under Churchill (1940–1), but he was not happy in this post, and knew he was not the right man to handle the inter-departmental clashes over propaganda and what information should be given to the press. He asked Churchill to find him another post.

In August 1941 he was sent to Singapore to report on conditions in the Far East, and after the Japanese attack of 8 December 1941 he was instructed to form a war council as Resident Cabinet Minister at Singapore for Far Eastern affairs. He was recalled in January 1942, since Wavell's appointment the previous month as overall commander made his post unnecessary. In June 1942 he presided over Lord Swinton's committee which had been established in 1940 to check all political prisoners in Great Britain. This occupied him for eighteen months.

In October 1942 Eden asked him to be the British representative on the French Committee of Liberation. Duff Cooper had always been convinced that de Gaulle was the only possible leader of the French Resistance. He set himself to work for the reconstruction of a powerful and friendly French nation. To do this he had to overcome the reluctance of many members of the British government who were hostile to France and to France's continued government of Syria. When de Gaulle returned to London in June 1944, Cooper did all he could to present the French case fairly, and to counter Churchill's and Roosevelt's doubts about Gaullism.

In September 1944 he was accredited to de Gaulle, now head of the French government. Cooper's ultimate aim was a treaty of alliance between the U.K. and

France, and he did everything in his power to further this at a time of tense relations between the Big Three, and of continued anti-Gaullist feeling. But he finally achieved his ambition with the Treaty of Dunkirk in January 1947. There is no doubt that this helped the shattered French to gain a new sense of prestige which made the resumption of normal relations after the war a much simpler task.

COURTNEIDGE, Cicely, b. 1893. A well-known actress before the war, chiefly in musical comedy, Cicely Courtneidge became a distinctive part of the war-time scene in Britain.

She gave frequent Sunday concerts for the troops with her Services Entertainment Unit. On tour she collected over £10,000 in two years to buy comforts for anti-aircraft gunners. She went with E.N.S.A. parties in 1945 to Gibraltar, Malta, North Africa, and, finally, Italy. Whilst there news of the cease-fire came through and, draped in a Union Jack, she led the audience in an emotional rendering of 'Home Is Where Your Heart Is'.

Lively, extrovert, with a huge and original sense of fun, Cicely Courtneidge related many amusing war-time anecdotes in her book *Cicely*. As well as her entertainment work for the troops she also appeared in three popular war-time shows: *Hulbert Follies* in 1940, *Full Swing* in 1942, and *Something in the Air* in 1943.

COWARD, Noël, b. 1899. One of the great names of the British theatre as an actor, a dramatist famous for his humorous and witty commentaries on English life and manners, and a composer of haunting and nostalgic songs, Noël Coward made an important contribution to sustaining the high morale of both civilians and members of the Services. In the making of his moving and inspiring film *In Which We Serve* (1942), based on the war-time life of a destroyer and her company, he was dramatist, director, producer, and actor. Two other famous Coward plays of the war years were *Blithe Spirit* (1941) and *This Happy Breed* (1942). He frequently used his position in the world of entertainment and his influence with people in various walks of life to help war charities and to bring cheer to the lives of those in the forces; he was, for example, instrumental in obtaining a constant supply of good films for showing in ships of the Royal Navy.

CRABB, Lionel, b. 1910. British naval officer, one of the first of the R.N. 'frogmen' during the war. His valour and enterprise earned him the nickname of 'Buster' Crabb. While he was serving in Gibraltar in 1942 as a mine and bomb disposal officer, he and his unit were given the task of disposing of bombs under water as well as on land. During these operations he pioneered the use of specialized under-water equipment. At the time of the Italian surrender in 1943 he was operating in northern Italy and was commissioned to take charge of anti-frogmen activities in order to keep the northern Italian ports clear for British warships and landing craft. Being something of a diplomat as well as a man of action, by purely friendly persuasion he arranged for Italian frogmen to clear Leghorn harbour of German mines. Commander Crabb was awarded the George Medal in 1944 'for gallantry and undaunted devotion to duty'.

CREASY, George, b. 1895. British admiral, in charge of naval planning for the Allied invasion of N.W. Europe in June 1944. At the beginning of the war he commanded the 1st Destroyer Flotilla in the Mediterranean. When his ship, H.M.S. *Grenville*, was sunk in 1940, it was three-quarters of an hour before he and other survivors were picked up. He then commanded H.M.S. *Codrington*, which took part in the Norwegian campaign, and for 2 months served as Chief of Staff to the First Sea Lord, Sir Dudley Pound.

In September 1940 Creasy was appointed Director of Anti-Submarine Warfare at the Admiralty, and held this critically important post until 1942, when he received command of the battleship H.M.S. *Duke of York*. Promoted rear-admiral, he headed the naval section of the Allied staff which under General Morgan developed the original plan for the invasion of Europe. General Morgan described him as 'the right man in the right place' for this assignment.

As Chief of Staff to the Allied naval C.-in-C., Sir Bertram Ramsay, Creasy was mainly responsible for the detailed naval planning preceding D-Day. One of his most difficult tasks—successfully accomplished—was the provision of navy-borne supplies for the ground and air forces of the invasion. He was promoted admiral in 1944.

CRERAR, Henry, b. 1888. Canadian general, a distinguished military thinker, and a brilliant commander in the field. He revealed great ability as an artillery tactician during World War I, and in the inter-war period he planned the reorganization of Canada's militia and served as Director of Military Operations and Intelligence from 1935 to 1938. In the latter capacity he drafted the Joint Staff Memorandum that repudiated isolationism, emphasized the deterioration of the international situation, and advocated a considerable expansion of the Canadian forces. He went to London on the outbreak of war to organize the Canadian military H.Q. there, but returned to Canada in 1940 as C.G.S. The programme he inaugurated aimed at building a mobile Canadian force based in the U.K., equipped for an offensive rather than a defensive role. He returned to London at the end of November 1940 for discussions with the British government on the Canadian military contribution, conferences which led to a modification of his proposed 1941 programme. Crerar resigned at the end of 1941, went to England, and dropped rank to become acting G.O.C. of the 1st Canadian Corps. In 1943 he led this force in Italy. When the 1st Canadian Army was formed in 1944 Crerar became C.-in-C., and commanded it throughout the campaigns in N.W. Europe. His forces first proceeded to clear the coastal belt, particularly the Pas de Calais, where important German flying-bomb and artillery installations were located. From September to November he cleared the Scheldt and freed Antwerp in the face of bitter resistance. On 8 February 1945 Crerar led his forces in an offensive S.E. of Nijmegen, in the Netherlands, beginning the Battle of the Rhineland. On 27 February his army stormed Udem in the outer defences of the last and weakest belt of the Siegfried Line between the Rhine and the Maas, and then advanced south and south-east. Reinforced by British troops the Canadian army advanced on two lines (9 April), thrusting into central Holland on the left to the Germans' last line of retreat, and on the right moving to Emden along the Dutch-German frontier. Pivoting on Arnhem, he cut off the Germans in a fast-closing pocket that contained most of the principal cities of Holland. After re-incorporating the 1st Corps from Italy in the Canadian army he proceeded to eliminate the remaining pockets of resistance in the Netherlands.

Although personally favouring conscription, Crerar was not involved in the crisis that developed in Canada on that issue. He brought sound judgment and tactical versatility to bear on the many complex problems and situations he encountered.

CRIPPS, Sir Stafford, b. 1889. Younger son of the 1st Baron Parmoor, Cripps belonged to the curiously élite group of Labour party intellectuals—idealistic, mostly churchmen, and solidly upper middle class. His pre-war reputation had been made as a barrister. His Socialism was so thorough-going that he had been expelled from the Parliamentary Labour party.

On the outbreak of war he was convinced that Anglo-Russian relations could and should be improved, despite the signing of the Nazi-Soviet pact in August 1939. In his opinion the pact was merely an attempt to buy time until Germany attacked Russia, and the events in 1941 proved him correct. Even Churchill, arch anti-Bolshevik, thought negotiation worth while.

Cripps set off on an unofficial mission to India, China, and Russia. He tried to assess the Indian political scene, and met the Hindu and Muslim leaders, before going on to China to gauge the situation there. He also visited Moscow, crossing the steppes of Asia during a bitter winter.

After Churchill became Prime Minister Cripps was sent to Russia as a special envoy in May 1940. By June 1941, when Germany was at war with Russia, he had effectively become ambassador. By nature he sympathized with Russian socialist ideals; he was therefore more welcome

than most other British representatives might have been, and though the alliance between Russians and the western Allies arose from the war situation itself, Cripps was rightly credited with working ceaselessly to prepare the ground and reached perhaps his highest peak of popularity on his return from Moscow.

While in Russia he had been appointed a Privy Councillor and when he returned to England he was determined to play an effective role in the War Cabinet. He refused a post as Minister of Supply, but in February 1942 accepted the positions of Lord Privy Seal and Leader of the House of Commons. In March he set forth on the 'Cripps Mission' to India to explain to the leaders of the Congress party and the Muslim League what practical steps towards Indian self-government the War Cabinet was prepared to take. But the draft declaration was rejected by them, albeit reluctantly.

In the House of Commons he spoke out stirringly as a Christian and as a socialist for spiritual and material reconstruction in the post-war U.K. Such ideals appealed to the young and he was made Rector of Aberdeen University in 1942. But he was a difficult and demanding leader of the House and was not happy in the War Cabinet, where his ideas on the direction of the war and the necessity for planning for peace were not acceptable to the Prime Minister. With relief he accepted in November 1942 the office of Minister of Aircraft Production which did not carry Cabinet rank. In this new post his organizing and administrative talents were given full play and he contributed significantly to the higher direction of the war.

CUNNINGHAM, Sir Alan, b. 1887. British general who commanded forces that helped to liberate Ethiopia from Italian occupation and who later commanded the 8th Army in the Western Desert. In 1940, after briefly holding a divisional command, he was appointed G.O.C. East Africa Forces.

In December 1940 it was decided to mount an offensive against the Italians in Eritrea, Ethiopia, and Somaliland to coincide with the offensive against the Italians in the Western Desert. Cunningham commanded the troops, including South Africans, who marched against the coastal towns of Italian Somaliland, working up from eastern Kenya. He had captured these towns by February 1941, and then began a 1,000-mile march to the Ethiopian capital, Addis Ababa. This operation was notable for the skill he showed in exploiting his force's mobility, and for the minimal loss of life. The capital was occupied on 6 April 1941, after the Italian commander, the Duke of Aosta, had agreed not to prejudice the safety of the civilian population. On 5 May the Emperor of Ethiopia returned to his throne in triumph and rejoicing. In two months, part of Mussolini's African empire had vanished, and the Red Sea was now safe for Allied shipping.

In August 1941 Cunningham left Ethiopia to take command of the new 8th Army in the Western Desert. He was now at the head of an almost entirely mechanized army, with about 30,000 vehicles at its disposal between Tobruk and Egypt. In the offensive of November 1941 against General Rommel's Afrika Korps, tank losses were severe, although the objective (the relief of Tobruk) was eventually achieved. Cunningham had felt inclined to break off the battle. But General Auchinleck would not agree, and replaced him on 26 November by General Ritchie. Tobruk was relieved on 10 December 1941 and Cyrenaica temporarily regained.

Cunningham returned to England as commandant of the Staff College, Camberley, in 1942. Subsequently he was G.O.C. Northern Ireland from 1943 to 1944, and G.O.C. Eastern Command from 1944 to 1945. At the close of the war he went to Palestine as the last British High Commissioner.

CUNNINGHAM, Sir Andrew, b. 1883. The outstanding British naval leader of the war. At the outbreak, he was C.-in-C. Mediterranean Fleet and, owing to his long experience in the area, few could have been better suited to this command. Essentially a man of action rather than an administrator (in which capacity he showed impatience), he quickly established complete ascendancy over the Italian fleet despite the actual superiority of the force

opposed to him. On the occasion of the defection of the French fleet he showed himself a diplomat by securing the effective immobilization of Admiral Godfroy's squadron at Alexandria, without bloodshed or rancour.

Within a few weeks of Mussolini's declaration of war Cunningham, in the action off Calabria, had chased a superior Italian fleet back into the shelter of its ports; in November 1940 the Fleet Air Arm attack at Taranto put part of the Italian navy out of action, and in March 1941, in the brief night action off Cape Matapan, three of the largest Italian cruisers were destroyed.

The establishment of strong land bases for the Luftwaffe on the shores of the Mediterranean and the loss of Cyrenaica, Greece, and Crete made it impossible for the British fleet, lacking air support, to operate freely or to keep the sea routes fully open.

Cunningham handed over his command to Admiral Harwood when he went to Washington as the British representative to the Joint Chiefs of Staff for six months. The expulsion of the Axis forces from North Africa beginning in late 1942 gave the British fleet sea-room once more. Cunningham returned as Allied Naval C.-in-C. under General Eisenhower and was promoted to admiral of the fleet.

He had the satisfaction of regaining complete control of the Mediterranean, and in September 1943 of receiving the surrender of the Italian fleet. In his history of the *War at Sea*, Captain Roskill remarked that Conrad's words describing the influence of Nelson in the same sea might be applied to Cunningham: 'Through the fidelity of his fortune and the power of his inspiration, he stands unique amongst the leaders of fleets and sailors.'

When Admiral Pound died in October 1943 Cunningham became First Sea Lord and until the end of the war he shared responsibility for its central direction.

Cunningham went to H.M.S. *Britannia* as a cadet in 1897 and by the beginning of World War I had gained great experience with destroyers. At the Dardanelles he was commander of the destroyer H.M.S. *Scorpion*. After his promotion to vice-admiral in 1936 it seemed unlikely that he would reach the top of his profession, but the war brought his undoubted gifts to

Cunningham

Curtin

fruition in a remarkable period of service to his country.

CUNNINGHAM, John, b. 1915. One of the most determined and successful night fighter pilots in the R.A.F., 'Cat's Eyes' Cunningham gained his first victory as a member of a Beaufighter squadron in November 1940 when he shot down a Junkers 88. In the following month he had 2 victories, and in the first 8 months of 1941 he destroyed 12 German aircraft. Before the war, Cunningham had been a test pilot to De Havilland Aircraft and he was a pilot of tremendous skill. One of his most famous exploits was a battle with a Heinkel 111 in which Cunningham so out-flew his adversary that, without firing a single shot, he forced him to crash.

CURTIN, John, b. 1885. Prime Minister of Australia from 1941 until his death in July 1945. When war was declared, as leader of the Australian Labor Party in Opposition, he refused to join a coalition government, but pledged his party's full support in a war against Germany. In October 1941 Arthur Fadden's ministry was defeated in a vote of censure, and Curtin became Prime Minister.

Japan entered the war in December, and Australia immediately took on an increased importance in Allied strategy. Curtin achieved a new stature of independence for his country by separately declaring war on Japan and frankly looking to the U.S.A. for support in the Pacific. This upset some people within the British Commonwealth, but Curtin considered it right and rational to seek such a relationship with the U.S.A., particularly at a time when British and Commonwealth forces were heavily committed in Europe and Africa.

The benefits of this attitude became clear at the only Commonwealth Prime Ministers' Conference held during the war, in May 1944, when Australia stood firm by the policies to be pursued by the U.K. in the S.W. Pacific. In late 1943 Curtin had proposed a Commonwealth Command in the S.W. Pacific, as a partner to the American Command. In July 1944 he wanted British sea power to balance the increasing successes of General MacArthur's campaign; another reason for this suggestion was his desire to satisfy public opinion in Australia, which wanted to see British forces re-conquer the Malay Peninsula.

Between 1941 and 1942 Curtin was Minister of Defence Co-ordination and chairman of the Advisory War Council. Then he became Minister of Defence in Australia, and was nominated to the Privy Council in 1942. He led the Labor party to victory in the 1943 general election, and this secured him from the parliamentary difficulties of his first years of office. He visited the U.K., the U.S.A., and Canada in 1944. In November of the same year he fell ill, and he died on 5 July 1945, one month before Japan sued for peace. Curtin was a man of great sincerity, and an inspiring war-time leader who faced up to Australia's own particular role and asserted it in the face of much opposition. In the past an anti-conscriptionist, nevertheless he introduced a measure of conscription when he considered that it was essential to his country's interest.

D

DALADIER, Édouard, b. 1884. Premier of France at the time of the German invasion of Poland on 1 September 1939. France, already bound to Poland, had been strengthened for war by the British-Polish Pact in August, but Daladier decided to wait on events. When the U.K. declared war on Germany on 3 September, France followed suit a few hours later. Daladier dissolved the Communist party on 26 September, 9 days after Russia's counter-invasion of Poland. Early in March 1940 he agreed to send 50,000 volunteers and 100 bombers to help Finland against Russia, but these plans fell through after Finland made terms with Russia. Criticized for inactivity, Daladier's government fell on 20 March 1940. As War Minister under his successor, Paul Reynaud, Daladier opposed Churchill's plan to put mines in the Rhine, for fear of German reprisals. From 18 May to 16 June he was Minister of Foreign Affairs. Attempting to help Georges Mandel's brief resistance in Casablanca, he was brought back as a Vichy prisoner. He was put on trial with others at Riom in February 1942, accused of leading France into war unprepared. He regained much of his reputation by his courageous statements. After the trial was suspended, he was kept in internment. He was deported to Germany in 1943, and freed in April 1945.

Daladier had become Premier of France in April 1938. In June he affirmed that his predecessor's pledge to Czechoslovakia was 'sacred, and cannot be evaded'. He believed that if Great Britain and France stood firm, Hitler would not attack. But he always followed Neville Chamberlain's lead, and told him that the entry of German troops into Czechoslovakia 'must at all costs be prevented'. Though convinced by late September that Hitler's real aim was to dominate Europe, he was a signatory of the Munich Pact.

DARLAN, Jean François, b. 1881. French admiral and politician, who, after the German occupation of France, at first pursued a policy of limited co-operation with Germany, but later aided the Allies. In August 1939 Darlan had become C.-in-C.

of the French navy. In the following June, as France collapsed under the German onslaught, he expressed determination, at a meeting attended by Churchill, not to let the French fleet fall into German hands. He considered, but rejected, plans to sail it to England, the U.S.A., or the French oversea ports. But he eventually accepted office as Minister of Marine in Pétain's Vichy government.

In February 1941 he became vice-premier, with responsibility also for foreign, home, and defence matters. At first he attempted to follow a policy whereby France through limited co-operation could keep her empire, fleet, and a semblance of free government. During this time he surrounded himself with young economists, and he gave support to the idea of French integration in Hitler's 'New Europe'. In May he met Hitler and agreed that German forces should have free use of facilities in Syria, but his offers of Dakar and Bizerta were vetoed by other Vichy members. In return, Darlan had hoped for major economic and political concessions from Hitler, giving all parts of France more freedom: but Hitler was vague about these and, even though Darlan offered to fight against England if necessary, Hitler treated further offers with disdain.

In the spring of 1942 Darlan lost his ministerial posts after Laval's return to power, but he was made head of all French forces. He was in Algiers as High Commissioner in Africa when the Allies landed in November. Darlan decided to co-operate with them, a decision reinforced by the German occupation of the Vichy zone of France. He alone had the authority to call a cease-fire, thus putting French forces in North Africa at the Allies' disposal; this he did. Co-operation with a 'Fascist' was much criticized in America and England, but the Allies wanted a quick end to resistance by the French forces, and only Darlan was powerful enough to issue the necessary orders. He was assassinated on Christmas Eve 1942 by a French monarchist.

DARNAND, Joseph, b. 1897. French soldier and administrator, one of the most hated of the 'collaborators' with the occupying German forces. He was head of the *Milice*, and one of the leaders of

43

French military organizations that openly fought for the Germans.

After the armistice with Germany in 1940 Darnand became one of Marshal Pétain's most enthusiastic supporters. He found an outlet for his militaristic and authoritarian ideas by forming the *Service d'Ordre Légionnaire* in July 1941. With Pétain's agreement this body of security police operated throughout the Vichy zone, and was endowed with considerable freedom of action and power under the name of the *Milice*.

Henceforth Darnand was in close co-operation with the Germans in tracking down members of the Resistance and agents dropped by S.O.E. and other organizations, and was responsible for much of the brutality of the Vichy régime. He arrested innumerable hostages, among them members of prominent Gaullist families, and was also largely to blame for the degrading conditions prevailing in the internment centres in North Africa for the thousands of foreigners who had volunteered in the early days of the war to fight for France. Darnand was the first Vichy minister to take an oath of allegiance to Hitler and to wear a German uniform.

After the re-establishment of a free government in Paris in 1944, Darnand and 6,000 of the most heavily compromised *Miliciens* fled to Germany, where he was complimented by Hitler, and various plans were made for utilizing his followers in operations against the Russians and as a pro-German 'underground' in France. Darnand himself became a member of the 'French government' of Sigmaringen. In 1945 he was put on trial in France for treason, and was sentenced to death. He went to his death calmly, crying 'Vive la France!' as the order to fire was given.

DE GAULLE, Charles, b. 1890. French soldier, statesman, and leader of the Free French. In the years up to and including 1940 de Gaulle urged on France a strategy of defence based on mobile tank units and aircraft in a professional army, rather than on fortifications (such as the Maginot Line) and a conscript army. When the Germans invaded France on 14 May 1940 he was a colonel in command of a tank brigade, part of the 5th Army in Alsace. On 24 May he was given command, as a

brigadier-general, of the 4th Division, an armoured division still in process of being formed. His troops made a good showing under great adversity. He won his first political post the following June when the new premier, Paul Reynaud, appointed him Under Secretary of State for War. In this capacity he visited London twice and met Winston Churchill. On 14 June the Germans entered Paris, and Pétain, who had replaced Reynaud, sought an armistice. De Gaulle fled from France to London where, on 18 June 1940, he made his famous radio appeal to the people of France to resist the Germans. He called on all Frenchmen to support him in his determination to keep fighting, saying: 'The flame of French Resistance must not and shall not die.' He made himself head of the Free French and was recognized as such by the British government on 22 June, the day that Pétain signed the humiliating armistice with Germany. His broadcasts fired the patriotic spirit of the French and helped keep up their morale. Thousands left France for Great Britain and North Africa to join the Free French forces. On 7 July de Gaulle was sentenced to death *in absentia* by a court-martial in France.

In September de Gaulle failed in an attempt to seize Dakar, capital of French West Africa, but managed to win the allegiance of other French colonies. In October he formed the Defence Council of the Empire as the governing body of Free French territories and by November he had over 20,000 troops, 20 warships, and control of all French Equatorial Africa.

In July 1942 Free France was renamed 'Fighting France'. In spite of their support of de Gaulle, the Allies did not include the Fighting French in their invasion of North Africa. A rival to de Gaulle's leadership had appeared in the person of General Henri Giraud. Giraud had been smuggled out of France by submarine and, after meeting Eisenhower, was put in command of all French troops in North Africa. For a time de Gaulle and Giraud co-operated, though without enthusiasm, functioning as co-presidents of the French Committee of National Liberation that had been formed in June 1943. But in the struggle between them for power Giraud was forced to resign. By the end of 1943 de Gaulle could claim control of all French colonies except the Japanese-occupied territories in Indo-China.

De Gaulle returned to France on 13 June 1944, going ashore in Normandy 7 days after the D-Day invasion. His greatest moment came on 25 August when he triumphantly marched into Paris with the liberating Allied forces. The Committee of National Liberation was established as the provisional government, with de Gaulle as president.

A series of setbacks ensued. First, he sought and was refused support by Stalin for France's boundary demands on Germany because the Soviet leader would not act independently of the U.S.A. and Great Britain. Secondly, he was not invited to the Yalta and Potsdam Conferences, at which post-war strategy was discussed. Thirdly, the French colony in Indo-China proclaimed its independence at the end of the Japanese occupation. Helpless in the first two instances, he chose to try to reassert France's status as a great power in the third instance. In 1945 he embarked on a disastrous 8-year war in Indo-China. In the same year he was made President of France by a newly elected constituent assembly.

The most dynamic if controversial leader of his country since Napoleon, de Gaulle never lost his vision of a France with a special—and exalted—destiny. His independent and uncompromising temperament created difficulties in foreign relations, but he championed his country and its cause with constancy and courage. Churchill described de Gaulle in these words: 'I always recognized in him the spirit and conception which, across the pages of history, the word "France" would ever proclaim. I understood and admired, while I resented, his arrogant demeanour. . . . Always, even when he was behaving worst, he seemed to express the personality of France—a great nation, with all its pride, authority and ambition.'

DE GUINGAND, Francis, b. 1900. British general, Chief of Staff to General Montgomery in the 8th Army in North Africa and later in 21st Army Group in N.W. Europe. It was one of the closest and most successful partnerships of the war. In 1939 de Guingand became military assistant to the Secretary of State for War,

Leslie Hore-Belisha. Later he was given an Intelligence appointment, and in 1942 was Director of Military Intelligence in the Middle East. In the same year he took up duties as Chief of Staff in the 8th Army. He remained there until 1944. De Guingand owed this appointment to Montgomery, who commented in his *Memoirs*: 'We were complete opposites; he [de Guingand] lived on his nerves and was highly strung; in ordinary life he liked wine, gambling, and good food. Did these differences matter? I quickly decided they did not; indeed, differences were assets.' Montgomery added that he never regretted his decision, and thereafter, wherever Montgomery went, so did de Guingand.

In 21st Army Group de Guingand's virtues as a diplomat proved almost as useful as his military talents. Montgomery did not always see eye to eye with General Eisenhower, the supreme commander in Europe, and, as he said himself, was not an easy subordinate. De Guingand's tact and his high standing with Eisenhower (who testified that de Guingand 'lived the code of the Allies') helped to smooth difficult passages between the two commanders.

DE VALERA, Eamon, b. 1882. Prime Minister of Eire from 1937, under the new constitution. He secured the neutrality of Eire for the whole of the war. This in 1940 was very difficult for Britain, which desperately needed the Irish harbours of Cobh (Queenstown), Berehaven, and Lough Swilly in defence of the North Atlantic routes. The British right to use these harbours had been surrendered in the agreement between De Valera and Neville Chamberlain in 1938. Churchill has many bitter words in his *History* about De Valera's neutrality, which meant that Britain could use neither ports nor airfields in Eire. He, and English public opinion, were convinced that De Valera was happy to sit by complacently as Britain was strangled—while enjoying British food subsidies. Churchill feared that rumours of U-Boats using Irish facilities might be true. De Valera, on the other hand, had no doubt that his was the right policy for Eire, so recently independent, needing peace and stability to heal the wounds of centuries. De Valera was not as convinced as the British that they were fighting for democracy and freedom. One British Cabinet Minister visiting Northern Ireland reproached the people of Eire in a speech for remaining neutral, and reminded them of their 'many battles for human freedom'. De Valera rejoined, 'Against whom?'

De Valera won the election of 1943, without gaining an absolute majority in parliament. Defeated twice on a Bill in 1944, he called a new election and won handsomely. He always maintained strict neutrality, including the retention of German and Japanese ambassadors in Eire. Churchill therefore cut off all normal civilian links between Britain and Eire by April 1944 for security reasons. De Valera (who in 1935 said he would never allow any foreign power to use Ireland as a base to attack England) had earlier sent the Dublin fire brigade to help Belfast during a blitz. 'These are our people,' he said.

DE WAVRIN, André. *See* BROSSO-LETTE, Pierre.

DEAN, Basil, b. 1888. British theatre and film manager and producer, founder of the Entertainments National Service Association (E.N.S.A.), which he headed from 1939 to 1946. One of the best-known men of the theatre in the years before the war, he had been the first director of the Liverpool Repertory Theatre in 1913 and joint managing director of the Theatre Royal, Drury Lane, in 1924–5. He knew a vast number of people in the theatre world, and after war began in 1939 he used his considerable organizing skill and all his powers of persuasion to enlist every kind of well-known and not so well-known actor, actress, and musician in the task of 'entertaining the troops'. At one end of the scale, theatres were taken over and ambitious performances mounted in liberated cities such as Amiens and Rome; while at the other, E.N.S.A. staged 'one-night stand' concerts in any place where Servicemen were stationed or happened to be. Many of these shows were given in the open air, often near the fighting line. The arrival of an E.N.S.A. concert party was an eagerly awaited event in Service units, and it not infrequently happened that troops who had been involved in fighting in the morning found themselves in the evening laughing at the jokes of a comedian on a hastily rigged-up stage.

DEMPSEY, Miles, b. 1896. British general, who commanded the 2nd Army in the 1944 D-Day invasion of the mainland of Europe. Previously he had commanded 13th Corps in the invasions of Sicily and Italy, and had established a reputation as a determined and successful leader. In the assault on N.W. Europe from D-Day onwards, Dempsey's army formed part of 21st Army Group under General Montgomery. This formation, in accordance with Montgomery's plan, had to hold the bulk of the German armour in the Caumont-Caen sector in order to allow the American formations to break out on the right. In the heavy fighting at Caen all Dempsey's resoluteness was called for, as it was again in the battles at Falaise and Mortain. Later his army had an opportunity to show its speed in the spectacular dash to Brussels.

In spring of the following year Dempsey's army was on the Rhine, ready for the crossing. When this had been achieved, airborne troops being employed in establishing a foothold, the 2nd Army was in the van of the advance into Germany. By the time of the German capitulation in May it had crossed the Elbe.

Dempsey's quiet and steady personality gave everyone—superiors and subordinates alike—great confidence in his judgment and leadership. He always took the trouble to get to know his troops, so as to take account of their strengths and limitations in the varied battle situations to be encountered.

DEVERS, Jacob, b. 1887. American general who directed the Allied landings in southern France in August 1944 and the subsequent push northwards to join the forces that had landed in Normandy. From 1940 to 1943 he gained experience in the handling of large formations, first as commander of an infantry division, and then in command of armoured forces. In 1943 he was in command of U.S. forces in the U.K. Although he had gained a reputation as a fine administrator, at the time he lacked battle experience, and General

Eisenhower decided not to include him in the organization for running Operation 'Overlord'. He was appointed deputy to General Wilson, Supreme Allied Commander in the Mediterranean. In this position he needed all of his administrative qualities to prepare for the Allied invasion of southern France in August 1944, which he commanded. His American and French armies drove up the Rhône Valley at great speed, co-operating with the *Maquis* and gathering thousands of German prisoners on the way. He took part in the assault in the Ardennes, having joined up with the main body of Allied forces in Europe. After the capitulation of the Germans in Italy in April 1945 he received the surrender of the German 1st and 19th Armies. This surrender was purely military in character, Devers making no commitments which could have embarrassed or limited the Allied governments in future decisions regarding Germany. So rapid were the ground advances of his group that he made no use of the U.S. 13th Airborne Division in the overrunning of Germany, although they had been assigned to him to ensure that he was not held up. It was the forces under his command that captured the city of Munich and Hitler's eyrie at Berchtesgaden.

DICKSON, Dorothy, b. 1900. American star of musical comedy who promoted and presided over the Stage Door Canteen, a nightly entertainment centre for Servicemen of all nations which was opened on a derelict site in Piccadilly, in London. To audiences of soldiers, sailors, and airmen on leave—or who had managed to snatch a night in London—she introduced many of the great names of show business, including Bing Crosby, Fred Astaire, Edith Evans, Marlene Dietrich, and Noël Coward, and she arranged visits to the Canteen by members of the royal family and by war leaders.

She was also typical of the numerous patriotic actors and actresses who 'did their bit' for the war effort by travelling around the various war fronts to entertain the troops. As a member of a company assembled by 'Binkie' Beaumont under the title *Spring Party*, she went to Gibraltar in early 1943, and then on a three-month tour across North Africa

playing to Service audiences. This company was the first group of show people to visit the Mediterranean after victory there, and its tour included E.N.S.A.'s first and only Royal Command Performance abroad when King George VI arrived to inspect his troops at Tunis in June 1943. The party went on to Cairo and Suez and was rapturously received: in the words of Eisenhower, they staged 'as beautiful a show as you would see in London, Paris, or New York'.

DILL, Sir John, b. 1881. C.I.G.S. from 1940 to 1941, and later British military representative in the U.S.A. In 1939 he commanded and trained 1st Corps in France, on the borders of Belgium, which was then neutral. Promoted general in October, Dill returned to England in the following April as Vice-C.I.G.S. In late May 1940 he reported from France on the German offensive, and succeeded Ironside as C.I.G.S.

Dill was the best officer for this post, and had the confidence of all the services. Unfortunately the war was at a critical stage, and Dill could only advise restraint. He was appalled at the dangers attending hasty action, which could lead to disaster or, at least, waste valuable resources which would be needed at a later, more propitious day. Churchill, as impetuous as ever, came to believe that Dill was being obstructive rather than wise. Over-strained, over-worked, depressed by his wife's illness and death, Dill's health began to fail.

In early 1941 Dill visited the eastern Mediterranean with Eden. He then advised against sending troops to Greece, on sound military grounds. He was persuaded to change his mind, but later came to regret this.

In December 1941 Alan Brooke succeeded him as C.I.G.S. Dill had been made a field marshal in November, and went with Churchill to America when Japan entered the war. He stayed on there as head of the British Joint Staff Mission, forming a joint staff with their American counterparts, until his death in November 1944. He became a personal friend of General Marshall, the American Chief of Staff.

Dill was a charming, kindly man; the President respected and trusted him. He

had many friends and extraordinary
prestige in American official circles.
Roosevelt called him 'the most important
figure' in Anglo-American military
co-operation.

DOBBIE, Sir William, b. 1879. British
general, Governor and C.-in-C. of Malta
during the Axis aerial onslaught on the
island. Under his determined and inspiring
leadership Malta withstood its worst
attacks of the war from June 1940 to
April 1942. He not only had to defend the
island but also to keep up the morale of
the citizens—both heavy tasks, with
thousands of tons of German and Italian
bombs being dropped night and day in a
desperate attempt to render Malta ineffective as an Allied offensive base. Strategically Malta was of vital importance to the
Allies for operations against enemy communications in the west Mediterranean,
especially for attacks on supplies bound
for the German and Italian forces in the
Western Desert. The chiefs of staff made
every effort to send aircraft and fuel and
food convoys, whatever the commitments
elsewhere. There were months when only
bare survival rations got through the heavy
enemy siege of the island but, by severe
rationing, Dobbie averted major fuel and
food crises.

Between January and June 1941 the
Luftwaffe had mounted an unceasing
attack, followed by a lull until December.
This initial baptism by fire taught the
civilian population how to live amidst
devastation and how to build and use the
sandstone shelters. But it was the much
respected Governor who kept up their
morale and endeavoured to ensure that air
and ground reinforcements came at .
crucial moments. To save paraffin and help
the homeless, he set up 'Victory kitchens'
towards the end of 1941. The heavy air-
raids of April 1942 caused vast destruction
and almost extinguished the R.A.F.'s
fighter defence; this was the island's worst
month. Morale was at its lowest, and the
supply of reinforcements and supplies able
to reach the island was minimal. For its
heroism and devotion, Malta was awarded
the George Cross on 15 April 1942.

On 22 April the Defence Committee
decided that Dobbie was worn out by
these crises and hardships and on 7 May

Lord Gort succeeded Dobbie. Dobbie
returned to England, taking with him the
admiration and gratitude of the people of
Malta. King George VI remarked in his
diary: 'He is a God-fearing man and lives
with a Bible in one hand and a sword in
the other.'

DOENITZ, Karl, b. 1891. German
admiral who held the chief command of
the German navy from 1943, and who, as
Hitler's designated successor, surrendered
Germany unconditionally to the Allies.
Doenitz was Flag Officer U-Boats until 30
January 1943 when he succeeded Admiral
Raeder as C.-in-C. of the German navy.
He was responsible for sinking some 15
million tons of Allied shipping. His
experiences during World War I had convinced him that the U-Boat was ineffectual
as a solitary raider in the face of the convoy system. In 1939 he wrote a book
about it, and was responsible for developing the concept of the 'wolf pack'. The
medium-sized boats which he had ready
when war broke out were devastatingly
effective in both short- and long-range
operations. Even before the early successes, Doenitz was convinced that
concerted U-Boat activities were capable
of winning the war for Germany and
constantly urged Raeder and Hitler to
spare no effort to build up a vast fleet of
submarines. By early 1943 he had 212
U-Boats operating in packs and 181 more
in training, and by 1944 the 'Schnorkel',
enabling submarines to charge their
batteries while submerged, had been
developed. But the invention of micro-
wave radar meant that the Allies were
capable of inflicting fairly substantial
losses on the wolf packs and, by that
stage of the war, German production was
not equal to the task of replacing them.

It was ironical that this talented officer,
whose ideas could have disrupted Britain's
supply routes, was called upon in May 1945
to order all U-Boats to cease operations
and return to their bases, and to supervise
the German capitulation as Hitler's
nominated successor. Fearful of the
intentions of the advancing Russians, he
attempted to end the war in the West
while continuing to fight the Russians, but
this proposal was rejected and on 7 May
an instrument of unconditional surrender

on all fronts was signed. Doenitz was sentenced by the Nuremberg Tribunal to 10 years' imprisonment.

DOMVILE, Barry, b. 1878. Retired British admiral, interned in 1940, together with his wife, under Regulation 18B as a person whose actions were prejudicial to the security of the nation. Domvile was founder member of an organization called the 'Link', whose professed purpose was 'to foster the mutual knowledge and understanding that ought to exist between the British and German peoples and to counteract the flood of lies with which our people [are] being regaled in their daily papers'. He believed in the existence of a mysterious power, which he named 'Judmas', its source being a Judeo-Masonic combination, whose aim was a world state kept in subjection by the power of money and working for its Jewish masters. According to Domvile, this secret and omnipotent organization had for many centuries wielded a baneful influence on world history, controlling the actions of those who were the ostensible governors and rulers. The latest stage in its nefarious design was the engineering of a war between Britain and Germany in order to weaken the resistance of the respective governments and to extend its own influence. In 1939 the 'Link' was denounced by Sir Samuel Hoare as 'an instrument of the German Propaganda Ministry' and the last number of the *Anglo-German Review*, the organ of publicity used by the 'Link', appeared a few days before 3 September 1939, the day on which Britain declared war on Germany, bringing the organization's brief and inglorious career to an automatic close. In 1943 an unreformed and impenitent Domvile was released from Brixton prison.

DONOVAN, William ('Wild Bill'), b. 1883. American lawyer and Intelligence chief. As President Roosevelt's special envoy to Europe in 1940–1, he stressed to the President, against the isolationists, the spirit of resistance to Hitler, and his belief that the U.S.A. should help the U.K. all she could. He visited all the then uncommitted countries, stating that the attitudes of Bulgaria and Yugoslavia reminded him

'of children looking into a shop window full of modern toys—tanks and aeroplanes —and complaining that their own military equipment was out of date'. He warned the Bulgarian king that if he let the Germans into his country, America would not intercede for him at the end of the war.

Donovan made many visits to Britain. In June 1942 he gave an exposition to the British chiefs of staff of the organization of the American Secret Service. After being Co-ordinator of Information he became the head of the American OSS (later the CIA). This body became increasingly active in the later part of the war in encouraging Resistance in the Axis-occupied countries.

DOOLITTLE, James, b. 1896. American Army Air Force general, one of the most successful exponents of strategic and tactical bombing.

In April 1942 he planned and led the first American bombing raid on Tokyo, a tactically brilliant low-level attack for which he received the Congressional Medal of Honor. Later in 1942 he organized and led the 12th Air Force in the Allied invasion of N.W. Africa. He was given command in 1943 of the Strategic Air Forces (with U.S. heavy and medium bomber units and British medium bomber units) which took part in long-range raids on Italian bases and shipping. In August of that year he led a devastating day-time bomber raid on Rome.

In 1944 Doolittle was promoted lieutenant-general and created Honorary K.C.B. by King George VI. In the Allied assault on Germany he commanded the 8th Air Force, and by bombing Germany's flying-bomb bases made a signal contribution to preserving morale in Britain. He then commanded the 8th Air Force against the Japanese in the Pacific, with similarly notable success.

Doolittle, one of the most versatile figures in American military aeronautics, was the only non-regular officer to command a major combat air force. His expansive character and aggressiveness won the loyalty of his men, and concealed a shrewd tactician, skilled and persuasive. Between the wars he had gained an international reputation as a record-breaking pilot and as a test pilot.

DOUGLAS, Sir William Sholto, b. 1893.
British air marshal who held some of the
highest posts in the R.A.F. At the outbreak of the war he was Assistant and
then (1940) Deputy Chief of the Air Staff.
In November 1940 he succeeded Dowding
as chief of Fighter Command, and ordered
strong air attacks over France which compelled the Germans to divert forces there
from other fronts.

In 1943 he was in command of the
R.A.F. in the Middle East and in 1944
became chief of Coastal Command. He
was then appointed commander of the
British Expeditionary Air Forces for the
D-Day landings and took an active part
as one of the 'Combined Commanders' in
the planning of the invasion. His particular task was of the greatest importance:
helping to ensure that the English Channel
was clear of U-Boats and any other enemy
vessels that could endanger the Allied
invasion fleet. He described this task as
'putting the cork into the bottle'.

DOWDING, Hugh, b. 1882. British air
marshal, the victor of the Battle of Britain
in 1940. Fighter Command, of which he
was chief, saved Britain from possible
invasion. In the battle he reaped some
benefit from pre-war foresight. In 1935,
on the Air Council, he had approved the
expenditure asked for by the Tizard
Committee to develop a radar early-
warning system, which was later supplemented by the Observer Corps. This
system enabled pilots to take to the air
only when raiders were approaching,
instead of wearing themselves out on
ceaseless patrols. And he had encouraged
development of the monoplane fighter
which emerged as the Hurricane and the
Spitfire.

Dowding's determination to check the
drain on Fighter Command in France
during May and June 1940 caused him to
warn Churchill that a minimum of 25
squadrons must be kept in reserve against
the eventuality of France's defeat. With
this force he was able to hold his own in
August and September when he actively
controlled and dispersed his meagre force
of planes and pilots. In November 1940 he

was succeeded in Fighter Command by
Sholto Douglas.

His unshakable if rather humourless
character (he was known as 'Stuffy')
proved rocklike in a time of great danger
for Britain and he may well be credited
with having prevented the war being lost
in 1940. He was the only man who ever
won a major fighter battle or, presumably,
ever will win one. As his biographer has
said: 'Whereas Dowding and Park proved
capable of standing up to men who
wanted them to do wrong things, their
German counterparts proved incapable of
standing up to Goering.'

Dowding retired in 1942 after special
duty for the Ministry of Aircraft Production in the U.S.A.

DULLES, Allen, b. 1893. American lawyer
and government official, and important
member of the OSS.

After the Casablanca Declaration of
1943, in which Churchill and Roosevelt
announced their determination to bring
about Hitler's unconditional surrender,
Dulles, as the President's special representative in Switzerland, held talks with
German emissaries, Prince Maximillian
Egon Hohenlohe and Dr Schudekopf.
German documents suggest that the discussions were not about unconditional
surrender but about compromise, possible
negotiations, eventual terms, and even the
preservation of Nazism. Such possibilities
were comforting for those Germans who
hoped for a 'political solution'. Dulles's
attitude to Hitler, and his assertion that it
would be impossible to maintain him as
head of the German State, gave satisfaction to Himmler and Schellenberg, who
saw themselves at the top of a transformed
Germany. Dulles's connections with the
S.S. were not confined to his talks with
Prince Hohenlohe. He had contacts with
Ernst Kaltenbrunner, as the latter himself
admitted at Nuremberg, and was in close
liaison with Wilhelm Hottl, a member of
the 'Austrian Catholic' group within the
S.S. He also worked, through the S.S.
general Karl Wolff, to bring about the
capitulation of the German troops in Italy
in 1945.

E

EAKER, Ira, b. 1898. American airman, a forceful and imaginative personality, who was Strategic Air Commander in Europe during the war. On 17 August 1942, with an established reputation as one of the USAAF's most outstanding pilots, he led 12 B-17 Flying Fortresses in the first U.S. bombing attack in western Europe. He attended the Casablanca Conference of January 1943, as commander of the U.S. 8th Air Force. He persuaded Roosevelt and Churchill to give daylight bombing an exhaustive trial before abandoning it (as had been urged), being convinced that heavily armed Fortresses in close formation could, without fighter escort, make long-distance raids into Germany. He aimed to prove this with the 8th Air Force by demonstrating that he could destroy specified targets in daylight. Eaker directed many such raids with worthwhile results, though he was not given the reinforcements for which he asked. It was mainly as a result of his persistence that the policy of continuous bombing of Germany was adopted—the USAAF bombing by day and the R.A.F. by night.

Promoted lieutenant-general in June 1943, Eaker was sent to Italy in 1944 to take command of the Mediterranean Allied Air Forces. From there he waged the Strategic Air Offensive against Germany and the Balkans. In August 1944 he was made Air C.-in-C. of the Allied air forces for the invasion of southern France. During the autumn, in spite of adverse weather, Eaker contributed greatly to the success of the Allied ground forces by his attacks on German communications and supplies.

EDEN, Anthony, b. 1897. British statesman, Foreign Secretary for the greater part of the war. A man of elegance and wit, his diplomacy and flair for persuasion when arguing from the position of his country's limited power and influence were probably his most remarkable talents.

In the war he became first Dominions Secretary and for a short period Secretary of State for War, but Churchill appointed him Foreign Secretary, in which post he distinguished himself. After the German invasion of Russia in 1941 Eden visited Moscow in December and learned of Stalin's acquisitive war aims; but in the interest of the prime requirement of defeating Hitler's Germany the principles of British policy had to be subdued. In May 1942 he negotiated the Anglo-Soviet 20-year mutual alliance against aggression. He supported Churchill with great skill throughout the negotiations with the Americans on strategy in the Middle East and Mediterranean theatres, and co-operated with the U.S. Secretary of State, Cordell Hull, in assuring the Russians of the Allies' intentions regarding the invasion of the Continent.

General Ismay's description of Eden at this meeting of Foreign Ministers in October 1943 is revealing of the latter's diplomatic mastery in, for example, explaining to Stalin that the invasion of N.W. Europe could not take place until June or July 1944: 'I had always liked and admired him but had hitherto been inclined to think that he was one of fortune's darlings . . . and that his meteoric success had been primarily due to charm of manner and a lucky flair for diplomacy. I now saw how wrong I had been. His hours of work were phenomenal and he was extremely thorough; he never went to a meeting without making sure that he had every aspect of a problem at his finger-tips. He could be tough when necessary, but he could also give way gracefully if the situation demanded it. He had a pretty wit and transparent integrity. His physical courage which had been fully proved in much front-line fighting in the First World War was matched by his moral courage.' Churchill advised the King that in the event of his death Eden should be his successor as Prime Minister.

Prior to the war Eden had been Minister for League of Nations Affairs in 1933, when he attempted to bargain with Mussolini over the invasion of Ethiopia. In December of that year he opposed the Hoare-Laval Pact, which resulted in Sir Samuel Hoare's resignation. Eden then became Foreign Secretary in Baldwin's government. In March 1936 Germany occupied the Rhineland and Eden offered to support France in hopes that the League would act. He refused to recognize Italian Ethiopia and deplored the Italian intervention in Spain. He resigned from the post of Foreign Secretary in 1938 in protest against what he regarded as Chamberlain's pusillanimous attitude towards Mussolini.

EICHELBERGER, Robert Lawrence, b. 1886. American general, one of the most successful of the field commanders in the war against the Japanese. When the U.S.A. entered the war Eichelberger was superintendent of the U.S. Military Academy at West Point. He was given command of the American 1st Corps and, the aim being at this time to halt the Japanese offensive before Australia was seriously in danger, took it to the Australian theatre. At the beginning of 1943 he was in action in New Guinea and achieved success in the attack on Buna; this victory, though minor, had an immense effect on the morale of the Allied troops. In September 1944 Eichelberger was appointed commander of the American 8th Army and led it in the invasion of the Philippines and the subsequent fighting up to the Japanese defeat. Eichelberger was a dedicated student of military science and was thought by some to have been capable of greater things than his commands permitted.

EICHMANN, Adolf, b. 1906. German S.S. officer, head of the Gestapo's department of Jewish affairs. In September 1941, shortly after his first official visits to the death camps in the east, Eichmann organized mass deportations from Germany and Bohemia, in accordance with a wish of Hitler, who had told Himmler to make the Reich free of Jews as quickly as possible. At the Wannsee Conference on 20 January 1942 his position as the authorized specialist in Jewish affairs of the Reich Security Head Office was confirmed and he was entrusted by Heydrich with the task of effecting the 'final solution'. Until the summer of 1944 when, behind Hitler's back, the 'final solution' was abandoned, he was entirely occupied with the macabre but immensely complicated problem of the organization of genocide. He was largely responsible for the introduction of gas chambers to replace the gruesome practice of mass shooting. At his trial in 1961 he testified that his knees had buckled at the sight of

an *Einsatzgruppe* (special extermination unit) engaged in this task near Minsk. He was, paradoxically, a mass murderer who never killed or even had the nerve to kill: 'I never killed a Jew or, for that matter, I never killed a non-Jew. I never gave an order to kill a Jew or an order to kill a non-Jew.' Yet, at all times, he did his best to make the 'final solution' really final. When Himmler became 'moderate', Eichmann sabotaged his orders as much as he dared, to the extent at least that he felt covered by his immediate superiors. This insubordination was not prompted by fanaticism but by his belief that Himmler's orders ran counter to the wishes of the Führer. This peculiar devotion to duty was reflected in his last words on the scaffold: 'I had to obey the laws of war and the flag.' He disappeared in 1945 after the Soviet army entered Czechoslovakia but was found 15 years later in Argentina.

Eichmann pretended to his S.S. comrades and his Jewish victims that he was born in Palestine (his birthplace was Solingen) and he was fluent in Yiddish. In fact his mother had Jewish relatives, one of whom got him a job with the Austrian Vacuum Oil Co., and this was one of his private reasons for not hating Jews. In 1932 he joined the Nazi party and entered the S.S. at the invitation of Kaltenbrunner. Two years later he became a member of Heydrich's Security Service. In Vienna, where he was so successful in arranging the forced emigration of Jews before the war, he had a Jewish mistress. Such contact with Jews was probably the greatest crime a member of the S.S. could commit. Thus his denunciations of Julius Streicher, the insanely anti-Semitic editor of *Der Sturmer*, were perhaps personally motivated.

EISENHOWER, Dwight D., b. 1890. American general and Supreme Allied Commander in Europe during the 'Second Front' operations on the European mainland in 1944 and 1945. Probably more than any other commander of World War II, 'Ike' Eisenhower—with his calm, friendly presence and air of mastery of the complex technicalities of war—exuded the very spirit of Allied co-operation. He was a 'soldier's soldier', a true professional who rose with extraordinary rapidity when war supplied the opportunity for him to exercise his capabilities. At the time of the Japanese attack on Pearl Harbor in December 1941 Eisenhower was a divisional Chief of Staff. He demonstrated his grasp of logistics, strategy, and tactics during the U.S. army manœuvres of 1941, and in the following year became Chief of Operations in Washington. In June of that year he was named as U.S. commander in Europe.

Eisenhower was in command of the U.S. forces that landed in N.W. Africa in November 1942. The American and British troops landed at Casablanca, Oran, and Algiers; by 10 November fighting around Oran ceased. On 15 November the Allied troops moved into Tunisia. Four days earlier Eisenhower and his advisers had persuaded the Vichy French High Commissioner, Admiral Darlan, to cooperate. Eisenhower's final settlement with Darlan was concluded on 13 November.

In February 1943 he was appointed Supreme Allied Commander in North Africa, a prelude to his direction of the Allied invasions of Sicily in July, and Italy in September. In December he was appointed supreme commander of the Allied Expeditionary Force in Western Europe, and arrived in Britain on 16 January 1944 to assume his duties. His task now was to mount the invasion of the western European mainland, an operation which the western Allies saw as the final and decisive one of the war against Germany. He had to weld together immense forces that included Americans, British, Belgians, Dutch, French, and Poles. Under him he had military commanders of several nationalities, many of them men of definite ideas and great experience. He had also to take account of the predilections of political leaders who by no means always saw eye to eye on aims or methods. By the exercise of tact and diplomacy, Eisenhower surmounted all obstacles, gaining in the process a respect and affection that few military commanders have enjoyed.

On 6 June 1944 he put into effect Operation 'Overlord', the greatest amphibious action ever seen. For this operation he commanded 176,000 troops, 4,000 invasion craft, 11,000 planes, and 600 warships. American and British parachute and glider troops also took part in the immense 60-mile-wide landing in Normandy. By July about 1 million Allied troops had disembarked in Normandy and, by the end of that month, a strong armoured thrust was being made into Brittany. After the breakout from the bridgehead, and the breaking of the 'hinge' at Caen, the operations gathered momentum. He commented in his book *Crusade into Europe*: 'The battlefield at Falaise was unquestionably one of the greatest killing grounds of any of the war areas . . . roads, highways, and fields were so choked with destroyed equipment and with dead men and animals that passage through the area was extremely difficult. Forty-eight hours after the closing of the gap I was conducted through it on foot to encounter scenes that could be described by Dante. It was literally possible to walk for hundreds of yards at a time, stepping on nothing but dead and decaying flesh.'

Eisenhower's broad-front strategy forced the Germans back relentlessly to the borders of their homeland by the end of 1944. In the early months of 1945, after the temporary setback of the German last-ditch counter-attack in the Ardennes, the war was carried into Germany itself, and, shortly, all was over. Despite its success, the merits of Eisenhower's strategy have been questioned—notably by Field Marshal Montgomery, the commander, under Eisenhower, of the British 21st Army Group. Montgomery's view was that a concentrated thrust into the German heartland would have achieved a more rapid victory. None, however, has doubted Eisenhower's supreme skill in carrying through the strategy adopted, his exceptional logistical gifts, or his unique achievements as an Allied commander in a situation fraught with so many possibilities of serious discord.

ELIZABETH, Princess, b. 1926. Elder daughter of King George VI and heir to the British throne. Her eighteenth birthday on 21 April 1944, although it did not constitute her majority, raised an issue of importance. Although she and her sister had spent most of the war at Windsor and in Scotland, the King realized that she would soon have to enter public life. Parliament was therefore requested to amend the Regency Act of 1937 to admit her among the Counsellors of State 'in order that she should have every opportunity of gaining experience in the duties which would fall upon her in the event of her acceding to the throne'. The Bill received no opposition and became law in November 1943.

Shortly after her eighteenth birthday she spoke in public, replying to her election as president of the Queen Elizabeth Hospital for Children. In December 1944 she launched the battleship H.M.S. *Vanguard*, and in March 1945 she was granted a commission in the A.T.S. and carried out normal training at the Mechanical Transport Centre at Camberley. At an earlier stage of the war, in October 1940, she had broadcast in Children's Hour to the children of the Commonwealth, linking herself, at the age of 14, to the men and women of the future in their common endeavours.

ELIZABETH, Queen, b. 1900. The consort of King George VI, throughout the war she was engaged in an endless round of visiting and giving encouragement to people in all parts of Britain; she broadcast to the women of the U.S.A., and was hostess to royal refugees—Queen Wilhelmina of the Netherlands, King George of Greece, and King Haakon of Norway.

In September 1940, when east and south London were staggering under the first shock of bombing, she and the King would appear in the bombed areas without formality to talk to those who had lost their homes, and to firemen, ambulancemen, and A.R.P. workers. Queen Elizabeth's sympathetic nature and charm were exemplified in the remark of a bystander on one of these occasions: 'For him we had admiration, for her adoration.'

The Queen and the King had narrow escapes when Buckingham Palace was bombed in September 1940. The Queen acted as a Counsellor of State when the King visited his troops in North Africa in June 1943, and she undertook lengthy investitures. Her support to the King throughout his reign was an undoubted factor in his accomplishments, and particularly so during the war.

ELLIOT, Walter, b. 1888. British politi-

cian who successfully organized the evacuation of children and others from areas likely to be bombed. A qualified medical practitioner, he had become Minister of Health in May 1938, and had already a 'skeleton' evacuation scheme ready at the time of the Munich crisis. England's unpreparedness for war led Elliot to support the Munich agreement, but by the time war broke out he had ensured that his own department was ready. With the aid of the Women's Voluntary Service, the voluntary evacuation of 1½ million townspeople (school children, mothers with infants, expectant mothers, and blind people) was put into operation on 1 September 1939, and successfully concluded 2 days later.

Elliot's specialized knowledge of nutrition contributed to the success of the food-rationing schemes, and he and Sir Arthur MacNalty were largely responsible for developing the Emergency Medical Service. In these fields preparations for war were singularly efficient; but when, in May 1940, Churchill replaced Chamberlain as Prime Minister, Elliot found himself rejected as a 'Municher'. He spent a few months as a staff officer at Chester, responsible for keeping the roads clear of refugees in the event of bombing or invasion, and he refused Churchill's offer of the governorship of Burma. Throughout 1941 he was Director of Public Relations at the War Office. In May 1941 he saved Westminster Hall from destruction by incendiary bombs, by smashing in the doors with an axe and directing the hoses himself. During 1942 he became known as a successful broadcaster and journalist and was chairman of the Public Accounts Committee. After a serious accident in 1943 he became chairman of a Commission on Higher Education in West Africa; its recommendations led to the establishment of university colleges in Nigeria and Ghana. Elliot was also a successful farmer, with special experience in breeding sheep.

EMBRY, Basil, b. 1902. British air force officer, the leader of three spectacular aerial attacks on Gestapo offices. On the outbreak of the war Embry was given command of a bomber squadron. He won a bar to his pre-war D.S.O. for attacks on Stavanger during the Norway campaign, and a second bar for operations over the Low Countries and France. In May 1940 he was shot down over St Omer and was taken prisoner. He managed to escape and after a series of adventures, during which he was twice recaptured, he succeeded in returning to Britain, and served in Fighter Command during the Battle of Britain. In June 1943 he was promoted acting air vice marshal, with command of a bomber group. The Germans had put a price on his head, but Embry continued to fly on operational sorties, leading three of the war's most exacting bombing raids: the pinpoint attacks on Gestapo H.Q. at Aarhus, Copenhagen, and Odense. The Copenhagen mission particularly demonstrated his skill. Important Danish Resistance members were imprisoned in the top storey of the Gestapo building, and Embry dive-bombed the side of the building and blew the door open. Embry once told his squadron that, since they'd got to have a war, 'they could damn well enjoy it'.

ESMONDE, Eugene, b. 1909. British naval airman, who gained fame for his leadership of what was virtually a suicide attack on German battle-cruisers. Esmonde, an Irishman, joined the Fleet Air Arm in 1939. He had previously held a short-service commission in the R.A.F.

He was appointed to H.M.S. *Courageous* (torpedoed soon after war began), then for a while trained pilots before joining H.M.S. *Victorious*. This vessel was still quite new and her squadrons only partly trained when, in May 1941, she was called from the Clyde to support Admiral Tovey in his chase of the German battleship *Bismarck*, on a sortie into the Atlantic. At 8 p.m. on 24 May, 120 miles from the enemy, 9 Swordfish torpedo-bombers took off in a storm and rising gale, led by Esmonde. They approached through heavy gunfire, but one torpedo struck the *Bismarck*; and then, with the help of radar, Esmonde led his squadron safely through storm and darkness back to the *Victorious*. The single hit failed to cripple the *Bismarck*, but Esmonde's gallantry earned him the D.S.O.

In August 1941 he joined H.M.S. *Ark Royal*, torpedoed in November near Gibraltar. In January 1942, commanding

825 Squadron of torpedo bombers, he volunteered to make a night attack on the German battle-cruisers *Scharnhorst* and *Gneisenau* and the cruiser *Prinz Eugen*, should they venture up-Channel from Brest; and he brought his half-formed squadron of six Swordfish to readiness at the airfield at Manston. Unexpectedly the enemy left Brest at night and passed through the Straits of Dover by daylight, undetected until 11.25 a.m. on 12 February. Thus Esmonde was faced with engaging the enemy immediately, without cover of darkness or the anticipated opportunity to attack from the bow. The decision was left to him and, promised an escort of 60 R.A.F. fighters, he agreed to attack. In fact only 10 Spitfires arrived in time, but he proceeded nevertheless in what he knew to be a desperate undertaking. The warships were protected by a screen of E-Boats, flak ships, and heavy destroyers, as well as a large air 'umbrella'; but Esmonde pressed in through a hailstorm of fire, followed by his other 5 Swordfish. All were shot down, only 5 men surviving, and none of the torpedoes found their targets. The fate of 825 Squadron and the escape of the warships was much criticized and the inquiry revealed a failure of air reconnaissance and the need for a single authority to control naval and air forces in a fast-moving operation of this kind. There was, however, nothing but praise for Esmonde's determined and gallant leadership, and he was awarded a posthumous V.C.

EVATT, Herbert, b. 1894. Australian lawyer and statesman. As Minister for External Affairs after 1941 he did much to increase the influence of Australia in international affairs, and to make his fellow countrymen more aware of Australia's place in the world. In March 1940 he entered the Advisory War Council and in the following year became Attorney General and Minister for External Affairs in the Curtin Ministry. It soon became apparent that he intended Australia to be the political representative of the British Commonwealth in the Pacific. In 1942 he advocated the establishment of a Pacific War Council sitting in Washington, at which the voices of Australia and the U.K. would carry equal weight. It was largely due to Evatt's advocacy that this body was in fact set up that very year. As Minister for External Affairs he gave his department its first major overhaul, increasing its oversea posts and enhancing its status at home. He travelled a great deal during the war and was Australian representative in the British War Cabinet and the leader of war-time missions to Washington, London and New Zealand. He was a strong proponent of Australia's right to be consulted in international affairs, and for his insistence that the governments of small nations may be just as well informed and perspicacious as those of the great powers he was awarded the Freedom of the City of Athens in 1945.

Evatt was a man of intellect and tremendous industry. In 1925 he was elected member for Balmain in the state parliament, standing as an independent Labor candidate against official Labor. In 1928 he dropped the prefix 'independent'. Later he became a judge of the High Court.

F

FALKENHAUSEN, Alexander von, b. 1886. German general, C.-in-C. in Belgium and North France from 1940 to 1944. He became a determined enemy of Hitler and a leading member of the conspiracy against him which culminated in the attempted assassination of July 1944. As C.-in-C. in Belgium, Falkenhausen employed the stock tactics to bring the Belgian patriots to heel; for example, he ruthlessly enforced the dreaded hostage system, used first in Norway, which was one of the instruments of Nazi terror. However, in mid January 1942 Falkenhausen became actively involved in the plans of the anti-Nazi plotters. Ulrich von Hassell, the former German Ambassador in Rome, already under surveillance by the Gestapo, used a lecture tour as the cover for a trip to Brussels, during which he initiated Falkenhausen into the conspirators' hopes and plans. At this stage Hassell discussed with both Falkenhausen and Witzleben, who had been commander of the Berlin garrison in 1938, vaiious schemes for assassinating Hitler. The details of these plans remain obscure, but Witzleben and Falkenhausen told Hassell that they were impracticable: they had at their disposal only troops of no great fighting value, and to base a revolution on such forces, even if Hitler were first eliminated, was out of the question.

It was Falkenhausen, together with Stülpnagel, military governor of France, who in January 1944 initiated General Rommel (then commander of Army Group B in the west) into the anti-Hitler conspiracy. Later in the same year Falkenhausen was one of the generals who were involved in the plot on Hitler's life. After the failure of the attempted coup of 20 July Falkenhausen was arrested and imprisoned.

From the Gestapo prison in the Prinz Albrechtstrasse in Berlin and then the concentration camp at Innsbruck, he was moved, together with other distinguished prisoners who had been involved in the revolt, to Niedernhausen in the South Tyrol. One of these prisoners, Fabian von Schlabrendorff, in his memoiis, described the unyielding spirit of Falkenhausen, and

the respect which he commanded, even at this time. Falkenhausen was wearing his *pour le mérite*—the highest German decoration for gallantry in World War I—and even the S.S. guards treated him with respect. Falkenhausen openly explained how near to collapse Germany was. The prisoners were freed by American troops on 4 May 1945; a liberation which almost certainly came just in time to save them from execution at the hands of the Gestapo guard.

Falkenhausen was later tried by the Belgians as a war criminal and was sentenced in 1951, after 4 years in prison awaiting trial, to 12 years' penal servitude. He was released, however, a fortnight later and returned to Germany.

FAROUK, b. 1920. King of Egypt, a somewhat reluctant ally of the British forces occupying his country. In September 1940 the Italians invaded Egypt, and the reinforcement of German troops meant that plans for British withdrawal were postponed, since it was vital to keep a foothold in the Mediterranean and to guard the Suez Canal route to India. Britain did not believe that it would be wise, in view of the anti-British feeling, to invite Farouk to lead his country in the struggle against the Axis Powers; consequently it was not until the end of the war that Egypt joined in the fight. Farouk's attitude and the strident pro-Nazi section of the Egyptian population were particularly worrying to the British at the time of the battle of El Alamein when the Italian and German forces were close to Alexandria. The Egyptians who were pro-Nazi claimed that the Germans would grant them the independence which the British were withholding. Although the extreme pro-Nazis were probably a minority, King Farouk decided that it was wise to identify himself with Egyptian nationalism and he showed this by appointing a pro-Nazi Prime Minister. The British could not accept the appointment and forced Farouk to dismiss him and to appoint instead a former Wafd Prime Minister. This appointment also created difficulties, for the Wafd party was discredited and lacked influence. There was great tension in Anglo-Egyptian relations during the war years, and when, just after the war, General Montgomery went to see Farouk during treaty negotiations, he found him uninterested in peacetime strategic considerations, constantly complaining of 40 years of British misrule in Egypt.

Farouk had succeeded as King of Egypt in 1936. Farouk's father, King Fuad, had been pro-British, but the growing dislike for British power in Egypt (which had led to the Anglo-Egyptian Treaty of 1936, providing for the phased withdrawal of British forces from Egypt) caused Farouk to become increasingly anti-British.

FEGAN. See FOGARTY-FEGAN, Edward.

FERGUSSON, Bernard, b. 1911. British soldier, one of the leaders of Wingate's 'Chindits' in Burma. He commanded No. 5 Column of the Wingate expedition into Burma in 1943 and the 16th Infantry Brigade in the 1944 expedition. After a short spell as brigade major of the 46th Infantry Brigade near the beginning of the war, he had been assigned to General Wavell's command in Palestine as a junior Intelligence officer. He continued to serve with Wavell in many capacities: as a liaison officer with the Turks in his Middle East Command, as his forward observation officer with the Free French during the Syrian campaign in 1941, and as a planner at G.H.Q. in India. Fergusson, however, felt uncomfortable in these posts, and did not realize himself until he joined Wingate's brigade in the autumn of 1942. He himself has described his motives for embarking on this hazardous adventure: 'I joined the expedition to exorcise the thought that I had spent almost all the war in safe places.' The Chindit expedition succeeded in doing some damage to Japanese communications and in distracting the Japanese from other operations. It captured the imagination of Churchill and Roosevelt, who arranged for Wingate to enter Burma in the following year, not with forlorn parties but with the best backing that the ingenuity of man could devise. After Wingate's death in an air crash in March 1944, however, three weeks after the fly-in, the strain on the Chindits became so severe as their campaign continued that 50 per cent proved

medically unfit for further service. Unfortunately for Fergusson he was placed in command of the only brigade which still had to walk instead of being flown in.

Fergusson once said that the most exhilarating experience of his life was serving under Wavell. This experience began at an early stage of his career, when he was A.D.C. to Wavell at Aldershot in the period from 1935 to 1937. It was at this time that he first encountered the notions of unorthodox soldiering which were to stand him in such stead in the jungles of Burma.

FIELDS, Gracie, b. 1898. An enormously popular variety artist who sang to thousands of British soldiers, sailors, and airmen in all theatres of war, bringing them reminders of home with her gay, warmhearted personality and Lancashire wit. She was recuperating at her home in Capri from a serious illness when war broke out, but she returned to England and set off to France with E.N.S.A. to entertain the troops. This she continued to do until the evacuation from Dunkirk.

There had simply been no time for convalescence. Like many other theatrical stars, she devoted her time for the duration of the war to entertaining troops and workers at home and abroad. She put her endurance down to a good Lancashire constitution. She sang her way round the world: in patches cleared in the jungle, on airfields, on ships, in football fields, and at railway stations she was joyfully welcomed by soldiers, sailors, and airmen, singing familiar songs like her signature tune 'Sally', 'The Biggest Aspidistra in the World', 'Wish me Luck', and 'There'll Always be an England'.

Gracie Fields gave a series of concerts in Canada which lasted for 13 months and earned 1½ million dollars for the British Navy League. As the strenuous tour ended in 1941 an American newspaper said: 'Britain wants fifty warships. If she will send us Gracie Fields, we will give Britain all the ships she needs.'

Gracie Fields's natural gifts and her technical ability enabled her to hold immense audiences, making her the 'true successor to Marie Lloyd'. Fame often overwhelmed her, but it did not change the basically shy, generous, and unaffected woman herself.

FINUCANE, Brendan, b. 1920. Irish fighter pilot in the R.A.F. who became one of the best known of the air 'aces'. In 1940 'Paddy' Finucane joined 65 Squadron, which was based at Hornchurch in Essex, and took part in operations over Dunkirk. Later this unit, after being presented with 6 Spitfires paid for by the East India Fund, fought as the 'East India Squadron' in the Battle of Britain, during which Finucane shot down 2 enemy planes and was credited with 2 more 'probables'. In the summer of 1941 he was posted as flight commander to 452 Squadron, the first Australian fighter squadron in Europe. This squadron made a great name for itself flying Spitfires on sweeps over enemy territory. In the space of 3 months Finucane shot down 18 aircraft and shared 2 more: he twice claimed 3 in 1 day. In January 1942 he was given command of 602 Squadron, and in June he became wing commander (flying) at Hornchurch, leading a wing of single-seat fighter squadrons. This was a newly created position at each fighter-sector station, and carried a unique privilege: instead of the squadron code letters, a pilot's own initials were painted on his aircraft.

Less than three weeks later Finucane lost his life while returning from a sweep over France: his radiator was hit by machine-gun fire, and he crashed into the sea and drowned. Altogether he had a confirmed score of 32 enemy aircraft.

FLANDIN, Étienne, b. 1889. French politician of the Centre group, a minister in the Vichy government, who pursued a somewhat equivocal course before and during the war. He held office as Premier in 1934 and 1935 and was Foreign Minister in 1936. As tension rose in Europe, and the French were trying to decide their policy in the event of war, Flandin was present with Pierre Laval at the Stresa meeting of April 1935 when the representatives of Britain, France, and Italy made the last display of Allied solidarity.

In March 1938 Churchill went to Paris to contact leading French personages. He found that Flandin—who had earlier advocated that war was inevitable unless Germany's aggression was stopped—was by then convinced that France's only hope lay in reaching an understanding with Hitler. After the Munich agreement of September 1938 he sent Hitler a telegram: 'Please accept warm congratulations on keeping the peace, in the hope that out of this historic act will come a trusting and cordial collaboration between those four European powers which met at Munich.'

On 21 March 1940 Paul Reynaud took over the French government after the fall of Édouard Daladier, and appealed for support from the Centre party. He received only individual promises of collaboration because the Centre leaders, including Flandin, accused Reynaud of warmongering. But speaking at Dijon on 15 November 1940 Flandin referred to the 'hidden forces' which had sent France to war, and then sent a telegram to Marshal Pétain concerning his hopes for the national revival of France as part of the great European family. This speech impressed Pétain (and Hitler), and three weeks later Flandin took office as Minister of Foreign Affairs in the Vichy government. On 13 December 1940 Flandin succeeded Laval as vice-premier, but he was replaced a little later by Darlan (February 1941). After the Liberation Flandin was called to appear before the French High Court; he was acquitted of serious guilt in collaboration, but was for a time excluded from political eligibility.

FLEISCHER, Carl, b. 1883. Norwegian general whose troops made a remarkable stand against the invading Germans, and who was later for a short time C.-in-C. of the free Norwegian forces. When the Germans entered Norway in April 1940 he was in command of the 6th Division, which had remained mobilized since the Russo-Finnish War. Stationed near Narvik, his job was to guard the northern provinces. He was unable to prevent the surrender of Narvik, but his troops menaced the German hold on the town and, while awaiting the assistance which the British had promised, prevented them from advancing farther northwards. After two naval attacks on Narvik the British landed at Harstad where, in view of the severe weather conditions, it was decided to wait for the thaw before launching an all-out attack on the Germans. To Fleischer, desperately holding the Germans at bay, it seemed that the British were not to be relied upon. In terrible weather conditions he managed to launch a counteroffensive, pressing relentlessly on the Germans' shrinking perimeter, but farther south the Germans had forced the British out of central Norway and were now advancing to relieve the garrison at Narvik. Fleischer felt betrayed and, when the Allies recaptured Bjerkvik, was bitterly unyielding towards their requests for cooperation. On 24 May the British, faced with the collapsing front in France and Belgium, decided to withdraw from Norway, after a final assault upon Narvik. Fleischer's troops took part in the battle, and the town was captured on 28 May. The Allies then withdrew, and further resistance by the Norwegians became pointless. Fleischer, whose troops had had the most continuous and determined fight of the campaign, was evacuated to London on 10 June with the King of Norway and members of the Norwegian government. So deep was his resentment of British actions in Norway that he formally protested against the inclusion of his forces under the title 'The Allies'. In London he was appointed C.-in-C. of the Norwegian army abroad. Later, he found himself at variance with certain members of the Norwegian government and in 1942, when the new post of Chief of the Defence Forces was established, he was passed over. Instead he became commanding officer of the Norwegian forces in Canada and military attaché in Ottawa, where he died later that year.

FOGARTY-FEGAN, Edward, b. 1895. British naval officer, awarded a posthumous V.C. for his sacrificial gallantry as commander of H.M.S. *Jervis Bay*, an armed merchant cruiser which was sunk while escorting a homeward bound convoy of 37 merchantmen in November 1940.

When the convoy was attacked Fogarty-Fegan steered straight for the enemy and engaged the German pocket battleship *Scheer*, knowing that his guns could do no real damage and that one broadside from the German ship could sink him. He thus made a calculated sacrifice of his ship in order that the majority of his 'flock' could escape. The *Jervis Bay* was hit early in the action, but although partly out of control

and on fire she continued to hold the enemy; and she was so successful in diverting attention that only 6 ships including the *Jervis Bay* itself were sunk.

FORRESTAL, James, b. 1892. American Under Secretary of the Navy until 1944 and later Secretary of the Navy. Although forceful and effective in his official life, he was unassuming by nature and shunned publicity. In the summer of 1940 he became one of President Roosevelt's assistants in national defence work, and when Congress created the position of Under Secretary of the Navy a couple of months later he was nominated by the President for the post. This made Forrestal a key figure, with responsibility for all material procured for the U.S. Navy. When Colonel Frank Knox died in 1944, Forrestal automatically became Acting Secretary and, shortly afterwards, his nomination for Secretary was approved by the Senate. This well-earned promotion stemmed from his ceaseless toil as Under Secretary to increase the production of ships, planes, guns, and other munitions vital to the war effort. He was already known personally to the British Admiralty because in 1941 he had gone to London to establish a closer liaison so that naval purchases and Lend-Lease problems could be sorted out more easily. On two occasions he visited the South Pacific war area, and was present at the attack on Iwo Jima. In August 1944 he visited the Mediterranean and watched the Allied landings in the south of France. He firmly believed that peace depended on the West maintaining its military strength, and in 1944 stated: 'Our progress towards world order must march with the maintenance of military power by the United States. Peace not backed by power remains a dream.'

During World War I Forrestal was trained as a naval aviator and spent 1918 in the Office of Naval Operations in Washington. Although he gave up his peace-time banking career in order to serve his country in World War II, he became a prime target of those who criticized the influence of finance in government, and he felt this abuse keenly.

FRANCO, Francisco, b. 1892. Spanish head of state, who succeeded in keeping his country neutral, or at least non-belligerent, during the war, despite strong pressure from the Axis side. His principal concern during the war years was to reinforce the national security of Spain. Initially, when it seemed that the Axis combination would succeed in dominating Europe, Franco declared his sympathy for Germany and Italy. He had an interview with Hitler on 23 October 1939 regarding the possibility of a Spanish-German attack on Gibraltar, to be followed by the seizure of the Azores, the Canary Islands, Madeira, and the Cape Verde Islands. But Franco's price for Spanish co-operation included Morocco and additional French territory in Africa, and Hitler would not agree to meet such demands in case he antagonized the Vichy government in France. Possibly Franco had realized that these demands would not be met. The recent devastating civil war had made him reluctant to be involved in more fighting. During 1940 and 1941 Hitler again tried to persuade Franco to put into operation the plan to bar the western approaches of the Mediterranean to Britain. But the scheme came to nothing, partly because Franco was impressed by Britain's staying power and therefore doubtful about the outcome of the war, but also because the strategic value of the plan was diminished after Wavell's resounding victories in the Western Desert. Britain had secured Benghazi in February 1941. It was generally assumed that Spain favoured the Axis powers during the war because of the material support that Germany and Italy had given to Franco's forces during the civil war; but in the event this partiality—even if a fact—was of little help to the Axis. To some extent Spain was liberalized during the course of the war. In 1942 Franco carried out a reorganization of the *Cortes*, and he approved a new constitutional charter in the same year.

FRANK, Anne, b. 1929. Jewish girl diarist, a victim of Nazi barbarism against the Jews. Through her diary she is the poignant symbol of Jewish suffering in the war. Anne Frank's family was living in Amsterdam when Germany invaded the Netherlands in May 1940. Anti-Jewish measures were progressively introduced and in late 1941 the two firms partly con-

trolled by Anne's father were taken over by non-Jewish colleagues to avoid confiscation on racial grounds. In July 1942 Anne's elder sister Margot was ordered to report at Westerbork Jewish Camp. The family immediately put into action a pre-arranged plan. They let it be known that they intended to flee to Belgium; then they vanished. They had gone into hiding in some empty rooms behind Anne's father's office on the Prinsengracht canal. Anne had already started a diary, which she kept up throughout the 25 months the family spent in hiding. In this diary she recorded not only a vivid day-to-day account of their secret life but also the heart-searchings and aspirations of a healthy and gifted girl in early adolescence, cut off from school and friends. The Franks were joined in their refuge by 4 others also threatened with deportation. The owners and staff of the premises at the front of the building ran enormous risks in harbouring the fugitives and in procuring for them the bare necessities of life. And since not all the employees or neighbours knew of their presence, the fugitives could make no noise during working hours, nor could they open any windows, except those in the attic, when the building was supposed to be unoccupied. Anne recorded in her diary, with honesty, humour, and optimism, the conditions they had to endure: the enforced silence, the cramped conditions, the hunger, the suffocating heat of a Whitsun holiday, and above all the inevitable friction between people living in such close proximity. It was her ambition to become a writer, and her diary shows that she had considerable ability. During the months in hiding she read widely the books brought in by faithful office staff—and wrote a number of short stories. Then, on 4 August 1944, the building was searched by armed German security police accompanied by Dutch Nazis. It is not known whether the occupants of the 'secret annexe' were betrayed or whether they had given themselves away. All 8 occupants were arrested, together with those responsible for sheltering them. The Frank family was sent first to Westerbork and then on 3 September in cattle trucks to Auschwitz in the last shipment of Jews out of Holland. Anne's mother died in Auschwitz in January 1945. Margot and

Frank

Fraser

Anne were transferred to Bergen-Belsen where, in February, both girls caught typhus. Margot died, and with her death Anne lost the will to live; she died in early March, only two months before Germany's surrender. The father of the family alone survived to return to Amsterdam after the war. The diary had been found by a cleaner on the floor of the annexe after the family's arrest. It has been published in many languages.

FRANK, Hans, b. 1900. Nazi lawyer and administrator, Governor-General of part of Poland. Shortly before the war Frank was Nazi Minister without portfolio and president of the Law Academy and the Bar Association. He was commissioned to take over the administration of Germany's conquered Eastern Territories from General Blaskowitz, C.-in-C. of a German army in Poland. In October 1939 Hitler appointed him to the so-called 'General Government'—that part of Poland that remained after Russia and Germany had annexed their respective shares of the country. There, installed in Wawel Castle, above Cracow, he ruled like an oriental despot, his declared mission being 'to make the Poles understand that a master race is ruling them'. He rounded up a steady supply of forced labour for Germany, saying: 'The Poles shall be the slaves of the German Reich.' He bled Poland of everything but the minimum necessary for the continued existence of its population. Briefed to reduce Poland's social, cultural, and political structure to 'a pile of rubble', he set about destroying the universities in November 1939, when all professors under his jurisdiction were deported or shot, and followed this up in May 1940 by instigating the 'Extraordinary Pacification Process', under which 3,500 of the Polish intelligentsia were liquidated. Although the suppression of the Polish Jews was the business of the S.S. who were only nominally responsible to him, Frank supported the S.S. with more enthusiasm than his post strictly required. He opposed the idea of the Lublinland Jewish Reserve, advocating instead deportation to Madagascar or migration to Russian-occupied Poland. Later he favoured confining the Jews to ghettoes. In 1941 he declared: 'The Jews

are a menace and they eat too much. . . . We cannot poison them but we will take action that will end in their extermination.' Under his authority hundreds of thousands of Polish Jews were dispatched to extermination camps such as Auschwitz and Treblinka. In 1942 he nearly lost his position when he crossed swords with Himmler's agent Krüger, but in the end it was Krüger who fell. He attempted 3 times to commit suicide; in 1944 the Polish Resistance tried to kill him. He made 14 attempts to resign his office.

Finally, in August 1944, he announced the collapse of his administration and left Cracow. Tried at Nuremberg as a major war criminal, he admitted his guilt and was hanged in October 1946. He left a record of his life in a diary of 42 volumes.

FRASER, Sir Bruce, b. 1888. British admiral, best known for his action off the North Cape, from which battle he took his title when elevated to the peerage. On 26 December 1943 in his flagship H.M.S. *Duke of York* with a cruiser and 4 destroyers he fought and sank the German battle-cruiser *Scharnhorst*. The engagement was conducted mostly in darkness and with the assistance of radar.

In 1944 Fraser was promoted to full admiral and became C.-in-C. first of the Eastern Fleet in S.E.A.C. under Mountbatten, and then of the British Pacific Fleet. His high regard for Admiral Nimitz greatly contributed to the success of inter-Allied naval relations in the Pacific and he also worked well with General MacArthur. In January 1945 he had a narrow escape when a Japanese *kamikaze* plane struck the American battleship *New Mexico* at a point where he had been standing a few seconds previously. On 2 September 1945, on board the USS *Missouri* in Tokyo Bay, he signed the Japanese surrender documents on behalf of the U.K.

Fraser was a highly professional sailor and strategist and combined this with good administrative abilities. He was much respected and liked throughout the navy. From 1939 to 1942 he had been Third Sea Lord and Controller at the Admiralty, and was to a major extent responsible for the expansion of the navy and its finances. In 1943–4 he was C.-in-C. Home Fleet, where he was chiefly concerned with protection of the convoys to Russia. In September 1943 he refused the position of First Sea Lord, offered to him by the Prime Minister, believing that Sir Andrew Cunningham was better qualified at that time to be the head of the navy.

FRASER, Peter, b. 1884. New Zealand statesman who became Prime Minister of his country in early 1940, after the death of Michael Joseph Savage. Fraser was a determined war leader, and also a strong and effective advocate of social reform. At the time he took office Fraser was already well known and highly respected throughout New Zealand and in many other countries. He considered that New Zealand should play the largest part she could in the war. In the use of the country's military resources he accepted Churchill's explanations of the strategies to be adopted, and did not complain when, because of urgent requirements elsewhere, the New Zealand islands were themselves apparently left open to attack at one stage. At the same time, Fraser insisted that, although New Zealand was always ready to accept the overall strategies, there was to be no question of New Zealand arms being used in any particular way without the expressed agreement of the New Zealand government. During the campaign in Crete and North Africa General Freyberg, the New Zealand C.-in-C., followed Fraser's directives.

During 1941 Fraser attended meetings of the British War Cabinet, both to give advice on Pacific policy and to help in planning future operations. In 1942 he visited President Roosevelt in Washington to discuss co-operation between the two countries. In 1943, in addition to his post as Prime Minister, he became Minister for External Affairs. In September of that year he was confirmed in office after a general election.

A strong individualist, Fraser started his working life as a dock labourer. His straightforward, determined, and friendly approach earned him a special place among war-time leaders.

FREYBERG, Sir Bernard, b. 1889. British general, commander of the New Zealand Expeditionary Force and one of the toughest and most admired soldiers of the war. Brought up in New Zealand, a holder of the V.C. and other decorations from World War I, Freyberg was chosen in 1939 to command the New Zealand forces overseas. Under his fearless leadership the New Zealanders became renowned for their heroic fighting. After action in Greece Freyberg retired with his division to Crete, and commanded the island's defence against the German invasion three weeks later (May 1941). This was the first large-scale airborne attack in history, and the defenders were overwhelmed after bitter fighting; but such was the battering suffered by the invaders themselves that Germany never attempted another expedition along these lines.

Aided by the navy, Freyberg evacuated 18,000 men from Crete, and his reconstituted division next took part in Auchinleck's Cyrenaica offensive in November 1941, but suffered crippling losses in the battle for Sidi Rezegh and the relief of Tobruk. Freyberg, critical of the command in the desert and responsible to the New Zealand government, secured temporary withdrawal of his forces to Syria; but in June 1942 they returned to stem Rommel's new advance. Freyberg was severely wounded at Minga Qaim but recovered in time for General Montgomery's El Alamein offensive, and fought with his division through to Tunis. He led a decisive flanking operation in the Battle of the Mareth Line (March 1943). In November the New Zealanders moved to Italy. After heavy fighting at the Sangro, Freyberg led the second offensive on Cassino in February 1944. His insistence on prior bombardment of the monastery proved a tactical error, for the rubble hampered his advance; but his capture of key positions enabled other forces to take Cassino later. In May 1945 he entered Trieste with the New Zealand troops and took the surrender from the German garrison.

Freyberg was a born fighter: likened by Churchill to a salamander because he 'thrived in the fire', he later chose two salamanders as supporters to his coat-of-arms. A somewhat formidable character, he inspired his men by commanding from the front line and by his concern for their welfare. New Zealanders looked upon his division as 'an outstanding example of democracy in action': he boasted that every officer had come through the ranks.

FRICK, Wilhelm, b. 1877. Nazi administrator. A member of Hitler's first Cabinet, in 1939 he still held the post of Minister of the Interior and was present at a meeting of the Reich Defence Council held on 23 June 1939 to co-ordinate mobilization measures for total war. Frick had the appearance of a medieval ascetic and was generally respected for his personal integrity, but he was uncritical in his ardour for the cause of National Socialism and could be taken advantage of. Although the police, which he had Nazified and centralized, were nominally under his control as Minister of the Interior, he had given up trying to control Himmler, who had been appointed chief of the German police in 1936. In August 1943 his diminishing competence allowed him to be ousted by Himmler, who was bent on more ruthless measures to curb growing defeatism in the Reich. Frick became instead Protector of Bohemia and Moravia, but he was really only a figurehead in the Protectorate, where effective power had been vested in Karl Hermann Frank. At the Nuremberg war crimes trials after the war it was established that Frick had known of atrocities committed in concentration camps in the Protectorate: he was convicted of helping to prepare a war of aggression and of committing crimes against humanity, and was executed in October 1946.

FULLER, John Frederick Charles, b. 1878. British soldier and military analyst. His reputation as one of the most eminent of military writers had been established well before the war. He was known as a leading advocate of the value of the tank in modern warfare.

Ironically it was in Germany that his principal influence on the war came to fruition. In 1916, as a staff officer in the Tank Corps, he saw the potentialities of the new weapon, and from that time he pursued his championship of it. His concept of a highly mobile warfare based on very fast tanks had caused the leaders of continental armies to pay attention, for once, to British military ideas. But in

England his trenchant observations were not appreciated, and 'the irrepressible Fuller' encountered much prejudice. (Liddell Hart suffered similarly.) Consequently, his 'Plan 1919'—explained in his *Memoirs of an Unconventional Soldier*, 1936—cut little ice with the War Office. But it proved to be the pattern of the German 'Blitzkrieg'. And although, in 1934, a permanent tank brigade was established in Britain which strikingly demonstrated the potentialities of armoured formations, it was Germany which took note of the lesson and created three armoured divisions in the following year.

FYFE, Sir David Maxwell, b. 1900. British lawyer and politician who took a leading part in the trials of the major war criminals. In February 1942 he became Solicitor-General, and was known for his extraordinary capacity for hard work (he was said to have as much energy as two ordinary men) and his prodigious memory.

Fyfe's work on the trial of war criminals also began in 1942, and after Churchill made him Attorney-General in the Caretaker government (May 1945) he became chairman of the War Criminals' Conference of the four major Allies. The general election in July 1945 removed him from this office, but the new Attorney-General, Hartley Shawcross, asked him to remain as Deputy Chief Prosecutor and in effect left him to continue as head of the British prosecuting team. His autobiography, *Political Adventure*, described the deep-seated differences of outlook and custom through which he led the four Allies' team of prosecuting lawyers to act as a coherent organization embodying the common principles of justice in the Western countries. Resolutely opposing the Russian view that the Nazi leaders were already convicted and only awaited punishment, he at length secured agreement that the defendants would be convicted only if certain charges were proved against them by evidence which they would have the chance of testing and answering. The trial of the 22 major Nazi leaders at Nuremberg lasted for 10 months. Maxwell Fyfe's brilliant cross-examination aroused general admiration, and the principles of impartiality and objectivity were rigidly adhered to.

G

GALE, Sir Humfrey, b. 1890. British general, Deputy Chief of Staff, and Chief Administrative Officer of General Eisenhower's H.Q. for the 'Second Front' invasion of N.W. Europe. His task was the extraordinarily complicated one of coordinating the operational logistics of the Allies and of supervising the work of the administrative staffs. He and his many associates had had to master, during the African campaigns, the novel art of dealing with immense forces of diverse nationalities operating under a single command. His name was virtually unknown to the general public, but he and his staff were as responsible for the teamwork out of which came the victories of Tunisia, Sicily, Italy, and N.W. Europe as were many others whose more spectacular accomplishments often made headlines. Gale's advice was indispensable to those in charge of the overall running of the war since his knowledge of available men and supplies had to be taken into account before any offensive could be launched.

GALE, Richard, b. 1896. British general, one of the war's most successful commanders of airborne troops. He raised and commanded the 1st Parachute Brigade. In 1944 he commanded the 6th Airborne Division, which was the vanguard of the force that had a most vital role to play in the scheme for the invasion of France. It was responsible not only for holding the left flank of the bridgehead against the onslaught of Rommel's Panzer divisions but also for capturing and holding a base to the east from which to expand the Allied bridgehead south-east beyond Caen. With only a small force, Gale seized the Orne crossings in the face of very heavy flak, proving that airborne landings should be made on or near the objective and that it was better to suffer land losses than to have to fight to reach the objective after landing. Although Gale looked every inch a 'Poona Colonel' (he had in fact been Master of the Delhi Foxhounds when serving in India), spare and straight with ruddy face, bristling moustache, and bushy eyebrows, this first impression was misleading. When he spoke, the power of his

blunt but lucid words disclosed a man who could both devise a plan of daring originality and infuse his men with the confidence and courage to carry it out. During the course of the landings in France, he was heard to mutter half to himself the words from Shakespeare's *Henry V*: 'And gentlemen in England now a-bed shall think themselves accursed they were not here.'

GALEN, Graf Clemens von, b. 1878. German churchman, Cardinal Archbishop of Munster. In 1933 he had taken the oath of allegiance to the Nazi régime, and he was opposed to Church interference in politics. But soon his contempt for Nazi propaganda against the Church established him as a force to be reckoned with. His attitude to the war was patriotic: resentful of the Treaty of Versailles, he exhorted his congregation to chivalry in defence of the Fatherland. However, his opposition to the régime grew, and by 1941 he had earned the nickname 'Lion of Munster' because of his sermons attacking the police state and the practice of euthanasia for mental defectives, urging his flock to do their Christian duty. Although leading Nazis pressed for action to be taken against him, the Gestapo merely confined him to Munster and kept track of his activities. However, confiscation of Church property ceased in his diocese, and the murder of the feeble-minded was temporarily stopped. Ulrich von Hassell, the former German ambassador in Italy, wrote in his *Diaries* (August 1941): 'Why does Rome let Galen fight all alone?'

GALLAND, Adolf, b. 1912. German airman, a leading fighter 'ace' of the war. With Werner Mölders and Helmut Wick he made a name for himself as one of the most successful Luftwaffe pilots during the Battle of Britain.

Galland had been a fighter pilot before the war, but during the German attack on Poland he had a staff post. He returned to fighters in April 1940 and served in France, and in August was appointed to lead a group during the summer battles over the Channel coast and England. After Mölders's death in November 1941 Galland became his successor as commander of the Fighter Arm. He was promoted to generalmajor in November 1942, and became, at the age of 30, the youngest general of the German armed forces.

In this position from 1942 to 1944 he experienced the gradual failure of the Fighter Arm and its eventual destruction as the Allied onslaught gained momentum. Beset by shortages of every kind, Galland was nevertheless able to inspire his pilots and he seized every opportunity for introducing new technical and tactical knowledge. As mediator between the front-line pilots and the Supreme Command, he invariably took the side of the fighting man. In consequence he was disliked and distrusted by some of his superiors, and in January 1945 he was relieved of his command.

Between 1937 and 1938 Galland had taken part in the Spanish Civil War and had there developed novel techniques of close support. Some of Galland's success as a fighter 'ace' was due to the fact that he never underestimated his enemies. He commented: 'We had no illusions about the R.A.F. We knew our opponents had to be taken very seriously.'

GAMELIN, Maurice, b. 1872. French soldier, C.-in-C. of the Allied armies in France, 1939–40. But after the French military reverses in the spring of 1940, Pétain dismissed Gamelin on 19 May and re-appointed the former C.-in-C., General Weygand. Gamelin was arrested on 6 September 1940. Later, at Riom in February 1942, he was accused—along with Blum, Daladier, Georges Mandel, and Reynaud—of responsibility for the French defeat. Also his strategy and control of French troops during May 1940 had been called into question. On taking over, Weygand had countermanded Gamelin's final order that the northern armies should fight back towards the Somme while the French 2nd Army, and the newly organized 6th Army, were to advance northwards. In fact Weygand very soon put Gamelin's order back into effect, but the delay was serious. In addition to difficulties created by Weygand's take-over from Gamelin, Gamelin had also been out of touch with his subordinate field commanders on a number of occasions. Enough material evidence was produced to support the accusation, and

Gamelin was imprisoned in various châteaux and finally in the fort of Portalet. He was summoned before the French High Court at Riom on 19 February 1942, but refused to defend himself or to take part in the judicial inquiry. Proceedings were adjourned on 11 April, and Gamelin was sent back to prison. He was deported by the Germans in March 1943 with other important French personages, and sent to Buchenwald concentration camp and to the Tyrol prison camp at Itter. He was set free by American troops in May 1945.

To some extent a defeatist, Gamelin appeared never really to have believed in the possibility of French resistance to the Germans.

GANDHI, Mohandas Karamchand, b. 1869. Indian political and spiritual leader, in his effect on events one of the great men of the 20th century. Gandhi, known by the title *Mahatma* (great souled) captured the Congress party in 1920 and retained its leadership until October 1934, ostensibly retiring to devote his time to social work but in effect continuing his leadership until the independence of India was achieved. He favoured passive resistance and the hunger strike as techniques to persuade the British to leave India.

When war broke out, tension on the independence issue grew rapidly in India. Some of the Indian politicians urged that Britain's preoccupation should be exploited in order to seize power, perhaps with Japanese assistance. The situation was exacerbated by the fact that, while Britain wanted to avoid the partition of India, the powerful Muslim League, led by Mohammad Ali Jinnah, demanded that the Muslims should be given a state separate from that of the Hindu majority.

The mission of Stafford Cripps to India in March 1942 studied the problem of Indian independence and the immediate requirement of winning the war. Cripps found that the old conflict between Muslims and Hindus had again raised its head. On the offer that the British government would grant independence to India after the war Gandhi refused to accept 'postdated cheques upon a bankrupt empire'. Congress did not want partition and decided to sabotage the British war drive, proclaiming passive disobedience (August 1942). Britain was therefore forced to declare the Congress party an unlawful organization and Gandhi, Jawaharlal Nehru, and others were imprisoned. Gandhi was arrested on 9 August 1942, and released on 6 May 1944.

Throughout the war, and until independence was achieved, Gandhi urged that although Britain must go she must be allowed to go in an orderly fashion. He had a sound sense of reality—not always apparent—but he interpreted every event in terms of its effect on his own self-imposed mission of reform. He never yearned for political power, only that those in power should be favourable to his ideals.

GEORGE II, b. 1889. King of Greece, an exile in London for much of the war. From there, with his government-in-exile, he continued to encourage the fight of his people at home against the occupying Axis forces.

When Italy invaded Greece in October 1940 the King and General Metaxas, the Premier, declared war, invoking Chamberlain's guarantee of April 1939. The King did not vacillate, and Mussolini was surprised to encounter an army pledged to defend a united nation. With the support of British and Commonwealth troops, the Greeks put up a heroic resistance, and succumbed to the Germans only in April 1941. Meanwhile in January Metaxas had died and internal dissension had grown—but the Greeks never wavered in loyalty to their allies.

When the new Premier committed suicide, the King took over his duties, rallying his people to meet the future. He transferred his government to Crete, but almost at once, in May 1941, there followed the German invasion of that island, and he narrowly escaped to Egypt. In September he was welcomed in London with his exiled government. Recent events had led to revived criticism of the monarchy, but he and his Premier, in broadcasts to occupied Greece, did what they could to encourage democratic principles and public confidence in a constitutional monarchy. In 1942 he visited his troops in the Middle East, and negotiated a Lend-Lease agreement with the U.S.A. In March

1943 he moved his government to Cairo, but political leaders in Athens strongly advised him not to return to Greece until a plebiscite had been held. The King offered the promise of a general election directly Greece was liberated, but this was considered insufficient, and political quarrels gradually turned into civil war. Ultimately, in December 1944, he yielded to Churchill's pressure—exercised in the interests of law and order—and appointed Archbishop Damaskinos as temporary Regent. He agreed not to return to Greece 'unless summoned by a free and fair expression of the national will'. He eventually returned as king in 1946.

Speaking good English, George was a popular social figure in England and had many friends there. He had already lived in England in exile from 1924 to 1935, and he was strongly pro-British. When war broke out, even though there were substantial pro-German trade interests in Greece and though General Metaxas was said to be Germanophile, Greece adopted a policy of neutrality.

GEORGE VI, b. 1895. Titular head of the British Commonwealth and Empire, King George, a modest, shy, and unassuming man, won by his conduct and example during the war the respect and affection of people in all walks of life. When war came he saw his role as that of leader of a Christian country morally committed to fight for Christian values and confident of the outcome of a just war. Through his personal humility he identified himself with the trials of his peoples, setting an example of courage and endurance and resolutely countering in public any sign of pessimism.

The King and Queen endured the rigours of the blitz and narrowly escaped injury when Buckingham Palace was bombed. Though politically impartial, the King developed a particular intimacy with Churchill, who scrupulously observed the King's right to be acquainted with everything and who remarked upon the extraordinary diligence with which he dealt with documents. As Head of State he showed a magnanimous understanding of the predicaments of the Heads of State of other Allied countries. He and the Queen made a significant contribution to Anglo-American co-operation and friendship through their relations with President Roosevelt.

In October 1939 he paid the first of several visits to the fleet and in December visited the B.E.F. in France, when he met French leaders. In the Battle of Britain he inspected defences up and down the country and was a constant visitor to London's bombed areas, and later to stricken provincial cities and towns. In Churchill's words: 'This war has drawn the throne and the people more closely together than ever before recorded.' But it was also the King's personal qualities which enabled him to move towards his people; in the grim early years his Christmas messages and other broadcasts touched the people of Britain and the Commonwealth. On these occasions he emphasized his unfailing belief in ultimate victory.

In June 1943 the King visited the troops in North Africa and also visited the island of Malta, to which he awarded his own order, the George Cross, for valour. In 1944 he travelled all over England inspecting the forces who were destined for the invasion of France. He kept in close touch with General Eisenhower and was present at the conference at St Paul's School in London on 15 May when the final plans for D-Day were explained. He visited the assault forces at the ports of assembly. Eager to witness the invasion himself he deferred to more cautious counsels; but when the bridgeheads were established he visited the troops in Normandy. In July he went to Italy, and in October to Holland.

He pondered the problems which would follow peace and was particularly concerned in trying to carry the war-time spirit into the future. His straightforward diary is a model of common sense and faith. At the announcement of the German surrender in May 1945 he and Churchill lunched together as they had done regularly throughout the war and then appeared on the balcony of Buckingham Palace with the Queen and the princesses. In August the King met President Truman in H.M.S. *Renown* at Plymouth when the President was returning from the Potsdam Conference at which the decision to release the atomic bomb on Japan had been taken.

The King had been at the head of his

people through the darkest days and had restored to the crown a prestige which had been partly lost through the abdication of King Edward VIII. He was admired for the way he learned to master a speech defect, in addition to indifferent health, which had impeded him since childhood.

GIBSON, Guy, b. 1918. Leader of the attack by R.A.F. bombers in 1943 on the Möhne and Eder dams, one of the most spectacular bombing feats of the war. For his part in the raid Gibson was awarded the V.C. Shortly after war broke out Gibson took part in the first British bombing raid of the war, on the Kiel Canal. Later he transferred to night fighters, but returned to Bomber Command and completed another tour of duty. He was offered command of 617 Squadron, which was then being formed for the task of attacking the Möhne and Eder dams. These dams were the source of electric power and water for part of the Ruhr, and were of great importance to the German war effort. The task posed unique problems. The artificial lakes formed by the dams were closely bordered by high mountains. Also, to destroy the dams bombs of special design were needed. These were constructed by the inventor Barnes Wallis. The pilots of 617 Squadron had to dive their heavily loaded planes steeply past the mountains, flatten out sharply at exactly 60 feet above the water, then drop the single spherical bomb that each carried so that it would bounce along the surface of the water and sink close to the dam wall. The pilots had to be expert at long-distance low-level night flying, to avoid detection by German radar; and they had to know in darkness when they were at the correct height above smooth water. To enable them to gauge their height, dual spotlights were fitted whose beams coincided at 60 feet beneath the planes. Gibson led in the squadron and dropped the first bomb. The water then had to settle again before another plane could attack. To distract the attention of the German anti-aircraft gunners from the other planes, Gibson flew repeatedly over the dam machine-gunning the German troops. The attacks on both dams were successful.

Gibson lost his life in September 1944

when he piloted a Mosquito as master
bomber, directing incoming planes to
their target. The task completed, he
wished the returning bombers 'Good
night' and turned for home. His plane
crashed in the Netherlands. Long before,
his house master at school had said that
Guy Gibson was 'strong minded without
obstinacy, disarmingly frank and of great
charm'—qualities that his associates in
later life could testify to.

GIFFARD, Sir George, b. 1886. British
general, a successful commander of the
old and conventional school. An expert on
African affairs, at the outbreak of war he
was Military Secretary at the War Office.
Appointed G.O.C. in Palestine and Trans-
jordan early in 1940, he was transferred to
West Africa as G.O.C. in June of the
same year.

Giffard had great success in building up
the West African regiments. The Gold
Coast and Nigeria regiments acquitted
themselves well in the East African campaign, helping to win back Addis Ababa
from the Italians. They proved themselves
determined and tenacious soldiers, though
fighting in unfamiliar terrain. Some of
their success resulted from Giffard's
understanding of his troops and his talent
for organization. In 1942 he went to India
as G.O.C. Eastern Army, and in 1943 it
was thought to use his knowledge in the
fighting in the East. He was appointed
C.-in-C. of 11th Army Group in S.E.
Asia, but held this command for only a
short period.

GIRAUD, Henri, b. 1879. French general
who competed with Charles de Gaulle for
leadership of the Free French forces in
North Africa. In May 1940 he was in
command of the French 9th Army when
its positions were fiercely attacked by
German armoured formations. Giraud
was forced to retreat, and was taken
prisoner by the Germans on 19 May 1940.
He was in captivity until April 1942, when
he managed to escape to Vichy France and
then to Gibraltar. In November 1942 he was
taken by British submarine to North Africa.

His two years of captivity had put
Giraud at a disadvantage as compared
with de Gaulle, who had been able to
operate in London since 1940. During this

interval de Gaulle had identified himself
with the Free French movement, and
stressed two main objectives: that political
resistance to the Vichy government should
be made through the *Conseil de Défense de
l'Empire*, and later through the *Comité
National Français*; and that military
resistance should be based on organizing
a Free French fighting command.

Thus after his escape Giraud was faced
by the fact that de Gaulle held a strong
position within the Free French movement. The Allies had not then irretrievably decided which French leader to support and build up as commander of the
French Resistance, so it is possible to
argue that Giraud still had a chance of
competing with de Gaulle. In the bargain-
ing which had earlier taken place with the
French leaders in order to win them
decisively to the Allied cause, Giraud had
received the impression that he was to
control the forces in North Africa. He had
escaped at a time when the North African
sector was crucial and, if he could have
made his claim effective, this would have
strengthened his challenge as leader. But
the Americans, who favoured him, found
that Giraud lacked political authority.
Even so they were unwilling to back de
Gaulle, and some effort was still made to
maintain Giraud's importance. After
Darlan's assassination in December 1942
he was made High Commissioner of
French North and West Africa.

When Roosevelt and Churchill met at
Casablanca in January 1943 strenuous
efforts were made to reconcile Giraud and
de Gaulle, but the latter would not accept
Giraud as supreme commander of the
French forces. In June of the same year an
apparent settlement was reached when the
French Committee of National Liberation
was established at Algiers with Giraud
and de Gaulle as joint presidents. But this
arrangement lasted only five months and
Giraud resigned, under pressure. De
Gaulle was accepted as the unquestioned
Free French leader, and Giraud had to
give up his political ambitions. In April
1944 he was forced by the Gaullists to
resign from his position as C.-in-C. of the
French forces in North Africa.

GLENDENNING, Raymond, b. 1907.
British radio commentator, one of the

best-known voices on the B.B.C. during the war. His commentaries covered many aspects of the war in Britain. He recorded vivid impressions of the 'Blitz' from the roof of Broadcasting House and from air-raid shelters; he described a training session of the National Fire Service from the top of a 100-foot ladder; and night training exercises of paratroopers and bomber crews. He also covered lord mayors' shows and the enthronement of the Bishop of Coventry in the ruined shell of Coventry Cathedral.

Glendenning's name was also associated with a number of popular programmes, including 'Theatreland', a programme for the Forces, 'Those were the Days', an old-time dancing programme, and 'Radio Allotment', which involved Glendenning and his team in the cultivation of an allotment behind Regent's Park station. On VE-Day he took his microphone to the belfry of the church of St Martin-in-the-Fields, and on VJ-Day he circled London in an aeroplane to link the progress of the victory processions.

GOEBBELS, Paul Joseph, b. 1897. Chief propagandist of the Nazi régime, in which he was one of the leading figures, Goebbels was probably the best educated and the most clear-minded of Hitler's close associates but was to the end an unswerving supporter of the Führer.

The war gave him his supreme opportunity to show his mastery of the techniques of mass communication, and he controlled every channel of propaganda and information in Germany. A skilled administrator and an orator of exceptional talent and power, he stamped his personality on press and radio and every other means of sustaining and advancing the myths of National Socialism. From his Propaganda Ministry he controlled an all-pervading mechanism of exhortation and vituperation that enabled him to play his role as 'the custodian of German knowledge and ideas'. When the occasion demanded it, he came to the microphone himself: in October 1939 when the *Athenia* had been torpedoed without warning by a U-Boat, with the loss of 112 lives including 28 Americans, Goebbels—remembering the lessons of World War I—accused Churchill of responsibility for the sinking

by having a bomb secreted in the ship. After the Casablanca Conference of January 1943 at which Roosevelt and Churchill agreed that the war could be ended only by the unconditional surrender of Germany, Goebbels sought to turn the declaration to the advantage of the régime, encouraging the German people to greater efforts since they now had only two choices: victory or utter destruction.

Completely cynical himself, Goebbels seems to have believed only in the self-justification of power. His *Diaries* revealed his adulation of Hitler, and his bitter contempt for mankind in general and the Jews in particular. 'I have learned to despise the human being,' he wrote. And again: 'After I have been with a person for three days, I no longer like him; if I have been with him for a week, I hate him.' In adversity his statements took on a whining note: thus, in 1943: 'The English Minister for Air made a speech that puts in the shade anything he ever said . . . he expressed the intention of the British of forcing a German exodus from the large cities. The cynicism underlying such a statement cannot be beaten!'

On the afternoon of the attempt on Hitler's life in July 1944 Goebbels's quick thinking and decisive action were largely instrumental in saving the day for the Nazis. Discovering where the nerve-centre of the conspiracy was located, he quickly organized a detachment of trustworthy supporters and isolated the plotters in the War Ministry.

Goebbels's last successful propaganda coup, which succeeded in altering Allied strategy, was his invention of a German 'National Redoubt'. This was a mythical impregnable fortress in the mountains, where the last stand was to be made.

As the Russians closed in on Berlin, Goebbels was invited with his family into the Führerbunker under the Chancellery where Hitler's last days were spent. After Hitler's suicide, Goebbels had his six children poisoned and then had himself and his wife shot by an S.S. orderly.

Goebbels was a graduate of Heidelberg University. A journalist, he was one of the earliest of Hitler's followers. He was elected to the Reichstag, and in 1933 became Minister for Public Enlightenment and Propaganda. He was a man of very small stature, and limped badly because of a childhood illness. In contrast to Goering, he had a reputation for leading a frugal life despite his partiality for lavish parties. Hitler used to hold up the Goebbels ménage as the ideal German family, but Goebbels was, in fact, involved in a constant succession of intrigues with women.

GOERDELER, Karl, b. 1884. German civil servant, former Lord Mayor of Leipzig, and a leader of the Resistance movement against Hitler. His rejection of Nazism, based primarily on ethical and political considerations, was made complete by the outbreak of war and by the news of the atrocities committed in occupied territories. In July 1940, at the height of the 'Blitzkrieg', he composed a memorandum originally intended for the officer corps of the German army. In this document he described the desolation of a Europe under Nazi domination. He had close connections with business leaders, officials, and diplomats, and possessed a tremendous knowledge of home and international affairs. He drew up detailed plans for the running of Germany after the overthrow of Hitler. At an early date he had drafted a new constitution envisaging almost complete decentralization of governmental power. He was convinced at the outset that Hitler could be removed from office only by the armed forces, and he had to battle hard to rouse the generals from their state of hesitation and vacillation. Although he possessed many qualities desirable in a Resistance leader, he was also dangerously over-optimistic and dangerously indiscreet. After the failure of the 20 July 1944 plot against Hitler, the Gestapo discovered a variety of documents incriminating Goerdeler, including the draft of his proposed radio address to the German people as Chancellor of the Reich and a list of the proposed members of his Cabinet. He was hanged in the Prinz Albrechtstrasse prison on 2 February 1945.

Elected Lord Mayor of Leipzig in 1930, Goerdeler was an established political figure before the Nazi seizure of power. In 1935 he resigned his position as Reich Commissioner of Prices in protest against the Nazi government, and in 1937 relinquished his post as Lord Mayor of Leipzig when the bust of Mendelssohn was removed from its place in front of the City Hall by order of the Nazi party. He then became the principal contact man abroad of the firm of Bosch, using his position to warn influential people in Europe and the U.S.A. of the menace confronting them in Nazi Germany.

GOERING, Hermann, b. 1893. German Nazi leader, responsible for the conduct of the war in the air. One of the main figures in the Nazi party, he had, for a time, a position of power second only to Hitler's.

Goering joined the Nazi party in 1922, and became one of the first commanders of the Stormtroopers. He rapidly rose in the ranks of the party, and was closely involved in the intrigues that finally brought Hitler to power in 1933. In Hitler's first Cabinet he was Minister of the Interior for Prussia, Germany's largest state. As such Goering had control over the Prussian police, which he skilfully organized into an instrument of Nazi tyranny to suppress all opposition to Hitler's policies. From the Prussian Secret Police, Goering organized the Gestapo. He also set up the first concentration camps.

In the mid 1930s Goering was Reichsminister for aviation. In this capacity he ordered the secret rebuilding of Germany's air force. His well-known catchphrase 'Guns before butter' symbolized the sacrifice of German well-being to an all-out scheme of rearmament. In 1935 he combined his ministerial position with that of C.-in-C. of the Luftwaffe (air force).

Goering supported Hitler's economic policy (to mobilize Germany's economy for war whatever the cost) and Hitler placed him in charge of the Nazi Four Year Plan, making him economic dictator of Germany. Goering was ill-equipped for this position, but his force of character produced results. In 1940 he became Germany's highest ranking officer, with the title of *Reichsmarschall*. The year before, Hitler had named him as his successor.

Goering had a great share in preparing Germany for a total war of aggression, but, ironically, the outbreak of war marked the beginning of his decline. As long as he had been successful his power had been unchallengeable. But Goering's failure to win the Battle of Britain frustrated Hitler's intention (the invasion of Britain), discredited the previously invincible Luftwaffe, and implicated Goering in its fall from favour. Constant intrigue against Goering amongst his enemies who were close to Hitler—and his own seeming disregard for other important Nazis—ensured that Goering's loss of influence was permanent. By 1943 Goering had lost effective power, retaining only his numerous titles, and there were frequent complaints that he was never to be seen. He retired to gloat over the treasury of art he had accumulated at his palatial mansion, 'Karinhall', named after his first wife. This vast collection of statuary, paintings, and jewels had been looted from all the German-occupied countries of Europe, where Goering's minions had selected for the *Reichsmarschall* the finest items from scores of museums and art galleries. The value of his haul was at least £20 million.

Despite his fall from favour, Goering remained faithful to Hitler to the end. But in April 1945 he sent a message to Hitler in the besieged Führerbunker in Berlin declaring his intention of taking over Hitler's function as Führer unless immediately assured that Hitler was neither dead nor incapacitated. This action was misunderstood by Hitler, and caused Goering's expulsion from the party and his arrest by his arch-enemy Martin Bormann. Soon afterwards he was taken prisoner by the Americans. At Nuremberg in 1946 Goering was condemned to death for war crimes, but despite the vigilance of his guards he committed suicide by taking poison in his cell the night before he was to have been executed.

Goering, known as 'the Fat One' because of his vast girth, was perhaps the most popular of the Nazi leaders because of his bonhomie and because he had been a hero of World War I, as the last leader of the famous Richthofen Fighter Squadron. He had a great love of parties and pageantry, and was famed for his flamboyant dress, ranging from his self-designed uniform as head of the Luftwaffe and as Chief Reich Huntsman to a wide variety

of fancy dress while entertaining his guests at 'Karinhall'.

GORT, Viscount, V.C., b. 1886. British general (field marshal, 1943), C.-in-C. of the B.E.F. in France in 1939. By 25 May 1940 the B.E.F. and the rest of the Allied northern armies were in immediate danger of being overwhelmed because of the rapid advance of the German Panzer divisions. The B.E.F.'s lines of communication to the Brittany ports had been cut by the German armour, and Gort decided to establish a defended line from Arras to the Channel coast. The 10 divisions of the B.E.F. were in fact caught in a pocket (with about 30 French divisions) and cut off from the main part of the French army to the south. Counter-attacks to effect a link-up were attempted unsuccessfully, but at the point where it seemed that the corridor to the Channel could easily be cut by the Germans, the German armour stopped and an infantry mopping-up operation was begun. Gort (with permission from London), seizing the unpalatable but—in the event—historic opportunity, withdrew, using the geographic defences, to Dunkirk; and beginning on 27 May, 848 ships evacuated some 340,000 men to England. About two-thirds of them were members of the B.E.F.; the others belonged to what was to become 'Free' Europe. It was the classic case of living to fight another day.

Back in the U.K., Gort became Inspector General to the Forces for Training until 1941, when he was appointed Governor of Gibraltar. He then went to the vital task of Governor and C.-in-C. of Malta at a critical time in the defence of that island. His unyielding and indefatigable approach to the situation in early 1942 was largely responsible for sustaining the inhabitants through the desperate months that saw the Luftwaffe's efforts to paralyse Malta's defences.

Gort was an Irishman. In World War I he served in the Grenadier Guards and gained the V.C., the D.S.O. and two bars, the M.C., and 8 mentions in dispatches. From being Director of Military Training in India since 1932 and commandant of the Staff College at Camberley 1936-7, he was brought to the War Office by the Minister for War, Leslie Hore-Belisha, as a new broom in the capacity of C.I.G.S. On the outbreak of war he went to command the B.E.F.

GRAZIANI, Rodolfo, b. 1882. Italian marshal. Renowned as a successful colonial soldier, in 1940 he was made governor of Libya and C.-in-C. of the forces in North Africa. Mussolini, having achieved no blazing victory in France, impatiently pressed for the invasion of Egypt. At first Graziani did not consider that his forces were ready, but in September 1940, under threat of dismissal, he complied and the British, heavily outnumbered, withdrew on Mersa Matruh; but at Sidi Barrani the marshal halted to build a chain of fortifications. On 9 December General Wavell suddenly struck back. Within two months, Graziani's army was hustled back across Cyrenaica, losing its equipment and 130,000 prisoners. He bitterly reproached Mussolini for forcing him into a struggle between 'a flea and an elephant'. Had his army been well trained and equipped, or eager to fight, he might well have defeated the British, but he could not, he said, 'break steel armour with finger-nails alone'. By early February 1941 the Italian 10th Army no longer functioned, and Graziani relinquished his command in North Africa. A court of inquiry censured his conduct of the campaign, though he produced the actual orders sent by Mussolini, whose strategy he claimed to have explicitly opposed.

In September 1943 Mussolini—having been deposed and arrested but rescued by the Germans—set up a republic in northern Italy under German protection, with Graziani as Minister of Defence. Graziani was always loyal to the German alliance, and denounced Marshal Badoglio and the King for seeking an armistice. But his efforts to create a republican Italian army were hampered by German distrust. In April 1945 Mussolini determined to make a last stand in the mountains, and Graziani went with him to Lake Como. Expecting Mussolini to escape over the border into Switzerland he returned to join his troops. He was taken prisoner by the Allies. Brought to trial by the Italian government for collaborating with the Germans after the armistice, he was sentenced to 19 years' imprisonment.

GRIGG, James, b. 1890. British Secretary of State for War. A civil servant by profession, and former Private Secretary to Churchill (1926), he returned from India to become Permanent Under Secretary of State for War just before hostilities started. Conscription had recently been introduced, the Territorial Army was in the process of being doubled, and at the War Office Grigg concentrated on administrative reforms leading to greater flexibility.

In February 1942 Churchill (who described Grigg as 'one of the finest of our civil servants') called him to ministerial office as Secretary of State for War. Disregarding his civil service future he accepted without hesitation. He declined a peerage, and won a by-election at East Cardiff. Then, with single-minded determination, he set out to produce and equip a first-class modern army so that, in 1944, Montgomery was able to declare: 'I doubt if the War Office has ever sent an army overseas so well equipped as the one fighting now in Normandy.' General Brooke had a high regard for him.

Grigg was a man from a humble background, with a passion for efficiency. Having found his own way to the top, he firmly believed in the individual helping himself. He was all against a country 'living beyond its means on its wits', and trying 'to make a community rich by calling a penny twopence'. He called his autobiography *Prejudice and Judgment*.

GROVES, Leslie, b. 1898. American general who headed the Manhattan Project for the construction of an atomic weapon. Groves was a professional soldier, an officer in the Engineer Corps, and before being assigned to the team working on the atomic bomb had played a major part in the construction of the Pentagon building. When he became director of the Manhattan Project in 1942 he had assembled the scientific and executive manpower adequate to one of the most exacting and complicated undertakings of all time. This he did with complete success. The project had a budget of some £150 million a year, employed 125,000 people, and involved every operation from finding the uranium and carrying out the necessary research to delivering the completed bomb.

Groves was a forceful and self-confident man. He also had considerable imagination and—when really needed—diplomacy. He succeeded in keeping his complex organization functioning under pressure without any major conflicts of personality or opinion.

GUDERIAN, Heinz, b. 1888. German general, perhaps the most brilliant commander of armoured forces of the war. Without him the 'Blitzkrieg' would not have been possible, and Hitler's early offensive efforts would have been frustrated, for in 1939 and 1940 Germany's forces in general were not numerically adequate to defeating the combined Allied strength. Germany's opening run of victories was primarily due to the Panzer units which Guderian had created and trained, and to his audacious leading of those forces. Guderian's breakthrough at Sedan (14 May 1940) and lightning drive to the Channel coast virtually decided the Battle of France. A year later, the drive he led into the east came close to producing the complete collapse of Russia's armies, but this time renewed hesitancy at the top imposed a delay that stretched the campaign into winter. This gave the Russians the necessary respite to raise fresh armies and to develop new arms factories to replace those that had been captured. On 25 December 1941 Guderian was dismissed for taking a timely step back instead of pandering to Hitler's illusions. He was recalled to service only when Germany's situation had become desperate. Eventually he was made C.G.S. (21 July 1944); but by then the position was hopeless. Guderian's appointment came just after the July plot failed. He became a member of a military court which expelled hundreds from the army, so that they could be degraded and sentenced as civilians by the People's Court. He warned all his staff officers to be good Nazis.

Guderian possessed most of the qualities that make for a great general: acute observation blended with swift, sure intuition; the ability to create surprise and throw the enemy off balance; the speed of thought and action that allows the opponent no chance of recovery; a combination of strategic and tactical sense; the power to win the devotion of troops and get the utmost out of them. He devoted himself single-mindedly to the progress of the technique of armoured warfare and did not question the purpose which such technical progress might serve. His attitude to Hitler was more favourable than that of most of the generals brought up in the old tradition, but this was mainly because both of them were in conflict with the General Staff and established conventions. His brusque honesty and pugnacity, however, often brought him into trouble, not only with his immediate superiors but with the Führer himself.

Guderian's early career alternated between regimental and staff duties. He was by training an infantryman, but his attachment to the 3rd Telegraph Battalion at Koblenz and an assignment involving work with radio enabled him to acquire a certain knowledge of communication techniques which was to stand him in good stead in the years to come. His main activity during the inter-war period was concerned with the creation of a German armoured force, and in 1936 he published a book called *Achtung! Panzer!* which told the story of the development of armoured forces and outlined his basic ideas as to how the German armoured units should be built up.

GUÉRISSE, Albert ('Pat O'Leary'), b. 1911. Belgian doctor and secret agent whose secret escape organization in France enabled hundreds of Allied Servicemen to evade the Germans and return to Britain. A medical officer in the Belgian army, Guérisse embarked at Dunkirk after Belgium capitulated. He was trained in Britain as an agent, and adopted the new *persona* of 'Lieutenant-Commander Patrick O'Leary, R.N.', with a French-Canadian background. In April 1941, while first officer of the 'Q' ship H.M.S. *Fidelity*, he was arrested on the south coast of France, imprisoned at Toulon and transferred to Fort Lamalgue and later to St Hippolyte du Fort. Escaping to Marseilles, he made contact with Ian Garrow, who had formed an escape organization to help Allied soldiers left behind at Dunkirk to travel south and cross the frontier into Spain. With authority from London, 'O'Leary' became Garrow's assistant, and, when Garrow was arrested later in 1941, took charge of what came to be known as

'Organization Pat'. A year later the organization, sponsored by M.I.9, stretched to the borders of Belgium, Italy, and Spain, and involved some 250 full-time agents. It produced forged papers, identity and ration cards, clothing, money, and black-market food; and its own transmitter (collected by 'Pat' from Gibraltar) kept it in touch with London. By this time most of the escapers were air crews that had been shot down: it was possible for an airman who crashed in northern France to be in England less than a fortnight later. Many airmen had been captured on landing, and had later escaped from prison; some prison breaks were arranged by the organization. As numbers increased it became difficult to depend on Spanish guides across the

Pyrenees, and 6 mass embarkations (each of 30 to 40 men) took place from secluded beaches in the south. When war ended, some 600 men had been returned down 'the line' to fight again. As the organization grew, so did the risk of detection and betrayal: many agents were arrested, and in March 1943 'Pat' himself was betrayed at Toulouse. Despite torture and imprisonment (at Fresnes, Nenebrenn, Mauthausen, Natzweiler, and finally Dachau) he gave nothing away. At Dachau he organized an International Prisoners' Committee which, by substituting corpses for the living, saved some 5,000 prisoners earmarked for the death convoys. On 29 April 1945 the Americans entered Dachau and 'Pat', reduced to half his weight, was flown to Paris. He was awarded the G.C.

H

HAAKON VII, b. 1872. Formerly Prince Carl of Denmark, he was the first King of Norway after the country's restoration to independence in 1905. When the Germans invaded Norway Haakon refused to parley, stating that he would abdicate rather than countenance arrangements contrary to the provisions of the constitution. When Vidkun Quisling's government was formed in April 1940, Haakon withdrew from Oslo under armed attack, and led a Resistance government from Trondheim. Under German pressure, the presidential board of the *Storting* (parliament) requested his abdication. Haakon's dignified refusal strengthened Norway's will to resist, of which the King soon became the symbol. He absolutely declined to accept the validity of Quisling's government, and when the British had to withdraw, Haakon and his ministers were evacuated with them.

In an influential broadcast to America on 2 September 1941, Haakon condemned the Germans as unfit to lead Europe or to rule any other nation. He continued broadcasting from London throughout the war. Speaking from London in 1943, he was able to say that Norwegians were actively resisting on the home front, while, in exile, Norway had a small navy and air force, as well as a considerable merchant fleet, all on active service. Haakon's exile government established warm relations with Sweden, to the anger of Germany.

In October 1944 Haakon's forces participated with the Russians in a joint attack from Finland on German positions in Norway. His arrival in liberated Oslo in June 1945 was treated as an occasion for national rejoicing.

HAILE SELASSIE, b. 1891. Emperor of Ethiopia. Driven from his country by the invading Italians in 1936, he regained his throne in 1941. A small man of immense dignity, his rule was all-embracing, shrewd, and enlightened.

Ethiopia's war began in 1935. When Italy attacked and overran Ethiopia that country was left to its fate even by those bound to it by treaty obligations. Against a 20th-century invader using modern weapons Ethiopia's only defence was the bravery and endurance of those tribes loyal to the Emperor. They had few and totally inadequate weapons. In May 1936, after seven months of bitter fighting and bloodshed, Haile Selassie was reluctantly persuaded that he could not save his country, and was evacuated by British warships into exile.

On 10 June 1940 Italy entered the war against the Allies. This event brought an immediate and fundamental reappraisal of the British official position regarding Ethiopia and her Emperor. The British government decided to assist him to return to his homeland before the collapse of France and the closing of the Mediterranean might make this impossible.

At first there were coolness and hostility on the part of civil and military officials after his arrival in Khartoum in the Sudan, but with backing from the U.K. a refugee Patriot Army was formed, chiefly as a result of the relentless energy of Orde Wingate, and on 20 January 1941 Haile Selassie raised the national flag once more on Ethiopian soil. As the Patriot Army advanced into the country other forces, under Generals Cunningham and Platt, fought their way into Somaliland to the south-east, and Eritrea to the north. A long, desperate struggle followed. Addis Ababa was taken on 6 April by Cunningham's troops, and Haile Selassie formally took possession on 5 May—five years to the day after Marshal Badoglio had captured it. The last Italian garrison had surrendered by the end of 1941. But the Emperor still had to fight for his 'independence' against a Britain not too certain of the stability of his régime. The initial outcome of this conflict was a victory for Haile Selassie with the Anglo-Ethiopian agreement on January 1942. Britain took steps to prevent Ethiopia from joining the United Nations, but the indomitable Emperor persisted and, in 1945, Ethiopia became a Charter Member. Britain had doubts whether Haile Selassie should be a signatory of the Peace Treaty, arguing that his country had been conquered before the real war began. But again the Emperor had his way, and duly signed the Peace Treaty along with his co-belligerents.

Haile Selassie, a member of the ancient Coptic Christian Church, made efforts to lead Ethiopia out of a state of tribal feudalism and into the 20th century. He steadfastly maintained the principles of the League of Nations and the United Nations: censure of the aggressor, with respect for the integrity of all. 'Apart from the Kingdom of the Lord, there is not on this Earth any nation which is superior to any other,' he told the League in 1936.

HALDER, Franz, b. 1884. German general, Chief of the General Staff, to which he was appointed in 1938 during the Sudeten crisis. He was leader of a rather half-hearted conspiracy to arrest Hitler, directly the final order was given to invade Czechoslovakia, but this plot collapsed when the Munich Conference gave Hitler a bloodless victory. In 1939 he sought assurance through a Vatican contact that there was still some hope for a German democratic government to secure a negotiated peace, and toyed with the idea of arresting Hitler before the Western offensive (planned for November 1939) could begin. This idea came to nothing because of the 'defection' of Field Marshal von Brauchitsch, the C.-in-C. of the army, who on 5 November 1939 had been exposed to such a storm of reproach and abuse by Hitler for his timidity and delay in launching an offensive that there was no more talk of rebellion. Halder lacked the conviction to take further active steps to overthrow the Führer, and told Ulrich von Hassell that Hitler should be given 'this last chance to deliver the German people from the slavery of English capitalism'.

He had an outstanding brain and tireless energy. Responsible for the Polish campaign, he insisted that 'housecleaning' (liquidation) measures be deferred until the army had withdrawn. He warned Hitler that a Western offensive in 1939 would be disastrous: when it took place in May 1940, Hitler personally directed the campaign and was responsible for the order (opposed by Halder) which halted the German armour outside Dunkirk, facilitating the Allied evacuation. Halder then set about planning the proposed invasion of England—followed by the attack upon Russia in 1941. He prepared for this campaign with enthusiasm, but his military Intelligence was faulty, and the strength of the Russian armies proved to be double

that anticipated. Then in August Hitler made, in Halder's words, 'the greatest strategic blunder of the Eastern campaign', by striking north to Leningrad and south to the Ukraine and the Caucasus, instead of heading for Moscow before the winter. Despite Halder's protests, the drive on Moscow was not resumed until October 1941. This had disastrous results. Halder himself took part, doing his best to encourage his exhausted troops. In December von Brauchitsch resigned and Hitler took over as C.-in-C. Halder agreed to continue as C.G.S., but he was dismissed in 1942, after disagreement over Hitler's determination to advance simultaneously on Stalingrad and the Caucasus. After the attempt on Hitler's life in July 1944 Halder was interned at Dachau as a suspect. Transferred south as the American armies advanced, he was freed by them in May 1945, and was to give important evidence at the Nuremberg trials.

HALIFAX, Earl of, b. 1881. British Foreign Secretary from 1938 to 1940, a strong advocate of the policy of appeasement, and Neville Chamberlain's choice for his successor as Prime Minister in May 1940. In the event, Halifax could not secure the support of Churchill, and stood down. He continued to serve as Foreign Secretary until the end of 1940, and was a member of the War Cabinet until this was disbanded in 1945.

In December 1940 Lord Lothian— British ambassador to the U.S.A.—died, and Halifax reluctantly agreed to take his place. The Embassy in Washington was particularly important to Britain at that time: American goodwill was essential and any overt attempts to manoeuvre the U.S.A. into the war would have outraged isolationist sentiment there and permanently damaged the relationship between the two countries. Halifax was not, on the face of it, the best man for the post, because his background and upbringing gave him an air of aristocratic detachment that might be mistaken for indolence and evasiveness. But in the event he adapted himself very successfully to the American scene and established a position of great authority and popularity. He was on friendly and confidential terms with Roosevelt and Cordell Hull, and the tours he made to every state in the country maintained and strengthened the support of a somewhat fickle public opinion. The fortitude with which he bore the death of one son and the crippling of another particularly impressed the Americans. Halifax was always sensitive to the 'conscience of the nation' and was inclined to take the moral line, as he had at the time of the Hoare-Laval plan in 1935, when he insisted on Hoare's resignation as Foreign Secretary.

HALSEY, William F., b. 1882. American admiral, a brilliant exponent of the use of naval air power. He was already an admiral when the U.S.A. entered the war, and he became commander in the South Pacific area in October 1942. Almost immediately the naval forces under his direction were involved in action against the Japanese, who still at this time had the advantage of the reflected glory of their early overwhelming victories. However, Halsey's men and ships tellingly demonstrated their fighting qualities and were the victors in several engagements, including the three-day Battle of Guadalcanal in November 1942. In June 1944 Halsey was given command of the U.S. 3rd Fleet. The carrier-based planes of this force were devastatingly successful in their attacks on Japanese vessels: in the Battle of Leyte Gulf in October 1944 they sank 4 aircraft carriers and a cruiser. Halsey believed that the old-style engagement between capital ships was obsolete, and that naval vessels had no effective defence against properly employed aircraft except the aircraft in their own force. The great battles of the Pacific demonstrated the reality behind this contention.

HANDLEY, Tommy, b. 1892. British radio comedian, a war-winner in his own line, whose name became a household word. The programme which made him famous was 'ITMA'—'It's That Man Again': 'That Man' was a slanting allusion to Hitler. The programme had skilful and original scriptwriters and was fortunate in its supporting team, but Handley's personality was responsible for the huge success it became. Listeners in every part of the U.K. and in every walk of life

looked forward to each programme. He himself played the irrepressible optimist in a series of unlikely situations: beset by mishaps and misunderstanding but always gaily coming back for more and winning through by sheer ingenuity and cheerful determination. Thus 'Tommy' seemed to personify the spirit of the country in the face of hardship, suffering, and sparse victories. His humour was just right for the moment. The programmes had great verve and energy, and their catch-phrases quickly became conversational currency: two of the most famous of them were 'Can I do you now, sir?' and 'I don't mind if I do!' Equally popular was 'This is Funf speaking': Funf, an enemy agent endowed with menacing diction, telephoned 'Tommy' at frequent intervals to predict disasters that never came about.

HARDING, Sir John, b. 1896. British general, a shrewd and exceptionally clear-thinking strategist, who played an important part in planning the campaigns of North Africa and Italy. As Chief of Staff he was one of General O'Connor's 'race of dwarfs in the desert' who planned the daring stroke that resulted in the victory of Sidi Barrani (December 1940) and enabled the Western Desert forces to push right through to Benghazi. Rommel succeeded in driving the British back to Egypt, but it was largely due to Harding that the decision to hold on to Tobruk was successfully implemented. In Auchinleck's November offensive (1941) Harding was with General Godwin-Austen commanding 13th Corps; and in the spring of 1942 Auchinleck appointed him Director of Military Training. In the Battle of El Alamein (October–November 1942) he was Deputy C.G.S.

In January 1944 Harding became Chief of Staff to General Alexander in Italy. The strategic aim of the Allies in Italy was to force the enemy to keep the maximum possible number of divisions engaged there during the Allied invasion of Normandy. Calculating the implications of this policy in an appreciation which he submitted in February 1944 Harding advised that further operations in Italy should be postponed until April so that rested, regrouped, and substantially increased forces would be available for a new

Italian offensive to coincide with the invasion of Normandy. These proposals, involving postponement of the projected landing in southern France, met considerable opposition but were eventually accepted; and by the time Rome fell on 4 June, 26 German divisions had been contained and routed in Italy. Had Harding's further recommendation been adopted (to push straight on to Bologna and the Ljubljana gap) the war in Italy might have been quickly ended; but General Alexander had to sacrifice 7 divisions to the postponed assault in southern France, and his final offensive was delayed until April 1945. When Alexander became Supreme Allied Commander in the Mediterranean (December 1944) he gave Harding command of 13th Corps.

Harding was a man of great physical and intellectual courage, strong-willed and persistent. Montgomery called him 'that little tiger'.

HARMON, Millard F., b. 1888. American general who commanded land and air forces in the Pacific. An experienced pilot and air commander, Harmon was given command in mid 1942 of U.S. non-naval forces in the South Pacific and it was his troops that took part in the fierce engagements in the Solomon Islands, including the epic struggle that wrested Guadalcanal from the Japanese. From July 1944 he was commander of the USAAF in the whole of the Pacific ocean territories, and he had primary responsibility for mounting the strategic air offensive against Japan, which rapidly gathered momentum and gave the U.S.A. crushing supremacy in the skies. Apart from his direction of actual aerial operations, he had the task of seeing that the logistical support was equal to the immense and expanding demands on his forces. He died in February 1945 when his plane disappeared while on a routine flight.

HARRIMAN, Averell, b. 1891. American businessman, distinguished as an overseas negotiator and administrator on behalf of the American government, and later as an ambassador. In 1940, as a U.S. representative in London, he smoothed the way for the Lend-Lease arrangements of the following year. In 1941 he was appointed

head of the Lend-Lease Administration in London, co-ordinating the flow of supplies from the U.S.A. to Britain and the Soviet Union.

On 29 August 1941 he headed the American mission to Moscow. There his industry at the 3-power conference of September, and assurances of Roosevelt's goodwill to Russia, pleased Stalin and helped to secure Russian co-operation with the U.S.A. and Britain. This he achieved in spite of the necessity, to placate American public qualms about the Russian alliance, of having to remonstrate gently with Stalin on the subject of religious freedom in Russia. In October 1943 he was appointed ambassador to Moscow. Granted an unprecedented monthly interview with Stalin, he worked closely with Russian officials on multifarious details and problems of Russo-American co-operation. In February 1945 he was a member of the 3-power committee that arranged for the establishment of a provisional government in Poland.

Harriman's calm, efficient diplomacy was a feature of all the major Allied conferences of the war, and greatly enhanced American prestige.

HARRIS, Sir Arthur, b. 1892. British air marshal, known as 'Bomber' Harris, who directed Bomber Command of the R.A.F. in its massive and successful onslaught on Germany from the air. He was a man of tremendous resolution, but a figure of some controversy because of the policies his command had to carry out. As Deputy Chief of Air Staff from 1940–1, Harris advocated the concentrated bombing of a limited number of enemy targets. In February 1941 he led a delegation to the U.S.A. to discuss air co-operation. Appointed C.-in-C. of Bomber Command in February 1942, when results had been very disappointing and the force was in need of positive leadership, Harris, a firm believer in the decisiveness of air power, immediately stepped up its offensive. On 30 May 1942 every available aircraft (1,046 planes altogether) was deployed in the first 'thousand-bomber raid', which devastated a third of Cologne, dropping an average 31 tons of bombs to the square mile.

With Churchill's close co-operation,

Harris continued to build up the intensity of the bomber offensive. In August 1942 he established a force of photo-reconnaissance aircraft to improve the accuracy of Bomber Command's raids. In September 1942 the first 8,000-lb. 'blockbuster' bomb was dropped on Karlsruhe. By 1943 the 32 operational squadrons of Bomber Command had risen to 50, with Harris insisting on more. Then he initiated the policy of night bombing, using illumination, as an alternative to vulnerable day raids.

On 18 November 1943 an unprecedented number of sorties were made against Berlin. Even the heavy damage occasioned was not up to Harris's expectations, who now began 'area' bombing of Germany in addition to depth bombing. In April 1944 Bomber Command dropped 4,500 tons in a single raid. Bomber Command was also successful at sea, laying mines that by 1945 had sunk more than 600 enemy ships.

A man not easily swayed from his convictions, and purposeful and resolute, Harris's spirit inspired Bomber Command. He was convinced that many civilian lives in Britain were saved by forcing the enemy onto the defensive by massive bomber raids. His remark during the German Blitz on London in 1940 that the Germans were 'sowing the wind' accurately prophesied the whirlwind that was reaped.

In retrospect, British war leaders, including Churchill, felt some guilt at the consequences of Harris's raids in terms of loss of civilian life in Germany, as measured against their effect in reducing Germany's war potential. Despite the fact that Harris's policies were endorsed by the government, he was almost alone among Britain's war leaders in not receiving a peerage.

HART, Basil Liddell, b. 1895. British military theorist whose ideas on warfare, largely disregarded in Britain in the inter-war years, helped to shape the methods adopted by the Germans with success in the early years of the war. He retired from the army in 1927 to devote himself to modernizing war tactics. His contributions to modern military science included the 'expanding torrent' method of attack, discarding the idea of static warfare of World War I with its heavy loss of life.

He elaborated his theories with reference to the use of air power with armoured forces, and was the principal originator of the theory of highly mechanized warfare.

In the inter-war period in Britain, Liddell Hart found difficulty in persuading people to listen to his ideas, and he was anathema to many professional soldiers who were conventional in their outlook. Liddell Hart's pronounced views were contrary to the current wish of the public who were reluctant to be forced to think seriously about war. Also money was short: this was a time of economic depression.

But, ironically, while the British neglected Liddell Hart's ideas (and the similar views of J. F. C. Fuller) the Germans paid close attention to them, and his views had an influence on German military policy in the war. Guderian in particular, the general who created and led the German Panzer forces, was affected by Liddell Hart's analysis of modern fast-moving attack.

From 1925 to 1935 Liddell Hart was military correspondent for the *Daily Telegraph* and from 1935 to 1937 for *The Times*, also acting as general adviser for defence with this newspaper. In 1937 he became unofficial adviser to the new War Minister, Leslie Hore-Belisha—nor did this endear him to the army—at a time when tardy attempts were being made to reorganize along mechanized lines. By 1938 Liddell Hart felt that this post impeded rather than assisted him in the fight to get Britain ready for the conflict which he believed was imminent; he resigned and pressed publicly for reforms. During the war years Liddell Hart wrote and lectured on modern warfare as a science but held no official appointment.

HART, Thomas C., b. 1877. American admiral who was in overall command of Allied naval forces in the Far East from the entry of the U.S.A. into the war until June 1942. Hart had been a member of the board of the navy from 1936 to 1939, in which year he was appointed C.-in-C. of the U.S. Asiatic Fleet. Japan attacked the U.S. Pacific Fleet at Pearl Harbor in December 1941, bringing the U.S.A. into the war, and shortly afterwards all Allied naval ships in the Far East were put under

Hart's direction. He was retired from service in 1942, but because of his vast experience in naval matters was at once brought back and appointed to a seat on the naval board. He held this appointment until 1945, when he again retired.

HARTLEY, Arthur, b. 1889. British engineer and inventor. From 1942 to 1945 he was Technical Director of the Petroleum Warfare Department and it was in large part due to him that the 'Pipeline Under The Ocean' ('Pluto') was laid across the Channel in order to supply the Allied invasion forces with oil for the assault on N.W. Europe in 1944. In the event, oil tankers were already bringing over sufficient fuel before Pluto began to function. Nevertheless the supply of fuel in bulk to the mainland of Europe by this ingenious means facilitated smooth operations in the subsequent build-up.

Hartley was also the originator of the 'Fido' airfield fog-clearance system. Churchill remarked on the result of Fido in April 1944: 'It is a fine reward to you and your department . . . in the saving of valuable lives and equipment.'

HASSELL, Ulrich von, b. 1881. German diplomat, a leading figure in the opposition to the Nazi régime. On 4 February 1938, the day that Ribbentrop became Foreign Minister, Hitler removed Hassell from his post as ambassador to Italy because of the open contempt shown in his embassy for the Nazi régime. Hassell also opposed the Italo-German *rapprochement*, which he predicted would lead to war. Thus disillusioned and rejected, he became (with Beck and Goerdeler) a leader of the anti-Hitler conspiracy based on Berlin, and recorded its development in his *Diaries 1938–1944*. In no sense a traditional 'revolutionary' figure, he exercised his role of go-between and co-ordinator under cover of a travelling appointment as lecturer and expert on economic affairs. From October 1939 onwards he pressed for a military *coup d'état* in which Hitler would be arrested and brought to trial. Meanwhile he looked for assurances that the British would grant favourable peace terms to an anti-Hitler régime. After sounding out various contacts, he gave up hope of active support

from the generals while their armies were victorious; even on the ominous Russian front, late in 1941, he found them held back by their oaths of allegiance to the Führer. It seemed clear that only with army support could Hitler be overthrown, but the generals' lack of firm resolve persisted throughout 1942.

Meanwhile Hassell's group was planning a restored Hohenzollern monarchy, and Hassell drafted an interim programme. Later a shadow government was formulated; Hassell was nominated as Foreign Minister. After April 1942 he was under suspicion by the Gestapo, and by early 1943 several in his group were being watched. From that time on the focal point of resistance moved to the eastern front where General Henning von Tresckow, anxious to end the war before the front fell to the Russians, had resolved to assassinate Hitler. Then Claus von Stauffenberg took command of the plot, which culminated in the unsuccessful attempt on Hitler's life on 20 July 1944. The Gestapo closed in speedily on the conspirators, and Hassell, calmly awaiting their arrival, was arrested at his office on 28 July. Confined for a time at Ravensbrück concentration camp, he was brought back to Berlin in chains, sentenced to death by the People's Court, and hanged two hours later.

'HAW-HAW, Lord'. *See* JOYCE, William.

HENDERSON, Sir Nevile, b. 1882. British diplomat, ambassador to the Third Reich from 1937 until the outbreak of war. He then turned his energies to assisting British refugees from the European mainland. Early in 1940 he founded the British War Refugees Fund, for which he earned large sums of money by writing and broadcasting appeals. His book, *Failure of a Mission*, was a description of his forlorn efforts to appease the Germans and preserve peace in Europe. It made more than £20,000, all of which he gave to the refugee fund. He also joined the Home Guard in which he became a group commander with the rank of colonel.

But his health was steadily declining. He had been seriously ill in 1938 and, although he seemed to recover, the events of 1939 had put an extra strain on him. His failure to avert the war, and to fulfil what he mystically believed to be his mission in life, caused him sadness and disillusion. This setback haunted him all the more because he was convinced that the people he had known in Germany were fundamentally honest and reasonable. He blamed the eventual outcome on 'the fanatical megalomania and blind self-confidence of a single individual', and on a 'small clique of his self-interested followers'. His decline was hastened by disappointment and he died at the end of December 1942.

Tall, lean, and fastidiously dressed, Henderson was said to have irritated Hitler by a somewhat talkative personality. His dispatches indicated his belief that by greater compliance with Hitler's wishes war might have been avoided; but according to Sir Robert Vansittart, the Permanent Under Secretary at the Foreign Office, the 'accidentalism' of events stressed by Henderson in his Final Report could not be further from the truth. From the advent of the Nazi régime there never was the least chance that any course would be pursued by the Nazis other than that which was in fact followed with fanatical determination.

'HENRI, Colonel'. *See* BLEICHER, Hugo.

HENSON, Leslie, b. 1891. British entertainer, whose 'cheerful croak' was heard in shows for the forces from Scapa Flow to Singapore. Probably the most popular musical comedy actor of the 1930s, he was planning with Basil Dean and others as early as 1938 the concert parties which were to develop into the war-time E.N.S.A. He remarked to Dean at that time: 'When will the first concert party be formed, as I've thought out a good gag about Hitler?'

He toured with his *Gaieties* to entertain members of the B.E.F. in France over Christmas 1939, and took part in the first E.N.S.A. broadcast in March 1940 with *Piccadilly Revels* before leaving with this show for France.

In 1943 Henson was one of a group of stars assembled to play a show called *Spring Party* in Gibraltar and North Africa; there they gave E.N.S.A.'s one

and only Royal Command Performance when King George VI visited his troops at Tunis in June. Thanks to the co-operation of Air Chief Marshal Tedder they proceeded along the North African coast to Cairo, Ismailia, and Suez and back again to Gibraltar. In 1944 Henson played to troops in Italy, Sicily, Malta, North Africa, Holland, Belgium, and France. Later he took a party to India, Burma, and, eventually, Singapore.

In Tripoli Henson opened with the time-honoured remark of the clown: 'Well, here we are!' To which he received the reply: 'Bit late, aren't yer?' When he arrived at Bari his Yorkshire musical director was rehearsing Italian musicians who knew no English. The conductor shouted louder and louder that he wanted so many bars played with more force and more abruptly. Henson decided to intervene: 'Why don't you say "staccato"?' to which the conductor replied, 'Eeh, but would they *understand*?'

HERBERT, Alan Patrick, b. 1890. Novelist, poet, humorist, barrister, and parliamentarian, famed as a witty and astringent commentator on the war-time scene in Britain. Since 1935 he had been Independent M.P. for Oxford University.

In 1940, as a petty officer, he commanded a Thames patrol boat, but still found time to ridicule either in Parliament or in the pages of *Punch* anything in the war-time emergency measures he thought ridiculous, untimely, or trivial. His eloquent denunciation of the proposed taxation of books, which were to be categorized as 'unnecessary', prevented this measure from ever becoming law. His protest against the 'in triplicate, quadruplicate, and even sextuplicate' mentality of the services was forcibly argued but less successful.

'A.P.H.', as he became known, wrote in an inimitable style, enjoyed by many in the war years. In particular his articles in *Punch* raised many a smile when the general situation provided little else to laugh at.

HERRIOT, Édouard, b. 1872. French statesman and scholar, an open opponent of the Vichy régime of Marshal Pétain. He was President of the Chamber of Deputies at the time of France's capitulation. On 13 June 1940 he assured Churchill of his country's determination to fight on, and on 15 June he endorsed Paul Reynaud's proposal to transfer the French government to North Africa. After France fell he remained in the country in order that he could help with the Resistance, and was one of the 17 members who abstained from the National Assembly's vote to give full powers to Marshal Pétain, having already protested that Pierre Laval's proposed régime would mean that the government would no longer be responsible to parliament. Consequently he was never associated with the collaborators.

In August 1942 Laval abolished the office of President of the Chamber of Deputies, and had Herriot placed under house arrest. Herriot rejected a request to give a written undertaking not to leave France. Later he was deported to Germany. His revenge came in July 1943, when he refused Laval's plan to take over leadership to bolster the tottering Vichy régime.

Freed by Russian troops in April 1945, Herriot was able to return to France free from the taint of collaboration. As leader of the Radical Socialist party, he was twice premier of France in pre-war years. His statesmanship, integrity, and patriotism made him one of France's most respected public figures.

HESS, Myra, b. 1890. A leading British pianist whose lunch-hour recitals at the National Gallery, London, became a wartime institution. She made her professional debut at the age of 17, and until 1939 she gave many concerts in Britain and abroad, particularly in the U.S.A. Immediately the war broke out, however, she cancelled all foreign engagements. There was little she could do immediately in the U.K. as most concert halls and galleries were closed down or requisitioned. However, she soon evolved the idea of lunchtime concerts at the National Gallery for Londoners harassed by bombing and deprived of most other forms of public entertainment. These concerts ran continuously for 6½ years, mainly because of her own energy and determination. In recognition of her work she was created D.B.E. in 1941.

HESS, Rudolf, b. 1896. Nazi leader, Hitler's deputy in party affairs, and (after Goering) next in line of succession to the Führer. A rather dull, unambitious man, Hess is interesting chiefly because of a single, sensational, and absurd act during the war.

On 10 May 1941 Hess left Germany secretly in a Messerschmitt fighter (which he piloted himself) and parachuted into Scotland. His alleged intention was to seek out the Duke of Hamilton, whom he had met briefly at the Berlin Olympic Games of 1936, and through him to arrange peace negotiations with the British government. His views were uncomplicated: Britain had no hope of winning the war; she faced only disaster and defeat; Hitler had no wish to destroy a fellow-Nordic nation, and was prepared to leave Britain alone as long as he was allowed a free hand in the East. This, Hess believed, was obviously to Britain's advantage, and he was prepared to open negotiations as soon as Churchill's government had been replaced by a more conciliatory body. The negotiations never had any hope of taking place, and Hess, to his astonishment, was treated simply as a P.O.W. After the war he was put on trial at Nuremberg with the other Nazi leaders and was sentenced to life imprisonment.

Hess was entirely sincere in his mission. He not only believed his own arguments, but was also endeavouring to confirm his position as Hitler's most trusted colleague and confidant. He was convinced that he was ordained to restore peace—a belief that had been encouraged by his astrologer. The bizarre incident of his peace mission stemmed from his ignorance of the actual situation in Britain and, it was said, from his mental instability. The question of Hess's sanity or otherwise has never been satisfactorily resolved.

Hess was one of Hitler's earliest followers, and took part in the attempted 'beer-hall putsch' in 1923. Hitler dedicated *Mein Kampf* to him.

HEWITT, Kent, b. 1887. American admiral, one of the Allies' chief authorities on the use of amphibious forces. He commanded the Western Task Force in the all-American landings round Casablanca in 1942. Having brought his various groups

Heydrich

across the Atlantic to a fixed time-table, he took the difficult decision to assault despite unfavourable weather forecasts received from London and Washington. His own meteorological staff predicted local moderating winds, and he backed their judgment. Had he acted with less boldness and adopted the alternative plan of landing near Spanish Morocco, the consequent delay would have made it impossible to win Algeria and Morocco simultaneously. In February 1943 Hewitt took command of the U.S. 8th Fleet in N.W. African waters. Then he commanded the Western Task Force in the American half of the invasion of Sicily in July, and in the Salerno landings in September. The latter operation, which in Hewitt's own words 'marked the beginning of the end of German military might', succeeded in the face of considerable opposition; but he was critical of the decision to forgo preliminary air and naval bombardments for the sake of achieving surprise. In August 1944, on account of his experience of similar operations, he was chosen to command the maritime side of the landings on the French Riviera, and this time the assault was preceded by heavy bombardments which enabled the troops to land with very few casualties. By a great feat of naval organization he landed on the beaches 86,575 men, 12,520 vehicles, and 46,140 tons of stores in a space of 64 hours.

HEYDRICH, Reinhard, b. 1904. Nazi administrator and policeman, one of the ablest and most ruthless of Germany's war-time leaders. He was, under Himmler, chief of the Reich Security Head Office, which comprised the Gestapo (secret police), the Kripo (criminal investigation department), and the S.D., the security service of the S.S.

Superficially a stronger man than his superior, Himmler, he was dangerously ambitious and pitiless in the use of power. Indeed had he lived longer he might well have attempted to replace Hitler. An intelligent man, contemptuous of the stupidity of most of his colleagues and superiors, he could nevertheless be clumsy in the use of force and was always in danger of overreaching himself. Although

he personally did not enjoy torturing and killing, he revelled in the Gestapo's reputation for brutality and inhumanity. Terror was an important weapon in his armoury, and he developed the S.S. weekly newspaper, *Das Schwarze Korps*, into a formidable instrument of blackmail and persecution.

From its earliest days it was used to smear and abuse the Churches, for which Heydrich had a pathological hatred. He even devised a plan for infiltrating the Churches with youths loyal to the S.S. and thus staging a revolt from within. Heydrich's most intensive schemes, however, were reserved for the Jews. At first he was content to follow the policy of blackmail and forced emigration whereby the Gestapo appropriated vast sums of Jewish money. His *Einsatzgruppen* (Action Groups) were originally intended not for the mass murder of Jews but for the spreading of terror and the liquidation of troublesome individuals. After the invasion of Russia, however, the *Einsatzgruppen* killed about three-quarters of a million Russian and Polish Jews by shooting.

On 31 July 1941 Goering instructed Heydrich to submit a comprehensive draft for the implementation of the 'final solution of the Jewish question'; the result was the Wannsee Protocol of January 1942. The action groups carried out mass shootings, and extermination camps began to replace deportation centres. Heydrich bears the responsibility for setting up and running the machinery for genocide in which Eichmann played an executive part. By way of reward for his efforts he was appointed Protector of Bohemia and Moravia to succeed von Neurath. On 4 June 1942 he died of wounds inflicted when his car was attacked by Czech Resistance fighters trained in Britain. The S.S. retaliated by murdering the inhabitants of the nearby village of Lidice and destroying the village.

Originally a naval officer, he was cashiered in 1931 by Admiral Raeder and expelled from the officer corps for 'conduct unbecoming to an officer and a gentleman': this was said to be in connection with a scandal involving the daughter of a dockyard superintendent. Filled with hatred for the corps, he joined the S.S., where he attracted the attention of

Himmler, who gave him the task of building up the S.D. By the end of the 1930s Heydrich was entrenched as Himmler's second-in-command and had transformed the S.S. from a small group of 'fair-haired morons' into the very nerve centre of the Nazi state. By 1939 Heydrich was important enough to be entrusted with the responsibility for faking the border incident at Gleiwitz, which was Hitler's excuse for attacking Poland.

HILLARY, Richard, b. 1918. British fighter pilot in the Battle of Britain who gained fame for his book *The Last Enemy*, published in 1942, in which he tried to describe some of the aspirations and feelings of the young men of his generation who had been caught up in the war.

When war broke out Hillary was an undergraduate at Trinity College, Oxford, and was a member of the University Air Squadron. He was commissioned in the R.A.F. Volunteer Reserve, and found himself one of 'the Few' when the Battle of Britain began in July 1940. At this time the R.A.F. was even more critically short of pilots than of planes. As the air offensive continued, it became increasingly difficult to replace the pilots that were lost: a fighter pilot's training took 11 months. With so much dependent on them, airmen needed not only courage but a kind of gay selflessness that did not count the cost. But Hillary, ironically, professed to believe only in 'the realization of one's self'—like an artist, using the world instead of being used by it. Later, when so many of the friends with whom he had argued about a philosophy of living had been killed, Hillary came to believe that man must give as well as take—that only the ideals he had scoffed at gave meaning to life.

Hillary was posted as a pilot to the hastily formed 306 Squadron. The squadron went into action for the first time on 28 August. By 6 September it had lost 16 aircraft and 12 pilots, Hillary amongst them. His plane was shot down in flames off the Kent coast and he was picked up by a lifeboat, his face and hands terribly burnt. He then spent many painful months in hospital with others who were maimed in the same way. Hillary's description of these months

made people aware of the price that was being paid in individual suffering, and, incidentally, how greatly medical techniques in the treatment of burns and in plastic surgery had been advanced by the necessities of war.

It was while convalescing that Hillary wrote *The Last Enemy*. The book was in part a personal tribute to his colleagues: an account of the beliefs and emotions of those who fought and an attempt, in the light of bitter experience, to conclude the enjoyable arguments of youth. Those who read it at the time were greatly moved by it. It did not tell of glory but spoke with compassion of the inner enemy who opposed each fighter: 'The last enemy that shall be destroyed is death' (1 Corinthians xv, 26).

After making a lengthy recovery Hillary, though disfigured and still partly maimed, eventually returned to active service. On 7 January 1943 he was killed when his night fighter plane crashed near Berwick while on a training flight.

HIMMLER, Heinrich, b. 1900. German National Socialist leader, the chief policeman of the Third Reich and, in effect, the most powerful man in the country after Hitler. He became Reichsführer S.S. in 1929, and was a close confidant of the Führer; with Martin Bormann and other trusted henchmen he formed the clique in Hitler's 'court' that came to be known as the Fireside Circle or the Midnight Club. Most of the vital and fundamental decisions of the Third Reich were taken by this small group of party intimates, Himmler and Bormann endeavouring to make sure that the Führer was isolated from all but the most official military contacts. Quite apart from his immense personal influence with Hitler, he possessed great official authority: as head of the Waffen S.S. he directed a powerful private army; through the Reich Security Head Office, with Heydrich and then Kaltenbrunner as his deputy, he controlled the criminal investigation department under Nebe, the Foreign Political Intelligence Service under Schellenberg, and the Gestapo (secret police) under Müller. The uniformed police also came under his command when he succeeded Frick as Minister of the Interior in 1943. Through the S.S. Himmler also controlled the concentration camps.

By the Führer's decree of October 1939 he had been charged with carrying out a principal part of the Nazi racial policy—the repatriation of Germans abroad and the elimination of 'the harmful influence of alien parts of the population, which represent a danger to the Reich and German folk community'. A fanatical disciple of the race theory, he possessed the inhuman nerve and unswerving dedication necessary to translate its dictates into stark reality. He ordered and supervised the extermination of millions of Jews and Slavs and had prisoners subjected to hideous medical experiments, listening with interest to reports about them as if they concerned experiments on bacterial cultures. His Central Office for Questions of Race and Settlement planned mass abortions, the sterilization of entire ethnic groups, and wholesale massacres of innocent civilians with the bureaucratic attention to detail of a town council planning a new road.

In a speech to S.S. leaders in October 1943 Himmler expounded his personal views on this subject: 'What happens to a Russian, to a Czech, does not interest me in the least. What the countries can offer in the way of good blood of our type we will take, if necessary by abducting their children and raising them here with us. Whether nations live in prosperity or starve to death interests me only in so far as we need them as slaves for our *Kultur* . . .' In the task of implementing the 'final solution' (the elimination of the Jews) Himmler demanded efficiency and thoroughness. Yet the man who could contemplate genocide with such dispassion was so appalled when he actually witnessed the spectacle of Jews being shot that he cried out and almost fainted. He recommended, as 'a more humane means', the use of poison gas, to be administered in specially constructed chambers disguised as shower rooms. In Hitler's eyes, Himmler's success in organizing the massacre of defenceless people contrasted favourably with the failures of the generals to produce military victories.

By 1943 Himmler was the second most powerful man in Germany and clearly saw

himself as the potential successor to the Führer, though, officially, Goering was the designated heir. Not content to bide his time, Himmler plotted the political downfall of his long-standing enemies, the generals, in order to add control of the army to his already substantial empire. The attempted army plot of 20 July 1944 to kill Hitler played right into his hands, and Hitler forced the army to accept Himmler as C.-in-C. of the Home Army. Without a German victory, however, his power was worthless to him. Dismissed by Hitler in Berlin and rejected later by Doenitz in Flensburg, his empire evaporated. He was captured by the British on 23 May 1945, and he took poison at Lüneburg before he could be brought to trial.

Though to people outside Germany Himmler's name had become irretrievably associated with murderous tyranny, he himself believed (or was persuaded by his subordinates) that the Western Allies would consider him an acceptable leader of a reconstituted Germany. In April 1945 he attempted to make peace, through the agency of Count Bernadotte. Himmler told the head of the Swedish Red Cross that Hitler was likely to die at any moment and that he, Himmler, would surrender the German armies on the Western front and those in Norway and Denmark to General Eisenhower, but that he would go on fighting on the Eastern front. Bernadotte replied that he must surrender to all three powers at once, as he knew that the U.S.A. and U.K. would not agree to such an arrangement. Stalin was assured by his allies that they would accept nothing but unconditional surrender to all three powers.

Himmler was the son of a Catholic Bavarian schoolmaster. Before joining the Nazi movement he had graduated from an agricultural school and operated a small chicken farm. With Goering he drew up the plans for the Blood Purge of 30 June 1934 in which Röhm and his associates in the rowdy S.A. ('Storm Troopers') were slaughtered. He was a very able administrator and organizer, and although he had many rivals he succeeded in maintaining his position with extraordinary dexterity.

Himmler was a small man, of hesitant, rather diffident, and pedantic demeanour.

To some his glance, through his thin-rimmed spectacles, seemed 'benevolent'; to others 'sharp'. Some of his associates complained of his lack of decisiveness; others saw in his refusal to be hurried another facet of his undoubted efficiency. Unlike some others of the Nazi hierarchy, he never used his vast powers for personal gain; and the man who was responsible for the deaths of countless innocent human beings and the torture and degradation of countless others was disgusted at what he regarded as Goering's cruelty to animals as chief huntsman of the Reich.

HIROHITO, b. 1901. Emperor of Japan from 1926, with the title 'Imperial Son of Heaven of Great Japan'. A moderate by inclination and temperament, he seemingly exerted little influence on the policies of his country.

Declaring war, concluding peace, making treaties, and the supreme command of the armed forces all lay within the royal prerogative. However, these powers were supposed to be exercised according to his ministers' advice. After France and Holland fell in June 1940 extremist elements (led by the army) urged an alliance with the Axis powers and the occupation of Indo-China. Warned by the Prime Minister, Prince Konoye, that the future of the dynasty was in jeopardy, Hirohito reluctantly agreed although he 'did not like playing the thief at a fire'. The Tripartite Pact was signed on 27 September, and northern Indo-China was occupied only two months later. Meanwhile militarist ambitions were growing, with the 'Great East Asia Co-prosperity Sphere' in view. At an imperial conference in July 1941 Hirohito sanctioned the resolution of his ministers to move southwards.

By agreement with the Vichy government in France, air bases in southern Indo-China were occupied. The U.S.A., the Netherlands, and the British Commonwealth responded with sanctions. Faced with the threat of economic strangulation, Konoye sought agreement with the U.S.A. But the Japanese army and navy were pressing for war. By September Konoye realized that the forces were bent on a southern war, and asked Hirohito to intervene. The Emperor summoned the Chiefs of Staff and urged that precedence be

given to diplomacy. But his lack of firmness and of political acumen made his attempts at restraint ineffective. Konoye resigned, General Tojo succeeded him, and plans for the attack on the American naval base at Pearl Harbor went ahead: the final decision for war was taken at an imperial conference on 1 December 1941.

While Japanese fortunes prospered, Hirohito was a figure in the background. But after the Japanese naval defeat at the Battle of Midway in June 1942, a turning point in the war, Tojo increasingly sought to involve him: reference was made to him in all public pronouncements, reminding the people of his divine destiny, which would ensure ultimate victory in the sacred war. In the imperial palace, Hirohito tried to introduce a régime of austerity—he even renounced his customary English breakfast. Assured through neutral sources that the imperial palace would not be bombed, he replied that he preferred to share the bombs with his people. In August 1945, when Japan was approaching defeat, Hirohito exerted some influence against the army and in support of those who advocated peace. Asked for guidance on what the Supreme Council's reply to the Allies' Potsdam Proclamation should be, he answered with a command: although the proclamation gave no guarantee of maintaining the imperial line, it must be accepted. On 15 August 1945, the day after the surrender, he announced it by radio; it was the first time in the history of his dynasty that an Emperor of Japan had spoken directly to his people.

Although named a war criminal by China, Australia, and New Zealand, he was nevertheless granted immunity from trial, and the official view of the Allied governments was that responsibility for the war did not lie with him. A self-effacing, rather nervous man, he was a marine biologist of some repute and wrote a book on shellfish, sea-diving for his own specimens. His advisers urged that such activities were out of place in war time, and the laboratories in the grounds of the imperial palace were temporarily closed. Until the end of the war, although himself sceptical of his legendary descent from the Sun Goddess, he nevertheless played his part as the Divine Ruler whose word was sacrosanct.

HITLER, Adolf, b. 1889. The founder and guiding spirit of Nazi Germany from the time of his grasping dictatorial power in 1933 to his suicide in 1945; a unique figure in his generation comparable to Attila the Hun or Napoleon in theirs.

At the outbreak of war Hitler wielded a degree of power that seems incredible in a modern industrial state. Since his appointment as Chancellor in 1933 he had become head of state and supreme commander of the armed forces; later he blatantly violated the traditional independence of the army General Staff by assuming the role of C.-in-C. of the army in the field. He made himself totally responsible for the conduct of the war: a powerful and organized nation was at the mercy of one man's will. The German successes of the early part of the war are a mark of Hitler's ability as a military tactician. In this respect his control was equalled by his virtuosity as a politician—he was a master of psychological warfare, fully aware of the value of bold and unexpected action. The German campaigns in Poland, France, and Norway were exemplary in conception and execution.

But one of the penalties of those early and heady successes was a growing enmity between Hitler and the General Staff. From the fall of France onwards, Hitler insisted on directing every campaign at almost every stage. Right or wrong, he remained dogmatic and minatory, incapable of listening to advice. In his view the General Staff was weak, indecisive, and incompetent. As his contempt for its members grew, so did his belief in his own infallibility. Hitler was convinced that he was a man of destiny—one of those whom Hegel called 'World Historical Individuals'.

In order to fulfil this destiny, to lay the foundations for the great German Reich that would last for a thousand years, Hitler finally put into action the plan that would make his dream of a European empire come true. In June 1941 he invaded Russia.

It was then that Hitler's military prowess was tested and found wanting. He lacked any grasp of overall strategy; he was stubborn and self-opinionated; he had no regard for facts, especially unpalatable ones; and he tended to

become carried away by unimportant questions of organization. In Russia he squandered his early advantages through sheer procrastination, and by constantly changing his mind about his objectives. He condemned his troops to a pitiless winter, deep in the Russian heartland, for which they were not equipped. Nor did he remedy the situation when the campaign was resumed in 1942; he made the same mistakes again.

What was more, some of Hitler's earlier errors were now beginning to have their effect. For example, he had neglected the vital Mediterranean theatre, and had bungled the situation in the Middle East, where the British still had a foothold. He had been unsuccessful in his attempts to make peace with Britain; he had failed to lure Franco into the war; and the clumsy mistakes of Mussolini's Italian troops had had costly consequences in Greece and North Africa.

Nevertheless Hitler had plenty to boast about. The German empire now extended from the Caucasus to the Atlantic, and from the Baltic to the Black Sea. It was an achievement that ranked with the conquests of Napoleon and Frederick the Great (as Hitler was fond of reminding his audience). But it marked the climax of German expansion. From 1943 onwards his empire fell into an accelerating decline.

During 1943 Hitler managed to maintain control, but he was almost entirely on the defensive. The Russians began to push the Germans back. In Italy, Mussolini had been overthrown and his successors had signed an armistice with the Allies. The Axis had lost North Africa and the battle of the Atlantic. Allied bombing was beginning to have a telling effect on industrial production. Germany just did not have resources equal to the struggle: the world alliance which Hitler had raised against himself, and which he had so much despised, was becoming too strong for him. By the beginning of 1944 it was clear that Germany could not win the war. If anything was to be retrieved from total destruction, Hitler would have to surrender.

It was at this stage that Hitler finally fell to his own overriding egotism. He refused to countenance defeat. He had been called to found a new 'European

Order'. This was his inexorable destiny. He cut himself off from the outside world, first of all at his dismal H.Q. at the 'Wolfsschanze' ('Wolf's Lair') in the east Prussian forests and then, after escaping assassination in July 1944, in the Chancellery and Führerbunker in Berlin. He avoided all contact with reality, refusing to believe anything that did not fit in with his selected picture of events. He grasped eagerly at last straws (so-called 'secret weapons') that could give him any hope—the U-Boats, the V-1, the V-2 rocket, even astrology. He was permanently suspicious of his associates. He dismissed his doctors, thinking they were trying to poison him, and retained only the services of an incompetent quack, Doctor Morell, who actually was poisoning him with some of his patent medicines. He constantly accused the army of treachery and cowardice. He even accused the German people of betraying him; they were not worthy to have him as their Führer.

During the closing stages of the war the real character of Hitler and of Nazi Germany became inescapably apparent. There was no well-defined Nazi creed at all: the bestial nonsense that masqueraded as the Nazi philosophy derived mainly from the prejudices Hitler had picked up in the streets of Vienna and Munich during his early years. The whole régime was nurtured on the grotesque ideas of a coarse and uneducated intellect. The basic article of Hitler's creed was a fixed belief in the ascendancy of the Aryan races and in the glorification of strength and the use of force.

His anti-Semitism was responsible for what must surely be one of the most horrifying episodes of history—the systematic attempt to wipe out an entire race, the 'final solution of the Jewish question'. But what stood out starkly during those last few months in the Führerbunker was the essential nihilism, the central core of sheer destructiveness, that inspired the whole Nazi movement. The sole alternatives were implicit: world domination or ruin. When Hitler realized that the former had eluded him, the frenzy to destroy possessed him. Almost his last words were a demand for more executions. His 'scorched earth' policy was a final

attempt to carry the entire nation with him to destruction.

On 29 April Hitler married his mistress, Eva Braun—a formal recognition of her devotion to the Führer. On 30 April they committed suicide together, and the bodies were burned in the Chancellery garden with Russian shells falling around them. It was the final symbolic act of destruction, and a logical finale.

HO CHI MINH, b. 1890. An Annamese by birth, and a leading figure in international Communism, Ho Chi Minh led guerrilla forces which fought the Japanese in Indo-China. With other leading communists he formed the Viet Minh league, ostensibly a Nationalist coalition, but actually a communist-dominated body. During the war in the Far East they induced the Allies to supply the guerrilla forces in French Indo-China with arms.

When Japan surrendered in 1945 the Free French were in no position immediately to assert their claims, and the Vichy French (who had been allowed by the Japanese to maintain their administration until 1945) had few friends in any camp. No other Vietnamese group other than the Viet Minh was adequately armed or organized, and in September 1945 Ho proclaimed the republic of Viet Nam.

HODGES, Courtney, b. 1887. American general and expert in infantry warfare. From 1941 to 1942 he was Chief of Intelligence and briefly in charge of the Replacement and School Command. In 1942 he was given command of 10th Army Corps. In 1943 he was promoted lieutenant-general with command of the 3rd Army at San Antonio. Later he joined the 1st Army in England, commanded by General Bradley and preparing for D-Day. As Bradley's deputy and understudy, he supervised the preparations for the invasion of N.W. Europe, and when on 1 August 1944 the American forces in Normandy were welded into the 12th Army Group under Bradley, Hodges took over command of the 1st Army. Despite supply shortages he led his troops through to Alençon and north-east to the Seine, Mons, and Liège. By October his army had freed the whole of Luxembourg and southern Belgium, pierced the Siegfried

Line, and captured Aachen—the first great city to fall. In December the full weight of the German counter-offensive in the Ardennes fell upon his army. When, after heavy fighting, the attack was repulsed, Hodges advanced to seize the Roer dams, fight his way to the Rhine, and capture intact the bridge across the Rhine at Remagen on 7 March 1945.

Having contributed to Germany's death-blow—the encirclement of the Ruhr—he pushed on to Leipzig and the Elbe and joined up with the Russian armies. After his great achievements in Europe, he went immediately to the Pacific theatre and took part in the battle for Okinawa. Hodges's reserved nature kept him from the limelight, but he was one of the great commanders in the field. His favourite recreation was rifle-shooting, for which he won many distinctions.

HOEPNER, Erich, b. 1886. German general, a specialist in armoured warfare, executed for his part in the July 1944 plot on Hitler's life. He took part in the invasions of Poland, Belgium, and Russia. His 4th Armoured Group came in sight of Moscow early in December 1941, but within a few days General Zhukov launched his fierce counter-offensive, and the Germans were compelled to retreat. Furious, Hitler dismissed Hoepner for ordering retreat without permission from above. Field Marshal von Kluge tried to save him by maintaining that the Führer's action was against military law, and threatening his own resignation, but Hitler was adamant: Hoepner, stripped of his rank and forbidden to wear uniform, was publicly disgraced.

Hoepner had been involved in conspiratorial activities against Hitler from pre-war days. He had been a key figure in the September 1938 plot to arrest Hitler, as soon as the final order was given to invade Czechoslovakia. The plot collapsed when the Munich agreement gave Hitler a bloodless victory, but Hoepner kept in touch with the other anti-Nazi leaders, Beck and Witzleben. He was nominated as a possible Foreign Minister in Goerdeler's provisional anti-Nazi government. He played an unfortunate part in the disastrous attempt to overthrow Hitler in July 1944.

The plan (under the code name 'Valkyrie') was that the Home Army should take over Berlin and other principal cities directly Hitler was assassinated. Hoepner's part was to replace General Fromm as C.-in-C. of the Home Army, if Fromm were to waver. Informed that Stauffenberg's bomb had gone off, but that Hitler was still alive, Hoepner and Olbricht did nothing to implement the 'Valkyrie' orders until personally instructed by Stauffenberg three hours later—by which time they should have had Berlin in their hands. Fromm refused to join in the attempted coup, and Olbricht arrested him. Later, Fromm was freed, and had Beck, Olbricht, and the other conspirators arrested. Hoepner was offered the choice of suicide or trial before the People's Court. He chose trial but, as a result of his ill-treatment by the Gestapo, made a poor impression in court. He was hanged at Plötzensee prison on 8 August 1944.

HOESS, Rudolf, b. 1900. German concentration camp commandant who brought to his horrifying business of mass degradation and murder the qualities of a conscientious civil servant. When war broke out Hoess was an adjutant at Sachsenhausen camp. In the spring of 1940 he was transferred to the newly built camp at Auschwitz (Oswiecim) in southern Poland, which was to be opened in June for Polish political prisoners. Later it was to become the most notorious of the extermination camps, and it was largely due to Hoess's devotion to duty that it gained such a reputation.

He had been brought up to believe that obedience and deference to his elders were the cardinal virtues, and throughout his life he willingly accepted subjugation to authority. His concern at Auschwitz was to run the camp along lines of maximum efficiency with regard to the purpose for which it was created. When ordered to set up extermination facilities he installed four huge gas-chambers and adjoining crematoria. He decided to use *Zyklon B* crystals in the chambers rather than the carbon monoxide gas used at other camps because this was 'an advance'. Later, before the International Military Tribunal at Nuremberg, he openly boasted of his superior methods and described in the most matter-of-fact way his detailed arrangements for the selection and disposal of victims; he even exaggerated the number of people killed, though there is now little doubt that at one time as many as 6,000 a day were gassed at Auschwitz.

After three and a half years at Auschwitz Hoess was withdrawn to become a chief inspector of concentration camps. He was dismayed to find that most of the camps were run with less conscientiousness and skill than his camp at Auschwitz, and that they were incapable of conversion to the same standard. For Hoess the matter of extermination was one of technical efficiency. When asked at Nuremberg whether he was convinced of his guilt he replied that he had 'really never expended much thought upon it'. An American psychologist at Nuremberg formed the opinion that Hoess would never have realized the horror of his crimes if their frightfulness had not been pointed out to him. Perhaps even then he did not fully understand. In April 1947 he was sentenced to death by the Polish People's Court and was hanged a fortnight later— at Auschwitz.

HOME, William Douglas-, b. 1912. British army officer, imprisoned for refusing to obey an order that he considered morally indefensible. Douglas-Home had been called up for military service and had joined the army, although he had foreseen the possibility of situations arising in which he would be given orders that he would not be willing to execute. He was granted a commission in the Royal Aimoured Corps. By standing as a candidate in parliamentary elections he reduced his contribution to soldiering, and at the same time gave himself a platform for his views. He stood for Cathcart, Glasgow, in April 1942, for Windsor in June 1942, and for Clay Cross in Derbyshire in April 1944. The political view he advanced was opposed to Churchill's autocratic conduct of the war—especially the doctrine of 'unconditional surrender'. Inevitably, Douglas-Home's standpoint brought him into conflict with the authorities, the crisis coming during the Allied attack on Le Havre in the summer of 1944, when the Allies refused a German

request to evacuate civilians from the town. Considering the Allies' action to be morally wrong, he refused to act on the order to take part in the battle. He wrote to the press about his decision, and news of his refusal was broadcast by the B.B.C. 12,000 civilians did, in fact, die in the battle, and in a similar situation later the civilians of Calais were evacuated. Douglas-Home was court-martialled and was sentenced to one year's hard labour, which he served in Wormwood Scrubs and Wakefield Prison.

Douglas-Home, a son of the Earl of Home, had joined the London Fire Brigade at the beginning of the war, and later worked as a journalist for the *Review of World Affairs.*

HOMMA, Masaharu, b. 1888. Japanese general who led the invasion of the Philippines in 1941, making a surprise attack on Luzon on 10 December, a few days after the Japanese air attack on Pearl Harbor. He was a forceful commander known for his ruthlessness.

Preliminary air bombardment had destroyed half the American aircraft on the ground, and the naval base in Manila Bay was wrecked shortly afterwards. Japanese troops landed in the north and the south of Luzon, the aim being to attract the defenders to these areas while the main Japanese forces landed in the centre of the island. This plan did not succeed. General MacArthur's forces withdrew to the Bataan peninsula and the island fortress of Corregidor, making a dogged stand there.

Homma was responsible for the notorious 'death march' which followed the surrender of Bataan. The American and Filipino survivors of the assault were taken prisoner and, although their commander had conserved enough petrol and vehicles to transport a large number of men out of Bataan, they were forced to march 75 miles in intense heat to San Fernando, Pampanga. Many were sick and wounded; those who fell by the roadside were shot or bayoneted. For the first 5 days they had no food; their only water was from ditches beside the road. On the 6th day, those who still had any valuables were given a cup of rice in exchange for

them. On the 9th day they were transferred to overcrowded railway coaches,
where many died of suffocation. Thousands
of prisoners perished on this terrible
journey. Later, Homma directed mopping-
up operations against stray American and
Filipino forces in Mindanao and the
Visayans.

In September 1945 Homma surrendered
to the Americans in Tokyo. He was taken
to Manila, brought to trial, and convicted
of ordering the march and condoning
other atrocities. He was sentenced to death
and shot in April 1946.

HOPKINS, Harry, b. 1890. American
administrator, Roosevelt's closest confidant, and supervisor of the Lend-Lease
programme. This exceptional man, of
humble background, was Secretary of
Commerce in 1939. During the war years,
contending with failing health, he undertook heavy responsibilities and long
journeys as the President's personal envoy.
Churchill first met him in January 1941
and recorded Hopkins's statement of his
mission to London: 'The President is
determined we shall win the war together.
Make no mistake about it. He has sent me
here to tell you that at all costs and by all
means he will carry you through, no
matter what happens to him.' Thenceforth
Churchill found Hopkins 'the most faithful and perfect channel of communication'
between himself and the President. In
March 1941 Roosevelt appointed Hopkins
supervisor of the Lend-Lease programme.
He came again to England in July, continuing to Moscow to ascertain from
Stalin the needs of Russia following the
German invasion. In the following month
he was present with Roosevelt at the
historic signing of the Atlantic Charter.
When America entered the war he became
an adviser on strategy and supplies, and
Chairman of the Munitions Assignment
Board. In 1942 he came twice to England
with General Marshall to discuss future
strategy, and addressed a private meeting of
M.P.s. He accompanied Roosevelt to the
Teheran Conference in 1943 and to Yalta
in February 1945. Shortly afterwards
Roosevelt died, but in May President
Truman sent Hopkins as his special envoy
to Moscow, to seek agreement on the Polish
question. Hopkins did succeed in breaking

this deadlock, but the journey was too much
for him. He could not attend the Potsdam
Conference in July, and indeed he had not
many months to live, but he was present
at the birth of the United Nations at San
Francisco and contributed to solving the
difficulty of the 'veto'. Among many
tributes that of Churchill is memorable to
'the priceless work of Hopkins . . . a soul
that flamed out of a frail and failing body'.

HORE-BELISHA, Leslie, b. 1893. British
politician, Secretary of State for War in
1939. Neville Chamberlain had given him
the War Office in 1937 with a brief to
modernize army methods and equipment.
Hore-Belisha brought in Lord Gort as
C.I.G.S., but it proved an uneasy relationship. Gort's successor in 1939, Sir Edmund
Ironside, made no secret of his hostility to
the Secretary of State.

Hore-Belisha had qualities of energy,
enthusiasm, and imagination, and he used
up-to-date publicity methods to make the
public more aware of the role and importance of the army. He also improved
conditions of service and made changes in
senior appointments that were very
necessary; but his choice in filling the
vacancies not infrequently provoked controversy. Hore-Belisha was among the
ministers who on the evening of 2 September 1939 agreed that Sir John Simon
should inform Chamberlain of their view
that war must be declared at once. The
Cabinet decided to give an ultimatum to
Germany, and this was sent at 9 a.m. on
Sunday the 3rd. The ultimatum expired at
11 a.m.; and at that hour—since no reply
had been received from the German
government—Britain was at war.

At the beginning of 1940 Hore-Belisha
went to inspect the fortifications constructed by the B.E.F. on the badly protected French-Belgian frontier. He considered them inadequate and inappropriate,
and expressed his disquiet. After protests
from some of the generals, Hore-Belisha
was dismissed. He stayed out of office for
the remainder of the war.

Hore-Belisha was best known to the
public for the 'Belisha beacons'—the
yellow globes with flashing lights to mark
pedestrian crossings—that he introduced
when he was Minister of Transport, 1934–
1937.

HORROCKS, Brian, b. 1895. British general, a forceful commander, particularly skilled in his use of armoured units. He came into prominence in 1942 when General Montgomery was preparing for the North African battles to prevent Rommel's advance to the Nile. Montgomery had considerably advanced Horrocks's career, as he recorded in his *Memoirs*: 'Horrocks had been in my 3rd Division as a battalion commander . . . I now wanted him to have a Corps in my Army. I knew I could not have a better man and so it turned out; he was exactly what was wanted for the job which lay ahead.' Montgomery ordered him not to let 13th Corps (and especially the 7th Armoured Division—the 'Desert Rats') be mauled by the opposing German and Italian armies. In the Battle of Alam Halfa in August–September 1942 Horrocks did all that was expected, and Montgomery commented: 'Horrocks fought his battle in full accord with the master plan and he deserves great credit for his action that day.'

After Alam Halfa, Montgomery made his final preparation for El Alamein: Horrocks's force was to operate in the south and break the enemy position; 7th Armoured Division was to draw off the enemy armour. After the Battle of El Alamein the Italian forces directly ahead of 13th Corps could only surrender because the escaping Germans had taken all available transport. Horrocks was detailed to deal with the Italians while Montgomery pursued Rommel's troops westwards. Later Montgomery transferred Horrocks to command 10th Corps, and this post meant that he carried responsibility for providing transport in the drive to Tripoli, a task which he accomplished with his customary efficiency. After this Montgomery transferred him to the 1st Army, where he dealt with the Tunis attack of 6 May; this episode ended the war in Africa.

In the operations in N.W. Europe in 1944–5, Horrocks commanded 30th Corps of 2nd Army (which was in Montgomery's 21st Army Group). The greatest achievement of the corps was probably the spectacularly fast advance into Belgium and the Netherlands, and it was 30th Corps that had the task of advancing to relieve the airborne troops during the Battle of Arnhem.

HORTHY, Miklos, b. 1868. Hungarian statesman, Regent of Hungary 1920–44. He was formerly an admiral in the navy of Austria-Hungary. Horthy was reluctant to involve Hungary in a war with the West, though he sympathized with Hitler's anti-Communism. This ambivalence of attitude characterized Hungary's policy during the war.

On 10 August 1941 Horthy ordered the Hungarian invasion of Yugoslavia and in the following month he held talks with Hitler resulting in a joint declaration of solidarity against Russia. This was reinforced at another meeting in April 1943. But the version of the declaration which was published in the Hungarian press omitted a hostile reference to the 'British and American allies of Bolshevism'.

In May 1943 Horthy refused Hitler's request for Hungarian reinforcements in Russia, and in March 1944 he went to Germany to plead for the recall of Hungarian troops on the Eastern front. He also asked that the Germans should cease to use Hungary as a base for military transport and operations. But, when Hitler threatened occupation, Horthy decided to co-operate.

With the agreement of collaborationist members of the government, the Germans began deportation of the Hungarian Jews. When this was reported to Horthy in June 1944, he stopped the deportation and saved the Jewish population of Budapest. But later, in August, German force prevailed; Horthy found himself powerless to prevent the Gestapo's persecution of the Jews. When Romania surrendered in August, Horthy tried to extricate Hungary from the war and submitted a preliminary armistice to Russia on 11 October 1944. Four days later he broadcast his intention to seek peace with the Allies, but was then deported by the Germans to Austria. He was freed by American troops in May 1945.

HORTON, Max, b. 1883. British admiral, whose long experience found its reward when he became C.-in-C. Western Approaches in 1942. As this year drew to its close the real issues involved in the Battle of the Atlantic seem to have been understood by the German leaders more clearly than before. The German U-Boat fleet numbered nearly 400 vessels, and Hitler was at last heeding Admiral Raeder's request for high priority submarine construction.

Horton was a submarine officer of long experience, renowned throughout the Royal Navy, and possessed of a ruthless determination, while his shrewd brain and knowledge of submarine tactics provided him with the right equipment to outwit Admiral Doenitz. He held the Western Approaches appointment until the end of the war, when he retired.

From 1937 to 1939 he had commanded the Reserve Fleet, and in the tense early days of the war at sea he fulfilled the onerous task of commanding the Northern Patrol. In January 1940 he became Flag Officer Submarines.

When he took over as C.-in-C. Western Approaches he was invited to lunch by the Lord Mayor of Liverpool. He wished to refuse but was persuaded to accept, and did so on one condition—that he could say grace. At the beginning of the lunch he said: 'If we eat while others starve may the Good Lord forgive us'—a view typical of his single-minded approach to the Battle of the Atlantic.

HULL, Cordell, b. 1871. American statesman, U.S. Secretary of State from 1933 to 1944. A strong believer in the necessity of international co-operation and organization to secure peace, Hull was intimately concerned in all the events that led up to U.S. participation in the conflict.

From 1937 onwards relations between the U.S.A. and Japan grew steadily more strained. At the end of December 1937 Japanese planes bombed an American river gunboat, the *Panay*, in the Yangtze River. The U.S.A. demanded apologies and guarantees against future similar incidents. The Japanese did apologize and their statement was accepted by Secretary of State Hull. But in the following year the Japanese, intent on the conquest of China, declared that the policy of the 'Open Door' to trade was now nullified. The State Department replied that the U.S.A. could not accept Japan's 'New Order' in China. By 1940 Hull was also perturbed about the future of the Nether-

lands East Indies, as Japanese power in the Far East increased; he declared that a change in the *status quo* of this area would prejudice the peace and security of the Pacific. Later he issued a similar warning to Japan concerning French Indo-China. But on 12 September 1940 the American Ambassador to Japan, Joseph C. Grew, told him that if America were to impose an embargo on oil Japan might regard this as a sanction and respond accordingly. The matter came to be of less importance soon afterwards, since Japan made an agreement with Vichy France and so gained air and troop bases in Indo-China. By 1941, however, American-Japanese relations were again tense, for the Japanese were now in effect demanding a free hand in China and particularly wanted to end the freezing of Japanese credits in America. Hull began negotiations with the Japanese on 20 November 1941 and suggested that agreement might be reached along specific lines, including the withdrawal of Japanese forces from China and Indo-China, and the pacification of Asia by making a multilateral non-aggression pact with stress on territorial integrity and sovereignty. Japan asked for a fortnight in which to consider the proposals, meanwhile going ahead secretly with her plans for the attack on the American Pacific Fleet at Pearl Harbor, which took place on 7 December 1941. On the following day, with only one dissenter, the American Congress declared war on Japan.

During the war Hull continued to play an important part as Roosevelt's Secretary of State. He attended the Moscow Conference of Foreign Ministers, which began on 19 October 1943 and was the first Three-Power Inter-Allied Conference; Hull was now in his 70s, so this was a gallant undertaking. In 1944 ill-health forced his resignation.

HUSSEINI, Amin el (the Grand Mufti of Jerusalem), b. 1900. Arab political and religious leader, a strong opponent of the creation of a Jewish state in Palestine; in furtherance of his aims he worked during the war for Axis support. In October 1939 he went to Iraq, where the pro-British Nuri es-Said was in power. The Mufti advocated Iraqi neutrality, and his presence strengthened the position of Axis supporters in the country. He sent envoys to Berlin seeking Axis recognition of Arab independence in return for pan-Arab support. In the spring of 1941 a favourable answer was received, and on 1 April of that year the government of Nuri es-Said was overthrown and a pro-Axis government established under Rashid Ali. The Mufti was the moving force in the plot, and had considerable influence on the resultant policy. Hostilities between Iraq and Britain commenced on 2 May. However, German arms were slow to arrive—Hitler in fact had little interest in Iraq—and the régime collapsed on 30 May. The Mufti fled to Iran, and finally to Europe, where he saw Mussolini on 27 October and Hitler on 28 November. But he failed to secure a firm declaration of

Arab independence until 5 April 1943. Complicated negotiations regarding the formation of Arab units under Arab flags were conducted against the background of a power struggle between El Husseini and Rashid Ali—finally resulting in Nazi recognition of the Mufti's claim to be the most widely supported pan-Arab leader. Hitler considered that the astute, red-haired, and blue-eyed Mufti must have had Aryan ancestry.

During the last years of the war the Mufti worked for the Nazi cause by forming S.S. units among Muslims in occupied countries, and by preventing Jewish emigration from Europe. He left Germany in 1945 and lived under house arrest in France until he escaped to Cairo in May 1946.

I

IBN SAUD, Abdul Aziz, b. 1880. King of Saudi Arabia. During the war he followed a policy of neutrality, but he sympathized with the Allied cause. He considered friendship with Britain vital to the prosperity and independence of his country. Against much opposition, he remained unshaken in his commitment to the treaty of 1927 with the U.K. A man of impressive presence and great ability, he had unified and modernized his kingdom, and fostered contacts with the rest of the world. Some people considered him the century's greatest figure in the Arab world.

In 1939 Germany and Japan were bidding energetically for concessions in the Arabian peninsula, where the presence of rich oil deposits was suspected. Ibn Saud ignored commercial considerations, and chose to lease the deposits less profitably to British interests. Later in the war he also entered into a close relationship with the U.S.A. As a result of his policies, Arabia was undisturbed by the war and was able to carry out considerable improvement plans under the guidance of an American technical mission.

In 1945, following the Yalta Conference, Churchill and Roosevelt visited Egypt and held independent conferences there with Ibn Saud. Churchill admired him 'because of his unfailing loyalty' and was much impressed by the meeting.

INÖNÜ, Ismet, b. 1884. Turkish soldier and statesman, President of Turkey throughout the war. The Axis powers and the Allies were each anxious to involve Turkey in the war as a co-belligerent. On the Allied side Churchill, in particular, considered that the winning of Turkish support was a goal to be strenuously pursued because of its implications for the great Mediterranean offensive that he advocated. But Inönü's government was made cautious by the disaster in Greece, the loss of the islands of the Aegean, the Allies' failure to take Rhodes, and the consequent German domination of this whole area.

At the Teheran Conference in November 1943 the Allied leaders discussed the possibility of persuading Turkey to support the Allied cause. Inönü met Churchill and Roosevelt at Cairo in December and made his position clear; the risk was too great to be acceptable. In the event, Turkey's rigidly maintained neutrality under Inönü's leadership may have been more useful to the Allied war strategy than hostilities in S.W. Asia would have been.

IRONSIDE, Sir Edmund (Lord Ironside, 1944), **b.** 1880. British general (field marshal, 1940), C.I.G.S. in the early months of the war. After the declaration of war Hore-Belisha, Secretary of State for War, who was on uneasy terms with Lord Gort, the then C.I.G.S., decided that he must have a C.I.G.S. with whom he could work. The result was that Gort was given command of the B.E.F. and Ironside, at that time Inspector-General of Overseas Forces, replaced him.

Estimates of Ironside's quality as C.I.G.S. vary, but there is fairly general agreement that the position was uncongenial to him. In May 1940 he went to France to see Gort, with instructions that a southward attack must be made in the direction of Amiens; Gort held that as 7 of his 9 divisions were fighting the Germans already it would be unwise to risk a southerly attack. Ironside agreed, and in the event Gort was able to save the remains of the B.E.F. by driving towards Dunkirk. This was possibly the only practicable policy under the strategic circumstances, since communication with the French was on the point of breaking down. On 27 May 1940 Ironside was succeeded by General Dill and became C.-in-C. Home Forces, to be relieved in July by General Brooke.

During the 'phoney war' months of September 1939 to May 1940, Ironside managed to inject into the preparations for active war a virility, force, and imagination that might have been lacking but for his strong presence in Whitehall.

ISMAY, Sir Hastings, b. 1887. British general, Chief of Staff to Churchill (as Minister of Defence) and consequently Churchill's channel of communication with many military leaders both at home and abroad. Having served only in Somaliland in World War I, despite his efforts to reach a major theatre of war, Ismay felt handicapped professionally and became a desk general. In 1939 he was head of the Secretariat of the Committee of Imperial Defence, which became the military wing of the War Cabinet Secretariat. In May 1940 Churchill became Prime Minister and assumed the office of Minister of Defence with Ismay as his Chief of Staff and a member of the Chiefs of Staff Committee. He linked the Prime Minister to the war machine, interpreting Churchill's flow of directives and queries. In the reverse direction he became the accepted channel through which controversial propositions were put to the Prime Minister. A member of the Chiefs of Staff Committee has described how he brought in certain bizarre messages from the Prime Minister in such a way that these would be least likely to annoy the committee; and when the chairman, General Brooke, sent back a terse answer, this was conveyed in such a way as to indicate that the Chiefs of Staff were impressed by his suggestion but greatly regretted there were not sufficient resources to implement it.

Ismay had a singular capacity for common-sense solutions acceptable to all concerned: in his own words, 'the resolution of a problem lies, more often than not, in the method of its presentation'. His infinite patience and skill in averting friction made him an admirable go-between in Churchill's relations with both British and American Chiefs of Staff. In September 1941 he took part in the difficult Anglo-American mission to Moscow, when agreement was reached on aid to Russia. He was also present at the Foreign Secretaries' Conference in Moscow in 1943. In general he took little part in formulating policy, but gave his time unsparingly to the Prime Minister, day and night. Affectionately known to his associates as 'Pug', he had an exceptional gift for friendship. At the Potsdam Conference Admiral King's toast was to 'Pug Ismay, whose contribution to our victory could never be properly rewarded'.

J

JACOB, Ian, b. 1899. British soldier, Senior Military Assistant and deputy to General Ismay in the military wing of the War Cabinet Offices—one of the select group that made up Churchill's 'handling machine'. He contributed greatly to the efficient operation of this organization during the war. He had been a member of the Committee of Imperial Defence since 1938. Jacob became a colonel in 1943, and a temporary major-general in 1944. He attended the major strategic conferences at Argentia, Newfoundland (the 'Atlantic Charter'), Washington, Casablanca, Quebec, Moscow, Yalta, and Potsdam.

Jacob's perceptive and entertaining war diaries were quoted extensively in Sir Arthur Bryant's *The Turn of the Tide*. One of his lighter memories was of Churchill's return flight from Casablanca in January 1943. His manservant Sawyers was helping the Prime Minister undress in the confined space of the aircraft. Jacob overheard Sawyers say: 'You are sitting on your hot-water bottle. That isn't at all a good idea.' Churchill's reply was: 'Idea? It isn't an idea. It's a coincidence.'

JAMES, Clifton, b. 1897. British actor with a remarkable physical resemblance to Field Marshal Montgomery. Just before D-Day in June 1944 the 'cover-planners' found James, a lieutenant in the Army Education Corps, at Leicester and briefed him to study Montgomery's appearance and mannerisms. Dressed in the latter's uniform, complete with the famous beret, he was sent to Gibraltar in the Prime Minister's plane accompanied by an imposing staff. On the way by car to the Governor's residence he was greeted by soldiers with the cry 'Good old Monty'. The Governor had been warned and had arranged that a Spaniard who was a well-known double agent should be present when 'Monty's' car arrived. The agent saw what he was meant to see and returned to Spain at top speed to inform agents in Madrid that he had seen Montgomery at Gibraltar. This information was passed on to Berlin. The false 'Monty' then continued with much ceremony to show himself in Algiers.

The ruse was successful in making the Germans believe that Montgomery, who was known by them to have been appointed commander of the initial assault, had left Britain and that therefore the invasion of the Continent could not take place until his return.

JODL, Alfred, b. 1890. German general, Hitler's main adviser on strategy and operations during the war. In August 1939 Jodl was appointed Chief of Staff to Keitel, the chief of the High Command of the Armed Forces (O.K.W.), and in this position directed under Hitler and Keitel all the German campaigns except that against Russia. In 1944 he was promoted to colonel-general. Intellectually Jodl was more powerful than Keitel, his superior, and involved himself less in political affairs. It is likely that he had more responsibility for the military conduct of the war than anyone else except Hitler. He himself maintained in his diaries that he often successfully opposed Hitler. But, from the fact that he retained his position for the duration of the war when so many others lost theirs, it would appear that Jodl's independence was less than he claimed.

In any case, examples of this vaunted opposition to Hitler show Jodl's powers of persuasion over the Führer rather than any particular military insight. His opposition to the Kursk offensive in 1943 enabled the Russians to mount a massive defensive operation, defeat the German army at Stalingrad and thus close another gap in the armed ring now tightening around Germany. Again, in the autumn of 1944, his faulty assessment of the situation on the Western front prevailed. The result was that the Ardennes offensive so stretched German resources in men and supplies that the collapse of the Western front elsewhere became inevitable. Jodl's refusal to base his strategy on the advice of commanders actually in the field (who frequently opposed his conduct of the later campaigns of the war) added to his share of the responsibility for Germany's ultimate defeat.

At Rheims, France, on 7 May 1945, a week after Hitler's suicide, Jodl signed the surrender of the German Army to the Allies, weeping as he did so.

During the course of the war Jodl condoned many illegal acts, such as the shooting of hostages. Because of this, and revelations (in his diaries) of complicity in Hitler's more nefarious schemes, he was tried for war crimes at Nuremberg, sentenced to death, and hanged.

JOHNSON, James ('Johnnie'), b. 1916. British R.A.F. officer, one of the top marksmen of the war in the air. He joined 616 (South Yorkshire) Squadron in 1939 and was still with it in 1941 when it became part of Douglas Bader's 12 Group Wing. He was on the mission during which Bader crashed. In 1942 he was sent to command 610 (County of Chester) Squadron, and while in this post took part in air operations supporting the raid on Dieppe. In the following year he was promoted to command the Canadian Spitfire wing at Kenley. Later, after a 6-month non-operational posting, he was transferred to 144 Wing, a Canadian fighter-bomber formation, and flew with it on many missions over France in preparation for the D-Day landings. Soon after 6 June the wing moved to St Croix-sur-Mer, the first airfield in France liberated by Allied forces.

On 30 June 1944 Johnson became the leading Allied scorer of the air war, with 33 enemy aircraft destroyed. Shortly afterwards he transferred to 127 Wing, another Canadian formation, and in 1945, as a group-captain, he was with 125 Wing when it was moved to Celle airfield, the Allies' first airfield east of the Rhine. Johnson was a cool and methodical fighter, detached and imperturbable in action.

JONES, Frederick, b. 1884. New Zealand statesman. He was a member of the Labour government and an ex-trade union leader. At the outbreak of war he gave up all portfolios except that of Minister of Defence. The army was at that time only 1,000 strong, but within a week New Zealand had promised to send a force for service overseas. Early in 1940 New Zealand troops were in Britain and in the Middle East. New Zealand ships were also sent to the Atlantic. The 2nd New Zealand Division under Freyberg fought in the Western Desert, Greece, Crete, and once again in North Africa. They took part in the swift advance to Tripoli in the autumn of 1942, and in 1943 Churchill said of them: 'The hearts of the British people go out in gratitude to the people of New Zealand for sending this blessed division to win glory on the battlefields of Africa.'

A man of action, Jones had by 1943 mobilized, trained, and equipped 80,000 men and 10,000 women in New Zealand. Minesweepers had been built to defend New Zealand waters. Another 80,000 men were serving overseas. Before the end of the war one-third of all men of military age were serving overseas: the 2nd New Zealand Division was fighting in Italy, while the 3rd Division was serving in the Solomons. Casualties (including P.O.W.s) numbered more than 39,000.

JONGH, Andrée de, b. 1916. Belgian Resistance leader who established an escape route for Allied P.O.W.s which later became known as the 'Comet Line'. She painstakingly organized a chain of contacts that ran from Brussels as far as Bayonne and St Jean de Luz on the Franco-Spanish border, and from there over the Pyrenees into neutral Spain. She personally escorted her first three escapers to the British consul in Bilbao in August 1941 and in the following three years the Comet Line snatched more than 800 Allied airmen and soldiers from German and French hands.

The Gestapo interrogated her as early as 1941 and, in the following year, put a price of a million Belgian francs on the head of her father, who had helped to establish Comet. He was eventually captured and executed by the Germans. Mlle de Jongh meanwhile moved to France, from where she continued to lead parties of escaping prisoners into Spain, making 36 frontier crossings in all. In January 1943 she was finally arrested at Urrugne, close to the Spanish frontier, and was imprisoned at Bayonne. Several unsuccessful attempts were made to rescue her there and at Biarritz, where she was later transferred. Eventually she was sent to Fresnes Prison, near Paris, and then languished for two years in a German concentration camp. Fortunately the Gestapo never seemed to realize what her true role in the Comet organization had been, for she managed to escape the death sentence passed upon 23 other Comet members. She was awarded the George Medal in 1946, and the story of her heroism has been told in the books *Little Cyclone* and *Saturday at M.I.9* by Airey Neave.

JOUBERT DE LA FERTÉ, Sir Philip, b. 1887. British air force leader (air chief marshal, 1941) who held many positions during the war. His career began in the Royal Flying Corps in 1913, and in 1930–1934 he was commandant of the Staff College. A.O.C. in India at the outbreak of war, he returned as Assistant Chief of Air Staff to advise on radar and air co-operation with the Royal Navy. From 1941 to 1943 he headed Coastal Command. Largely due to Trenchard's attitude towards sea warfare, the peace-time training of Coastal Command had been deficient and no proper anti-submarine weapon was available. As a result it was in 1939 badly hampered in its reconnaissance role. In August 1942 Joubert initiated a 'planned flying' scheme. This increased the efficiency of the limited number of aircraft available for the Battle of the Atlantic. By February 1945 air domination had been achieved over the eastern part of the North Atlantic. In the autumn of 1943 he was appointed Deputy Chief of Staff for Information and Civil Affairs on Mountbatten's staff in S.E. Asia.

Joubert's career was varied, but not always satisfactory, because his outspokenness made his relations with politicians difficult.

JOYCE, William ('Lord Haw-Haw'), b. 1906. British Fascist and political agitator who gained notoriety during the war because of his venomous propaganda broadcasts to Britain over the German radio. A great number of people in Britain listened to Joyce's broadcasts, and his rasping and ironic accents became almost as familiar as the voices of the country's leaders, of the B.B.C. announcers, or of the entertainers who strove to keep people's spirits up; one of the popular catch-phrases of the time was 'This is Jairmany calling', in imitation of the way in which Joyce began each instalment of

invective. Few of those who listened knew the broadcaster's real name, and the sobriquet 'Lord Haw-Haw', invented by a journalist, quickly gained currency and seemed appropriate to his portentous (though by no means lordly) tones.

To most Britons he was a comic, but at the same time menacing, figure. Strangely, although it was generally taken for granted that Joyce's broadcasts were a hotch-potch of fact and fancy—with the fancy greatly predominating—he acquired at one time a reputation for having an up-to-the-minute knowledge of local affairs in some parts of the country. Stories were current of allusions in his broadcasts to such local trivia as defective traffic lights at a particular road junction or a dance to be held on a certain night; the implication was that Joyce had widespread and detailed sources of information and that his truthfulness and prescience were to be respected. These stories do not survive comparison with the record; doubtless some of them were the products of deliberate rumour-mongering by the disaffected, and others were tales of the kind with which people like to frighten themselves.

Joyce was arrested at Flensburg by the British shortly after the end of the war; he had been recognized by two army officers with whom he had, quite gratuitously, entered into conversation. He was put on trial at the Old Bailey, in London, for high treason, and was found guilty and sentenced to death. His defence was that he was an American citizen; but during the first nine months of his war-time activities in Germany he had been the holder of a valid British passport and the court held that this entailed a duty of allegiance to the Crown. Appeals to the Court of Appeal and the House of Lords were unsuccessful, and he was executed.

Joyce was very small in stature and his most distinguishing physical characteristic was a deep scar on the right side of his face, running from his ear to the corner of his mouth; this scar is said to have been a legacy of a fight at a political meeting in London. His demeanour was friendly, and he could be extremely humorous and witty in conversation. He was born in Brooklyn, New York City, of an English mother and an Irish father who had become an American citizen. The family moved from the U.S.A. to Ireland and then, in 1921, to England. William Joyce attended a college of London University, and obtained a degree in English language and literature with first-class honours. He joined Sir Oswald Mosley's British Union of Fascists in 1933, and after Mosley 'purged' him founded the British National Socialist League. On the eve of the outbreak of war he and his wife left England for Germany.

JUIN, Alphonse, b. 1888. French general, a tough and courageous commander in the field. He began his military career with flying colours, passing out top of his year at the St Cyr military academy in the class that included de Gaulle. As a divisional commander of the French 1st Army in 1940, he was captured by the Germans, but after the armistice was soon released at the personal request of Pétain. He then replaced Weygand as C.-in-C. in North Africa, after refusing the offer of a post as Minister of War in the Vichy government. Now torn between his strong army

loyalties and his dislike of Vichy, Juin was in a quandary that made him somewhat ineffectual. After the Clark-Darlan agreement of 1942, Juin and his troops attached themselves to the Allies. Once fully committed to the Allied cause, he proved a strong and reliable ally. Juin distinguished himself in the desert campaign against Rommel's Afrika Korps. He later led a French expeditionary force into Italy with great success, as at Monte Cassino where the ruthless *élan* of his 'Goums' (Moroccan troops) intimidated the Germans. Juin's advance to Rome some months later was described as 'one of the most daring and brilliant advances of the war'. Kesselring, his opponent in Italy, had a high opinion of his spirit and aggressiveness as a commander.

In 1944 Juin was promoted Chief of Staff of France's National Defence Committee. He raised fresh French troops to help the Allied advance across France. In fact it was at de Gaulle's insistence that the 4 French divisions under Juin took part in the liberation of France.

K

KAIN, Edgar, b. 1918. 'Cobber' Kain, a New Zealand fighter pilot in the R.A.F., was one of the war's early aces. He gained his first success in November 1939, 2 months after the beginning of hostilities, when he shot down a German bomber. By the time of his death, 7 months later, he was credited with 17 victories. On one occasion, when he was on patrol accompanied by another aircraft, he pursued 7 German bombers over enemy territory. He was attacked by a German fighter and his aircraft set on fire. Kain shot down his adversary and flew his burning aircraft back over the Allied lines before baling out. In May he scored 12 victories over France, including 3 in one day. In June 1940 he was killed accidentally while going on leave when a wing tip touched the ground after taking off.

KAISER, Henry, b. 1882. American industrialist who made a major contribution to Allied victory by developing revolutionary methods of shipbuilding. In 1941 the U.S. government embarked on an unprecedented shipbuilding programme to provide the vast number of merchant ships needed to sustain the Allied supply lines. About a third of these 'Liberty' ships were constructed in shipyards organized by Kaiser. They were produced in what was then considered an amazingly short time by using new techniques of prefabrication and welding, and Kaiser became probably the most famous shipbuilder in the world.

Before the war made new demands on his drive and imagination, Kaiser had worked chiefly on the construction of roads, bridges, and dams.

KALTENBRUNNER, Ernst, b. 1902. Austrian Nazi leader and Heydrich's successor as chief of German security, in which position he was responsible for many of the worst Nazi atrocities. From the earliest days an extreme supporter of National Socialism, he was head of the Austrian S.S. at the time of the *Anschluss*, and later became chief of police in Austria. In 1943 Hitler himself chose Kaltenbrunner to replace the assassinated Heydrich (who had been Kaltenbrunner's bitter enemy) as

head of Reich security. In 1944 he also became head of the Abwehr (military Intelligence). Himmler officially headed these organizations, but real control was exercised by Kaltenbrunner, who by this time was a close confidant of the Führer, with great influence over him. To the bitter end of the war Kaltenbrunner remained steadfast, and instigated, with Hitler, many of the last desperate executions intended to eliminate the living evidence of Nazi bestiality.

Kaltenbrunner hounded all opponents of Nazism relentlessly and without mercy. 'Oppression', he said to Himmler, 'is the essence of power.' He resisted all attempts to lighten conditions in Nazi-occupied countries. He caused the death or imprisonment of many of the 'July Plotters' against Hitler, including von Moltke, Bonhoeffer, and Canaris. He sanctioned the murder of P.O.W.s and captive airmen. To the end he opposed all attempts at conciliation, such as the release of Jews and prominent persons, and frustrated the Abwehr in the peace moves that it initiated. On Kaltenbrunner's orders the prison camps that lay in the path of the advancing Russians and Western Allies were evacuated in a last attempt to conceal what had happened in them.

Kaltenbrunner was a drunkard, and it has been said that he was the only man whom even Himmler feared. He was described as 'a tough, callous ox . . . a block of wood would be more sensitive. He is coarse, hard-bitten, probably only capable of thinking when he is drunk.' Another description likened him to an old gorilla. Nominally Himmler's deputy, Kaltenbrunner was without doubt personally responsible for millions of deaths. At his trial in Nuremberg in 1946 his denials and evasions reached a grotesque level, including even the refusal to acknowledge his own signature. But there was ample evidence to prove his guilt, and he was condemned and executed.

KEITEL, Wilhelm, b. 1882. German general, Chief of the High Command of the Armed Forces (O.K.W.). A man of poor mental and moral calibre, in the opinion of many in a position to judge, he apparently was able to sustain his role as Hitler's chief military adviser partly because of the Führer's dislike of more able and independent officers, and partly because of the ability of his Chief of Staff, Jodl. He was the perfect lackey, justifying the pun which Berliners made on his name on the announcement of his appointment in 1938 (*Lakaitel*, meaning 'little lackey').

There is no evidence that he ever queried any of Hitler's decisions; far less did he dare to contradict the Führer he idolized. In Keitel's view, the traditional loyalty due to the sovereign had been transferred to Hitler, and to voice criticism of him, either in private or in public, was dishonourable and treasonable. His deficient intuition prevented him from understanding Hitler's character and limitations. Keitel's only moment of doubt came when his Führer committed suicide, thereby evading the sole responsibility which he had so often passionately declared was his.

There are many examples of Keitel's lack of character and cringing adulation of the Führer. In 1938 Hitler developed a plan for the invasion of Bohemia and Moravia. The heads of the General Staff expressed grave doubts as to its viability, doubts which Keitel later admitted sharing. But at the time he vehemently upbraided the General Staff, declaring that he would not brook 'criticism, scruples, and defeatism'. In the following year he showed his failure of comprehension when, advised by alarmed colleagues that Hitler's policy towards Poland would lead to a world war for which Germany was ill-equipped, he replied that there was no such danger since France was too degenerate, Britain too decadent, and America too uninterested to fight for Poland. Even Hitler had small regard for him, describing him on one occasion as 'a man with the brains of a cinema usher'. Some of the worst of his deeds, however, cannot be put down to stupidity; in signing the orders for the conduct of the German forces in Russia, he willingly sacrificed the honour of the army to the ambitions of the Nazi party. He was sentenced to death by the Nuremberg Tribunal for planning and leading a war of aggression and for crimes against humanity, and was hanged on 16 October 1946.

Keitel came from a middle-class Hanoverian family with a marked anti-Prussian tradition. He served in World War I with an artillery regiment and was seriously wounded. In 1930 he was appointed head of the organizational department of the armed forces, and from this post was promoted Chief of the High Command.

KELLER, Rodney, b. 1900. Canadian general who distinguished himself in the Allied invasion of N.W. Europe. In 1942 he had been given command of his regiment, Princess Patricia's Canadian Light Infantry, and in September 1943 he became G.O.C. 3rd Canadian Division. McNaughton, the C.-in-C. of the Canadian army overseas, had said in 1941: 'Through the long months on watch and in repeated routine training, there have been many disappointments at action deferred, and great patience has been required.' Keller had to wait for four and a half years before going into action. The 1st Seaborne Canadian Infantry went ashore north-west of Caen at 8 a.m. on D-Day, 6 June 1944. Against strong German resistance the infantry and tanks battled through, captured two coastal towns, and pressed on inland. Keller and his headquarters were constantly on the move to keep up with the advance. They later had to meet a German Panzer attack on their beachhead perimeter. The division went on to attack Caen and the Falaise area, but Keller was wounded and returned to Canada. Keller was a democratic commander who believed that troops should know as much about what they were doing as was possible within military security.

KENNEDY, Joseph, b. 1888. American business magnate who as American ambassador to the U.K. from 1937 to early 1941 did much to encourage American isolationism—at a time when Britain most urgently needed American help.

In August 1939 Kennedy transmitted Chamberlain's appeal to President Roosevelt for the U.S.A. to put pressure on Poland to concede Germany's territorial demands. This message seemed to be counter to Britain's guarantee to support Poland's integrity, and it was probably one of the reasons why Kennedy was unable to understand Britain's motives for entering the war.

Although Kennedy seems to have been well disposed towards Britain at the

beginning of the war, he also seems to
have been certain that Germany would
win. On returning to the U.S.A. in 1941
he supported the Lend-Lease Plan, but he
was still convinced that Britain would lose,
and declared: 'This war is not our war
and Britain is not fighting our battle.'
Largely because of this counsel, Kennedy's
political influence declined after America's
entry into the war in December 1941.

KENT, Duchess of (Princess Marina), **b.**
1906. When war broke out the Duke of
Kent was about to go to Australia as
Governor-General. The appointment was
postponed, and he and his wife dedicated
themselves to war work. The duchess
became commandant of the W.R.N.S. and,
apart from her duties in this connection,
worked also as a nurse at University College Hospital in London, and travelled
extensively on visits to hospitals, factories,
and bombed areas. On 4 July 1942 her
third child, Michael, was born. Seven
weeks later her husband was killed in an
air crash over Scotland. The duchess continued to devote herself to her children
and to public service for the remainder of
the war. She was well known for her
beauty, stylish appearance, and charm.

KENT, Duke of (Prince George), b. 1902.
Accomplished, handsome, and charming,
the Duke of Kent, fourth son of King
George V, came into his own during the
war. At the outbreak he was Governor-
General designate of Australia, but he
asked for a job more directly concerned
with the war effort. He was given an air
commodore's appointment (he waived his
honorary rank of air marshal) and was
engaged on welfare duties, eventually
becoming chief welfare officer for R.A.F.
Home Command.

In 1941 the duke toured the various
centres of the Empire Training Scheme in
Canada, and ended the tour by staying with
President Roosevelt, who had great affection for him and became his younger son
Michael's godfather. In August 1942 he
went on a tour of R.A.F. establishments.
Flying from the U.K. to Iceland on 25
August in bad weather, he was killed when
his flying-boat crashed in Scotland. There
was only one survivor of the accident.

KERR, Sir Archibald Clark, b. 1885.
British diplomat, between 1938 and 1942
ambassador in China and then in Russia.
In China Clark Kerr's relations with
Chiang Kai-shek were good, and in
Russia it was largely due to his tact and
diplomatic skill that Anglo-Soviet relations did not totally collapse. The Moscow ambassadorship was probably Britain's
trickiest war-time diplomatic mission.
Although Britain was now his ally, Stalin
mistrusted and disliked the British intensely,
and this influenced the Russian conduct of
the war. But Clark Kerr's unfeigned
admiration for and understanding of
Stalin made it possible for him to mitigate
somewhat the hostility of Stalin's approach
to the Allies. By accurately gauging the
extent to which Stalin's rhetoric indicated
his intentions, and by teaching Churchill
some of his own respect for the Russian
leader, Clark Kerr averted many major
crises in Anglo-Soviet relations. But when
Clark Kerr was a member of the ill-fated
Moscow Commission on Poland, he was
unjustly blamed by Stalin for its failure to
find a solution to the Polish question.

At Clark Kerr's urgent prompting the
meeting of the 'Big Three' took place at
Teheran in 1945. This meeting went some
way towards creating or restoring mutual
confidence.

KESSELRING, Albrecht von, b. 1885. One
of the most able German generals of the
war, who took a major part in nearly
every campaign in Europe. Originally an
artilleryman, he later transferred to the
air force.

He commanded the operations of the
German air force in the invasions of
Poland in 1939 and of Belgium in 1940. He
then ordered the Luftwaffe's heavy
bombing of the B.E.F. during its retreat
to Dunkirk. Later in 1940, from his
H.Q. in Brussels, Kesselring directed the
German attack on the R.A.F. during the
Battle of Britain, which by highly success-
ful attacks on air bases in S.E. England
gave the British great cause for alarm.
This advantage was thrown away by
Goering's decision to redirect the Luft-
waffe onto London.

In 1941 Kesselring, as C.-in-C. in the
south, shared the direction of Rommel's
North African campaign, assuming com-

plete control during the latter's absence. He was also in charge of the Axis withdrawal from Tunisia.

In 1943 Kesselring was made C.-in-C. in Italy. It was in Italy, a country he knew and loved, that he came into his own as a strategist and tactician, conducting a superb defensive campaign in the face of heavy odds. Kesselring had long complained about Berlin's apparent indifference to Allied superiority in the air. But his repeated pleas for air reinforcements failed, and the numbers of troops and the arms made available to him were inadequate to the type of campaign he thought appropriate. Nevertheless he conducted a brilliant retreat and skilfully rebuilt his defensive line after the delayed Allied success at Monte Cassino. For more than a year he stubbornly resisted the Allied advance northwards. Most of those who opposed him there paid tribute to his military genius. Many considered that if Kesselring had been given a free hand and proper support in Italy the outcome of the Italian campaign might have been less of a disaster for the Germans.

In March 1945 Hitler ordered Kesselring to take over the Western front and do what Kluge, Rommel, Rundstedt, and Model had all failed to do—halt the Allied advance. But the situation had deteriorated beyond repair, and no amount of military skill could prevent the Allies continuing their drive into the German homeland.

The fact that Kesselring was ultimately unsuccessful in each of the campaigns he fought does not detract from his great military skill. General Brooke rated Kesselring as the greatest of his opponents. In spite of several attempts to win his support by the anti-Nazi camp Kesselring remained loyal to Hitler to the last, and it was only after hearing of Hitler's death that he acknowledged the war lost.

After the war Kesselring received the death sentence from a British military court for having ordered the execution of Italian hostages. His sentence was later commuted to life imprisonment and he was freed in 1952 on grounds of his ill-health.

KEYES, Geoffrey, b. 1917. British Commando leader who received a posthumous V.C. for his bold attempt to assassinate Rommel. He typified the daring and enterprising character of the men who made up these groups of 'leopards' so highly admired by Churchill. An officer in the Royal Scots Greys, he joined one of the first Commando units to be trained for attacks behind enemy lines.

In 1941 Keyes was part of 'Layforce' in the Mediterranean, and took part in attacks in Syria and Crete. In June 1941 he commanded one of the three units that carried out raids in Syria with the aim of assisting the advance of Allied forces invading the country to deprive the Germans of the use of Vichy French airstrips there. The operation was abortive; of the three Commando groups which had set out only Keyes's achieved its objective, at the cost of many casualties.

The Desert Commandos' most remarkable exploit was their bid to disrupt German command and communications before Auchinleck's offensive to relieve Tobruk in November 1941. Keyes, now a lieutenant-colonel at 24, received the most dangerous assignment—to penetrate Rommel's headquarters and to kill or capture the general. Keyes and a small party landed from the submarine H.M.S. *Torbay* near Apollonia on 17 November, and despite serious setbacks managed to enter what they believed was Rommel's house, killing a number of the occupants. Keyes was killed and his party scattered, and the operation achieved nothing: the house was not in use by Rommel, though he had once lived there.

KHAN, Noor Inayat ('Madeleine'), b. 1914. An agent of the British S.O.E. working with the Resistance in France, 'Madeleine' was a shy and gentle girl of mixed Indian and American parentage. In 1940 she had escaped from France with her mother and a brother, and was working as a wireless operator in the W.A.A.F. before her transfer to S.O.E. in February 1943. Her training revealed a determined but temperamental character. On 16 June 1943 she was landed by Lysander aircraft in France. Her task was to ensure continued radio transmissions between London and an organization of the Resistance in the Paris area. During the weeks immediately following her arrival the German security police made mass arrests in the Paris circuit to which she had been assigned. Although given the opportunity of returning to England, she refused to leave her French comrades without communications. The Gestapo, possessing a full description of her and knowing her code name, deployed considerable forces in an effort to catch her and so break one of the last remaining links with London. In July 1943 she and some comrades were ambushed at Grignon but managed to escape, killing some of the Germans who tried to stop them. But about three months later she was betrayed to the Gestapo and taken to their H.Q. in Avenue Foch. With her were captured not only the transmitter but also a book in which she had recorded the messages she had sent and received since her arrival in France. Brutally interrogated for several weeks, she revealed no information of any kind. After two unsuccessful attempts at escape, she was sent to Germany for 'safe custody'. She was considered a dangerous and unco-operative prisoner and on 12 September 1944 she was taken to Dachau concentration camp where she was shot on arrival.

A direct descendant of Tippoo Sahib, the warlike 18th-century Sultan of Mysore, she was born in the Kremlin. Her mother was a cousin of Mary Baker Eddy, the founder of Christian Science. She had spent much of her life in France and was almost bilingual in French and English. Prior to the outbreak of war she was engaged in writing children's stories for Radio Paris and the Sunday *Figaro*.

KILMUIR, Earl of. *See* FYFE, Sir David Maxwell.

KIMMEL, Husband E., b. 1882. American admiral who was in command at Pearl Harbor at the time of the Japanese air attack on the U.S. Pacific Fleet there in December 1941. Kimmel had held the appointment for ten months and was removed from command almost immediately after the attack. He was strongly criticized in some quarters for allegedly neglecting to take precautions that were obviously necessary to safeguard his ships, considering the dangerous tension between the U.S.A. and Japanese governments. It

was pointed out that the Japanese planes found all the battleships of the fleet in port, that the warning system was ineffective, and that the U.S. planes on the ground (which were not Kimmel's responsibility) were disposed in a way that made them vulnerable to attack from the air. Kimmel and his many supporters vigorously rebutted his culpability. He maintained, it seems with some justice, that he had not been properly apprised of the seriousness of the situation and was not made aware of the urgent need to guard against sudden attack—a danger that Washington knew to exist.

KING, Ernest, b. 1878. American admiral who masterminded the triumphant American naval campaign in the Pacific. When the U.S.A. entered the war, he was C.-in-C. of the U.S. Fleet; in 1942 he also became Chief of Naval Operations (he was the only man ever to hold both appointments). A member of the Joint Chiefs of Staff Committee throughout the war, he was given the rank of fleet admiral in 1944.

King devoted himself single-mindedly to the energetic waging of the Pacific war. He considered the war in Europe to be merely a distraction from the more vital tasks of removing the threat to American security posed by Japanese imperialist aspirations in the Pacific. This attitude did not endear him to the leaders of America's allies, one of whom described him as 'rude, chauvinistic . . . conscious of only half the facts'. His strong, often successful insistence that the Pacific campaign should not take second place to European objectives was sometimes damaging to the conduct of the war in Europe.

Most of the war leaders who knew him recognized King's qualities as a commander. General Brooke, often the butt of King's strictures, paid him an elegantly English compliment in stating that 'the Pacific campaign in size and brilliance of execution rivalled that of Trafalgar'.

More than anyone else, King was the architect of the eventual defeat of the Japanese in the Pacific. The sheer weight of the achievement of the American forces in the Pacific campaign has never been exceeded in the history of naval warfare. To implement his masterly strategy King had to cope with problems of supply on a scale never before envisaged. By building up relays of supply and repair ships, he made it possible for battleships and carriers to stay at sea for months on end. King, in solving these problems, became a pre-eminent figure in the development of modern naval logistics.

KING, William Mackenzie, b. 1874. Liberal Prime Minister of Canada throughout the war. A shrewd politician, he remained in office longer than any other Prime Minister in the English-speaking world. During the pre-war years he had been a strict isolationist. Until hostilities appeared inevitable he pursued a policy of non-commitment, ever keeping in mind the bitter conscription controversy of 1917 which had torn apart French and English in Canada. Responding intuitively to aroused and changed public opinion, he rejected the advice of his extreme isolationist advisers and led Canada into the war, maintaining national unity at this crucial moment. King saw his principal contribution to the war effort as the preservation of this national concord. Initially therefore he sought to delay the formation of a Canadian expeditionary force and concentrate on building up air and naval strength. Expenditure of man-power overseas he knew would raise the spectre of conscription, and so commitments must be avoided if possible. The idea of an 'Imperial War' was especially rejected, and King's role in no way comparable to that of Sir Robert Borden's struggle to secure a voice in the decision-making of World War I. He opposed the suggestion for an Imperial War Cabinet and refused to support Robert Menzies of Australia, who sought a place in the inner war councils through such a body. King experienced opposition from members of his Cabinet and from some higher civil servants for his failure to take a firmer line during the war. Part of his own assessment of his war-time role was the need to bring the U.S.A. into closer co-operation with the U.K.

Before Churchill and Roosevelt had personal meetings, King played something of the role of intermediary, though tending to overestimate its importance. The formation of the Joint Defence Board of the two countries (1940), and the Hyde Park Declaration (1941), were facets of this policy. He was host to two international conferences at Quebec, in August 1943 and September 1944, but had no hand in the political or military strategy evolved at them. Having won a General Election in 1940, King made a successful appeal to the country in a plebiscite (27 April 1942) seeking release from his promise of 'no conscription'. The potential crisis did not materialize until the large forces Canada had built up experienced heavy casualties. In late 1944 his Defence Minister resigned, but early in 1945 King had to send some conscripted home defence forces to Europe. Delay, however, had proved successful; the demand for men abated, and with it the crisis. By 1943 his traditional isolationism began to decline in favour of an active, enlarged role for Canada in the post-war world. Basically a functionalist in his view of the United Nations, he aimed at clarification of the smaller states' position, and representation of middle powers on the Security Council.

KIPPENBERGER, Howard, b. 1897. New Zealand general, a distinguished and outstandingly successful infantry commander. A solicitor by profession and a Territorial officer, Kippenberger commanded the 20th Battalion when war broke out. After a year's training in Egypt the battalion saw action in Greece and Crete. It was there that Kippenberger briefly took command of a composite brigade. His battalion transferred to Libya in 1941 where it was severely mauled in the fighting around Belhamed at the beginning of December. Kippenberger himself was wounded in the battle and later taken prisoner.

He escaped to the Allied lines, and was given command of the 5th Infantry Brigade, first in the Western Desert and then in Syria. His brigade distinguished itself in the fighting at Mingar Qaim, at the battles of El Mreir and Ruweisat Ridge, and at the crucial battle of El Alamein in October–November 1942. Kippenberger, acting as commander of the New Zealand Division during General Freyberg's absences at corps H.Q., chased the fleeing Germans across North Africa to Takrouna in Tunisia.

After a spell of leave Kippenberger resumed command of the 5th Brigade, this time at the Sangro in Italy, before taking command of the New Zealand Division at Monte Cassino in 1944. On 2 March he stepped on a mine. The explosion cost him one foot immediately; his other foot was amputated later. Although his active career was thus suddenly ended, after convalescence he was given control of the repatriation scheme for New Zealand P.O.W.s. He returned to New Zealand in 1946 to become editor-in-chief of the nation's war histories.

KIRKPATRICK, Ivone, b. 1897. British diplomat who in September 1941 became Controller of the European Service of the B.B.C., in charge of propaganda broadcasts in Europe. Earlier he had been Director of the Foreign Division of the Ministry of Information and the B.B.C.'s Foreign Adviser. Kirkpatrick performed perhaps the strangest mission of his war career in 1941 when he was sent to Scotland to identify, interview, and report on Rudolf Hess, after the latter's bizarre arrival by air from Germany. Kirkpatrick had known Hess in Germany before the war. In 1944 Kirkpatrick was given the job of setting up the British Element of the Allied Control Commission in preparation for the occupation of Germany at the end of the war.

KLEIST, Paul von, b. 1885. German general, a skilled and devastatingly successful commander of Panzer forces in the early part of the war, who again demonstrated exceptional competency in Russia. It was Kleist's troops who in May 1940 broke through the Ardennes and into France, reaching the Meuse in two days and starting the progressive rout of the French army that ended inexorably in France's collapse. Kleist put the 'Blitzkrieg' into effect in the West, to the horror and amazement of conventionally minded generals on the Allied side who had expected to fight with a defined and relatively static front line. At Sedan one of Kleist's corps, under the command of Guderian, crossed the river with the support of a thousand aircraft, some of them the morale-shattering dive bombers, and consolidated their position with a

speed that allowed of no effective countermeasures; in two days they had broken through the French defences and turned for the Channel ports. On the German side, too, the speed of this operation had surprised many commanders, and on several occasions in the war the Sedan was remembered when planners advised caution.

In 1941 Kleist had command of a Panzer group in the invasion of Russia. The German 6th Army crossed the Bug, south of the Pripet Marshes, allowing Kleist's forces to pass through. In a very short time they had taken Lutsk and Rovno. They then made for Kiev but were slowed down by some resistance and heavy rain which upset the German time-table for reaching the Dnieper. The Germans captured Kiev on 19 September.

In the 1942 summer offensive Kleist led the armoured drive to the Caucasus as part of the newly created Army Group A. In six weeks the Germans had reached and taken the first airfields, but then their fortunes changed. Kleist himself attributed the German failure to a shortage of petrol, because of which he was unable to maintain the speed and power of his drive, and to the gradual erosion of his formation, units of which were diverted to support the army attacking Stalingrad (autumn 1942).

By some of his colleagues Kleist was considered a commander of the old school who did not take kindly to innovation. The record, however, shows him capable of using the new techniques of the war of movement with expertise, force, and, occasionally, verve. He was lucky in his subordinates, such as Guderian, and knew when to give a subordinate his head.

KLUGE, Günther von, b. 1882. German general who commanded Army Group Centre on the Eastern front with outstanding success in the great defensive battles of 1942–3, and who for a short time was C.-in-C. in the West. From 1939 to 1940 he led the German 4th Army with conspicuous success in the Polish and French campaigns. As a result he was given command of Army Group Centre facing Moscow in the Kursk offensive. He distinguished himself in the long-drawn-out defensive battles that ensued, and when Runstedt fell from favour because of his realistic advice to Hitler in the impossible situation on the Western front, Kluge was sent to replace him on 1 July 1944 and had to face the rapidly growing strength of the Allied armies in Normandy. Although he was fighting such a critical battle, he was not made fully aware of Hitler's intentions and was simply ordered to 'hold on everywhere'. He attempted a counter-offensive at Avranches (where the American 3rd Army had broken out), but had not the strength to sustain it. He then had to mount a series of withdrawals—each of them too late to be tactically effective. He saw clearly what would be the fate of his men trapped near Falaise in Normandy, and said as much in his dispatches to Hitler, which urged surrender. On 17 August he was relieved of his command and replaced by Model.

Like many other army leaders, Kluge knew by this time that Germany had lost the war and realized that the only way of saving even part of the army was to surrender. His dispatches were too outspoken in this advice (though he continued to obey his orders to hold on) and Hitler came to believe that Kluge had not only made an approach to the Allies but had also been involved in the assassination plot of July 1944. Depressed by his failure in the field, and realizing that he was suspected of treachery by the Führer, Kluge committed suicide by poison on 18 August on his way back to Berlin, leaving a letter in which he defended his actions and proclaimed his loyalty.

Though Kluge understood and agreed with the opinions of those who were working against the régime, he was not a party to the assassination plot. However, he knew that records existed of his conversations with the conspirators and that this evidence against him was bound to be discovered. He had little interest in affairs outside his profession and considered that a soldier should not involve himself in politics. But he saw clearly that the war was lost and wanted it brought to an end before the country and army were destroyed.

KNOX, Jean, b. 1908. Chief Controller and Director of the A.T.S., the women's service of the British land forces, 1941–3. She had held various appointments in the

Service before succeeding Dame Helen Gwynne Vaughan as Director in July 1941.

In 1942 the problem of man-power in Britain was becoming more and more acute. With increasing war commitments, and with the prospect of an all-out attack on the Axis forces on the mainland of Europe, there was a crucial need for more men in the fighting corps and regiments. It became obvious that a better organized and more effective use of women was necessary than could be achieved by a voluntary system of service. For the first time in the U.K. the conscription of women was introduced, though not without much heart-burning and some opposition to the idea. During this period of expansion Mrs Knox was faced with complex problems of administration and welfare. But gradually women in the A.T.S. took over more than a hundred army trades previously reserved for men.

KOENIG, Pierre, b. 1898. Free French general in North Africa and later commander of the Free French Forces of the Interior.

In 1939 Koenig served in Norway as a captain. After the Allied collapse there he returned to France, and when France fell escaped to England and joined de Gaulle's supporters. He was sent to French Equatorial Africa, where his capture of Libreville in November 1940 helped to provide a welcome base for the Free French forces.

In the following year Koenig took part in the desert campaign in North Africa against Rommel. In June he and a small force were besieged in the fortress of Bir Hakeim on the Gazala Line. For 10 days Koenig resisted the determined attacks of the German Panzers, supported by Stuka aircraft. Ordered to abandon Bir Hakeim on 10 June, Koenig escaped with the greater part of his force. The newspaper headline 'Rommel Beaten by de Gaulle's Troops' was, if not the exact truth, at least an expression of the psychological effect of Koenig's stand. It was the first time that Free French forces had opposed the Germans in a major battle, and Allied propaganda turned a defeat into a 'famous victory'.

Later Koenig served under Eisenhower

as commander of Free French forces in France, and co-ordinated the Resistance in preparation for the D-Day invasion of 1944. After the liberation of Paris he became military governor of the city. One of his chief tasks was the re-establishment of law and order: many of the Resistance groups were not inclined to accept the authority of de Gaulle's provisional government.

KOGA, Mineichi, b. 1882. Japanese admiral, until 1944 C.-in-C. of the Japanese combined fleet. Koga succeeded Admiral Yamamoto as head of the Japanese navy after the latter's death in April 1943. But he developed no new strategy to halt the steady deterioration of the Japanese position in the Pacific, choosing instead to follow his predecessor's policy of defending the Pacific Islands at all costs.

Koga tried to reinforce the Japanese troops at Rabaul, but suffered a crippling defeat and was obliged to retreat. At the same time he failed to beat back the American attack on the Gilbert Islands, suffering heavy losses—over 20,000 tons of shipping sunk in 12 hours. Koga himself retired to Singapore, where he began to prepare the Japanese fleet for a confrontation with the U.S. fleet, realizing that this was inevitable sooner or later. Before his plans could be put into effect, Koga died in an air accident in March 1944.

KONOYE, Prince Fumimaro, b. 1891. Japanese statesman who, although he ceased to be Premier before the Japanese attack on Pearl Harbor, was listed by the Allies as a war criminal. He became Premier in June 1937, and although he adopted an expansionist policy he was not among the extreme militarists. At the time of his taking office he seemed, to the moderates, a good choice, those close to the throne considering that Konoye was a man of sufficient standing and reputation to be able to exercise the restraint that the militarists were not prepared to accept from an ordinary politician. But he did not succeed in preventing the war with China which broke out in the following month.

By 1938 Konoye was a very discouraged

man; he had failed in his aim of playing off one extremist faction against another and in January 1939 he resigned, to be recalled to the premiership in July 1940. He concluded the Tripartite Pact with the Axis powers, but his failure to reach agreement with the U.S.A. led to his resignation two months before the Japanese attack on the American Pacific fleet at Pearl Harbor in December 1941; he was replaced by General Tojo, who had been War Minister and who had no fear of extending the war.

In July 1945 Konoye was selected as a peace envoy to Moscow, but by 8 August Hiroshima had been laid waste by the atomic bomb and Russia shortly declared war on Japan. Konoye became vice-president of the post-war Cabinet, but when he found himself listed for trial as a war criminal he committed suicide.

He was posthumously condemned by a war crimes tribunal, chiefly on the grounds that he had borne a major responsibility for the setting up of a totalitarian state; his negotiations with the U.S.A. in 1941 were declared to be 'solely for the purpose of furthering Japan's own aims in conjunction with those of Germany and Italy'; and he was 'the chief protagonist of the plot to seize all territory between eastern India and Burma on the one hand and Australia and New Zealand on the other'.

KRAMER, Josef, b. 1906. Nazi official, one of the most notorious of the concentration camp commandants. A member of the S.S., Kramer entered the concentration camp service in 1934, and remained in it until his arrest in 1945. He spent some time at Natzweiler camp, where he supervised the construction of the gas chamber and was personally responsible for the gassing of 80 people. In May 1944 he was put in charge of an extermination camp at Auschwitz, in Poland.

In November 1944 Kramer became commandant of Belsen camp in N.W. Germany. Belsen, heretofore a relatively innocuous place of detention for Jews to be exchanged for German nationals abroad, was at the same time classified as a *Krankenlager*—a camp for sick prisoners transferred from all the other concentration camps in the area. Conditions in Belsen deteriorated rapidly as the number

of inmates increased. . from approximately
15,000 to more than 40,000. . with no
increase in food or accommodation.
Kramer tried to close the camp when
spotted fever swept through it, but was
thwarted by orders from Berlin. When the
camp was eventually liberated its inmates
were dying at the rate of several hundred
a day, and 13,000 corpses were found
lying unburied, along with the emaciated
survivors.

Although Kramer was called the 'Beast of
Belsen' in contemporary newspaper headlines, few substantiated charges of personal
cruelty were brought against him at his
trial. He seems rather to have been a
blindly obedient and totally conscience-
less functionary, who carried out all
orders as efficiently as possible. He was
found guilty of war crimes in November
1945 and executed.

KRETSCHMER, Otto, b. 1912. German
U-Boat commander who, before his capture
in 1941, was credited with sinking almost
350,000 tons of Allied shipping, including
3 armed merchant cruisers and a destroyer.
He was, in the words of Admiral George
Creasy, Britain's head of anti-submarine
warfare at the time, 'the most efficient and
the most competent U-Boat commanding
officer that Germany produced'. At the
outbreak of war he was given command of
the *U-23*, a small coastal attack submarine, and after 9 patrols with this (on
one of which he sank the destroyer H.M.S.
Daring) he was transferred to the ocean-
going *U-99*. It was at this time that he
began to employ the tactics of convoy
infiltration and surface attack that became
his trademark. After one patrol, during
which he sank 7 ships, he was awarded the
Knight's Cross for the greatest tonnage
sunk by a submarine commander in one
voyage. Later in the same year he won the
Oak Leaves, Germany's highest decoration
for valour in the face of the enemy. After
a number of Atlantic patrols round the
south-western approaches to the Channel
and the Irish Sea, he gained the distinction
of being the first German submarine
commander to sink more than a quarter
of a million tons of shipping.

On 27 March 1941 the *U-99*, in company with the *U-100* (commanded by
another 'ace', Schepke), was trapped by

the destroyers H.M.S. *Walker* and H.M.S.
Vanos while returning from an Atlantic
patrol. Kretschmer and his crew scuttled
their boat and surrendered. He spent the
remainder of the war in P.O.W. camps in
Britain and Canada.

KRUPP von BOHLEN, Alfried, b. 1907.
German arms manufacturer. In 1939 he
was one of three deputy directors of the
vast Krupp concern whose Essen armament factories had contributed immeasur-
ably to the military strength of Germany.
He was in charge of the cardinal department of Mining and Armaments. His
father had actively ingratiated himself
with the Nazis, but, although still theo-
retically in control, was by that time
senile. Alfried's position was challenged
only by the rivalry of Loesser, another
deputy director.

Between 1939 and 1943 Alfried Krupp
von Bohlen was chiefly responsible for
incorporating industries within German-
occupied territories into the Krupp
industrial empire; he also had to ensure
that a continuous and increasing supply
of Krupp's armaments reached the German forces. Entire factories were dis-
mantled, transported to Germany, and
there rebuilt. In 1942 Krupp travelled to
the Ukraine to supervise the take-over of
its iron and steel industry. The Mariupol
electro-steel works were reconstructed at
Berthewerke, Breslau. That was the year
in which 'Fat Gustav', an enormous
siege-gun, made its bow. It had been
ordered originally for use against the
Maginot Line, but was completed too late
even for use against Stalingrad. However,
Krupp eventually supervised its delivery
and installation, and watched it go into
action against Sebastopol, which it
devastated with 53 7-ton shells.

In July 1942 at a meeting with Speer,
minister for armaments and war production, Krupp agreed to the forcible employ-
ment of 45,000 Russian civilians in his
steel plants and 120,000 P.O.W.s, plus
another 6,000 Russian civilians in the coal
mines; all of these people were at a lower
standard of physical fitness than would be
acceptable in German civilians. Some
Germans were reluctant to use impressed
labour, but Krupp was even willing to use
the inmates of concentration camps. For

example, the Mariupol project was manned by 5,000 prisoners from a nearby camp which Krupp visited on one of his tours of inspection. In accordance with the policy of establishing factories 'near known sources of labour', a shell-factory was set up at Auschwitz, the site of the notorious concentration camps, during 1943. Many of the occupied countries were visited by Krupp officials in order to recruit labourers, and Krupp female employees were trained by the S.S. as guards for Romanian and Czechoslovak female slave labourers.

In 1943 the 'Lex Krupp' was passed, exempting the Krupp concern from inheritance tax. Bertha Krupp von Bohlen, Alfried's mother (and a Krupp by birth), renounced her title of inheritance, and Alfried became sole proprietor of the entire industrial empire. In the same year he was awarded the Nazi Cross for meritorious war service and was made War Economy Leader, responsible for the mobilization of the full resources of the German armament industry. But in March 1943 Essen suffered its first major air attack, and by 1944, when Krupp was arrested by a unit of the U.S. army, the works there had been largely destroyed and other Krupp works badly damaged. In 1948 Krupp was charged as a war criminal. Evidence of the barbarous treatment accorded to inmates of the 53

Krupp labour camps secured a verdict of guilty, and Krupp was sentenced to 12 years' imprisonment with confiscation of his property.

KURIBAYASHI, Tadamichi, b. 1885. Japanese general responsible for the defence of Iwo Jima. The island, between the Japanese islands and the Marianas, was of great strategic importance. Kuribayashi started to build a third airport on the island and to construct vast and intricate defences. Several miles of tunnels were constructed as fortresses, and the order to troops was: 'Each man will kill 10 of the enemy before dying.' There were 23,000 Japanese soldiers on the island when U.S. forces landed on 19 February 1945. Despite fierce opposition the U.S. troops occupied an airfield and the mountainous south of the island within 5 days. The battle for the central areas was bitter, and although the island was declared secure on the 16th it was not until 26 March that all resistance ended. Only 1,000 Japanese survived, while the Americans suffered 26,000 casualties, including 6,800 dead.

Kuribayashi telegraphed on 15 March: 'Am determined to go out and make banzai charges against the enemy at midnight on the 17th.' But on 23 March another message came: 'To all officers and men of Chichi Jiwa, goodbye.'

L

LACEY, J. H. ('Ginger'), b. 1917. British fighter pilot who destroyed more enemy aircraft during the Battle of Britain than any other pilot in Fighter Command.

Lacey was a Yorkshireman and a pre-war flying instructor. He joined 501 Squadron in 1939. During his time with the squadron he shot down 27 enemy air-aircraft. It was probably Lacey who accounted for the Heinkel that bombed Buckingham Palace, though he lost his own plane in the operation and had to bale out. Between August and October 1940 Lacey regularly flew some 4 to 8 flights daily and destroyed 18 enemy air-craft, with 6 damaged and 4 others probably destroyed.

After leaving 501 Squadron in August 1941 Lacey spent a period of 19 months on non-operational postings in various parts of the U.K. In March 1943 he was transferred to India. There, too, he was kept off operational duties. But in November 1944 he was given command of No. 17 Squadron in Burma. Their task was to maintain the air-lift which was supplying the Allied troops with much-needed food and weapons. The air-lift at that time was being threatened by the Japanese offensive. Lacey survived a total of 87 combats during the course of the war.

LANGSDORFF, Hans, b. 1890. German naval officer, captain of the pocket battle-ship *Graf Spee*, which he scuttled after being trapped in Montevideo harbour by units of the Royal Navy.

At the outset of the war the *Graf Spee* was sent to prey on Allied shipping routes in the Atlantic to prevent food and other supplies from reaching the U.K. The Royal Navy searched for the *Graf Spee* for nearly three months before she was finally located—by intelligent anticipation—and forced to action by three cruisers, H.M.S. *Exeter*, *Ajax*, and *Achilles*, off the coast of Uruguay on 13 December 1939. The action became known as 'The Battle of the River Plate'.

The British cruisers inflicted consider-able damage in spite of the *Graf Spee*'s heavier armament. Langsdorff put into the harbour of Montevideo to effect

repairs at midnight on 13 December. He mistakenly supposed that the British had sent naval reinforcements and that a con-siderable force now awaited him at sea. On 17 December he landed his 300 P.O.W.s and most of his crew, took his ship out of port, and scuttled her at the mouth of the River Plate. He then com-mitted suicide. He left a note in which he said: 'I can now only show by my death that the fighting forces of the Third Reich are ready to die for the honour of the flag . . . I shall face my fate with firm faith in the cause and the future of the nation and of my Führer.'

Before the Royal Navy tracked him down Langsdorff and the *Graf Spee* had sunk 9 British ships totalling 50,000 tons —quite a considerable loss to Allied shipping. But he had not found a way of enabling the many German merchant ships in neutral South American ports to cross the Atlantic safely, carrying badly needed supplies to Germany. A humane man, Langsdorff was careful of the lives of his own and of the enemy's men. Not one British life was lost through his actions against merchantmen.

LARSEN, Leif, b. 1906. Norwegian fisher-man, whose exploits as a member of the Royal Norwegian Navy's Special Service Unit made him an almost legendary figure. After the occupation of Norway by the Germans in 1940 Larsen worked with the British S.O.E. In the course of its secret war S.O.E. organized the escape of hun-dreds of Norwegians to Britain. Many of these patriots later returned to their home-land trained to encourage resistance and sabotage. Larsen himself took an active part in running the celebrated 'Shetland bus', which carried arms, men, and sup-plies to Norway from Britain.

The service was born in December 1940, when Captain Larsen, with a volunteer crew, joined the planners in Britain. At first all they had at their disposal were 4 ancient, rather unseaworthy, boats. Eventually they were able to build up a small fleet of Arctic whalers, British motor torpedo boats, and American submarine chasers. The crews were all Norwegian, and Larsen himself led many expeditions, performing acts of great gallantry. The Norwegians laid mines, carried arms and explosives for the Norwegian Resistance, and ferried S.O.E. agents to Norway. On the return journeys they never failed to bring back eager Norwegian volunteers for training in Britain. Frequently Norwegian V.I.P.s were among the passengers.

After 1942 the service was expanded rapidly. More than 80 voyages were made during the winter of 1943–4 without a single loss. In the following summer business boomed.

'Shetland bus' boats were also involved in spectacular raids—such as those on the Lofoten Islands and Vagso. A year before midget submarines crippled the German battleship *Tirpitz* at Altenfiord in 1943, Larsen was involved as a guide to even smaller under-water craft, the 'Chariots', in an attempt to sink the battleship. The Chariots were 'human torpedoes'—two men in diving gear riding astride a tiny craft—towed by Norwegian fishing vessels. This attempt was unsuccessful because of rough weather.

Larsen continued with his daring exploits until the end of the war. He became one of the most decorated men in the entire Allied forces.

LASSEN, Anders, b. 1920. Danish commando who won the V.C. for extraordinary gallantry. Working as a cabin boy when the war broke out, he went to Britain where, in January 1941, he and 13 other Danes swore to fight with the Allies to free Denmark. After joining a Commando special unit, he saw action in West Africa, where he was decorated for his part in hijacking the Italian ship *Duchessa d'Aosta*. In 1942 he took part in several raids on the Channel Islands and the French coast.

Late in 1942 Lassen was transferred to the Special Boat Service, a Commando unit operating in the Mediterranean. He led an attack on the Kastelli Pediada airport in German-occupied Crete, damaging or destroying German bombers there. Lassen was later posted to the Aegean, where he took part in raids on the Dodecanese Islands. After his unit moved its base to Italy in August 1944 Lassen led a successful raid on Karasovici in Yugoslavia. In Greece, when Athens was liberated, Lassen and a handful of men entered Saloniki (Thessalonica) before the Germans had evacuated it. He was then

made commandant of Crete with the rank of major before again transferring to Italy in February 1945. While leading an attack upon the Germans at Lake Commacchio, he was killed. For this exploit Lassen received a posthumous V.C.

LATTRE de TASSIGNY, Jean de, b. 1889. French general, commander of the Free French forces which landed with the Allied invaders of Normandy in 1944. Already a general and Chief of Staff to the French 5th Army in 1939, at the start of the war he took a field command and acquitted himself with distinction at the head of the 14th Division at Aisne.

After France's capitulation in 1940 de Lattre considered that his loyalty was to the army and to the Vichy régime. He was sent to a command in Tunisia, but because of his supposed Allied sympathies was soon recalled. In 1942 he was sentenced to 10 years' imprisonment for his denunciation of the German violation of unoccupied France.

In 1943, after escaping from Riom prison, de Lattre was secretly flown to Britain by the R.A.F. He then returned to North Africa as commander of the French 1st Army. He took a major part in the Allied liberation of France in 1944, leading his troops up the Rhône, across the Rhine, and finally to the Danube. In Berlin he signed the German capitulation on behalf of France.

De Lattre was highly conscious of the role of his army as being that of French soldiers fighting for France. His troops displayed traditional French military qualities of spirit and tenacity, with impressive results. Churchill praised de Lattre's achievements: 'I send all my congratulations on the brilliant exploits of your young army.'

As early as November 1943 de Lattre had stated the view that Germany would not be overcome until the Allies had crushed its forces on their own territory. He predicted Hitler would hold on till the last and finally 'go up like a volcano'.

LAVAL, Pierre, b. 1883. French politician, one of the chief figures of the Vichy régime for much of the war. Together with Vidkun Quisling in Norway, Laval was regarded by the Allies, perhaps unjustly, as the most notorious collaborator of the war.

On 23 June 1940, the day after the signing of the Franco-German armistice, Laval convened the Assembly which made Marshal Pétain head of the government. He himself was chosen *Président du Conseil*, and he served as foreign minister and deputy to Pétain. In July Laval successfully persuaded the National Assembly at Vichy of the necessity for ratifying the armistice with Germany, and abiding by it in letter and spirit. He could at this stage see no possibility of Germany losing the war, and he urged Frenchmen to face the facts and make sure that France had a proper share in Hitler's 'New Order' in Europe. Laval was dismissed in December 1940, but was recalled in April 1942. By now it seemed to him that Germany's victory was no longer a foregone conclusion. He now took the line that France was able to bargain with Germany, and this he attempted to do, with some small success. The result was that both sides viewed him with distrust. Laval seems genuinely to have worked in what he saw as the country's best interest, but in doing so he made concessions to the German occupiers that many Frenchmen considered totally unacceptable. He took strong measures against the Resistance in France and assisted the Germans in rooting out all those who worked actively against them.

At a late stage of the war—the end of 1943—the writing was on the wall for all to see, and Laval, who would probably by now have liked to seek some accommodation with the Allies, was forced instead to bolster the Vichy government by accepting the help of the extreme pro-Germans. In August 1944, after the Allied invasion of N.W. Europe, he tried to convene a meeting of the National Assembly in Paris. But, under German pressure, he was obliged to move his virtually defunct government to Sigmaringen in Germany. He escaped to Switzerland and thence to Spain, where he mistakenly expected to be welcomed. He was put on trial in France for treason and was found guilty and sentenced to death. He was executed by shooting after an unsuccessful bid at suicide.

Laval took an essentially practical view of his responsibilities as a politician, and maintained that his empirical approach to France's political problems was unimpeachably patriotic. He had as little respect and liking for the reactionary idealism of the Pétainists as he had for those to whom France's honour was the most important of her possessions. His pre-war notoriety as co-author of the Hoare-Laval pact in 1935 (which proposed to appease Italy at the expense of Ethiopia), the shifting policies consequent on his 'practical nationalism', and even his small and swarthy appearance made him anathema to those who looked to the resurgence of a self-respecting and purified France.

LAYCOCK, Robert E., b. 1907. British Commando leader, Chief of Combined Operations during the D-Day invasion of France in 1944.

In June 1940, at the request of Churchill and Admiral Keyes, Laycock raised one of the first Commando units from the Household Brigade; he was an officer in the Royal Horse Guards. In 1941 he was given command of a Special Service brigade assigned to General Wavell's Middle Eastern army. The job of this assault force was to make raids behind enemy lines. But from the start 'Layforce', as it soon became known, was hampered by the chronic shortage of British manpower in the Middle Eastern theatre. After the failure of an attack in Crete in May 1941, which Laycock led personally, Layforce was disbanded. Laycock led the unsuccessful attack on Rommel's supposed H.Q. in which Geoffrey Keyes won the V.C. and was killed. After it he spent several weeks wandering in the desert before he was found by the advancing 8th Army. Laycock had had with him a copy of *The Wind in the Willows*. This he had read aloud to Sergeant Terry, his only companion, to while away the boredom. Terry's first words on finding himself in safety were: 'Thank God I shan't have to hear any more about that bloody Mr Toad!'

Laycock later led a Royal Marine Commando battalion in the invasion of Sicily and of the Italian mainland. In 1943 he was promoted to major-general and succeeded Mountbatten as Chief of Combined Operations, and held this post for the rest of the war. His main job was to integrate forces for the D-Day landings.

LAYTON, Sir Geoffrey, b. 1884. British admiral, C.-in-C. in Ceylon during the period of consolidation against the Japanese advance in Asia. Layton took part in the Norwegian campaign of April 1940, and shortly afterwards was appointed C.-in-C. Eastern Fleet. He was relieved for a few days by Admiral Phillips in December 1941, but, after the sinking by the Japanese of H.M.S. *Prince of Wales* and H.M.S. *Repulse*, in which action Phillips was killed, Layton was again C.-in-C. of what was now a virtually non-existent fleet. He set up his H.Q. in Colombo, Ceylon, and was technically responsible for 'China Force' under Wavell, but could do little to help in Burma.

Immediately after his arrival in Ceylon, in mid January 1942, Layton signalled to London the need for a powerful central authority. On 5 March, after the fall of Singapore, he was appointed C.-in-C. Ceylon, with wide-ranging powers; the Governor, the civil administration, and all naval, air, and civil authorities in the area (which included the Maldive Islands) came under his authority. Layton set to work energetically: the island's defences were properly established; the port was reorganized; the race-course was turned into an air-strip; and civil defence measures were inaugurated. On 26 March Admiral Somerville took over as C.-in-C. Eastern Fleet. On 5th April 1942 Ceylon was attacked by carrier-borne Japanese aircraft, and two cruisers, an aircraft carrier, and some other naval vessels were sunk. Admiral Nagumo, the Japanese commander, then withdrew to the Pacific and Admiral Somerville to East Africa. In May Layton reported 'the people have got their chins up and are pulling well together', and by then the danger to Ceylon was receding.

At a later stage Mountbatten set up his H.Q. in Ceylon as Supreme Allied Commander, S.E. Asia. However, Layton remained in his post as C.-in-C. Ceylon for some time after Mountbatten's advent.

LEAHY, William, b. 1875. American admiral and diplomat who in 1940 became ambassador to Vichy France. After the U.S.A. joined the war in 1941 he became personal Chief of Staff to President Roosevelt, and in this capacity took part in all the major policy decisions. He attended the Teheran Conference in November 1943, and in 1944 was honoured with the newly created title of fleet-admiral. After Roosevelt's death Leahy stayed on as personal Chief of Staff to President Truman.

Leahy's position as ambassador of a neutral power in Vichy France was difficult. He handled the situation tactfully but with no real insight. Roosevelt's orders were to approve French resistance to Hitler without doing injury to American neutrality, and to prevent the French fleet from falling into German hands. Leahy fully realized the danger to American security of German naval power and supported all aid to the British, short of involving the U.S.A. in the war. But his disapproval of de Gaulle (who, he thought, was 'lusting after power') caused Leahy badly to misjudge the French situation. He remained oblivious to the growing support for de Gaulle and could not see that the pliancy of Vichy to Germany's growing demands meant that to support Vichy was to support Germany. Even after returning to America in 1942 Leahy continued to advocate support for the Vichy régime in France and its colonies.

As Roosevelt's Chief of Staff, Leahy was responsible for liaison between the President and the chiefs of the armed services. He was extremely successful as chairman of the American Joint Chiefs of Staff Committee, and had a greatly admired gift for distilling an agreed policy from a variety of strongly held opinions.

LECLERC, Jacques Philippe, b. 1902. French general, a daring and skilful soldier, who commanded the French armoured units participating in the D-Day invasion of France in 1944.

Captured by the Germans at Lille in May 1940, Leclerc escaped and rejoined the French army, but was again captured. After another escape he joined de Gaulle in England. He went to Africa, where he was first military governor of Chad and

Cameroun and then G.O.C. French Equatorial Africa. Here he did much to rebuild French self-respect and to create a French base for Free France.

In December 1942 Leclerc led a Free French force from Chad on a 1,500-mile journey across the desert, attacking various Italian garrisons on the way before at last joining the British 8th Army in Libya in January 1943. His most important command came in 1944 when he was given charge of the 2nd French Armoured Division for the Normandy invasion. This, at Churchill's express wish, was 'to give real significance to the French re-entry into France'. In August 1944 Leclerc's troops entered Paris and he took the formal surrender of the city. His forces continued with the Allied advance across France, liberating Strasbourg and finally reaching Berchtesgaden, Hitler's Bavarian eyrie. In 1945 Leclerc was sent with a French force to Indo-China, but he was able to do little to resolve the confused situation there.

Leclerc's escapes from German captivity made him a legendary figure to Frenchmen. He carried out some of the most audacious actions of the war, and had a preference for situations where the odds were against him. General Brooke considered him 'the best type of French soldier . . . hard-bitten, capable, and of great charm'. An American war correspondent summed him up as 'a sophisticated d'Artagnan come to life again in the twentieth century'. His real name was Philippe, Comte de Hauteclocque. He adopted the name Leclerc during the war.

LEESE, Sir Oliver, b. 1894. British general, Montgomery's successor as commander of the 8th Army, and in the last stages of the war C.-in-C. of Allied land forces in S.E. Asia.

Leese was brought in to command the 30th Corps of the British 8th Army in North Africa after Montgomery's 'purge' of the older men whom he considered responsible for the army's poor performance in the Desert. He proved an able tactician, and his corps distinguished itself in the Battle of El Alamein. In spearheading the Allied invasion of Sicily Leese gained further distinction. As C.-in-C. of the 8th Army in Italy Leese

pressed the Germans under Kesselring into gradual retreat. A capable and popular leader, Leese was assiduous and resourceful in battle. To Harold Macmillan, who saw him in action, Leese typified the 'new general . . . driving along crowded and muddy roads, which the enemy may actually be shelling as he drives, waving and calling to the men', very different from the 'remote, blimpish figures of 1914–18 . . . in limousine Rolls'.

LEIGH-MALLORY, Sir Trafford, b. 1892. British air marshal, commander of the Allied air forces in the D-Day invasion of France in 1944.

At the outset of the war as commander of No. 12 (Fighter) Group his chief task was to defend the Midlands and the east coast shipping routes from the German Luftwaffe. He took a leading part in the Battle of Britain. In December 1940 he was transferred to No. 11 (Fighter) Group and overcame strong opposition, switching the R.A.F. from defensive to offensive tactics. This move was amply justified by the course of the war in the air.

In November 1942 Leigh-Mallory became head of Fighter Command, and was an early choice as Air C.-in-C. for the planned 'Second Front'. By December 1943, when he became air chief marshal, few German aircraft dared to approach the British coast, and no enemy aircraft penetrated his air defence of the D-Day invasion preparations. When the invasion began Leigh-Mallory commanded 9,000 British and American aircraft. This force cleared the Luftwaffe from the skies and severely hampered German land forces by disrupting their road and rail communications. Leigh-Mallory directed the operation with the sure touch of a master.

In November 1944, with the war in Europe almost over, Leigh-Mallory was appointed Air C.-in-C. in S.E. Asia. While on his way there he and his wife were killed in an air crash.

LEMAY, Curtis, b. 1906. American air general who developed a number of advanced bombing tactics that were a major contribution to the success of the Allied air offensives against Germany and Japan. The best-known of Lemay's innovations were the technique of pattern bombing—employed with devastating effect against Germany in the later years of the war—and the 'combat box' formation. These tactics were put into effect by Lemay while with the U.S. 8th Air Force in Europe from 1942 to 1944. Subsequently he commanded the B-29 formations in India, and at the beginning of 1945 was appointed to the U.S. 21st Bomber Command in the Mariana Islands. With this force he was engaged in attacks on Japanese cities and he developed techniques of low-level attack which greatly increased the effectiveness of bombing, and made the attacking force difficult to intercept.

LEOPOLD III, b. 1901. King of the Belgians, who surrendered his country unconditionally to its German invaders in May 1940.

When German forces invaded Belgium in 1940 Leopold assumed command of the army and appealed to the Allies for help. French and British troops were sent to aid the Belgian army, but by 28 May Leopold felt that Belgium had no chance and ordered his forces to surrender. There was considerable opposition to the King's capitulation, headed by Pierlot the Prime Minister. The surrender was declared illegal, ministers were released from allegiance to the Crown, and the army stated its intention to resist. But it was too late for effective action. The King was captured by the Germans and confined in the Palace of Laeken near Brussels. When the Allies invaded Europe in 1944 Leopold was taken to Germany, and was liberated by the Americans in 1945.

Leopold's surrender in 1940 inevitably left France open to the German invader. As a result his action was strongly criticized in France and Britain as well as Belgium. In the light of post-war evidence, much of this criticism was probably not justified.

Many Belgians were opposed to Leopold's moves to return to Belgium after the war, and his brother Charles's regency was extended. In 1950, after a commission had examined his actions of 1940 and exonerated him from guilt, Leopold was finally allowed to return to Belgium.

LEY, Robert, b. 1890. German Nazi leader and head of Hitler's Labour Front from 1933 until his death in 1945. A chemist by profession, he was one of Hitler's earliest followers, his membership in the Nazi party dating back to 1924. During the war he supervised the mobilization of foreign, as well as German, manpower for war work. His close personal friendship with Hitler, which lasted until the Führer's suicide, led to a wealth of appointments for him—director of the Union of Germans Living Abroad, head of the Strength through Joy recreational movement, and, finally, in 1945, chief of the Adolf Hitler Volunteer Corps of guerrilla fighters.

Referred to contemptuously by Fritz Thyssen, head of the steel trust, as 'a stammering drunkard', Ley had an unstable personality and was erratic and inept as an administrator. In 1944 he joined Goebbels in a radical group that called for even more extreme measures. He also ingratiated himself with Hitler by accusing the Officer Corps of collective guilt for the abortive bomb plot on Hitler's life in July 1944.

In 1945 he sought to escape from the Allies by fleeing to the mountains near Berchtesgaden, but was captured by U.S. troops. On 25 October 1945 he hanged himself in the Nuremberg prison before he could be tried as a war criminal. Among Ley's effects was a political testament in which, despite a lifetime of bitter anti-Semitism, he recommended a complete reconciliation between Germans and Jews.

LIDDELL HART. *See* HART, Basil Liddell.

LILLIE, Beatrice (Lady Peel), b. 1898. British comedienne who became one of the greatest war-time entertainers. Already internationally noted for her wit and sophistication on the stage, 'Bee' Lillie gave her first war-time shows at Scapa Flow and Rosyth. In 1940 she followed these with a tour, with John Gielgud, of camps throughout the U.K., when they presented plays by Noël Coward.

In December 1942 'Bee' Lillie gave shows at Malta and Gibraltar. She followed these up in the Mediterranean theatre by appearing with such other stars as Dorothy Dickson, Vivien Leigh, and Leslie Henson.

A war-time story about 'Bee' Lillie concerns the occasion on which she and some other entertainers were flying to Tripoli. One of the engines of their aircraft spluttered and stopped. To a hysterical girl who wanted to know what would happen if they crashed 'Bee' Lillie, with great aplomb, answered 'Two minutes' silence in the Ivy, dear.' (The Ivy restaurant in London—a popular resort of theatre people.) Beatrice Lillie helped to found London's 'Stage Door Canteen' for all ranks and nationalities of Allied Servicemen.

LINDEMANN. See CHERWELL, Lord.

LOTHIAN, Lord, b. 1882. Journalist and statesman, British ambassador to the U.S.A. from 1939 to 1940. Lothian's service as ambassador during the crucial first 15 months of the war was the culmination of a lifetime's study of international affairs.

In spite of this background, the announcement in 1939 of Lothian's appointment as ambassador came as a surprise, for he had had neither diplomatic training nor the experience of high political office. The assets which he brought to his new job, however—his knowledge of foreign affairs and, most important, his familiarity with American life and thought—compensated for his lack of official qualifications. As a journalist and as secretary of the Rhodes Trust he had spent much time travelling in the U.S.A. and meeting the country's leading men. He liked Americans and was able and willing to appreciate their points of view. This, coupled with his affable personality and his tolerant, 'democratic' attitude, made him popular with an American public distrustful of the British—especially those with titles.

Lothian saw his main task in America as that of dispelling the age-old suspicion of Great Britain which had overshadowed relations between the two countries. He set out to accomplish this by presenting the American public with a frank and clear picture of the reasons for the U.K.'s involvement in the war, the sacrifices her people were making, and the goals for which she was fighting. He also pointed out the danger to the interests of the U.S.A. which a Nazi victory would

involve, but he never pontificated or tried to tell the Americans what to do.

Lothian's approach was tremendously successful. In 17 speeches and a broadcast he helped to evoke a climate of opinion favourable to the U.K. and her struggle against Hitler, a change of public attitude that was of immense importance for the later American entry into the war.

Lothian's death in December 1940 was mourned in both the U.S.A. and the U.K., for his loss as a bridge of understanding between the two nations seemed irreparable at the time. On the day before his death he made his last appeal to the American people: 'If you back us you won't be backing a quitter. The issue now depends largely on what you decide to do. Nobody can share that responsibility with you.'

LOVAT, Lord, b. 1911. British soldier, one of the most successful of Commando leaders. He was the 24th chief of the Clan Fraser, and from 1934 to 1937 served in the Scots Guards. From 1939 he commanded the Lovat Scouts, first as a captain and then with the rank of brigadier. His father had raised the Scouts for service in the Boer War.

In 1942, at Churchill's suggestion, the Scouts were made a Commando unit 'by reason of their origin, traditions, and composition'. The new unit replaced Laycock's 'Layforce' in the Middle East. In 1942 Lovat led the 4th Commando in the Dieppe raid. In the Normandy landings in 1944 he commanded the 1st Special Service Brigade, attended by his personal piper. But he sustained wounds that forced him out of active service. He later accompanied General Laycock to Moscow to discuss river-crossing techniques with the Russians. He favourably impressed the inscrutable Stalin, who allowed that he was 'drawn to these young military types'.

From May to July 1945 Lovat was Joint Under Secretary at the Foreign Office in Churchill's caretaker government.

LOW, David, b. 1891. Political cartoonist, a New Zealander by birth, who became one of the most influential commentators on public affairs in pre-war and war-time Britain. His mordant observations were effected by means of familiar, standard figures who appeared in his cartoons and whose personalities embodied complete (real or supposed) ways of life and thought. Among the best-known of these were 'Colonel Blimp', whose fat, apoplectic person represented reactionary Toryism, and the amiable cart-horse that represented the T.U.C. Low was political cartoonist of the *Evening Standard*, and lived in London throughout the war. His work was also syndicated in free Europe and the Commonwealth, and was published in *Colliers* and the *New York Times*.

Early in the war he produced a Penguin book of cartoons, *Europe Since Versailles*, which sold a quarter of a million copies. Two other books of cartoons followed. As an independent and uncommitted commentator he had the knack of expressing the mood of the British people in moments of crisis as, for example, in his cartoon *All Behind You, Winston*. During the Nazi-Soviet *détente* he tried to condemn the Russians without irretrievably alienating them. Late in the war an exhibition of his cartoons was mounted in Russia, and he contributed to the humorous magazine *Krokodil*. His correspondence with a Soviet cartoonist, Efimov, was given wide publicity.

Political cartoonists are invariably controversial figures, and during the latter part of the war Low was widely criticized in the House of Commons and elsewhere. But as a self-appointed gadfly he did not worry unduly about adverse reactions to his stings.

LYNN, Vera, b. 1916. British radio singer, known as 'the Forces' Sweetheart'. During the war she starred in a radio programme called 'Sincerely Yours', the first of a now traditional pattern, which sent a message and a song to Servicemen abroad. Her most famous song, 'We'll meet again', had tremendous poignancy in a time of so many partings. Her voice, also, had a quality that was in accord with the hopes and yearnings of men a long way from home: it was warm and endearing, and it was also the voice of 'the girl next door'. Vera Lynn broadcast for E.N.S.A. from 1942 to 1944, and she took part in the final broadcast in November 1945. She made several tours abroad to entertain the troops, reaching India in 1943 and taking part in camp concerts within a few miles of the fighting line in Burma.

LYTTELTON, Oliver, b. 1893. British industrialist and statesman, a member of the War Cabinet from 1941 to 1945. His family was distinguished not only for its ancient lineage but also for generations of public service. Before the war he had achieved great success as the managing director of the British Metal Corporation. His expertise in this field was put to good use during the war when, as Controller of Non-Ferrous Metals, he was responsible for the purchase, licensing, and allocation of metals necessary for the production of war supplies.

In 1940 he was appointed President of the Board of Trade, and took on a range of duties which included such diverse matters as the rationing of clothes and the control of exports. This was followed in 1941 by his appointment as Minister of State in the Middle East, with a seat in the War Cabinet. His job in the Middle East was one of enormous scope and difficulty, to relieve the C.-in-C.s of all unnecessary political and economic responsibilities and, in matters of military policy, to furnish them with any relevant political information and guidance. He also acted as overall co-ordinator and arbiter for the Service and other authorities in the Middle East.

He knew the ways of Whitehall inside out, and his work in this post was of immense value to the war effort. This was followed by an equally distinguished tenure of office as Minister of Production between 1942 and 1945. In that position he was the minister holding responsibility for all aspects of war production. His recognition of the need to co-operate with trade union leaders, coupled with the fact that he made no pretension to control labour, resulted in a refreshing and workable partnership.

M

MacARTHUR, Douglas, b. 1880. American general who, in 1942, directed the dogged but unsuccessful defence of the Bataan peninsula and Corregidor in the Philippines against the Japanese after the U.S.A. had entered the war, and who, in 1945, as Allied Supreme Commander in the Pacific, received the Japanese surrender on behalf of the Allies. MacArthur, who had been military adviser to the Philippine government, was recalled to active duty in the U.S. army in July 1941 and appointed commanding general of the U.S. army forces in the Far East. The Philippine army, by an earlier agreement, was incorporated in the forces that he now directed. The Japanese, by their success at Pearl Harbor, had been enabled to establish a blockade of the Philippines, and in December 1941 they landed 200,000 soldiers on Luzon. MacArthur's forces were less than half this number. He adopted the defensive strategy of retiring to the Bataan peninsula and the island of Corregidor, while declaring Manila an open city. Although poorly supplied, he fought a delaying action against the Japanese that lasted well into the spring. President Roosevelt then ordered MacArthur to go to Canberra in Australia as C.-in-C. of the newly named S.W. Pacific Area and on 11 March 1942 he left Luzon for Australia, where he declared: 'I came through and I shall return.'

He soon won the confidence of the Australian Prime Minister, John Curtin, and made the bold decision to defend Australia from New Guinea, establishing his base at Port Moresby. After the great naval battle of Midway in June 1942 had changed the balance of power in the Pacific, MacArthur gained control of Papua by late January 1943, using ground, sea, and air forces. In this campaign he worked out a strategy, which he later used with great effect in 'island hopping' to the Philippines. His aim was to flush out the enemy, or render him impotent, by severing his lines of communication rather than by direct frontal attacks. The result of this strategy, summarized as 'hit 'em where they ain't', was that he achieved his aims with comparatively low casualties. His

plan for the 1943 offensive was to advance simultaneously along two lines from Guadalcanal and from Papua, securing northern New Guinea and the Solomons group, and then converging to pinch off the Japanese stronghold at Rabaul. By the spring of 1944 Rabaul was cut off and there was no longer any need for an assault on it. The Japanese 18th Army was surrounded in New Guinea and had ceased to be a threat.

In July 1944 MacArthur and Admiral Nimitz attended a conference with Roosevelt and General Marshall at Pearl Harbor. MacArthur's plan for the re-conquest of the Philippines was adopted. MacArthur and President Osmena landed with advance forces on Leyte on 20 October 1944. The naval battle of Leyte Gulfe on 23 October lasted for three days and preceded further fierce fighting against General Yamashita's army. But Leyte was conquered by 26 December. The Luzon landings took place on 9 January 1945. The Americans entered Manila on 4 February, and on 28 February constitutional government was restored to the Philippines. On 6 April MacArthur was given command of all ground troops in the Pacific, while Nimitz controlled all naval units. The island conquest continued: Iwo Jima was captured by 16 March, and Okinawa by 21 June. When, in August 1945, atom bombs forced the sudden surrender of Japan, MacArthur, as supreme commander for the Allied powers, was the chief Allied signatory at the formal surrender on 2 September 1945 on board the battleship *Missouri* in Tokyo Bay.

The military strategist Liddell Hart, one of MacArthur's greatest admirers, summed up his achievements in these words: 'MacArthur was supreme among the generals. His combination of strong personality, strategic grasp, tactical skill, operative mobility, and vision put him a class above Allied commanders in any theatre.'

McCREERY, Sir Richard, b. 1898. British general, highly successful as a strategic planner in the North African campaign, and later distinguished as a field commander. In 1940 he was in France with the B.E.F. and, after Dunkirk, in the Home Forces. In May 1941 General Brooke, the C.I.G.S., sent McCreery to North Africa to advise General Auchinleck on tank warfare. However, McCreery's vociferous opposition to Auchinleck's proposals for the reorganization of his armoured forces lost him this post. But he was appointed Chief of Staff to General Alexander, Auchinleck's successor, in August 1942, and served with him for the rest of the Desert campaign. Alexander described him as 'one of those rare soldiers who are both exceptionally fine staff officers, and fine commanding officers in the field'. McCreery took a key role in the latter part of the Battle of El Alamein, in which his battle plan was adopted. Alexander stated: 'His was the key decision of the Alamein battle, nor have I any doubt that Monty was suitably grateful to his Chief of Staff.'

McCreery went with the 8th Army to Sicily and commanded the British 10th Corps in the Salerno landings of September 1943. He later led this corps to Cassino where, on 17 January 1944, he began the onslaught on the Germans. McCreery and the 10th Corps made an important contribution to the hard-won victory in the lengthy battle that followed. In November 1944 McCreery was appointed commander of the 8th Army in succession to General Leese, and continued to force Kesselring's German troops north towards the River Po. The Italian campaign ended with the German surrender on 2 May 1945.

McEWEN, John, b. 1900. Australian statesman, from 1937 to 1939 Minister of the Interior, and then Minister for External Affairs and Air Minister. From 1941 to 1945 he was on the War Advisory Council, the coalition body that managed Australia's conduct of the war.

McEwen was a farmer and a leading member of the Country party, which represented rural as against commercial and industrial interests. The party's rather uncertain attitude to Australia's involvement in the European theatre finally lost it electoral support, and McEwen lost his ministerial offices.

In his term of office McEwen acquitted himself well as Air Minister, in which capacity he administered the Dominions Air Training Scheme. Australian air squadrons already made a valuable contribution to the Allied war effort in the critical early stages of the war—the Battle

of Britain and the North African offensive being two contests in which they particularly distinguished themselves.

MacFARLANE, Sir Frank Mason-, b. 1889. British general and diplomat. Early in the war he was head of Intelligence with the B.E.F. in Belgium. There was already much confusion on the Allied front, and this appears to have been aggravated by the operation of Intelligence. According to General Brooke, the C.I.G.S., the blame for this state of affairs lay mainly in the unsuitable organization of G.H.Q.: this was not attributable to Mason-MacFarlane. After the British evacuation from France and Belgium Mason-MacFarlane was posted to Gibraltar. After a short period there he led a British mission to Moscow with the job of studying conditions on the Eastern front and of reassuring Stalin of Britain's 'best intentions at all times'. He concluded that the Russians were unable to resist the Germans without American and British aid.

From 1942 to 1944 Mason-MacFarlane was Governor and G.O.C.-in C. of Gibraltar. There he received the Allied leaders at the time of the invasion of N.W. Africa in November 1942. In 1944 he was appointed Chief Commissioner of the Allied Control Commission for Italy following the Italian surrender. He incurred Churchill's anger for his rather uncompromising attitude towards Italy's political leaders. His policy was eventually endorsed by the Allies, and Bonomi, a socialist opponent of the Fascists, became Italy's Prime Minister. In 1945 Mason-MacFarlane returned to England, his health having deteriorated. He was elected Labour M.P. for North Paddington in the 'Forces' election of 1945, but had to retire because of poor health next year.

McGRIGOR, Rhoderick, b. 1893. British admiral, a determined fighting sailor. He commanded the battle-cruiser H.M.S. *Renown* in Admiral Somerville's famous 'Force H', based on Gibraltar. He helped to guard many convoys to Malta and the *Renown* also guarded the convoy route to West Africa against the German battle-cruisers *Scharnhorst* and *Gneisenau*. In May 1941 *Renown* was involved in the

pursuit of the *Bismarck*. McGrigor was
shortly afterwards promoted rear-admiral,
and served 1941–3 at the Admiralty as
Assistant Chief of Naval Staff (Weapons).
He planned and executed the naval attack
on the island of Pantellaria in 1943, and
later commanded one of the beaches in
the Sicily invasion. He was wounded
during operations off Calabria. After
four months in Sicily he became Flag
Officer at Taranto. He returned home in
March 1944 to command the 1st Cruiser
Squadron in the Home Fleet. In this
capacity he escorted convoys to Russia
and harassed the enemy in Norwegian
waters. He directed naval air operations
against the German battleship *Tirpitz* at
Altenfiord in April 1944, and in November
1944 he destroyed 10 of an 11-ship enemy
convoy off the Norwegian coast.

McGrigor was a determined Scotsman,
of very small stature, popular with his
officers and ratings. His fighting approach
was typified in an incident that occurred
while he was escorting a convoy to Russia.
McGrigor was informed of a U-Boat
pack converging on his ships, and signalled
back: 'Damn the U-Boats, cleave a way
through.'

McINDOE, Archibald, b. 1900. New
Zealand surgeon in Britain, famous during
the war for his work in rehabilitating the
badly burned. In September 1939 he went
to the Royal Victoria Hospital at East
Grinstead in Sussex as Consultant to the
R.A.F., and there set up an emergency
clinic for the treatment of burns and facial
injuries. His original team consisted of
anaesthetist John Hunter, theatre sister
Jill Mullins, and assistant surgeon Percy
Jeyes. McIndoe retained his civilian status
and with it a freedom of action that
enabled him to fight many crusades on
behalf of his patients. His work really
began during the Battle of Britain, when
large numbers of badly burned R.A.F.
men came under his care.

In the course of the war McIndoe was
responsible for the introduction of new
techniques in plastic surgery, but the most
revolutionary aspect of his procedure lay
in the fact that he took responsibility for
the mental well-being of his patients. For
example, the nature and probable length
of treatment were explained to them, dis-

cipline in the wards was relaxed, and the
men were encouraged to make use of the
facilities in East Grinstead, where, thanks
to McIndoe's initiative, a friendly welcome
awaited them. Again, thanks to his efforts,
the '90-day rule'—by which an injured
Serviceman after 90 days' absence was
invalided out of the service with consequent loss of pay and no possibility of
return to active service—was abolished.
Several ex-patients, indeed, later distinguished themselves in action.

He became president of the 'Guinea-
Pig Club' formed by airmen who had
passed through his hands and whose
high spirits were expressed in their anthem:

'We are McIndoe's army,
We are his guinea pigs,
With dermatomes and pedicles
Glass eyes and teeth and wigs.
And when we get our discharge,
We'll shout with all our might:
"Per ardua ad astra!"
We'd rather drink than fight.'

Funds which McIndoe raised for the
Guinea-Pigs were later converted into a
Trust Fund. He also raised money for
essential equipment and facilities at his
hospital, and succeeded in adding two new
wings—one paid for by Canada and the
other by the U.S.A.

McIndoe was a man of strong will, with
great energy and ability. The plight of the
burned flier ('one moment has turned him
from a Don Juan into an object of pity—
and it's too much [for him] to bear')
enlisted all his powerful compassion, and
his life was channelled into schemes for
his patients' welfare.

MACLEAN, Fitzroy, b. 1911. Leader of
the British Military Mission with Tito's
Partisans behind the German lines in
Yugoslavia. Maclean already had a
reputation as a linguist and an explorer
when, in 1941, he left the Foreign Office
to enlist in the army. In January 1942 he
joined the S.A.S. in Cairo, and took part
in two raids on Benghazi. From September
1942 he served in Iran, and organized the
kidnapping of General Zahidi.

In September 1943 Maclean was dropped
by parachute into Yugoslavia as leader of
the British Military Mission accredited to

General Tito. In 1943 the Partisan Resistance fighters in Yugoslavia numbered about 150,000 and were distributed throughout the country. They were organized in formations ultimately responsible to Tito, and they engaged in guerrilla warfare against German targets. In November Maclean reported to Anthony Eden in Cairo: he stressed the military effectiveness of the Partisans compared with General Mihajlović's rival Resistance group, the Četniks, and suggested that they be given supplies and air support. He returned with a Partisan delegation to see Churchill in Cairo and Marrakesh in December 1943; also to talk with King Peter, who described Maclean as 'self-confident and forceful'. Maclean's suggestions were adopted, and his mission was enlarged. He returned to Tito's new H.Q. at Drvar. In June 1944 German attacks forced Tito to move his H.Q. to the island of Vis.

In October Maclean took part in the fighting which led up to the liberation of Belgrade. He became British representative there and remained until the Tito-Šubašić government was formed in March 1945.

MACMILLAN, Harold, b. 1894. British statesman who played a major part in shaping Allied policies in the Mediterranean area during the war. A supporter of Anthony Eden at the time of the Munich crisis in 1938, he became an opponent of Neville Chamberlain and joined in the vote of censure which brought about Chamberlain's fall and Churchill's appointment in 1940. He served in the National government as Parliamentary Secretary, Ministry of Supply, from 1940 to 1942, and after a short spell at the Colonial Office became Minister Resident at the Allied H.Q., N.W. Africa.

The complex political situation in French North Africa, an American sphere of influence, gave Macmillan scope for his flair for diplomacy. He worked closely with the Americans, and won the confidence of Eisenhower and de Gaulle.

He was involved in the Casablanca Conference of January 1943 and in the negotiations leading to the Italian armistice of September, at which time he was advising Churchill concerning the sur-

render, signed at Malta by Marshal Badoglio on 28 September. In November he became British High Commissioner for Italy while retaining his post as Minister Resident, now at Naples. In November 1944 he became head of the Allied Commission in Italy. He thus had a powerful voice in the reconstruction of the Italian government, and was a force in the Yugoslav and Greek settlements, remaining in Greece until the peace treaty was signed in the spring of 1945.

Macmillan was one of the survivors of the so-called 'lost generation' who fought in World War I. He once said that the art of politics was to make angles into curves. The impression of arrogance he gave to some people was ill-founded; he possessed great tenacity of purpose and an unruffled temperament. His chief contributions to the war were his undoubted skill in negotiation and his solution of the many political problems which arose in the Mediterranean theatre of operations.

McNAIR, Lesley, b. 1883. American general who virtually completely reorganized the systems of training in the U.S. army. At the outbreak of war the U.S. army, like other armies on the Allied side, was still thinking in terms of the static warfare of World War I; military training consisted largely of the inculcation of basic skills, the belief being that ultimately the soldier learnt his art on the battlefield. In 1940 McNair was appointed Chief of Staff at the U.S. army G.H.Q., and he set out to establish training schools that could simulate modern battle conditions and to develop a system of training in units and formations that would familiarize soldiers with the requirements and circumstances of life in the fighting line. All active troops were made to take part in strenuous obstacle courses and exercises in which live ammunition was used, and formation exercises were held in which units of various arms learnt how to work together in action. At the same time McNair worked for more general coherence of organization and methods throughout the army. McNair was killed in 1944 while making a tour of observation of U.S. formations during the Normandy fighting; a unit he was visiting was bombed in error by Allied planes.

McNARNEY, Joseph, b. 1893. American general and a dynamic military administrator responsible for important innovations in the American military system during the war years. McNarney, who became a member of the U.S.-Canadian Joint Board of Defense in 1940, was appointed chairman of the U.S. War Department Reorganization Committee in March 1942. He thus became the agent of changes which replaced a near-obsolete system of command by a simplified and more effective structure. He was then appointed Deputy Chief of Staff of the U.S. army; his administrative abilities being needed in this capacity, he did not obtain a command until October 1944, when he became acting Supreme Allied Commander in the Mediterranean and commander of all U.S. forces in that theatre. In December 1945 he succeeded Eisenhower as C.-in-C. of American occupation forces in Germany.

At the end of 1941, when America found itself suddenly and disastrously in the war, it had an army command system more appropriate to 1918. The whole system was so out of date in a multitude of details that a fundamental replanning was essential. This McNarney essayed, and his committee's recommendations were implemented by the President in March 1942. The changes, which were basic and drastic, proved in the event to be justified and effective. The extent to which he was personally responsible was revealed in his writings of the time. The efficiency of the American command system in the years that followed was a tribute to his comprehension of military requirements and also to his foresight.

McNAUGHTON, Andrew, b. 1887. Canadian general, whose reputation was made as commander of the Canadian Corps Heavy Artillery during World War I, and who was described during World War II by General Pile as probably the best and most scientific gunner to be found in any army in the world. In 1923 he was joint inventor of the cathode ray direction finder, the direct forerunner of radar. He served as C.G.S., 1929 to 1935, and as president of the National Research Council, Canada's top scientific post, 1935 to 1939. On the outbreak of war he was given command of the 1st Canadian Division, and from 1939 to 1943 he devoted his keen intelligence, forceful personality, and great energy to building the Canadian military force in Europe which became in 1942 the 1st Canadian Army. Believing that Canada's war effort should be concentrated as an independent national force for participation in the eventual invasion of N.W. Europe, he opposed the decision to split the army he had created by diverting one of its three divisions to the Mediterranean theatre under British command in April 1943. His retirement followed on the Canadian government's acceptance of this plan as a permanent arrangement, and on his failing health.

In the summer of 1942 McNaughton had been requested by Churchill to examine the possibilities of operations in northern Norway. He advised strongly against an invasion. His proposed visit to Moscow for discussions with Stalin on the matter was vetoed by the Canadian government which feared unwanted commitments. Promoted general on his retirement (27 September 1944) he first accepted Prime Minister King's proposal that he succeed the Earl of Athlone as Canadian Governor-General. Believing, however, that the crisis posed by the increasing need for recruits could still be remedied by voluntary means, and conscription for overseas service with its potential threat to national unity avoided, he accepted instead King's offer of the Ministry of Defence (2 November 1944), succeeding J. L. Ralston who resigned on the conscription issue. His appeals among conscripted forces in Canada had little effect, and it was necessary to transfer some home defence troops to Europe early in 1945, though improvement in the military situation then alleviated the demand. As minister, McNaughton was able to remove from Italy the detached Canadians, now a corps in strength, and reunite the army. He left the government on 21 August 1945 after failing to secure a seat in the Commons at a by-election (5 February 1945) or the General Election (11 June 1945).

MAISKY, Ivan, b. 1884. Russian diplomat, ambassador in London until 1943. He was an intelligent, well-informed observer, and by the time of the outbreak of the war

already had many friends in Great Britain.
The autumn of 1939 was a difficult one
in Anglo-Soviet relations. The Soviet-
German Non-Aggression Pact was signed
on 23 August and was followed by the
Russian occupation of eastern Poland and
the war with Finland. The relationship
improved somewhat when Churchill's
government was established. When the
fall of France seemed imminent in May
1940 Maisky sought the opinions of the
Foreign Office, Lloyd George, and the
Webbs before advising his government of
his conviction that the U.K. would continue the war alone. He conveyed messages
to Stalin in June from the British government, indicating that Germany was about
to attack Russia, but Stalin made little
response.

Soon after the German invasion of
Russia in June 1941 Maisky opened the
question of a 'Second Front' with Lord
Beaverbrook, an old friend of his. This
question continued to dominate Anglo-
Soviet relations for the next two years
and was one on which Stalin, through
Maisky, constantly badgered Churchill.

In July 1941 Molotov, the Russian
Foreign Minister, and Sir Stafford Cripps,
the British ambassador to Russia, signed
the Anglo-Soviet Mutual Assistance Pact;
similar pacts were made in London by
Maisky with the émigré governments of
Czechoslovakia and Poland. Maisky met
Harry Hopkins, the American emissary,
on his visit to London and persuaded him
to visit Stalin. This meeting led to the
eventual decision by the U.S.A. and U.K.
to send supplies to Russia under a Lend-
Lease agreement. Maisky accompanied
Anthony Eden on his visit to Moscow in
December 1941, but agreement on the
terms of an Anglo-Soviet Treaty was not
reached until May 1942 when Molotov
was in London. In June 1943 Maisky and
the Soviet ambassador to the U.S.A. were
recalled for consultations in Moscow.
While in Russia Maisky was informed of
his new appointment as Deputy Commissar for Foreign Affairs. He returned
to London to wind up his affairs, took the
opportunity to establish diplomatic relations between Egypt and Russia, and was
back in Moscow in October. He remained
in his new post for the rest of the war, a
somewhat deflated figure.

MALAN, Adolph ('Sailor'), b. 1910. South
African fighter pilot, one of the most
successful aces of the R.A.F. He first saw
action at Dunkirk, where he accounted
for 5 enemy planes. He became commander
of his squadron in August 1940, and soon
afterwards took his 'Tigers' to Kirton-
in-Lindsey for re-equipping and training
new pilots. Malan took the opportunity
to write *Ten Rules for Air Fighting*, which
was later distributed throughout the R.A.F.
In October the squadron transferred to
Biggin Hill in Kent, where he saw intensive action, being decorated for 'commanding his squadron with outstanding success'.
In 1941 the R.A.F. went on offensive
expeditions over northern France, and in
May Malan was promoted to command a
wing. He was still capable of taking on 6
Messerschmitts single-handed, and by
July had destroyed a total of 32 planes, a
record that stood for 3 years.

After lecturing in the U.S.A. he spent
some time as a gunnery instructor. He was
promoted group-captain in October 1942,
and in January 1943 took over command
of the Biggin Hill fighter station. He
trained a fighter wing for the invasion of
Europe. In July 1944 he was given command of an advanced gunnery school at
Catford, where crack pilots were called
in to pool ideas, try out new weapons, and
evolve new combat techniques.

MANSTEIN, Fritz von, b. 1887. German
general, considered by many of his colleagues to have been the ablest German
commander of the war. In September
1939 he was Chief of Staff to Rundstedt.
He suggested the plan, which Hitler
adopted, for the invasion of France. This
was the highly original idea of a thrust
by concentrated armour through Luxembourg and the wooded hill defiles of the
Ardennes, to seize the Meuse crossings
between Dinant and Sedan in the centre
of the Allied line.

He himself commanded an infantry
corps during the campaign with great
distinction. In the spring of 1941 he was
appointed commander of the 56th Panzer
Corps in East Prussia. From late June to
September he fought in Russia with conspicuous success, advancing on Leningrad
in late July. On 11 September he was given
command of the 11th Army on the south-

eastern front. In the next ten months, with numerically inferior forces, he defeated the Red army in the Crimea and took 430,000 Russian prisoners. He stormed Perekop, Parpatsch and, finally, Sebastopol, maintaining his isolated armies throughout the severe Crimean winter. On 6 July he was promoted field marshal and put in command of Army Group Don.

From now on Manstein had to contend not only with Russian counter-offensives but also with Hitler's notions of strategy —chief among them being a reluctance to retreat at any cost. Although in constant disagreement with Hitler he eventually succeeded, by personal interviews, in obtaining permission to retreat to the Mius (after Stalingrad) and to the Dnieper (after the failure of the Kursk offensive, July 1943). In each of these cases he was able to consolidate his position and fight an offensive action. On 25 March 1944 he again sought permission to retreat, and in early April he was dismissed by Hitler. He lived quietly on his estate for the rest of the war.

Manstein inspired devotion and respect in those who served under him. Liddell Hart, the British military writer, described him as 'the Allies' most formidable military opponent—a man who combined modern ideas of manœuvre, a mastery of technical detail and great driving power'.

MARINA, Princess. See KENT, Duchess of.

MARSHALL, George, b. 1880. American general and administrator, one of the ablest strategic thinkers of the war; he built up the war-time army of the U.S., and his contribution to Allied victory was described as 'irreplaceable and unexcelled'. He was appointed Chief of Staff of the U.S. army on 1 September 1939; at that time it consisted of fewer than 200,000 men. His task was to enlarge, re-organize, equip, and train it so as to create a fighting force equal to any demands that might be made on it. This was a task difficult to achieve in the conditions of American neutrality.

Marshall soon won admiration both in and outside the army for his ability to grasp wide issues, his powers of rapid thought, and his quick decisions. He repeatedly addressed senators and congressmen, explaining the necessity for building up the country's defences. In May 1940 the authorized strength of the army was raised to 375,000. In July 1941 Marshall made a report to the Secretary of War which emphasized the need to extend the Selective Act of September 1940. This was finally passed in Congress by one vote.

At the top-level meeting of December 1941, after Pearl Harbor had been attacked by the Japanese, Marshall was insistent from the start, as was General Dill, on the importance of the unification of Allied commands: General Wavell was appointed the first Allied Supreme Commander in the S.W. Pacific. Marshall then turned his attention to simplifying the U.S. command structure. In January 1942 the army was grouped into three major components: the army ground forces under McNair, the army air forces under Arnold, and the services of supply (later called the army service forces) under Somervell. The war plans division remained at H.Q. directly under the Chief of Staff. Marshall became chairman of the Joint Chiefs of Staff Committee, the President's advisory body which included Admiral King, General Arnold, and Admiral Leahy, the presidential representative.

In December 1941 the Washington conference had confirmed the decision that the destruction of Nazi Germany should take precedence over other war aims. During 1942 Marshall repeatedly pressed the British for agreement on the early invasion of Europe. In July a compromise decision for the invasion of North Africa under Eisenhower was reached.

During 1943 Marshall accompanied Roosevelt to the Casablanca Conference in January, to the 'Trident' Conference held in Washington in May (where it was agreed to postpone the invasion of N.W. Europe), and to the first Quebec Conference in August. It was generally assumed that he would become the overall commander of the Allied invasion of Europe. But eventually the view prevailed that a top-level strategist of Marshall's calibre should stay in Washington. He attended the Cairo and Teheran Conferences and then made a short trip to India, Australia, and the Pacific. He was also present at the second Quebec Conference (September 1944), and attended the Yalta (February 1945) and Potsdam (July–August 1945) Conferences. Towards the end of the war he spoke of the need to keep the U.S. 'citizens' army' in being. On 20 November 1945 he retired, to be succeeded by Eisenhower.

Marshall was awarded an Oak Leaf Cluster to his Distinguished Service Medal. The citation began: 'Statesman and soldier, he had courage, fortitude, and vision, and best of all a rare self-effacement. He has been a tower of strength to two commanders-in-chief.'

MASARYK, Jan, b. 1886. Czechoslovak statesman, a leading figure in the Czechoslovak government-in-exile in London. He was Czechoslovak ambassador in London at the time of the Munich agreement and the partition of Czechoslovakia. At the beginning of the war he was one of the most important figures among the Czechoslovak exiles in Britain, along with Eduard Beneš. The B.B.C. invited Masaryk to broadcast daily to his compatriots, and he became one of the most successful Allied broadcasters of the war. His name had particular significance to his oppressed countrymen because his father, Tomáš Masaryk, had been one of the heroes of Czechoslovak independence.

Masaryk acted as mediator between Beneš and the British government, and the status of the Czechoslovak exiles vis-à-vis the British government gradually improved. On 3 July 1940 Beneš was recognized as head of a provisional government of Czechoslovakia, in which Masaryk was Foreign Minister. On 19 July 1941 full recognition was given to the Czech government in London, and to Beneš as its President. In 1942 Anthony Eden formally renounced the Munich agreement in the House of Commons.

Masaryk spent much of his time fulfilling speaking engagements in Britain and in the U.S.A. He represented his country at the creation of the United Nations Relief and Rehabilitation Association in Washington in the autumn of 1943, which saved many Europeans from starvation. Relations with the Soviet Union were cordial. On 18 July 1941 a mutual aid agreement was reached between the

two countries, providing for the exchange of ministers and for the formation of Czech units under the supreme command of the Soviet army. The agreement was signed in London by Masaryk and Maisky. Beneš visited Moscow in December 1943, and a pact of friendship was also signed there. Masaryk was an extremely popular man and did much to gain sympathy and understanding for his country. He was not a narrow nationalist, and felt himself to be 'a citizen of the world'.

MASON-MacFARLANE. *See* MacFARLANE, Sir Frank Mason-.

MATHEWS, Vera Laughton, b. 1900. Director of the W.R.N.S. Born into a naval family, she was already widely experienced as an administrator when she was appointed in 1939. The W.R.N.S. at the time she became Director was still lacking both professional organization and a role. Mrs Mathews rapidly developed it into an efficient and purposeful body. By performing vital shore jobs, and thereby freeing men for service at sea, the 'Wrens' made a major contribution to the war effort. Although the W.R.N.S. depended on voluntary enlistment throughout the war, it was never short of recruits, and after the war it was established as a permanent part of the R.N. Mrs Mathews became first president of the W.R.N.S. when she retired in 1945, and she was created D.B.E. in recognition of her services.

MENZIES, Robert, b. 1894. Australian statesman, Prime Minister at the outbreak of the war. In April 1939, as leader of the United Australia party, he became Prime Minister in a minority government which was, however, to last for two years. War seemed inevitable, and preparations were duly made: the Defence department was reorganized, and Service departments were created; a Ministry of Supply was set up; and compulsory military training was re-established. On 3 September 1939 Menzies broadcast the announcement that Australia had entered the war: 'It is my melancholy duty to inform you officially that in consequence of a persistence by Germany in her invasion of Poland, Great Britain has declared war upon her, and that, as a result,

Australia is at war.' A few days later Parliament met and approved this action.

Shortly afterwards 3 Australian divisions were sent to the Middle East; a cruiser and some destroyers went to the Mediterranean; and food supplies and raw materials were dispatched to Britain.

A Coalition government was formed in August 1940 through an alliance between the United Australia party and the Country party. But in the September general election the alliance had only a tiny majority over Labor. Menzies set up an Advisory War Council, consisting of four members of the government and four members of the Opposition.

In January 1941 Menzies travelled to London, by way of Singapore, Palestine, and Egypt. His purpose was to discuss the Japanese threat and the state of the Singapore defences. He took part in discussions at the Foreign Office on 26 February, but found that there was no clear policy in relation to Japan. However, he was greatly impressed by morale in Britain despite the low ebb of the country's fortunes.

In June 1941, after his return to Australia, Menzies announced the creation of 5 new ministries: of Aircraft Production, Transport, War Organization of Industry, Home Security, and External Territories. But war measures were becoming unpopular, and on 22 August he suggested an all-party government with Curtin as Prime Minister. The offer was rejected, and Menzies resigned as Prime Minister on 28 August. But his successor's government lasted only until 6 October and Labor came to power under Curtin for the rest of the war. Menzies resigned the leadership of his party and sat in Parliament as a private member.

Menzies later declared that, despite his disappointment, everything had turned out for the best both for Australia and for himself. In Opposition he had the opportunity to discover 'that human beings are delightfully illogical but mostly honest', and to realize that 'all-black and all-white are not the only hues in the spectrum'.

MERRILL, Frank, b. 1903. American soldier who led a legendary group of jungle guerrillas, known as 'Merrill's Marauders', in operations against the Japanese in northern Burma in 1944. The members of the group were all Americans and volunteers, and were part of the army commanded by General Stilwell. Merrill had been on Stilwell's staff, and believed that a determined force, marauding behind the Japanese lines, could play havoc with the enemy's communications. The 'Marauders' set off from Ledo in Assam in February 1944 and, living off the land, travelled for hundreds of miles through the forests, attacking Japanese dumps and isolated units. Though they marched and fought themselves almost to a standstill they achieved the remarkable feat, with help from Chinese units, of wresting the airfield at Myitkyina from the Japanese. The eventual capture of Myitkyina city in May 1944 enabled a vital juncture to be made between the Ledo and Burma roads. Many observers considered the 'Marauders' the best and most effective of the troops under Stilwell's command. Later Merrill became Chief of Staff in the U.S. 10th Army in the Pacific.

MESSE, Giovanni, b. 1883. Italian general who commanded Axis troops in the Western Desert. Messe was one of the most experienced and skilful of the Italian senior commanders. He had fought in Libya in 1911, and had taken part in the Italian conquest of Ethiopia (1935–6) and Albania (1939). After World War II broke out Messe took part in the invasion of Greece, and then, when Germany invaded Russia in 1941, he went to the Eastern front as commander of the Italian Expeditionary Corps. However, he found himself in disagreement with the German command, and was eventually recalled to Italy. At the beginning of 1943 he was sent to Tunisia as C.-in-C. of the Italian 1st Army which now had fallen back to the Mareth Line. He arrived at a time when little could be done: the Axis troops were steadily giving way in the face of relentless pressure from the superior Allied forces, which now included the Americans. The end came in May when Messe, obeying cease-fire instructions from Rome, ordered his troops to lay down their arms. More than a quarter of a million prisoners were taken by the Allies, including Messe himself.

MESSERVY, Frank, b. 1893. British soldier who fought in the East African and North African campaigns, and later conducted the epic defence of the 'Admin Box' in Arakan. When Italy declared war in June 1940 he became a staff officer with the 5th Indian Division in the Sudan. From October 1940 he commanded a mechanized raiding group, 'Gazelle Force', which acted as a reconnaissance, fighting and pursuit formation during the East African campaign. In March he took part in the assault on Keren. In the North African campaign, as commander of the 4th Indian Division, he was involved in the second invasion of Cyrenaica under Auchinleck. His division entered Benghazi on Christmas Day 1941. He took over the command of the 1st British Armoured Division in January 1942, and of the 7th Armoured Division (the 'Desert Rats') in March.

After Rommel's counter-offensive Messervy returned to India, where he was Director, Armoured Fighting Vehicles, until given command of the 7th Indian Infantry Division in 1944. During the Japanese offensive in Arakan in February 1943 this division was cut off, but Messervy formed a defensive strongpoint in the famous 'Admin Box' (originally the 7th Division's administrative base, with clerks, signallers, mule companies, road-builders, ordnance units, field ambulances, and a large collection of vehicles that Messervy called 'The Ascot car park') and held it, with air supply, for 18 days, before being relieved to help in mopping-up operations.

General Slim, commanding 14th Army, made Messervy commander of 4th Corps in September. He was chosen, wrote Slim, because 'he had the temperament, sanguine, inspiring and not too calculating of odds, that I thought would be required for the tasks I designed for 4th Corps'. These tasks included the invasion of Burma with Slim's army and the capture of Rangoon.

MIHAJLOVIĆ, Draža, b. 1893. Yugoslav soldier, leader of the Serbian Četnik Resistance forces in Yugoslavia. Strongly royalist and a Serbian nationalist, he eventually found himself in opposition to the Communist Partisans. German troops invaded Yugoslavia on 6 April 1941, and

the Yugoslav High Command capitulated 11 days later. Germany, Hungary, and Italy annexed parts of the country, and four puppet regimes were set up in Serbia, Croatia, Montenegro, and Slovenia.

Mihajlović, a Serbian army officer, took to the woods with some other soldiers and organized guerrilla groups to resist the occupation. These groups were called Četniks, the name of similar groups that had operated in the Balkan Wars and World War I. The Germans were also opposed by another Resistance group, the Communist Partisans led by Tito. The aims of these two movements were ultimately incompatible. Mihajlović was fighting for a Serbian-dominated Yugoslavia—he increasingly felt it to be primarily the task of the Allies to defeat the Germans while he prepared to form a government when that became possible. Tito was fighting to create a Communist state.

During 1941 the Četniks and the Partisans fought together, and Mihajlović favoured a less active resistance to the Germans than Tito advocated, since he did not wish to provoke reprisals on the civilian population. Also their plans for the administration of regained territories differed widely. By November Mihajlović had decided that the Communists were as much a menace to the future of Yugoslavia as the Germans. The Partisans were driven out of Serbia by the Germans' 'first offensive'. Since both the Četniks and the Axis forces hated the Partisans, various understandings were arrived at between them, and as time went on most of the active resistance to the Germans came from the Partisans. Meanwhile Mihajlović was in contact with the British by wireless. In September 1941 a British liaison officer was sent to join him, and he began to receive Allied supplies and arms. In January 1942 he was appointed War Minister by the Yugoslav government-in-exile in London. But a British Mission reached Tito in mid 1943, and in November the British warned the Četniks not to collaborate with the Nazis. Eventually official British support of Mihajlović was withdrawn, and British missions operating in his territory were recalled by May 1944.

Mihajlović sponsored a conference at which a Yugoslav Democratic Popular

Committee was formed; but he himself
was unable to stage a political comeback.
Tito signed an agreement with Šubašić,
the head of the Yugoslav government in
London, in June, and Mihajlović was
deprived of his post. By September Partisan activity forced Mihajlović to leave his
headquarters in Ravna Gora. By early
1945 Tito had political control of Yugoslavia, while Mihajlović remained in the
mountains. He was captured by the Communists in March 1946, tried, and executed.

MITCHELL, Reginald, b. 1895. British
aircraft engineer who designed the Spitfire
fighter, which was developed from fast
seaplanes of the Schneider Trophy period.
The prototype, powered by a Rolls-Royce
engine, flew in March 1936, and deliveries
to Fighter Command of the R.A.F. began
in 1938. By August 1940, the critical
month of the Battle of Britain, the Command had 19 Spitfire squadrons operational. It also had 30 squadrons of Hurricanes. The Hurricane, designed by Sidney
Camm and the prototype of which had
flown in November 1934, could not have
successfully engaged the best German
fighters. Its performance was 317 m.p.h.
at 17,500 feet compared with the Spitfire's
355 m.p.h. at 19,000 feet. Altogether over
22,000 Spitfires and Seafires (the naval
version) were produced in 32 types. Over
a period of 15 years the engine power was
doubled and the speed raised to 450
m.p.h. without radical departure from
Mitchell's original design, and the Spitfire
was recognized as one of the most remarkable aircraft ever built. Though he died
in 1937, Mitchell's genius was a vital part
of the British war effort.

MITSCHER, Marc Andrew ('Mich'), b.
1887. American admiral who commanded
the famous Task Force 58 in the South
Pacific. From January to October 1944
his force of aircraft carriers, battleships,
cruisers, and destroyers sank or damaged
795 Japanese ships and destroyed 4,425
enemy planes.
    Mitscher had taken command of the
aircraft carrier *Hornet* in October 1941.
It was from the decks of the *Hornet* that
Doolittle's bombers had made the first
air raid of the war on Japan, on 18 April
1942. In June 1942 Mitscher played an

important role in the U.S. victory at the
Battle of Midway, when aircraft from the
carriers *Enterprise, Hornet,* and *Yorktown*
sank 4 Japanese carriers and destroyed a
large part of the Japanese air arm. For
several months in 1943 he commanded all
air forces in the Solomon Islands. In April
and May 1945 Mitscher's force took part
in the operations at Okinawa in support
of the ground troops. The Japanese were
able to mount attacks on the American
invaders of Okinawa from airfields in
Japan. Task Force 58 had to minimize
these attacks and attacks by naval forces.
Among the greatest dangers they had to
endure were *kamikaze* (suicide) raids.
    Mitscher graduated from the U.S. Naval
Academy in 1910, and was one of the first
U.S. navy officers to adopt aviation as a
career.

MODEL, Walther, b. 1891. German
general, an energetic, thrusting commander, greatly favoured by Hitler, but
one of the few senior generals to stand up
against the Führer's military opinions. He
was Chief of Staff to the 4th Corps
during the Polish campaign, and later to
the 16th Army in France. He was then
given command of the 3rd Panzer Division,
and led the drive beyond the River Dnieper
during the Russian campaign. Model was
a 'new man' whose fortunes were bound
up with the Nazi régime rather than with
the established army hierarchy. Hitler made
him commander of the 9th Army in 1942.
    When the Kursk offensive of 1943 was
planned Model declared that strong tank
reinforcements would be necessary for its
success. As a result the operation was
postponed until July against the advice
of Kluge and Manstein. In the event the
offensive was broken up by the Russians.
    Model's qualities as a front-line leader—
he was known as 'the lion of defence' by
his troops—were not good enough to
stem the Russian offensive and Orel had
to be abandoned. Despite this failure
Model still retained the Führer's confidence. He was switched from place to
place during the 1944 Russian advance:
first, as commander of Army Group North,
checking the Red army's drive towards
the Baltic states, and then with Army
Group South fighting against Zhukov at
Lwow in Poland; his last exploit was as

commander of Army Group Centre when he halted the Russian offensive near Warsaw. After the Allied invasion of N.W. Europe, Hitler hailed Model as the 'saviour of the Western front' and on 17 August 1944 appointed him Supreme Commander in the West, replacing Kluge. But on 4 September Rundstedt relieved him of this appointment and Model was left free to concentrate on Army Group B.

This army group had been driven out of Belgium into Holland. On 4 September Model wrote: 'The unequal struggle cannot long continue.' On 17 September, when the Allied attempt to establish a bridgehead at Arnhem took place, Model was only a few miles away at Oosterbruk. As a result he was able to concentrate his troops and defend Arnhem successfully. On 16 December, after long arguments with Hitler, Rundstedt and Model launched the Ardennes offensive. Manteuffel's army broke through the American lines and marched into Belgium. But by January 1945 the offensive had been contained and Model's forces retired into the Ruhr pocket where they were quickly surrounded. Model refused to surrender, but on 15 April formally dissolved Army Group B.

He had said of Field Marshal Paulus, whose army had surrendered before Stalingrad in February 1943: 'A field marshal does not become a prisoner. Such a thing is not possible.' He shot himself on 21 April 1945.

MÖLDERS, Werner, b. 1913. German fighter pilot, one of the leading 'aces' of the war. During the battle for France he was in command of a fighter group. He destroyed 25 enemy aircraft before he was shot down by a French fighter and forced to bale out.

Mölders was an accomplished tactician as well as a brilliant pilot, and he invented the 'finger four' fighting formation which was used by the Luftwaffe and later adopted by the R.A.F. in the Battle of Britain. During this battle Mölders was in command of approximately 100 Me 109s. On 19 August, when some of the deficiencies of the German air force had become apparent, Goering promoted him to command a group. He had shot down 45 enemy aircraft by October 1940.

On the Russian front in the summer of 1941 he accounted for more than 100 aircraft and was decorated with the Jewels to the Oak Leaves, and with Swords to the Knight's Cross. He was then appointed Inspector of Fighter Aircraft at the Luftwaffe H.Q. In November, while he was in the Crimea, Goering summoned him to the state funeral of Ernst Udet, the Luftwaffe general. Despite engine trouble Mölders hurried home in bad weather, and crashed while attempting to land at Breslau. He was killed outright. Goering stage-managed his state funeral a few days later.

Mölders was a calm and skilful leader, concerned more about the efficiency of his unit than about his own success score. He had first made his name fighting in Spain in 1938.

MOLOTOV, Vyacheslav, b. 1890. Russian statesman, Foreign Minister throughout the war. He replaced Litvinov in this post (then titled People's Commissar of Foreign Affairs) in 1939, and for the next two years he was involved with Stalin's labyrinthine diplomacy, playing the Western powers off against Germany. When the German-Soviet Non-Aggression Pact of August 1939 was signed Stalin consented to the division of Poland, took over the Baltic states by plebiscite, and in November 1939 began the war on Finland.

During 1940, when German troops appeared in Romania and Finland, the relationship between Russia and Germany became somewhat strained. On 9 November Molotov went to Berlin where Hitler suggested a four-power pact between Germany, Russia, Italy, and Japan. Stalin agreed so long as German troops were withdrawn from Finland—a condition that Hitler saw as a suspicious rebuff. A major success for Molotov was the signing on 13 April 1941 of a pact of neutrality and non-aggression between Russia and Japan. On 22 June 1941 Molotov announced to the Russian people the invasion of Russia by Germany.

War changed the entire aspect of Soviet diplomatic policy. Stafford Cripps, the British ambassador to Russia since May 1940, gave promises of military assistance, and in July Molotov signed a Mutual Assistance Pact with Great Britain.

Molotov became a member of the five-man State Defence Committee, with Stalin, Voroshilov, Beria, and Malenkov. He worked relentlessly to promote the war effort, relaxing only occasionally for a game of chess. In May 1942 he went on missions to London and Washington, where, in those days, his elaborate security precautions amazed his hosts. On 26 May an Anglo-Soviet treaty, a 20-year alliance against Germany, was signed. Molotov obtained assurances from the Americans that the invasion of Europe would be launched in 1942, but in August Churchill himself went to Moscow to explain why this, never a reasonable proposition, was impossible to realize.

The year 1943 was the turning point of the war for Russia. During October Anthony Eden and Cordell Hull went to Moscow for the Foreign Ministers' conference, with Molotov acting as chairman and impressing the others by his total competence and grasp of affairs. The ground was prepared for the top-level Teheran Conference of November, where agreement was finally reached on the timing of the 'Second Front' invasion of the European mainland.

Churchill visited Moscow in October 1944 to discuss Poland and the Balkans. Molotov attended the Yalta Conference in February 1945, and was sent by Stalin to the United Nations Assembly in San Francisco in the following April as a good-will gesture to President Truman. Molotov also played an important part at the Potsdam Conference (July 1945). As Stalin's health began to fail, more and more responsibility was delegated to this loyal subordinate.

Molotov was able and hardworking. He had devoted himself to the Communist cause since joining the party in 1906. His personal life was subordinated to these ends.

MONTGOMERY, Bernard Law, b. 1887. British general (field marshal 1944), probably the finest British field commander of the war. Relentlessly professional in his attitude to soldiering, austere in his personal life, and with a sure touch for capturing the imagination and confidence of the men he led, he became a legendary figure after his success against the German

General Rommel, the 'Desert Fox', in North Africa.

At the beginning of the war Montgomery commanded the 3rd Division in the B.E.F. which fought in France until the evacuation from Dunkirk. During the next two years he was successively commander of 5th Corps, 12th Corps, and South Eastern Army in England; these appointments gave him the opportunity to develop his tough training methods and put them into practice.

In August 1942 he took over command of the 8th Army in North Africa under the overall command of General Alexander. At this time Rommel had pushed the British back about 250 miles into Egypt. Montgomery infused into his army a sense of common purpose and carried out a complete reorganization. He made an immediate impression on the troops by ordering the cessation of defensive planning and work: his army was going to attack.

Rommel's offensive to the gates of Cairo was blunted at the Battle of Alam Halfa, and then Montgomery began his offensive at El Alamein on 23 October 1942. The Afrika Korps was routed, the Italians were divided from the Germans, and a pursuit followed. Egypt was free of the enemy by 12 November and Cyrenaica by 17 December. Tripoli was taken on 23 January 1943. Although the victory was undoubtedly Montgomery's, some credit for the success belonged to his predecessor, General Auchinleck, who had paved the way by the punishment he had meted out to Rommel and the Afrika Korps.

In April the 8th Army made contact with the Allied forces operating in N.W. Africa, and entered the sphere of Allied co-operation, which (in Montgomery's view) was apt to involve poor planning and lack of co-ordination. In July it landed with the 7th U.S. Army in Sicily, and on 3 September the 8th Army went on to southern Italy. Montgomery was ordered north to assist the 5th U.S. Army at Salerno and then fought in S.E. Italy up to the River Sangro, which was reached on 8 November 1943.

In January 1944 Montgomery returned home to command the 21st Army Group. He worked on the plans for Operation 'Overlord', the invasion of N.W. Europe, and on D-Day, 6 June 1944, was field commander of all the land forces. His immediate chief was General Eisenhower, the Supreme Allied Commander in Europe. Montgomery remained in command of all land forces until August, after which he led 21st Army Group. In the early phase Montgomery's plan was sustained—the weight of the German opposition was held by the British and Canadians on the east, while the Americans broke out on the west. By the end of August the first phase was over. The plan for the assault on Germany was, as proposed by the supreme commander Eisenhower: first, to close the Rhine along its whole length; secondly, to cross the river at several points; and thirdly, to advance on a wide front into Germany. Montgomery, on the other hand, argued that Germany was already beaten; the plan was too cautious and might result in the Russians getting to Berlin first. He advocated an all-out advance on Berlin via the Ruhr by a force of some 35 to 40 divisions who would be given all the logistic support they required. The Americans totally disagreed with 'a pencil line thrust on Berlin'. The merits and demerits of the rivals plans are still argued; but from the military point of view Eisenhower's plan, which was the plan put into effect, proved to be completely successful. Whether it unduly prolonged the war is a matter of opinion.

In September Montgomery took Antwerp. On 16 December the Germans initiated the Battle of the Ardennes and 2 American armies came temporarily under Montgomery's command while the front was restored. On 8 February 1945, 21st Army Group began its thrust to the Rhine and crossed the river on 24 March, reaching the Baltic on 2 May. On 4 May, at Lüneburg Heath, Montgomery took the surrender of all German forces in the Netherlands, Denmark, and N.W. Germany.

Although Montgomery showed himself on more than one occasion quick to exploit a favourable situation, his professional skill showed to greatest advantage in his direction of the 'set piece' battle. He believed that careful planning and calculation combined with the disciplined use of power saved lives and prevented future reverses. He was not too concerned to dis-

guise his scorn for commanders who relied heavily on luck and dash, even when they were successful. He was an inspiring leader, who seldom failed to reach his objective when given a free hand and in fact 'never lost a battle'. His American allies on the whole disliked his distinctly abrasive and irrepressible self-confidence. The fact that he was rather ostentatiously a teetotaller and non-smoker set him somewhat apart, as did his choice of headwear: he wore a tank-man's beret and badge, with his general's badge added. His troops respected and trusted him and he made it his business to show himself to them on every possible occasion. But his military thinking combined simplicity with force and clarity, and he was intensely thorough in the preparation and administration of all his battles—this was the real secret of his outstanding success.

MOOREHEAD, Alan, b. 1910. Australian journalist, war correspondent for the London *Daily Express.* He arrived in Cairo in May 1940 and spent the next 3 years following the campaigns in North Africa. He published three widely discussed books about his experiences: *Mediterranean Front, A Year of Battle,* and *The End in Africa.* After a brief visit to the U.S.A. in 1942 he returned to the 8th Army after the fall of Tripoli, remaining with Montgomery's H.Q. for the rest of the war, first in Tunisia, Sicily, and Italy, and later in Normandy, Belgium, the Netherlands, and Germany, until the German surrender.

At the time of the fall of Tobruk in June 1942 he wrote for the *Daily Express* that the army, in Libya at any rate, was 'not equipped for the job'; that it was inferior to the Germans in tanks, in guns, and in dive-bombers. His reports are thought to have had some effect on the future equipping of the Desert armies.

MORGAN, Sir Frederick, b. 1894. British general in charge of planning for Allied landings in Normandy on D-Day 1944. In January 1943 Morgan was appointed Chief of Staff to the Supreme Allied Commander for the proposed invasion of France, with instructions to produce a detailed plan for an invasion of Europe for May/June 1944. He was henceforth known by the short title COSSAC, and his task was a daunting one. Resources were scarce, and when Morgan was appointed there was not yet an actual Supreme Allied Commander. Morgan's scope for action was small (in spite of his impressive title) but he consulted all the different groups involved with the invasion and produced a plan—at first an inadequate one, as he himself was aware. The plan met with strong opposition and was hedged around with many 'ifs' and 'buts'. Morgan needed more landing craft for the invasion and went to the U.S.A., without success, to try to get them. Only when General Eisenhower became Supreme Allied Commander were the essential craft released.

Morgan's final plan was adopted at the Largs Conference called by Lord Louis Mountbatten, the Chief of Combined Operations, in June/July 1943. Over the next year the plan was worked out in detail, under Morgan's unflagging supervision. In June 1944, when the invasion took place, Morgan's plan proved to be a remarkable success. The achievements of Eisenhower and the field commanders on D-Day depended on the thorough groundwork of Morgan, the architect of 'Overlord'.

MORGENTHAU, Henry J., b. 1891. U.S. Secretary of the Treasury during the war; he had to devise the means of raising revenues unprecedented in the history of any country. In September 1939 Morgenthau had already been Secretary of the U.S. Treasury for five years. In view of the economic depression, providing the necessary subvention for the effective defence of the U.S. presented him with difficult problems. Government spending programmes accelerated greatly, and the trend in government fiscal affairs was one of sharply rising revenues, even more sharply rising expenditures, and vast increases in the public debt through deficit financing.

A concomitant problem was how to evolve a tax system that would increase revenues to the limit of economic safety and yet contrive to curb the threat of inflation. Morgenthau recognized the risk and guarded against it. Defense (later 'War') Savings Bonds were sold to finance the war effort. Meanwhile, as business improved, the Treasury tax income increased. Treasury activities also included the purchase of non-military materials for the United Nations under the terms of the Lend-Lease Act, and economic measures designed to block trading with enemy-controlled companies.

As Secretary of the Treasury, Morgenthau had a seat in the Cabinet and he was an old and influential friend of President Roosevelt. He is best remembered for the so-called 'Morgenthau Plan': at the second Quebec Conference in September 1944 he put forward a plan that would render post-war Germany industrially ineffective. Roosevelt and Churchill—who was influenced by Lord Cherwell—signed a document which contained the statement: 'This programme for eliminating the war-making industries in the Ruhr and in the Saar is looking forward to converting Germany into a country primarily agricultural and pastoral in its character.' This policy meant that 40 per cent of the German population would have been unable to support themselves on German territory. The plan aroused strong opposition in the Cabinets on both sides of the Atlantic and proved good propaganda material for Goebbels when it was reported in the press, especially since Morgenthau was Jewish. But by the time of the Truman administration economic vengeance on Germany was no longer part of Allied policy.

Morgenthau was a shy, hard-working man, considered to be good at his job but not at public relations. Roosevelt called him 'Henry the Morgue'.

MORRISON, Herbert, b. 1888. British politician who had the responsibility for directing many of the measures for civilian defence during the war. In 1939 he was leader of the London County Council and Chairman of its General Purposes and Civil Defence committees. As a leading member of the Labour Opposition in Parliament, he was largely responsible for the 'No-confidence' motion of 8 May 1940 that led to the fall of Neville Chamberlain.

Churchill made him Minister of Supply in the new Coalition government; the principal problem which faced him was the shortage of raw materials, especially steel. In October 1940 the Prime Minister asked him to take over from Sir John Anderson as Home Secretary and Minister of Home Security. In this capacity Morrison inaugurated the National Fire Service and organized the system of compulsory fire-watching—the nightly guard on industrial and public buildings as a precaution against air attacks using incendiary bombs. He was responsible for all the varied activities of Civil Defence and the Home Guard. As Home Secretary Morrison had to take difficult, and sometimes centroversial, decisions on more specific matters, particularly those relating to censorship and the internment or release of people whose actions were considered prejudicial to the war effort.

In January 1945 he was appointed chairman of the Labour party special campaign committee, and he drafted the Labour declaration 'Let Us Face the Future'. Churchill objected to what he called the over-political nature of his speeches at this time, and Morrison offered to resign from the Coalition; but this was not accepted. The Labour party adopted his programme in 1945. It included nationalization measures and promises of a new deal in the fields of health, education, and social insurance.

MOUNTBATTEN, Lady Louis, b. 1901. Superintendent-in-chief of the St John Ambulance Brigade, she was responsible for saving the lives of many P.O.W.s in the hands of the Japanese after the surrender in 1945.

Married to Lord Louis Mountbatten, then a naval lieutenant, in 1922, she had travelled widely in the 1930s, making a number of journeys to the East and becoming at the same time a noted hostess and organizer of charities in London. At the outbreak of war in 1939 she threw herself into work for the Women's Voluntary Service and later the St John Ambulance Brigade, of which she became Superintendent-in-chief in 1942. Early in 1945, after indefatigable work for her organization, she embarked on a round of hospital inspections for her husband, then Supreme Allied Commander, S.E. Asia, which took her through India and Burma and into China. Her unique achievement

came towards the end of this year when the atom bomb had brought the war with Japan to a sudden and unexpected end.

When the Japanese revealed the existence of 250 unsuspected P.O.W. camps, Lady Mountbatten travelled by plane with medical services and supplies, investigated the situation and signalled to Singapore for requirements. The conditions she discovered were appalling: the prisoners had been starved and ill-treated, and many were near to death. So successful were her drive and initiative that within six weeks R.A.P.W.I. (Recovery of Allied P.O.W.'s and Internees) had cleared 90,000 men and women from camps sprinkled over a front of 3,000 miles.

Her strong personality, gift for organization, and genuine concern for human beings endeared her to people of all races and classes.

MOUNTBATTEN, Lord Louis, b. 1900. British admiral, one of the most resourceful, personally daring, and successful of war leaders. After a distinguished career in the Royal Navy in which he specialized in communications, Mountbatten was appointed to command of the 5th Destroyer Flotilla early in 1939. This flotilla was a unit in the defence of Britain and took part in the evacuation of Allied troops from Norway. H.M.S. *Kelly*, the flotilla leader, was both mined and torpedoed but was recommissioned after repairs. In April 1941 *Kelly* arrived in Malta. In May she took part in naval action off Crete during the battle for that island, but was herself dive-bombed and sunk. The crews of H.M.S. *Kashmir*, also sunk, and *Kelly* were rescued by another ship of the flotilla, H.M.S. *Kipling*.

Appointed to command the aircraft carrier *Illustrious*, under repair in Norfolk Navy Yard, U.S.A., Mountbatten flew to Pearl Harbor where he was invited to lecture on the war at sea. He met President Roosevelt before his urgent recall by Churchill to be given the important post of Adviser on (later Chief of) Combined Operations and to plan the invasion of Europe with preliminary raids on the French coast. In this capacity Mountbatten made full use of a probing mind, initiative, and diplomacy to create a new command vital to the war effort. His responsibilities included development of the Mulberry harbours, the artificial ports used in the 1944 invasion. In March 1942 Churchill made him a member of the Chiefs of Staff Committee. His plans included the raids on St Nazaire (March) and Dieppe (August); the latter caused heavy loss of life and many participants were taken prisoner; but as General Morgan, the planner of 'Overlord' (the invasion of N.W. Europe), said: 'Without Dieppe "Overlord" would have proved impossible.' He was also engaged in planning the successful North Africa landings of November 1942. He attended the Casablanca Conference of January 1943 and accompanied Churchill to the Quebec Conferenee after the Sicily landings in July.

He was next made Supreme Allied Commander, S.E. Asia, arriving in Delhi in October 1943. (The S.E.A.C. H.Q. moved from Delhi to Ceylon in the spring of 1944.) Starved of landing craft and ships for the envisaged sea operations, the command changed to that of a land campaign, and into this Mountbatten threw new ideas and techniques and raised the morale of the Allied forces under him. The 14th Army attacked in the Arakan, and in February Orde Wingate with his long-range penetration groups went into Burma. The great counter-attack against the Japanese offensive at Imphal and Kohima began at the same time. Mountbatten was suffering from a severe eye injury, but ignoring this went to his H.Q. to order planes, over which he had no jurisdiction, to be sent with troops to the relief of Imphal. By May the Japanese were in retreat.

Mountbatten still failed to receive his promised equipment, but the 14th Army fought through Burma and by March 1945 had taken Mandalay. He attended the Potsdam Conference in July. By August the atom bomb had made the Japanese surrender imminent.

Lord Louis was an inspiring leader of men as he showed in his relationship with his ships' companies and with the 'forgotten' armies in S.E. Asia. The American leaders were prepared to work with him. His gift for showmanship and reputation for glamour earned him both friends and enemies, but he 'produced the goods'

through sheer ability. As General Slim said: 'When you saw Dickie it was good for your morale.' And this was echoed by thousands in his various commands.

MUFTI of Jerusalem. *See* HUSSEINI, Amin el.

MÜLLER, Heinrich ('Gestapo Müller'), b. 1896. Senior S.S. leader, and head of the Gestapo from 1936 until its collapse. A talented administrator who admired the methods of the Soviet secret police and endeavoured to improve on them, he built up an internal spy system in Germany that paralysed opposition to the Nazi régime by making every man feel himself to be under constant surveillance by informers. Müller staged the border 'incidents' that were the prelude to the invasion of Poland, and gave the orders for many of the atrocious acts of the Nazis. It was Müller who issued the *Kugel Erlass*, or Bullet Decree, under which countless Russian, Polish, and other P.O.W.s were killed, Müller whose Gestapo agents spread terror throughout the German-occupied countries, Müller whose subordinate Adolf Eichmann had the task of delivering the Jews of Europe to the extermination camps, and Müller who was called to Hitler's bunker two days before the end to question and condemn the Führer's aide-de-camp Herman Fegelein for supposed treachery. After the German defeat he disappeared, and was never brought to justice. Müller was a policeman in Munich until he attracted Himmler's attention. Like his master Himmler, he was efficient, loyal, and generally mild-mannered, and in his hands murder was reduced to a problem in administration. He was refused membership of the Nazi party until 1939, presumably because of his work against the Nazis during his Munich days. Remarkable though it may seem, a British officer who was once his prisoner said of him: 'In my experience I always found Müller a very decent little man.'

MURPHY, Audie, b. 1924. American war hero who enlisted in the infantry soon after his 18th birthday and was to become the most decorated American soldier of the war. Murphy's qualities were not immediately apparent to his superiors. He earned the nickname 'Baby' because of his youthful looks, and had difficulty in retaining combat status. In the spring of 1943 he was posted to North Africa as a replacement in a unit of the 3rd Infantry Division. He did not see action until the Sicilian landings of 1943. Promoted corporal, he was at Palermo and Messina, took part in the Salerno landings and was in the 5th Army front line until mid November. After a spell in Naples he went to the Anzio beach-head. At the end of the campaign in June, after several daring exploits, he reached Rome. By this time he was a sergeant.

Murphy landed with his unit in southern France in August 1944. A close friend was killed and Murphy, in a white rage, attacked the gun crew responsible from the rear and killed them all. The 3rd Army marched across France to the Vosges and, in September, Murphy's company was involved in a prolonged action for command of a strategically placed quarry near Cleurie. This was finally taken by a full-scale assault. Later Murphy was shot in the hip, and the wound became gangrenous. But in January 1945 he returned to the front (by this time in Strasbourg) as a lieutenant. His division was then engaged in clearing the Colmar pocket and lost 4,500 men in seven weeks. Murphy was made a liaison officer, but hearing that his company was pinned down in the Siegfried Line he made an opportunity to lead the frightened men to safety.

By the end of the war Murphy was credited with having killed, wounded, or captured 240 enemy soldiers. For his exploits he was awarded 21 medals, including the Congressional Medal of Honor. He was a modest hero, attached to his comrades, impatient to get on with the job, and resourceful in every crisis.

MUSSOLINI, Benito, b. 1883. Italian dictator who led his country into war on the side of the Nazis, and who before the war's end had been driven from power and ignominiously executed. In May 1939 in Berlin, Ciano and Ribbentrop—representing, respectively, Italy and Germany—had signed the so-called 'pact of steel', a military alliance between their countries. Mussolini had allowed the Germans to

draft the pact, and had approved it swiftly, impatient to share the fortunes of a rising star. But when it appeared that Hitler was about to attack Poland the Duce became indecisive; he had been led to believe that war would not start until 1942. Eventually he opted for Italian neutrality because he was disturbed by the German-Soviet pact and the Russian invasion of Finland. Before long, German military successes persuaded him to climb on the bandwagon. He was ageing. The American diplomat Sumner Welles described him at this time as follows: 'The man I saw before me seemed fifteen years older than his actual age of 56. He was ponderous and static rather than vital. He moved with elephantine motion: every step appeared an effort. He was heavy for his height and his face in repose fell into rolls of flesh. His close-cropped hair was snow white.'

Mussolini met Hitler at the Brenner Pass on 18 March 1940 and committed himself to the Axis cause. The successful German invasion of the Low Countries and France proved the catalyst. On 10 June he declared war on 'the plutocratic and reactionary democracies of the west'.

The war began well for Italy. Italian troops crossed the Egyptian frontier from Libya on 13 September and advanced to Sidi Barrani. But the successes were short-lived, and the Italian invasion of Greece proved disastrous almost from the beginning. By early December Italian troops had suffered reverses not only in Greece but also in North Africa. Mussolini appealed to Hitler for help and had to accept a humiliating agreement which entailed sending labour to Germany in exchange for goods.

During 1941 Italian dependence on Germany became even more marked. In April General Rommel, employing the skilful and determined troops of the Afrika Korps, regained Cyrenaica, which had been lost by the Italians. The Germans also lent support in Greece with outstanding success. In June, when Hitler invaded Russia, Mussolini was informed of the attack only after it had started. By the time that Mussolini was invited to tour the Eastern front with Hitler in August, he was ill and depressed by the death of his son Bruno, killed in an air crash. On 11

December Italy, following the German lead, declared war on the U.S.A. But soon the Italian people were tired of the war; there were reports of the ill-treatment of Italians in Germany, and German-Italian friction increased in the Western Desert. In June Mussolini spent three weeks in Libya without even seeing Rommel. The Allied landings in French North Africa in November added to his depression.

Mussolini formed a new government on 5 February 1943, in which he was himself Foreign Minister. He met Hitler in Salzburg on 6 April and attempted to persuade him to make a settlement with Russia. By May Hitler, suspicious of Italian intentions, was making plans to occupy Italy if she withdrew from the war. On 19 July, after the Allied landings in Sicily, Mussolini met Hitler once more. He was presented with a virtual ultimatum, making the defence of southern Italy conditional upon German control of the Axis forces. Meanwhile Mussolini's own position in Italy was in peril. A conspiracy to depose him was well under way. Both politicians and generals were involved. The King had agreed to remove Mussolini and appoint Marshal Badoglio as head of the government. A meeting of the Fascist Grand Council was convened on 24 July, and at it Count Grandi presented a motion demanding that all existing organs of government should be revived and that the King should assume command of the armed forces. The motion was passed by 19 votes to 7, but Mussolini, though ill, appeared calm during the meeting. On the following day, after an interview with the King, Mussolini was arrested in the palace gardens, and the new government under Badoglio exiled him to the island of Ponza. After some time, to guard against German rescue attempts, they took him to an hotel in the Gran Sasso (in the Abruzzi mountains). On 8 September 1943 the Badoglio government surrendered to the Allies, but three days later the Germans seized Rome. Mussolini was rescued from his prison on 12 September by a daring aerial Commando-style raid led by Otto Skorzeny.

After talks with Hitler, Mussolini announced the revival of the Fascist party, and reaffirmed Italian-German solidarity, absolving officers of the armed forces from their oath of allegiance to the King. His new Cabinet met on 27 September at La Rocca, and Mussolini wrote to Hitler asking that German military forces should allow Italian civilian authorities civil jurisdiction. But Hitler had no intention of relaxing his grip on Italy and did not answer the letter.

Mussolini settled down to conducting the affairs of a phantom government. The trials of leaders who had been engaged in the July coup took place in January 1944. Ciano, Mussolini's son-in-law, was among those executed for treason. But there was little support for Mussolini: it was estimated in June 1944 that there were 82,000 Italian partisans actively fighting against him, and Hitler complained of the unreliability of Fascist troops and refused to permit Mussolini an Italian army. The last meeting of the two dictators took place in Germany on the day of the July assassination plot against Hitler. After an emotional tea-party the Führer saw the Duce to his train, calling him his 'best and possibly only friend' and said goodbye. More powerless than ever, Mussolini spent the rest of the year reminiscing and holding meandering and contradictory conversations. 'Death has become a friend who no longer frightens me,' he said. But he had sufficient interest in the world outside to seek peace with the Allies through the mediation of Cardinal Schuster. In April 1945, as the German forces in the north of Italy collapsed, Mussolini left for Como after writing a farewell letter to his wife. He was joined by his mistress, Clara Petacci. On 26 April Italian partisans arrested the couple, and on 28 April shot them unceremoniously. The bodies were taken to Milan and hung, upside-down, in a public square.

To the end, despite the fact that Italy was very much a junior partner in the Axis (and in the latter months scarcely even that), Hitler in his personal relations with the Duce treated Mussolini with deference. Mussolini was, of course, chronologically the senior dictator. Despite the Duce's megalomania he never permitted among his Fascist followers the extraordinary barbarities endemic to the German Nazis.

N

NASH, Walter, b. 1882. New Zealand statesman, the architect of New Zealand's 'welfare state'.

At the outbreak of war he held the portfolios of Finance and Customs and was responsible for initiating much remarkably far-reaching financial and social reform. In 1939 he pushed through Parliament the bitterly contested social security legislation which made New Zeaand a prototype welfare state. As Minister of Finance he brought in legislation which placed the Reserve Bank under state ownership and control, acquired for the state privately owned shares in the Bank of New Zealand, and nationalized the major domestic airlines.

His influence upon the policies and fortunes of the Labour party was profound. The exigencies of war finance caused him to be regarded as a stern tax-gatherer, but his uncanny success in handling New Zealand's war-time finances more than compensated for the lack of public appeal of his policies.

In 1940 Nash took over the Deputy Premiership, and in 1942 he was appointed New Zealand Minister in the U.S.A. and a member of the Pacific War Council. He continued to hold, however, the position of Minister of Finance and in 1944 was the leader of his country's delegation to the International Monetary Conference. Tenacious and confident in politics, all his energies were devoted to his work. Despite his practical grasp of politics, he remained throughout his career an idealist and visionary, fired with zeal for the alleviation of suffering and the correction of economic injustice.

Nash was born in Kidderminster in England and emigrated to New Zealand in 1909.

NEBE, Artur, b. 1896. S.S. leader, head of the German criminal investigation department (Kripo). An enigmatic character whose true affiliations are a matter for conjecture, he was certainly in close contact with the conspirators against Hitler, passing on to them information about Gestapo activities. His contact, von Schlabrendorff, considered him 'a resolute and determined anti-Nazi', but it has also been argued that he was merely an unscrupulous careerist concerned to hedge his bets.

After the Wannsee Protocol of January 1942, Heydrich put Nebe in charge of one of the *Einsatzgruppen* entrusted with the task of exterminating the Jews of Russia. It is possible that Nebe contrived to thwart Himmler's orders for wholesale murder by faking the numbers of those executed, but it is still an undeniable fact that he was responsible for the execution of thousands of innocent and defenceless people.

In 1943 he returned to his post as head of the criminal police in Berlin, and became involved in the July 1944 plot to kill Hitler. After the failure of the plot he was arrested by vengeful Gestapo colleagues and executed in Plötzensee prison on 3 March 1945.

Nebe was a member of the Prussian criminal police long before 1933, when it was taken over by the S.S., and was an expert in the field of crime prevention and detection. In 1929 he joined the Nazi party and the S.S. in defiance of a law forbidding membership of political parties to members of the civil service. He was, however, never obviously an ardent Nazi and long before the outbreak of war had joined the ranks of Hitler's opponents.

NETTLETON, John, b. 1917. South African airman in the R.A.F., awarded the V.C. for a bombing attack on Germany of extraordinary daring. On 17 April 1942, as a squadron-leader, he led an attack by Lancaster bombers on the submarine diesel engine works at Augsburg in southern Germany. It was thought that the destruction of these works would severely hamper German war production. The attack, although successful, had little effect on the German war effort, but the courage of Nettleton and his squadron provided an example of selfless bravery which lifted the morale of their countrymen.

The feat was one of the most hazardous ever attempted by Bomber Command. Nettleton, leading a squadron of 12 Lancasters, had to take them on a round-trip flight of 1,250 miles, mostly over enemy territory. Only 8 planes reached Augsburg, and there they bombed the target, a single building situated within a huge factory complex. In addition to the necessity for a precision attack, the operation meant that the aircraft had to fly at low level during daylight amidst a heavy barrage of flak. Only 5 of the Lancasters, Nettleton's among them, returned from the Augsburg mission.

On the night of 12 July 1943 Nettleton was killed in action during a Bomber Command attack on Turin.

NEURATH, Konstantin von, b. 1873. German diplomat and former Foreign Minister, appointed Protector of Bohemia and Moravia after the German invasion of Czechoslovakia in 1938. Towards the end of 1939, on Hitler's instructions, the Czech parliament was dissolved, political parties were forbidden, the freedom of the press was abolished, and the Nuremberg racial laws were adopted. Student resistance was brutally crushed, Czech universities were closed down, along with numerous schools, and the Churches were persecuted, many eminent churchmen being imprisoned or even executed. Even so, Hitler considered that Neurath was not sufficiently dedicated and strict, and he was replaced by Reinhard Heydrich in 1941. Neurath later became involved in clandestine opposition to Hitler. After the war he was sentenced to 15 years' imprisonment at the Nuremberg Trials as a war criminal.

NICHOLSON, J. B., b. 1917. R.A.F. officer, the first pilot of Fighter Command to win a V.C. during the war. He had been a Spitfire pilot with 72 Squadron, but before the Battle of Britain had been promoted flight-commander with 249 Hurricane Squadron. On 16 August 1940 he was patrolling the Southampton area. He closed in with two other Hurricanes to attack three Junkers 88 bombers, but was anticipated by a Spitfire squadron. As he turned for base he was hit by cannon shells from a Messerschmitt 110; two struck him and a third set fire to the reserve petrol tank behind his instrument panel. Although wounded and half blinded by fire in his cockpit, Nicholson realized that the Me 110 was in a vulnerable position, delayed baling out until he had attacked it, and shot it down. His face

and hands were severely burned, but he succeeded in parachuting to safety.

NIEMÖLLER, Martin, b. 1892. German Protestant churchman, regarded by many as a symbolic figure of the suppression of liberty under the Nazis. He was, in World War I, celebrated as a U-Boat commander. He then became a Lutheran clergyman and was pastor of Berlin-Dahlem from 1931 to 1937. In the early days a supporter of the National Socialists, he soon came into conflict with the Nazi régime. Hitler had at first encouraged 'positive Christianity', and had declared that Christianity could play an important part in the realization of the destiny of the German people—a welcome change in Niemöller's eyes from the neutral attitude of the Weimar Republic. However, it soon became clear that Hitler visualized a Church that was a willing agent of the Nazi party. A Protestant 'German Christian Church' was established under Nazi patronage, and, in opposition, Niemöller organized the 'pastors' emergency league'. In 1933 he and his supporters founded the Confessional Church, which declared itself the true German Lutheran Church at the Synod of Barmen in 1934. Later it gave way to the Lutheran Council, which took a less intransigent line towards the State Church.

In November 1933 Niemöller was suspended by the Reichsbishop of the German Christian Church for his anti-Nazi attitude, which included opposition to laws discriminating against Jews. Niemöller spoke out fearlessly against the philosophy and excesses of the National Socialist Party and in July 1937 he was arrested and sent to Moabit prison. Later, after a trial, he was imprisoned in Sachsenhausen and Dachau concentration camps, where he remained until 1945. In 1941 he asked, unsuccessfully, to be allowed to serve again in the German navy, believing that in wartime this was his duty.

NIMITZ, Chester, b. 1885. American admiral who commanded the naval forces in the Pacific for most of the war. He was appointed C.-in-C. of the Pacific Fleet shortly after the Japanese attack on Pearl Harbor in December 1941, and later became commander of the Pacific Ocean

area and the Central Pacific area. These
commands raised problems connected with
inter-service relationships, and Nimitz controlled the operations of the marine corps
as well as naval forces.

Nimitz's first task was to defend the
approaches to Hawaii and to secure communications with General MacArthur in
Australia—MacArthur being responsible
for the S.W. Pacific land theatre. Initially
he engaged in submarine warfare and
naval bombardment of Japanese island
bases. But by May 1942 he was ready to
engage in a major battle. The Battle of
the Coral Sea, which was decided by air
power, lasted for 4 days. The U.S. forces
consisted of the aircraft carriers *Yorktown*
and *Lexington*, with 3 cruisers and 6
destroyers. Planes from the carriers
destroyed or damaged a number of
Japanese ships at Tulagi and sank the
Japanese carrier *Shoho* on 7 May. Japanese
planes sank the *Lexington* and damaged
the *Yorktown*, but they abandoned their
plan to attack Port Moresby.

Meanwhile U.S. Intelligence had cracked
the Japanese naval code, and was aware
of plans for a Japanese offensive at Midway. Nimitz collected a large fleet, with
3 carriers, 8 cruisers, 14 destroyers, and
20 submarines, supported by air forces
based on Midway and Hawaii. He directed
the battle from his land H.Q. at Pearl
Harbor. Admiral Yamamoto's fleet was
heavily defeated, with the loss of 4
carriers, a cruiser, and a destroyer. The
Americans' worst loss was the carrier
Yorktown. The Battle of Midway transformed the balance of naval power in the
Pacific. The U.S.A. was now safe from
direct naval attack.

In July 1942 the Japanese began to build
up a base at Guadalcanal in the Solomons.
The Americans retaliated by landing a
Marine division and other troops. A series
of bitter naval, air, and land engagements
followed, as each side built up its forces
and tried to protect its supply lines. By
December the Americans had gained control of the southern Solomons, and the
Japanese were gradually forced out.

Thereafter Nimitz held the initiative in
the Pacific. His fleet and air arm were
considerably enlarged and were divided
into four task forces. Nimitz used his
forces in helping to eliminate gradually

the enemy strongholds and push the
Japanese westwards. Makin and Tarawa
in the Gilberts were taken in November
1943, followed by Truk, and then by Saipan
in the Marianas by February 1944. After
the end of the Marianas campaign Nimitz
successfully proposed that the next steps
should be the capture of Luzon and then
of Okinawa. Subsequently it was realized
that Iwo Jima, in the Volcano Islands,
should also be taken to provide an inter-
mediate base for bombers operating
against the Japanese islands. Iwo Jima was
captured in February 1945; the campaign
for Okinawa, 350 miles from the Japanese
mainland, ended on 21 June. By 16 July
Nimitz could say: 'We have paralysed the
will and ability of the Japanese navy to
come out and fight.'

The bombardment of Japan reached its
climax with the atom bomb attack on
Hiroshima on 6 August. Nimitz, the quiet
and efficient fleet admiral who had directed
the navy in the Pacific from the prospect
of disaster to ultimate victory, saw his
Japanese opponents surrender formally on
2 September 1945 on board the USS
Missouri in Tokyo Bay.

NORTH, Sir Dudley, b. 1881. British
admiral. At the outbreak of war he became
Flag Officer, North Atlantic, at Gibraltar
and was there at the time of the abortive
Allied attack on Dakar, which failed
partly because the Vichy French were
informed of the impending operation and
sent naval reinforcements.

The French colonial port of Dakar, in
Senegal, on the west coast of Africa, was
of great strategic importance to the Allies,
and the possibility of the Vichy government's allowing Germany the use of the
port caused the dispatch of a largely
British expedition to establish de Gaulle's
Free French forces in Senegal. On 11
September 1940, when the troop convoys
were approaching Dakar, Admiral North
at Gibraltar reported that 3 French cruisers
and 3 destroyers from Toulon had been
observed heading out of the Mediterranean
into the Atlantic. The Admiralty blamed
North for letting the French squadron
pass Gibraltar unmolested. At Churchill's
instigation he was relieved of his command.

An impartial review of the orders
previously sent to him showed that his

belief that he was not required to stop French ships sailing to West African ports was reasonable. In any case he did not have the strength to intercept them had he wished to do so.

North served as Flag Officer at Great Yarmouth from 1942 to 1945. He loyally kept quiet for the duration of the war, but afterwards he and his friends tried to reopen the question of his war-time dismissal without inquiry. It was not until 12 years after the war that his name was cleared. Then, in 1957, Prime Minister Harold Macmillan at the First Sea Lord's suggestion held an inquiry. As a result of the inquiry North was publicly acquitted of any charge of dereliction of duty in 1940.

NYE, Archibald, b. 1895. British general, Vice-C.I.G.S. 1941 to 1946. His partnership with General Brooke, the C.I.G.S., was remarkably harmonious and successful. Nye had been in India in command of the Nowshera Brigade at the outbreak of war. Back at the War Office, in 1940 he became Deputy Director, then Director, of Staff Duties. In 1941, when Churchill wished to replace General Dill as C.I.G.S., Nye was one of several candidates for the post. In the event General Brooke, the senior and more experienced officer, was appointed.

Nye's first mission as Vice-C.I.G.S. came in December 1941, when he accompanied the Foreign Secretary, Anthony Eden, to Moscow. The German front line was then little more than 25 miles away. The conduct of the war and Anglo-Soviet relations were discussed, Stalin proposing that Britain should recognize Russia's new western frontiers as they existed before the German invasion. The talks were inconclusive, and agreement postponed until May 1942, when Molotov signed the Anglo-Soviet treaty in London.

In March 1942 the C.I.G.S. could not leave England, so Nye joined Sir Stafford Cripps in Cairo for discussions with General Auchinleck, C.-in-C. Middle East. Here there was a critical military situation. Churchill was urging Auchinleck to attack and drive the Axis forces west to Tripolitania, while Auchinleck maintained that he was not in a position to do this without endangering Egypt and his army. Cripps, Nye, and the Service chiefs reported to Churchill that Auchinleck's views were sound, and that an immediate attack would involve an unwarrantable risk.

Nye's most important contribution, probably, was to lift much of the routine administration from Brooke's shoulders. Brooke later wrote of his deputy: '. . . a first-class brain, great character, courage in his convictions . . . a quick worker with very clear vision . . . a man I trusted implicitly. I could not have wished for anyone better. I could leave the country with the absolute confidence that he would do his best to maintain the identical policies which he knew I wanted.'

O

O'CONNOR, Sir Richard, b. 1889.
British general, one of the most successful
of the Desert commanders. He was
military governor of Jerusalem and
commander of the 7th Division in September 1939. In June 1940 the 7th Division
was moved to Egypt, and O'Connor, an
old friend of General Wavell, was appointed
commander of the Western Desert forces.
On 8 December Wavell launched the great
offensive which was to take Tobruk
within 6 weeks and to reach Benghazi
and El Agheila by 5 February 1941.
O'Connor, who led the seaward flank of
the attack, was principally responsible for
planning and carrying out the operation,
which brought the whole of Cyrenaica into
British hands. The whole operation went
exactly to plan. The motto of this
determined soldier was 'offensive action
wherever possible'. After the advance to
El Agheila had been made, Wavell was
obliged to send a large part of the army to
Greece, under General Wilson's command.
O'Connor accepted this decision stoically.
He was made G.O.C. British troops in
Egypt under General Neame of the Cyrenaican command.

On 30 March Rommel launched a heavy
counter-attack, and the skeleton British
forces in Libya, now on the defensive,
were forced to withdraw. In April
O'Connor and Neame were taken
prisoner when surprised by a German
motor-cycle patrol near Derna. They were
sent to captivity in Italy.

In December 1943, after the capitulation
of Italy, O'Connor, Neame, and Air
Marshal Boyd escaped. In June 1944
O'Connor went to Normandy in command
of 8th Corps and directed tank operations
from a mobile H.Q. It has since been said
that, but for his misfortune in being taken
prisoner, he might have become the
greatest of all the 'Desert generals'.

ODETTE. *See* SANSOM, Odette.

OLBRICHT, Friedrich, b. 1886. German
general, one of the leading members of
the July 1944 conspiracy to assassinate
Hitler. As head of the Supply Section of
the Home Army, and personal deputy to

General Fromm, the C.-in-C. of the Home
Army, Olbricht had direct authority over
all troops stationed in the Reich for
garrison and replacement purposes.

He was not deeply involved in the early
conspiracies to overthrow Hitler. But in
February 1943 he agreed to co-operate in
building up a military organization in
Berlin, Vienna, Cologne, and Munich to
take control after the planned assassination of Hitler. The first attempt during the
war took place in March 1943, and failed;
many of the conspirators were arrested.
Claus von Stauffenberg then became
associated with the plot, and Operation
'Valkyrie' was planned. Olbricht gave the
'Valkyrie' alert (which involved a move
on Berlin by troops) on 15 July 1944—
but the attempt on Hitler's life, which
was a prerequisite, had not in fact taken
place, and the operation had to be explained to Fromm as a 'surprise exercise'.
On 20 July Stauffenberg's bomb exploded
in Hitler's conference room at Rastenburg.
However, the planned disruption of communications did not take place. Olbricht
gave the 'Valkyrie' signal and arrested
Fromm—who had already telephoned
Rastenburg and knew that Hitler had
escaped serious injury. The machinery of
the take-over was not put into operation
with sufficient speed and force. The situation in the Bendlerstrasse (the War
Ministry, and the plotters' H.Q.) became
more and more confused, as the conspirators only gradually realized that all was
lost. Fromm was released, and had
Olbricht, Stauffenberg, and others shot
immediately.

'O'LEARY, Pat'. *See* GUÉRISSE, Albert.

OPPENHEIMER, J. Robert, b. 1904.
American physicist whose name is permanently linked with the development
of atomic weapons. As Professor of
Physics at the University of California
from 1936, Oppenheimer established the
first important school of theoretical
physics in the U.S.A., a school that was
greatly strengthened by the work of
refugees from Hitler's régime. After war
began Oppenheimer was appointed by the
government to the directorship of the
Los Alamos laboratory in New Mexico,
where his task was the design and con-

struction of an atom bomb. This Oppenheimer and the team of scientists working
under him achieved in time for the new
weapon to prove a decisive factor in
bringing to an end the war with Japan.

ORR, Sir John Boyd, b. 1880. British
biologist, an expert on problems of
nutrition and government adviser on food
production and rationing. At the beginning of the war he was head of the Rowett
Research Institute in Animal Nutrition.
He was already known for his report
Food, Health and Income (published in
1936) in which he demonstrated that a
third of the population of Britain was
unable to afford an adequate diet. He
next published a book, *Feeaing the People
in Wartime*, which pointed out the dangers
of food shortage and recommended that
every family should grow some of its own
food. As the result of an interview with

Orr, the Minister of Food set up a scientific advisory committee on food production. Orr joined the Cabinet Food Committee and the system of rationing during
the war was based on his recommendations and those of other experts on nutrition.

Orr was made Professor of Agriculture
at Aberdeen University in 1942 where he
amalgamated the College of Agriculture
Farm with the Institute Experimental
Farm. He visited the U.S.A. in 1942 at
the invitation of a group of scientists who
were interested in setting up a world food
plan. This idea was put into cold storage,
but was revived after the war when
Orr was made Director-General of the
newly created Food and Agriculture
Organization.

Orr was a Scot from a working-class
background, a hard-working idealist, with
great tenacity of purpose.

P

PACELLI, Eugenio. *See* PIUS XII.

PAGET, Sir Bernard, b. 1888. British general who played a large part in re-shaping the army after the earlier reverses of the war. As commander of the 18th Division he took part in the Norwegian campaign of 1939–40. After the Royal Navy's successes at Narvik it was decided that in order to complete the operation successfully by landing troops the important city of Trondheim would have to be captured. Paget commanded 'Sickleforce', which was to advance on Trondheim from the south. But, because of the rapid German tank advance and heavy air attacks, the whole of central Norway had to be evacuated. It was this disaster which precipitated the downfall of Neville Chamberlain and his replacement by Churchill. Paget became C.G.S. Home Forces in 1940; C.-in-C. South Eastern Command in 1941; and C.-in-C. Home Forces from December 1941 to 1943. (He had been among those considered for the post of C.I.G.S.) During this latter period he greatly improved the standards of training throughout the army. As chairman of the 'Combined Commanders'—the others being Sholto Douglas and Mountbatten—he was involved in drawing up the early plans for a return to the Continent and thus laid the foundations for the final 'Second Front' plan, Operation 'Overlord'. From June to December 1943 he was C.-in-C. 21st Army Group, which was to be the British component in the invasion force, but was transferred to the Middle East when Eisenhower was appointed Supreme Allied Commander in Western Europe. He was perhaps not given full credit for the manner in which he fashioned the formation which, under Montgomery's leadership, proved to be probably the finest the British had ever marshalled. Paget forged a magnificent weapon, and Montgomery imparted the final polish to it. While in the Middle East he dealt successfully with the mutiny of the Greek Brigade instigated by Communist elements; and also with the delicate situation arising from France's attempts to reassert her former authority in Syria and the Lebanon. For these diplomatic and military manœuvres he received much praise from Churchill.

PAPAGOS, Alexander, b. 1883. Greek general who was C.-in-C. when the Italians invaded Greece from Albania on 28 October 1940. He not only repulsed the attack but drove the Italians back into Albania. As a follow-up attack by the Germans seemed likely, the British government instructed General Wavell, C.-in-C. Middle East, to give the defence of Greece precedence over all other operations.

A meeting was held with Papagos in Athens on 22 February 1941. The British offered a land force with intensified naval and air support. They decided to defend the so-called Aliakmon Line. But on returning to Athens on 28 February the British party (led by Anthony Eden) found that Papagos had waited to see what Yugoslavia's attitude would be, and had not withdrawn his troops to the Aliakmon Line. It was by then possibly too late to do so. Papagos urged a joint defence of the Nestos Line in Eastern Macedonia, but a compromise defence, based on the Aliakmon Line, was agreed upon.

On 9 March 1941 a new Italian offensive began in Albania and, in early April, the Germans invaded Yugoslavia and Greece in quick succession, forcing a British-Greek withdrawal. An army coup by General Tsolacoglou on 21 April preceded a Greek surrender, with Athens in German hands on 27 April. Papagos was arrested by the Tsolacoglou regime in May. He was taken to Germany as a hostage by the Nazis in 1943, and was eventually liberated from Dachau concentration camp in 1945 by the Americans.

PAPANDREOU, George, b. 1888. Greek politician, a former leader of the Social Democrat party who, after the mutinies in the Greek armed forces in April 1944, was brought out of Greece by the Allies to form a Greek government in exile in Cairo. He assumed office as Prime Minister on 26 April, and issued a proclamation which was to be the agenda for a conference of members of all the patriotic groups, including guerrilla leaders from the Greek mountains. The delegates met in the Lebanon in May when it was agreed—though not without doubts and misgivings on the part of some speakers—to set up an administration in Cairo in which all groups would be represented under the premiership of Papandreou, while in Greece a united military organization would continue the fight against the Germans.

In October 1944, on the withdrawal of the Germans from Greece, Papandreou returned to Athens as Prime Minister in the Cabinet of National Union.

PARK, Keith, b. 1892. British air marshal, commander in some of the greatest battles by fighter aircraft in the war. A New Zealander, he became A.O.C. No. 11 Fighter Group under Dowding in 1939. He was responsible for providing air cover during the Dunkirk evacuation. With only 200 planes at his disposal he nevertheless claimed fighter ascendancy over the German bombers. His tactics in the Battle of Britain were criticized, but proved successful.

In the autumn of 1941 he was appointed A.O.C. at Allied H.Q. in Egypt. On 15 July 1942 he took over as A.O.C. Malta. The island had been short of supplies since September 1941, and was very much on the defensive against attacks by Axis aircraft. Park adopted offensive tactics: his Spitfires intercepted the enemy at sea, and regular bombing raids on German convoys to North Africa were ordered. He gave air support to the Allied landings in North Africa in November 1942. In January 1943 the Malta air command became part of the Mediterranean air command, under Sholto Douglas. By June Park had built up a huge air base in Malta to support the Sicily landings of July and the Italy landings of September. In January 1944 he took over supreme command of the air in the Middle East, and in February 1945 he became Air C.-in-C. S.E.A.C. He provided the vital air support for the 14th Army during the capture of Rangoon and the Battle of the Sittang Bend in the summer of 1945.

Park was an officer of great initiative and energy, and his command in Malta, specially, with his fighters putting up a magnificent defence of the island, showed his talents to their best advantage.

'PASSY, Colonel'. *See* BROSSOLETTE, Pierre.

PATCH, Alexander, b. 1889. American general who, after a victorious campaign against the Japanese as commander of U.S. forces at Guadalcanal in the South Pacific 1942–3, led the 7th Army in the Allied invasion of southern France. In 1941 Patch was in command of the Infantry Replacement Center at Camp Croft, North Carolina, and in the spring of the following year became commander of the Task Force assembled to take over the defence of New Caledonia, in the South Pacific, on behalf of the French. On 9 December 1942 he took over as commander in Guadalcanal in the South Solomons, where the Americans were making plans for their final offensive. By 4 January 1943 the Japanese were withdrawing, and on 9 February Patch announced the end of the campaign in Guadalcanal. In March 1944 he was designated commanding general of the 7th Army, which was due to take part in the invasion of southern France. The U.S. 7th Army landed between Toulon and Cannes on 15 August 1944. They quickly took Toulon and Marseilles and then advanced along the Rhône valley in pursuit of the German 19th Army. During October they were delayed in the Vosges, but had contacted the American 3rd Army and taken northern Alsace by the end of December. On 15 March 1945 Patch opened the battle for the Saar against the much-weakened German Army Group G. He crossed the Rhine on 26 March. In late April, to prevent the formation by the Germans of a national redoubt, Patch turned southeast from Munich and headed for the Brenner Pass via Salzburg. The instruments of surrender were signed by Army Group G delegates on 5 May.

PATTON, George, b. 1885. American general, a bold and resourceful tactician and an outstanding practitioner of mobile tank warfare. He commanded, under Eisenhower, the U.S. forces that landed in Morocco in November 1942 and held command of the 2nd Army Corps in Tunisia in the early months of 1943. Later that year Patton commanded the

U.S. 7th Army during the invasion of
Sicily; he used his armour in a rapid drive
that captured Palermo. The high point of
his career was the summer of 1944, when
his 3rd Army, part of the invading Allied
forces in N.W. Europe, raced across
France. His army forced its way to Metz,
raised the siege of Bastogne, and swept
on to Czechoslovakia in a campaign
which was marked by great initiative and
disregard of classic conventions. In his
thrust across France he exploited many
situations to his advantage and showed
a ruthless determination to press forward
at any cost. These characteristics earned
him the nickname 'Old Blood and Guts'
from his troops. He had scant regard for
field regulations and textbook rules, and
on a number of occasions seemed to show
little respect for his superiors. Once, when
his main force had ground to a halt on the
Meuse for two days because there was no
petrol, while his superiors were giving
priority to the capture of Antwerp, Patton
had no hesitation in appealing to Eisenhower for petrol so that he could continue.
He very quickly came to resent Montgomery, and complained, with some other
American commanders, about his allegedly
over-studied warfare. Patton differed
from Montgomery in outlook and method
on a number of points, especially where
reserves were concerned. Patton impatiently asserted that attack was always
the best method of defence; he thought
that all available force should be used in
the fighting line. Patton acted on this
principle in his advance from the Marne
to the Moselle, and somewhat disrupted
the Allied front in the process. Under
Patton's leadership the 3rd Army siphoned
forces and supplies from what Eisenhower
had declared be the main drive; and
Patton was himself unscrupulous about
getting what he wanted. He recorded as a
rumour what his staff boasted as a fact,
that 'some of our ordnance people passed
themselves off as members of the 1st Army
and secured quite a bit of gasoline from
one of the dumps of that unit'. Patton's
comment was: 'This is not war but it is
magnificent.'

Patton was known for his flamboyant
appearance and assumed a 'tough guy'
attitude, typified by his sporting of a pearl-
handled revolver. This pose, together with

his recklessness and daring as a commander,
made him immensely popular in the
American press. While he had marked
eccentricities, he did not provoke resentment, and was admired by his colleagues
and men. Dogmatic though he could be,
he commanded in a 'democratic' way,
and consulted with his staff in daily conference. One of his principles was: 'Never
tell people how to do things, tell them
what to do and they will surprise you with
their ingenuity.'

Patton's professional interest and expertise in the new tank arm and in mobile
tank warfare stemmed from battle experience with the U.S. tank corps in World
War I; between the wars his fascination
with tank warfare had continued. He died
as the result of an accident in Germany
in December 1945.

PAUL of Yugoslavia, b. 1893. Prince
Regent for the young King Peter II from
1934 until his enforced resignation on 27
March 1941. An amiable and unambitious
man, Paul's main concern on the outbreak
of war was to maintain Yugoslav neutrality. He eschewed a more positive
attitude because of internal unrest and lack
of military preparedness.

Paul soon decided that the only way of
saving Yugoslavia was to come to some
agreement with the Axis powers. Early in
March 1941 the British government tried
to win him over, telling him that Greece
and Turkey were prepared to fight if
attacked. But Paul was already in contact
with the Germans, and paid a secret visit
to Hitler at Berchtesgaden on 4 March.
Under extreme pressure he consented to
Hitler's demands. In the face of strong
opposition from within the Royal Council
and among the political and military
leaders, the Yugoslav government decided
on 20 March to adhere to the Axis pact.
On 25 March the Prime Minister and the
Foreign Minister signed the pact with
Hitler in Vienna.

But national feeling was outraged, and
a bloodless coup (planned some months
earlier in the event of such a sell-out) was
successfully initiated on 27 March by
officers of the armed forces, led by General
Simović. Various members of the government were arrested, and when Prince Paul
returned to Belgrade from Slovenia he

and the other two regents were forced to sign an act of abdication. That night, accompanied by his family, Paul left Yugoslavia for Greece.

PAULUS, Friedrich von, b. 1890. German field marshal whose defeat by the Russians at Stalingrad marked the turning-point of the war. As Chief of Staff of the 6th Army under Reichenau, Paulus took part in the German army's victorious drives through Poland, Belgium, and France in 1939 and 1940. He also helped in preparations for an invasion of England. Towards autumn 1940 Paulus was appointed Deputy Chief of the General Staff under General Halder. In that capacity he was responsible for planning the invasion of Russia, Operation 'Barbarossa', which began in June 1941. Hitler and his advisers on the one hand and the General Staff of the Army on the other were deeply divided over operational objectives—the former favouring concentration on the flanks, the latter preferring to launch a thrust on Moscow. The army's advice was ignored and an attack on Moscow was deferred until it was too late to achieve success. Both before the invasion and during its early stages a number of extraordinary orders were issued, including the 'Commissar Order' which directed that Soviet political commissars were not to be treated as P.O.W.s but should be shot out of hand; and the 'Severity Order' which encouraged savagery in dealing with Russians and Jews. As soon as Paulus became commander of the 6th Army he cancelled those two orders on his own initiative. The new appointment gave him great satisfaction, because he had long been hoping for an operational command.

During the course of the German advance into Russia in the summer of 1942 victory followed victory, though casualties were colossal. Eventually the 6th Army advanced on Stalingrad, encountering dogged resistance at Kalach. Paulus intended to occupy the part of Stalingrad that stretched along the Volga, and then surround the whole city. There followed weeks of exhausting house-to-house fighting. Paulus begged for more troops, for arms, fuel, food, and winter clothing, all of which he urgently needed; but no aid was forthcoming. By November 1942

the 6th Army found itself surrounded by the Russians—the only alternatives being to attempt to break out and retreat, against Hitler's express orders, or to stand firm and risk complete annihilation. In the bitter winter Paulus decided to hold out, but by the end of January 1943 his army had virtually disintegrated and when, on 31 January, Soviet troops entered Red Square, where his battle headquarters were, he had no option but to surrender.

PEIERLS, Rudolf, b. 1907. British scientist of German birth who made one of the most important contributions to the development of the atomic bomb. Educated at Berlin, Leipzig, and Zürich universities, he became Professor of Applied Mathematics at Birmingham in 1937.

At the time war broke out in 1939 the idea of producing an 'atomic bomb' of immense destructive power was under active discussion, but there were formidable obstacles in the way of making a practicable weapon. Though uranium fission and the emission of neutrons had been achieved, physicists were working chiefly with natural uranium: the chain reaction could be attained only with thermal neutrons, and it was calculated that impracticable amounts of uranium would be needed to make a bomb. In February 1940, however, Peierls and Otto Frisch, in a paper, set out calculations which seemed to show that if uranium-235 were used the amount needed would be small. The paper was shown to Sir Henry Tizard, the chairman of the Committee for the Scientific Survey of Air Warfare, and as a result a committee (the Maud Committee) was established to study the possibilities of separating isotopes. The committee came to the conclusion that the creation of an atomic bomb could probably be achieved on the basis of the Peierls-Frisch observations, and government support was given to work on the separation of isotopes. In 1943 the British government decided—for reasons of economy and war-time practicality—to merge the work being done in the U.K. with that being carried out in the U.S.A. Peierls and other British scientists concerned with research on the atomic weapon were transferred to the U.S.A to help on the Manhattan Project.

PEIRSE, Sir Richard, b. 1892. British air chief marshal who directed the Allied air forces in S.E. Asia. At the outbreak of the war he was Deputy Chief of Air Staff and in 1940 Vice-Chief of Air Staff. He succeeded Portal as C.-in-C. Bomber Command in October 1940. Bomber Command was handicapped in those early years of the war by the necessity for night flying, lack of training for crews, and inadequate radar equipment. Consequently there was lack of precision in hitting targets and a very high casualty rate. At first the priority targets were synthetic oil plants, but the emphasis changed to attacks on U-Boat installations and area bombing. Peirse was told to conserve his command in November 1941, and was relieved of his post in January 1942.

He was then made A.O.C.-in-C. India, arriving in Delhi in March. His first task was to reorganize the existing air forces, and to prepare for expansion by providing maintenance facilities and new airfields. A H.Q. of a new Bengal Command was set up in Calcutta to help operations in N.E. India. In May 1943 Peirse attended the Washington Conference, and returned to speed the development of air facilities in Assam so that the China airlift could go forward. Under Mountbatten he became Allied Air C.-in-C. S.E.A.C. in December 1943, with an American as his second-in-command. The air forces played a vital part in the reconquest of Burma. Mastery in the air was achieved by late 1943, and maintained by continual offensives against Japanese targets. Air supply of the invading 14th Army hence became possible. Peirse's term of office expired in November 1944, and he retired shortly afterwards.

PENIAKOFF, Vladimir, b. 1897, known as 'Popski', founded and commanded Popski's Private Army, a British raiding force operating in North Africa and Italy. PPA, which consisted of about 200 men, was highly mobile and, travelling in armed jeeps, carried out reconnaissance duties and attacked petrol dumps and other military installations behind the enemy lines. 'Popski', despite the splendidly irregular nature of his unit's work, claimed that its success depended on cautious preparation and denied any qualities of dash or spontaneity in his own make-up.

By birth a Belgian of Russian parentage, 'Popski' became a sugar manufacturer in Egypt in the inter-war years. He found enjoyment in travel in the desert, and made himself extraordinarily proficient in the difficult art of desert navigation. Popski greatly admired the English approach to life, and had been a student at Cambridge for some months before joining the French army in World War I; when World War II broke out, he joined the British army and was commissioned in the Libyan Arab Force. His desire was to join the Long Range Desert Group, but he was persuaded to form his own small raiding unit, at first known as No. 1 Long Range Demolition Squadron but soon officially recognized as Popski's Private Army. For its badge 'Popski' chose an astrolabe.

PERCIVAL, Arthur, b. 1887. British general, in command of the forces in Singapore at the time of the surrender of the island to the Japanese in 1942. Early in 1940 Percival commanded first the 43rd Division and then, after the fall of France, the 44th Division, which was employed in defending the coast of Great Britain. In April 1941 he was made G.O.C. Malaya. He had previously served in this theatre from 1936 to 1938.

Percival informed the War Office in 1941 that he would need at least 6 divisions with supporting troops and aircraft to undertake the defence of Malaya; but no reinforcements were afforded to supplement his 2½ weak divisions. He was handicapped in the disposition of his forces because he was not permitted to enter neutral Siam, where the Japanese were (correctly, as the event proved) expected to land. News of Japanese fleet movements came in on 6 December. But the defence operation was not authorized, and the alternative defence plan was set in motion only on 8 December, by which time the Japanese had already gained the initiative. They controlled the air by 10 December. There followed a long series of defensive battles and hurried retreats, beginning with the battle for Jitra on 10 December. Percival finally ordered the retreat to Singapore island on 27 January

1942. On 5 February the siege began. Singapore had inadequate defences to the north, and there was a large civilian population. Churchill ordered Percival to fight to the bitter end, but, when it became apparent on February 15 that the island was faced with a potentially disastrous shortage of water and supplies, he surrendered to General Yamashita with 85,000 troops. He was interned in Singapore and later in Manchuria, but was released in time to be present at the formal surrender of Yamashita in the Philippines in September 1945.

PÉTAIN, Henri Philippe, b. 1856. French army commander and politician, and head of the Vichy government in France. Ambassador to Spain from 1939 to 1940, he returned to Paris after the German invasion to become a member of the government of Paul Reynaud. The authority of Pétain, the veteran hero of Verdun, had greatly influenced French military thought, which remained staunchly conservative, especially by his opposition to the use of 'offensive weapons' and to extending the Maginot Line. Pétain's name was almost legendary, and at the time of France's greatest need he was the obvious choice for leadership.

In May 1940 Paul Reynaud recalled Pétain from Spain, and he was appointed Vice President of Council. Churchill met him at a meeting of the Supreme War Council and later commented on the influence Pétain's personality, reputation, and acceptance of successive disasters had on those under the 'Pétain spell'. By the meeting of 11 June it was clear that France had almost reached the end of organized resistance. Reynaud told Churchill that Pétain was convinced that an armistice was inevitable, and had prepared a paper on the subject; but, Reynaud commented: 'He has not handed it to me—he is still ashamed to do it.' When the Germans entered Paris on 14 June Reynaud realized that the battle for France was over, but, with Admiral Darlan and General de Gaulle behind him, he felt that they could still carry on the war from Africa and the French Empire, using the French fleet. Darlan assured Churchill that the fleet would never be allowed to fall into German hands. But Pétain was now convinced that peace must be made. It was his duty to save as much of France as possible from systematic destruction. Many members of the Cabinet supported him. Churchill said of his attitude: 'There can be no doubt that Pétain is a dangerous man at this juncture; he was always a defeatist, even in the last war.' Reynaud had real hopes that the proposed 'Declaration of Union' with Britain would enable France to keep fighting, but Pétain declined even to look at the proposal. He claimed that it was a humiliation for France; and he also thought that England was on the verge of defeat: 'To make union with England was fusion with a corpse.' Pétain and the other defeatist ministers vowed to stop the fighting, and behind them was Pierre Laval, who had made his position ominously clear: France must not only make peace, she must change sides, ally herself with Germany, and by her service against Britain save her interests and her territory and emerge on the victorious side. Pétain's threat to resign over the 'Declaration of Union' meant the end of the proposal and on 16 June Reynaud himself resigned. President Lebrun immediately called on Pétain to form a new ministry; and on the following day France offered to surrender. Pétain broadcast to all French forces, ordering them to stop fighting pending an armistice and thus abandoning the British forces in France and leaving them to save themselves as best they could in the face of an unopposed triumphant German army. Amid near chaos and military defeat, Pétain made an armistice with Germany on 22 June, and on 24 June signed an armistice with Italy.

France was allowed to retain her colonies and fleet intact. Two zones were established: German forces continued to occupy the northern region, which also included the Atlantic coastline; while Pétain's government was permitted to control the southern 'unoccupied' zone, which included the Mediterranean area. Vichy was also allowed a maximum force of 10,000 men to maintain law and order at home. After the National Assembly had ratified the armistice terms on 10 July, Pétain was armed with 'temporary' emergency powers and forthwith appointed himself Chief of State. The severance of diplomatic ties with the U.K. followed.

Pétain maintained his position as Chief of State from that date until 1945, when France was liberated. During those years the aged Vichy leader walked a diplomatic tightrope in his twin efforts to exclude France from all fighting commitments and at the same time to hold Hitler as much as possible to the terms of the armistice. Some collaboration with the occupying forces was inevitable, and in October 1940 he appeared to endorse the plan for the conquering of Britain that Hitler and Laval put to him. Pétain is said to have remarked on his return to Vichy: 'It will take six months to discuss this programme and another six months to forget it,' but the transaction caused alarm among the Allies and dismayed many in France. The status of the French fleet became vitally important and the Allies constantly reminded Pétain of Admiral Darlan's promise that it would never fall into German hands. Churchill said: 'Pétain has always been an anti-British defeatist, and is now a dotard. The idea that we can build on such men is vain.' Pétain, however, became increasingly fearful of Laval's pressure to pursue a policy that could lead to war with Britain and he objected to the German occupation of the North African colonies. He dismissed Laval in December 1940, replacing him by Flandin. The Germans managed to free Laval, but Pétain refused to take him back in the government; it seemed that the limits of Franco-German collaboration had been reached. In addition Hitler's failure to overcome Britain and his preoccupation with the attack on the Soviet Union meant that the terms of the armistice were proving increasingly favourable to France, and Roosevelt's intervention over the *Dunkerque* in April 1941 made relations between the Vichy government and the British a shade friendlier. But after 1942 the Germans demanded more and more in the way of manpower from France, and with the occupation of the whole of France by the Germans, and Laval's return to power in April 1942, Pétain's authority was considerably undermined. With his physical and mental powers steadily declining, it is possible that Pétain no longer knew or cared much about the decisions taken in his name. But the

disservice done to France by the blatant collaboration that took place in the later stages of the war remained his responsibility as nominal Chief of State.

Pétain was arrested by the Germans in August 1944, and chose to return to France in April 1945. The provisional government under General de Gaulle put him on trial, and on 15 August 1945 a High Court of Justice sentenced him to military degradation and death, though de Gaulle had the sentence commuted to life imprisonment. His trial led to the expression of extreme opinions in France: some hailed him as a self-sacrificing patriot; while his detractors accused him of gross treachery.

Pétain's heroic record in World War I, especially as the hero of Verdun, won him the acclaim and unstinted admiration of most Frenchmen; and though it is difficult to understand the power of the myth that surrounded him, he was hailed as the supreme military genius and the only man who could save France in a crisis. Throughout the war his guiding principle was determination that France should not suffer again as she had in the earlier war. Intensely patriotic, the aged general nevertheless declined into a pathetic and ineffectual figure, but the myth lived to the end.

PETER II, b. 1923. King of Yugoslavia, who spent most of the war in exile and was deposed after peace had been declared. He had ruled through the Regency of his cousin, Prince Paul, since 1934, but assumed full royal powers after the revolt of the armed forces and overthrow of the Regency and government on 27 March 1941. The revolt had been occasioned by the signing of adherence by Prince Paul's government to the Axis powers' Tripartite Pact (25 March 1941).

Germany's rapid invasion of the militarily unprepared country forced the King and his government to leave Belgrade. They moved to Athens, but were obliged to move again—this time to Palestine. They were followed there by the Yugoslav forces that had managed to escape. Peter next moved to England, where his already immense difficulties were further exacerbated by conflicts in his government-in-exile between Serb and Croat members.

Two distinct Resistance movements
emerged in Yugoslavia, one led by
Mihajlović, the other by Tito. Peter soon
found himself at loggerheads with the
Allies, who increasingly relied on Tito
and wanted the King to drop his support
of the less effective, but non-Communist,
Mihajlović. Despite considerable pressure
he refused to do this, and less and less
attention was paid to his wishes: for
example, the news that he was to form a
new government under Šubašić in May
1944 was first announced in the House of
Commons, and took Peter completely by
surprise. Soon afterwards he was at length
forced to disown Mihajlović.

The Tito-Šubašić agreement of 1
November 1944 obliged King Peter to set
up a regency council to represent him in
Yugoslavia; but Tito failed to carry out
his part of the agreement. A republic was
proclaimed on 29 November 1945 and
Peter was deposed.

PILE, Sir Frederick, b. 1884. British
general responsible for the anti-aircraft
defence of Britain throughout the war.
He commanded the 1st Anti-Aircraft
Division of the Territorial Army from
1937 to 1939, and was then appointed
G.O.C.-in-C. of Anti-Aircraft Command,
a post which he held for the duration of
the war. He exploited to the full the skill
of teams of scientific advisers such as Sir
Henry Tizard and P. M. S. Blackett in
order to meet the German attacks in
various forms from the air. One serious
problem that had to be overcome was
the German invention of long-distance
'flying on the beam', or radio directional
navigation for bombing at night.

His first challenge in the war was the
Battle of Britain, in which A.A. Command
was responsible for giving support to the
R.A.F., a task which Pile performed with
success, ingenuity, and a notable disregard
of red tape. His greatest contribution to
the war effort came shortly afterwards
with the 'Blitz', when he made use of
large batteries of rockets which produced
a greater volume of concentrated fire power
than did the normal A.A. artillery.

In 1944–5, when Hitler sent his 'secret
weapons' against London, it was Pile who
remained responsible for the defence
tactics that beat the menace of the V-1

flying bombs and the V-2 rockets. Churchill
wrote of Pile that he was 'an officer of
great distinction . . . ingenious and ser-
viceable in the highest degree'.

PIUS XII, b. 1876. Pope throughout the
whole course of the war. Eugenio Pacelli
was elected Pope on 2 March 1939. Earlier,
in 1937, he had been responsible for gathering the detailed information embodied in
Pius XI's encyclical of March 1937 which
openly condemned the Nazi régime and
which brought violent protests from the
German ambassador to the Vatican.
During the months immediately before
and after the outbreak of war Pius XII
redoubled his diplomatic activities in an
attempt to bring the major world powers
together. He spoke out against aggression,
though without naming names, hoping by
this means to retain some influence with
Hitler and Mussolini, each of whom was
endeavouring to obtain the goodwill of
the Holy See. After Italy's entry into the
war his relations with Mussolini deteriorated rapidly, but he was still able to preserve the Vatican's neutrality and give
sanctuary to many thousands of refugees,
including Jews. A Pontifical Relief Committee was also formed, supplying war
victims of all countries with medicine,
food, and money. As the Allied troops
approached Rome Pius made strenuous
attempts to have the capital declared an
open city. The Germans repeatedly begged
him to leave, so that they could turn the
city into a fortress, but the Romans
regarded him as their best anti-aircraft
defence and Marshal Kesselring finally
agreed to withdraw his troops.

Despite Pius's official neutrality, priests
were permitted to help the Resistance
movement, and many Allied soldiers
hiding in Rome possessed identity cards
supplied by the Vatican. Pius's war-time
encyclicals included one on the unity of
the human race (1939). The question of to
what degree Pius used his authority in
aid of the oppressed peoples under Hitler's
sway became a point of controversy after
the war and is so far unresolved.

**PLACE, Godfrey, b. 1921; and
CAMERON, Donald, b. 1919.** British
submarine officers who severely damaged
and immobilized the German battleship

Tirpitz by what Admiral Horton described as 'a magnificent feat of arms'.

On 11 September 1943 six X-craft (midget submarines) started from harbour in Scotland for Altenfiord in northern Norway to penetrate one of the world's most strongly defended harbours. Their mission was to sink the *Tirpitz*, which was anchored 50 miles up the fiord. Each X-craft was towed by a large submarine. One X-craft was lost during the tow and another had to be abandoned. By the early hours of 22 September Cameron in 'X6' and Place in 'X7' were ready for the final approach to the *Tirpitz*.

The Germans were alerted to their danger when 'X6' accidentally broke surface, but Cameron submerged again, probed his way beneath the battleship, and placed his 2-ton explosive 'side-charges'. He then surfaced and scuttled his craft. He and his crew were taken prisoner. Place had a similar experience: 'X7' also surfaced accidentally, but Place submerged again and released his charges. He then tried to force his way out through the submarine protective nets, but was still entangled when the charges exploded. His craft went out of control and sank, but Place and one of his crew managed to escape and were taken prisoner.

On board the *Tirpitz* there was consternation: the explosions caused the immense ship 'to heave several feet out of the water'. The gravest damage was to the main turbines, all of which were effectively put out of action. The success of the attack on the *Tirpitz* had far-reaching results. Allied plans to revive the Arctic convoys to Russia, suspended because of the threat of the *Tirpitz*, were pressed ahead, and in November the American squadron detailed to reinforce the British Home Fleet at the time of its lowest strength was able to return.

Place was a midshipman R.N. as late as 1940 and a lieutenant at the time of the operation: Cameron was a lieutenant, Royal Naval Reserve. Both received the V.C.

PLATT, Sir William, b. 1885. British general who played a leading part in the defeat of the numerically greatly superior Italian forces in eastern Africa in 1941. Platt was G.O.C. Sudan and commandant

of the Sudan Defence Force from 1938 to 1941. In December 1940 it was decided that an offensive should be mounted against the Italians in Eritrea, Somaliland, and Ethiopia to coincide with the attack on the Italian forces in the Western Desert. Platt's first objective was Kassala in the Anglo-Egyptian Sudan, which had been taken by the Italians at the same time as their drive into British Somaliland. Simultaneously with Platt's offensive, other British, South African, and Ethiopian forces were to fight their way into Somaliland and southern Ethiopia. The Italians abandoned Kassala early on 19 January 1941, considering their position there untenable, and Platt's two Indian divisions were ordered to advance on Massawa, in Eritrea. The Italians made a determined defence of Keren, but were overrun on 27 March. In a matter of days Asmara was taken from them, and by 9 April Platt's troops had taken Massawa. Platt then advanced southwards, with a smaller force, and took part in the decisive Battle of Amba Alagi, which broke the power of the Italians. After the battle the Italian C.-in-C., the Duke of Aosta, surrendered with more than 18,000 troops on 16 May. From 1941 to 1945 Platt was G.O.C.-in-C. East African Command.

'POPSKI'. *See* PENIAKOFF, Vladimir.

PORTAL, Charles, b. 1893. British air marshal, and Chief of Air Staff from 1940 to 1945. Previously, for a short period, he had been A.O.C.-in-C. Bomber Command. At the Air Ministry he directed the policy and operations of the R.A.F., and he also had a major role in the important Allied conferences as the Air Member of the Chiefs of Staff Committee, under the chairmanship of General Brooke.

Until the summer of 1941 Britain's hope of winning the war lay in the aerial bombardment of Germany. After victory in the Battle of Britain, and when fighter ascendancy over the Channel had been gained, the next step was to bomb Germany as often and as heavily as possible. This meant building up an adequate force of four-engined bombers and, under Portal's direction, far-reaching preparations were put in hand. But after the U.S.A. entered the war at the end of 1941 there were inevitable readjustments of policy and tactics.

Portal made a valuable contribution to the Casablanca Conference in January 1943. It was largely his attitude that gained American support for the British point of view, and it was he who usually formulated the arguments which were acceptable all round. Colonel Ian Jacob said of him: 'The Americans put their money on Portal. They would accept him as Commander-in-Chief over everything. They would put all the Allied air forces from Iceland to Bombay under his control. His great asset was his unshakable honesty of thought and deed. They knew he knew his stuff, and they trusted him one hundred per cent.'

In May 1943 he accompanied Churchill to the Washington Conference, and at the Quebec Conference of August, where the 'Second Front' invasion of the European mainland became a live issue, Portal's views commanded great respect.

POUND, Sir Dudley, b. 1877. British admiral, First Sea Lord from 1939, and Admiral of the Fleet from 1939 until his resignation in September 1943 due to ill-health. He brought both wisdom and experience to the immense task of conducting the war at sea. Because of the nature of his responsibilities at the Admiralty (where he had to conduct naval operations and at the same time cope with internal administration) Pound virtually worked himself to death. But, as General Ismay recorded, he was a master of his profession and a sailor to the depths of his being: a brave and generous character.

According to the official naval war history, there is little doubt that during the first two years of the war the Admiralty intervened in the day-to-day conduct of operations to an unjustifiable extent, and that on some occasions Admiralty signals caused confusion and on one occasion brought about a disaster of some magnitude. But Pound's career as First Sea Lord was rich in achievement. To him more than any other must go the credit for the change of fortune at sea by 1943 which opened the way to victory. The successes gained by the Royal Navy— among them Cape Matapan, the breaking of the U-Boat peril, the sinking of the

Bismarck, and the regaining of supremacy in the Mediterranean—were in large measure due to his firm overall control in Whitehall.

Pound did not live to see the final victory of the Allies. He died a few weeks after resigning as First Sea Lord, on 21 October 1943—Trafalgar Day.

PRIEN, Günther, b. 1908. German U-Boat commander whose submarine penetrated Scapa Flow only six weeks after Britain's declaration of war on Germany and sank a British battleship. In the autumn of 1939 Admiral Doenitz entrusted Prien of the submarine *U-47* with the planning and execution of an attack on Scapa Flow, the base of the British Home Fleet. As it happened after an operation most of the fleet had returned to Loch Ewe on the east coast of Scotland, but the battleship H.M.S. *Royal Oak* had anchored in Scapa. The attack took place on the night of 13 October. Prien penetrated a tide-swept, narrow passage between two islands which was incompletely blocked. At 1.30 a.m. on 14 October he torpedoed and sank *Royal Oak*, and then successfully withdrew by the way he had come.

This daring act so early in the war was a shock to British morale, though it had the salutary result of hastening measures to bring the defences of the anchorage up to standard. The German crew celebrated by painting 'The Bull of Scapa' on the conning-tower of *U-47*.

Prien was also active in the Atlantic and the Channel, and at Narvik, where he attempted but failed to sink ships landing British troops. On 8 March 1941, after a long chase, Prien's *U-47* was sunk by the British destroyer H.M.S. *Wolverine* with the loss of all hands. The German authorities kept the loss a secret for several months, knowing the effect the news of the death of a popular hero would have on people in Germany.

Prien came from a poor family and struggled to acquire his naval training. His childhood hero was Vasco da Gama, and throughout his life he retained a love of adventure and a distaste for civilian life. Churchill admired his skill and daring as one of the most outstanding of the U-Boat commanders: he called him 'the redoubtable Prien'.

PRIESTLEY, J. B., b. 1894. English novelist and playwright who became one of the most popular figures in broadcasting during the war. His wise yet chatty commentaries (notably his 'Portraits' in 1940) were heard by millions of people, and Priestley's effect on the national morale was inspiring; it has been said that as a broadcaster he commanded almost as large an audience as Churchill. The B.B.C. had asked Priestley for a novel to be serialized, and the first instalment of the extremely popular 'Let the People Sing' was broadcast on the day that war was declared.

Priestley, in his broadcasts to the U.S.A. as well as to the U.K., described aspects of the war as he saw them, 'in their simplest but profoundest terms'. He wrote a number of highly popular novels with a war-time background, including *Blackout in Getley* (1942), *Daylight on Saturday* (1943), and *Three Men in New Suits* (1945). But it was as an entertainer and broadcaster that Priestley had his greatest war-time effect.

PYLE, Ernest, b. 1900. American journalist and famous war correspondent. Beginning his career as a small-town newspaper reporter, he had by the time war broke out acquired a roving assignment for the Scripps-Howard newspaper chain, and his syndicated articles appeared in hundreds of newspapers all over the U.S.A. In 1941 he made his home in London, enduring the 'Blitz' of that year. His vivid accounts of the campaigns in North Africa, Sicily, Italy, and France earned him a Pulitzer Prize in 1944, as well as many other awards. He covered the war against Japan, accompanying the U.S. forces in the Pacific on Iwo Jima and Okinawa. During the latter campaign he visited the nearby island of Ie Shima and was killed there by Japanese machine-gun fire on 18 April 1945.

'Ernie' Pyle began life as an Indiana farm boy, and throughout his career retained his sympathy for ordinary folk. He was a personal friend of Generals Eisenhower, Bradley, and Doolittle, but, as a war correspondent, he was not interested in the overall strategy or the planning and execution of campaigns, but concentrated instead on the life of the common soldier—the boredom, discomfort, and danger of war at the front, as well as the heroism and companionship. He uniquely conveyed to his readers the atmosphere of the front. In all he spent more than three years in combat areas, and his greatest pride was to think that 'every G.I. regarded him as a friend'.

Q

QUEZÓN, Manuel, b. 1878. Philippine statesman. After the Japanese attack on Pearl Harbor on 7 December 1941 the Philippines—an American dependency with a number of American bases in its territories—inevitably found itself at war with Japan, fighting alongside the U.S.A.

Quezón, who had been elected President of the Commonwealth of the Philippine Islands in 1935, was a firm believer in U.S.-Philippine co-operation, and devoted his energies to boosting his people's morale. During the first week of aerial bombardment, for example, he drove through the streets of Manila every day, to let the people see he had not deserted his post. He assured the U.S.A. of the Filipinos' determination to fight on, and urgently called for reinforcements to help them.

On 24 December 1941, following the advice of his military adviser General MacArthur, he moved to the island fortress of Corregidor as the Japanese took over the main island of Luzon. It was on Corregidor that Quezón's second term of office as President was inaugurated, the ceremony taking place in an air-raid shelter as Japanese bombs were falling. In March 1942 he decided to leave the Philippines for Australia, where he felt he might be able to do more for the liberation of his people. On his arrival in Australia he discovered that the reinforcements arranged for the Philippines were now needed for the defence of Australia. He decided that the best he could do was to go to the U.S.A. and there plead the Filipino cause. He was given an official reception by the House of Representatives, and addressed them on 2 June. During the course of his speech he again promised that the Filipinos would fight to victory. He did not live to see, in March 1945, the last Japanese soldier leave his islands; on 1 August 1944, after much ill-health, he died at Saranac Lake, New York.

QUISLING, Vidkun, b. 1887. Norwegian army officer and political leader whose name became synonymous with 'traitor' —particularly a traitor who works openly in support of his country's enemies. Before the war Quisling had been instrumental in launching the Fascist movement in Norway, although on an insignificant scale. Norway was traditionally neutral, although the Germans had assiduously sought for friendship and cultural ties with her. However, when war began the country was betrayed by a small but well-organized internal pro-German faction under Quisling's leadership.

Since 1936 Quisling had been in touch with Alfred Rosenberg, and he had visited Hitler on 14 December 1939, with Admiral Erich Raeder acting as intermediary. He showed Hitler his detailed plans for a *coup d'état* in Norway. Hitler, in order to camouflage his own plans for Norway, appeared reluctant to discuss Quisling's scheme. He said he favoured a neutral Scandinavia. But, according to Raeder, on the same day he gave orders to the Supreme Command to prepare for an invasion of Norway, which took place on 9 April 1940. Hitler had preferred not to rely on a coup, which might have been unsuccessful, but to use Germany's overwhelming armed superiority in the subjugation of Norway. In the event Quisling promptly collaborated by proclaiming himself the pro-German ruler of the conquered nation, and countermanded Norwegian mobilization orders. His régime so infuriated most Norwegians that it lasted barely a week—almost all Norwegian officials refusing to serve under him. But the German invasion had been well planned: the country was taken completely by surprise, and the occupation carried out swiftly and smoothly. Quisling continued to lead the Nasjonal Samling, the only party permitted by the Germans.

However, he soon found himself at variance with the occupiers. In September 1940 Quisling was deprived not only of the premiership but also of such powers as he had by the German occupation chief. And although he became head of the government again, when Reichskommissar Joseph Terboren named him Minister President in February 1942, he failed to achieve any real authority.

Quisling's efforts to steep the Norwegian Church, the schools, and young people in Nazi propaganda merely incensed his countrymen. He started an anti-

Semitic pogrom, sending about a thousand Jews to their deaths in concentration camps, and in spite of increasing difficulties with the Germans and with his own party he clung to office until Norway was liberated in May 1945. Quisling then gave himself up to the police, and at his trial was found guilty of treason, for which the penalty was death. He was executed on 24 November 1945. His blatant collaboration in the conquest of Norway, and his conduct as a puppet prime minister during the years of the German occupation, earned him the loathing of his Norwegian countrymen and the contempt of the free world. Yet, as his behaviour in his last days showed, he was a brave man; and, according to the testimony of many who knew him well, one who was not prepared to subordinate to the interests of Germany what he conceived to be those of his own country.

R

RAEDER, Erich, b. 1876. German admiral, C.-in-C. of the German naval forces until 1943, and an advocate of aggressive naval warfare.

In October 1939 he submitted a proposal to Hitler for acquiring bases in Norway, pointing out that this would give Germany control over the approaches to the Baltic and also provide a launching area for air attacks on the U.K. Shortly afterwards he was given orders to plan the operation against Norway; the attack actually began in April 1940.

From the outset the Germans had decided that sooner or later they might have to invade Great Britain, but Raeder insisted on many pre-conditions before he was prepared to act, including complete control of the French, Belgian, and Dutch coasts. After the French surrender these conditions were fulfilled, and in May, and again in June, Raeder discussed prospects of invasion with Hitler. Hitler, however, still hoped the British would sue for peace. It was not until 2 July that the first directive was issued for planning an invasion of England. Raeder was by then highly pessimistic about the outcome, and was convinced that Hitler had grossly underestimated Britain's strength. After the Luftwaffe's abortive attempt to eliminate the R.A.F., he managed to persuade Hitler to shelve the idea (and in February 1942 it was abandoned completely). Hitler turned in 1941 to the invasion of Russia with the intention of later returning to the attack on the U.K. Raeder was strongly against this dispersal of German forces on two fronts, and thought that they should conquer the U.K. first.

Raeder had overall responsibility for the war at sea and, because the submarine arm was the strongest element in the navy, he decided that the most effective way of weakening the U.K. would be to sever her overseas communications and deprive her of vital supplies. He aimed to make his submarine fleet as mobile as possible, always keeping the initiative, and striking swiftly and unexpectedly, thus forcing the enemy to weaken her forces by guarding too many vulnerable fronts. But Hitler favoured direct engagement and did not understand the military value of dislocating an enemy's communications.

Raeder had been supreme naval commander under Hitler for 10 years, and had therefore been responsible before the war for building up the German navy. He considered Hitler too nervous in naval strategy, and he pressed for the introduction of unrestricted U-Boat warfare. As a result of Hitler's fury against the navy and Raeder himself after British successes in the Arctic, Raeder resigned as supreme commander on 30 January 1943 to be replaced by Doenitz. After the war he was sentenced to 10 years' imprisonment as a war criminal.

RAMSAY, Sir Bertram, b. 1883. British admiral, who, as Flag Officer at Dover, was in charge of the vast evacuation operation at Dunkirk in 1940, and who later became a successful practitioner of amphibious warfare.

In April 1942 he began work on the first of a number of amphibious operations which were to be his concern for the rest of the war. He was appointed Naval Force Commander for the preliminary plans to invade the mainland of Europe, and from this he switched in July to responsibility for the Algerian landings in the invasion of North Africa, which took place in November 1942. His next concern was with the Sicily landings of July 1943, for which he became Naval Commanding Officer, Eastern Task Force, with responsibility for British landing operations.

Ramsay's appointment as naval C.-in-C. for the 'Overlord' operation was welcomed by General Eisenhower, the Supreme Commander. Eisenhower testified to Ramsay's 'resourcefulness and tremendous energy'. Operation 'Overlord' was planned for May 1944, and in fact began on 6 June. One million soldiers were landed in France in just under a month. Ramsay's next task was the invasion of the flooded Isle of Walcheren in the Netherlands. On 2 January 1945 he left his H.Q. at St Germain-en-Laye to confer with General Montgomery in Brussels. His plane crashed on take-off near Paris and all its occupants were killed instantaneously.

Ramsay was a brilliant organizer and innovator in the untried field of major amphibious operations. His personality was unobtrusive, and his strong feelings were seldom expressed. He was much respected by senior officers of the other Services, American as well as British.

REITZ, Deneys, b. 1882. South African politician. When the Union of South Africa declared war in September 1939 General Smuts appointed Reitz (an old associate of his) Minister of Native Affairs and Deputy Prime Minister and then, in October, sent him to London as South African delegate at the Empire War Conference. On his return to the Union he did a great deal to win the general support of the Africans for the war. He encouraged them to volunteer—there was no conscription in South Africa—both for the Services and for industry. They were further induced to join by the knowledge that Reitz was also working for improved conditions at home: he wanted not only higher wages, but also wages in kind—improved social services, housing, and a voucher system to prevent the misappropriation of money in urban areas. Under his vigorous direction a committee was set up to investigate the conditions of Africans in such areas.

In January 1943 Reitz was appointed High Commissioner in London. He had fought against the British in the Boer War, and for them in World War I; he now took up his new position with zest. British-South African relations were exceptionally close during the war. He died suddenly in office in October 1944.

REYNAUD, Paul, b. 1878. French statesman who succeeded Édouard Daladier as Premier on 21 March 1940, and who, as France collapsed, brought in Marshal Pétain. As well as being Premier, he was Foreign Minister and War Minister until 16 June 1940, when Pétain took over from him.

During the months following the outbreak of war Reynaud was in the forefront of those politicians who urged aggressive action against the Germans. On 28 March 1940, a few days after he had become Premier, Reynaud met Churchill in London and agreed on a joint declaration with Britain to bar a

separate armistice or peace. Some days after the Germans had crossed the Meuse at Dinant, and made the decisive breakthrough at Sedan on 15 May, Reynaud reorganized the French Cabinet and High Command, appointing Marshal Pétain as vice-president of the Council and replacing General Gamelin by General Weygand. When Italy looked like joining the attack on France Reynaud sought to placate Mussolini by offering him concessions in the Mediterranean, but his overtures were rejected. On 11 and 12 June British leaders under Churchill conferred with Reynaud and other French leaders, and learned that a number of them—especially Pétain and Weygand—felt that they had no choice but to seek an armistice, although Reynaud preferred to fight on. On 13 June the French government asked to be released from the agreement with the U.K. barring a separate armistice, but this request was rejected. On 16 June Reynaud put before his Cabinet the British proposal for an Anglo-French union, which he himself supported. Such was the hostility accorded this proposal that Reynaud promptly resigned, to be succeeded by Pétain. Reynaud was arrested by the Vichy government on 6 September 1940 and was among those put on trial at Riom in early 1942 for leading France into war without adequate preparation. The trial was adjourned when the defendants managed to turn the tables on their accusers. In 1943 he was deported to Germany. He was released in 1945.

REYNOLDS, Quentin, b. 1902. American journalist, associate editor of *Collier's Magazine*, who covered the war from 1940 onwards, travelling widely and seeing action on a number of occasions. In April 1940, sent to report the war in France, he was at the front in the Ardennes at the attack on Beauvais, and in Paris just before the Germans marched in. Reynolds stayed in London for most of the 'Blitz' and was impressed by the doggedness and courage of the British. His direct, sympathetic descriptions of London at that time were widely read in the U.S.A., and he was the commentator for the film *London Can Take It*, made in 1941, which became a hit in the U.S.A. and U.K. and brought in considerable revenue for British

war charities. His first-hand experiences—
he joined a convoy across the Channel to
see the Luftwaffe's activity for himself and
spent some time at an R.A.F. base in
Dover—did much to put his fellow countrymen in the picture about the British war
effort when there was genuine scepticism
about Britain's chances of survival. His
war articles dealing with the fall of France
and the London 'Blitz' were republished
in a book, *The Wounded Don't Cry* (1941),
which became a best-seller. Reynolds also
made some highly popular broadcasts for
the B.B.C. which brought congratulations
from Churchill.

When the Germans invaded Russia he
went to Moscow, and in November 1941
was with the Desert army in action at
Sidi Omar. While there he was so impressed by the fortitude of the 1st Battalion
the Royal Sussex Regiment, in the face of
superior German forces, that he broadcast
his admiration and made the battalion
famous. *Only The Stars Are Neutral* (1942),
covering his later experiences, again joined
the best-seller lists. He went on the ill-
fated Dieppe Raid in August 1942 and
wrote a moving account of it in a further
book, *Dress Rehearsal* (1943). He covered
the destruction of Vyazama in Russia;
and in July 1943 he joined the 7th Army
in Sicily to produce first-hand accounts of
the Salerno campaign. Returning to the
U.S.A. in 1944, he spoke at the Democratic Convention and subsequently made
several broadcasts in his own country.

Reynolds was a highly talented, well
liked, and universally respected journalist
who, among other things, did much to
help the United Jewish appeal in America
when the war ended.

RIBBENTROP, Joachim von, b. 1893.
German Foreign Minister, one of the
earliest of Hitler's adherents, and a
trusted adviser of the Führer. He was
appointed Minister for Foreign Affairs in
February 1938; previously he had been
an ambassador-at-large and, from 1936 to
1938, ambassador to the U.K. This latter
appointment had engendered in him a
strong Anglophobia; he considered Britain
effete, and although he believed that
Germany must eventually fight Britain
he held that the German invasion of
Poland would not provide a *casus belli*.

He signed the German-Soviet non-
aggression pact in Moscow in August
1939 at which the partitioning of Poland
was agreed.

Ribbentrop's influence declined steadily
during the war; neither liked nor respected
by his associates, he was dependent on
Hitler's good graces. The assassination
plot against Hitler of 20 July 1944 discredited the German Foreign Office and
this affected Ribbentrop's influence. After
the fall of Berlin he disappeared, but was
found by the British at Hamburg in June
1945. Brought to trial at Nuremberg for
war crimes, and convicted, he was hanged
in October 1946.

After serving in World War I Ribbentrop worked as a salesman for a champagne firm, and married the daughter of a
German wine manufacturer, adding 'von'
to his name. In 1935 he negotiated the
Anglo-German Naval agreement and in
1936 became the German ambassador to
Britain. Most people who came into contact with him found him tactless, full of
preconceived notions, and not too intelligent. But he had won Hitler's regard by
his social accomplishments and international contacts, and the echoing of
Hitler's extreme philosophy. His constant re-
assurances to Hitler that Britain would not
implement her guarantees to Poland did
much to strengthen plans for the invasion
of that country.

RIDGWAY, Matthew, b. 1895. American
general, a calculating, adventurous, and
successful commander of airborne troops.
Before Pearl Harbor Ridgway worked
with the war plans division in Washington,
D.C. In the spring of 1943 he became
commander of the 82nd Infantry Division,
which was converted to an airborne force.
It then consisted of one glider regiment and
two parachute regiments. The division
arrived in North Africa in May 1943, and
on 10 July the invasion of Sicily began,
despite adverse weather conditions.
Ridgway himself landed on 11 July and
accompanied his advance guard to Trapani.
On 12 September he took his troops into
Italy at Salerno and fought his way up to
Naples. The 82nd Division subsequently
trained in the U.K. in preparation for the
Normandy invasion. On 6 June 1944,
D-Day, Ridgway went into France to

spearhead the assault on the Cotentin Peninsula. He was later promoted commander of the 18th Airborne Corps, part of the 1st Allied Airborne Army. In September he took part in the airborne invasion of the Netherlands, fighting in the Eindhoven area. On 18 December 18th Corps was called in at short notice to help block the German breakthrough in the Ardennes. Ridgway helped to restore order to a confused situation and his troops were engaged in some of the heaviest fighting of the war. Eventually he initiated an offensive across the Siegfried Line.

In March 1945 he distinguished himself in action in the Wesel-Hamminkeln area. His last mission in Europe involved crossing the Elbe and moving north to link up with the Russians on the Baltic, on 2 May. Shortly afterwards he returned to the U.S.A. on leave, and was later ordered to the Pacific not long before the Japanese surrender. He was greatly admired and respected as a soldier, and had all the qualities that make a great leader—courage, foresight, and the understanding of men.

RITCHIE, Douglas ('Colonel Britton'), b. 1905. War-time broadcaster on the B.B.C. who became known to millions of people in the German-occupied countries of Europe as a voice encouraging resistance to the enemy, and whose instructions were a central component of the famous 'V campaign'.

In July 1941 'Colonel Britton' launched his war of the air when he asked his listeners throughout occupied Europe to tap out the 'V sound'—the opening notes of Beethoven's 5th Symphony—whenever Germans were within earshot; the 'V sound' of course, stood for 'Victory'. In one of his broadcasts he said to his audience across the Channel: 'You are the unknown soldiers; millions of you. Men and women. A great silent army, waiting and watching. The night is your friend, the V is your sign.' He gave advice on minor practical pieces of sabotage that would aid the Allies and hinder the Germans; workers could, for example, lose their tools, cause stoppages and muddles in offices, and make deliberate miscalculations. In August he asked for a 'go slow' and called for a 'tortoise day' on 15

September to celebrate the anniversary of the Battle of Britain.

The broadcasts were extremely effective; as well as helping the Resistance to establish its identity and encouraging countless ordinary people to feel themselves part of the Resistance movement, 'Colonel Britton' did much to undermine the morale of the German forces of occupation. His announcement of the mobilization of the V army was taken so seriously by the German propaganda ministry that it endeavoured to adopt the V sign as its own, saying that the letter stood for the German word 'Viktoria', meaning 'the celebration of a victory'. The German attempt was largely unsuccessful, but there was enough argument to cause some confusion.

Instructions for the V campaign were put out weekly by the B.B.C. to its English-speaking listeners on the Continent, and then re-broadcast in the language of each of the occupied countries. The first V campaign ended in May 1942 when 'Colonel Britton' explained that he would not speak again 'until the moment comes to indicate a particular line of action which is needed'. By this time he had already made a solid contribution to keeping the flame of Resistance alight and convincing the temporarily defeated that the war was by no means lost. He returned to the air in 1944 as the voice of S.H.A.E.F. before D-Day. The identity of 'Colonel Britton' was a carefully guarded secret until after the war, when the B.B.C. identified him as Douglas Ritchie, at that time Director of its European News Department.

RITCHIE, Neil, b. 1897. British general who commanded the 8th Army in North Africa from 26 November 1941 to 25 June 1942, and who later commanded 12th Corps in the 'Second Front' campaign in N.W. Europe. Ritchie served as General Brooke's Chief of Staff in Belgium and France during the first half of 1940. In 1941 he was appointed to the Middle East as Deputy Chief of Staff to General Auchinleck, the C.-in-C.

Auchinleck decided in October 1941 to launch a Desert offensive, but the attack, which began on 18 November, faltered, and General Alan Cunningham in command of the 8th Army proposed to disengage. The C.-in-C. was opposed to the idea and replaced Cunningham by Ritchie, who mounted an offensive that resulted in Rommel's withdrawing west of Cyrenaica for a short time. By December 1941 the British had recovered all their lost territory and Tobruk had been relieved after a siege of ten months.

On 21 January 1942 Rommel began a major counter-attack and by 28 January had re-taken Cyrenaica and stood on the El Gazala-Bir Hacheim line. In May he attacked again in strength and with crushing effect, aiming at the Nile valley. On 21 June Tobruk fell to the all-conquering Germans and General Brooke remarked in his diary: 'Rommel is outgeneralling Ritchie.' On 25 June Auchinleck took over from Ritchie. Auchinleck retreated as far as El Alamein, where he made a stand.

Ritchie was unlucky in his command in that he was called upon to direct the 8th Army in a time of emergency: he was under the crushing disadvantage of having no time to gain the requisite experience, while Rommel, his adversary, was a brilliant, forceful, and highly experienced tactician of mobile warfare. Ritchie later commanded with distinction the 12th Corps of the British 2nd Army in the operations in N.W. Europe. Brooke said of him that he was '. . . a very fine man, who did a wonderful "come-back" after suffering a serious blow'.

ROEY, Joseph van, b. 1874. Belgian cardinal, Primate of Belgium and Archbishop of Mechelen. He continued to advocate Belgian neutrality even after the French and British declarations of war on Germany, and he advised preachers to avoid jeopardizing their country's position by incautious statements. In May 1940 he supported the King's decision to capitulate because of the impossible situation in which the Belgian army found itself. Under the German occupation he encouraged resistance to German attempts to make the Church a tool of the occupying power, to introduce Nazi propaganda into schools, or to restrict freedom of worship in any way.

When the Germans began the mass deportation of Belgian civilians for forced labour in Germany Cardinal van Roey did his best to intervene, but with little success. He found homes with Belgian families for Jewish children whose parents had been deported, maintained homes for elderly Jews, and did what he could to help others who were in hiding.

His Pastoral Letter of 17 January 1943 condemned attacks on German soldiers because of the serious reprisals on the Belgian people, and thereby he was instrumental in delaying introduction of a more repressive régime for 18 months. When Allied night bombing began to cause high civilian casualties he became worried about the possible effect of this slaughter on Belgian morale and, by apparently condemning the Allies from the pulpit, was able to discourage this method of warfare which was beginning to erode Belgian sympathy for the Allies.

ROKOSSOVSKY, Konstantin, b. 1896. Russian marshal, famous for his defence of Moscow and Stalingrad. He was also the commander on the central front who could have aided—but failed to aid—the people of Warsaw in the uprising of summer 1944.

Having distinguished himself in the defence of Moscow in November–December 1941, Rokossovsky found himself a year later, in 1942, opposing the German 6th Army, which was trying to take the city of Stalingrad. The fierce battle for the city lasted from August until November, when a massive and determined Russian counter-offensive saved Stalingrad and proved the turning point of the war in Russia—indeed possibly the turning point of the whole war. Three Russian army groups were involved, with Rokossovsky, commanding the forces on the river Don front, attacking from the north-west. Within five days the three army groups had encircled the German 6th, 9th, and 4th Panzer armies. Even so, it was not until 31 January 1943 that the German forces under General von Paulus finally abandoned the city to Rokossovsky.

During 1943 and 1944 the Russians continued to drive the Germans back. Rokossovsky, commanding on the Belorussian front in the south, reached Poland and took Lublin and Brest-Litovsk. Then came the tragedy of Warsaw: on 29

July Moscow radio had broadcast an appeal to the inhabitants of the city, urging them to rise against the German occupying forces. The Poles assumed that the Russian armies would shortly come to their aid; but the Germans halted Rokossovsky's advance and turned furiously upon the insurgents. The Poles fought bravely for two months though desperately short of arms and supplies. But eventually, since the Western Allies could not, and the Russians would not, assist them, they were obliged to surrender. Three hundred thousand Poles had perished, and the city was almost completely destroyed.

The Russians' behaviour, which brought disaster to the Poles, raised many questions. The explanation possibly lay partly in the age-old bitterness and distrust between Russian and Pole, and in the Russian repudiation of the Polish government-in-exile in London. Nevertheless after the end of the war Rokossovsky became Minister of Defence and chief of the armed forces in Poland. He was himself of Polish blood.

The Russian advances continued throughout 1944, and a vast offensive was launched in 1945. Rokossovsky swept across northern Poland to take Danzig, which fell in April. Striking westwards, he made contact in May with the British army at Wittenberg near Lübeck on the Baltic. In the same month Marshal Zhukov in Berlin received the surrender of Field Marshal Keitel.

In 1938 Rokossovsky had been removed in a political purge of the Red army. But after Russia's near defeat by the Finns in the winter of 1939 he and many others were recalled to duty.

ROMMEL, Erwin, b. 1891. German general, outstanding field commander and Desert warfare tactician. At one time in the Desert he was almost as much admired by his opponents as by his own troops. He was one of Hitler's early supporters, and commanded his bodyguard battalion in Austria and Czechoslovakia and in the Polish campaign. He served in France in 1940, where he led a Panzer Division with such flair that he was given command of the Afrika Korps in 1941. His almost unbroken series of successes against the weakened British 8th Army earned him the epithet 'Desert Fox'.

He recaptured Tobruk in June 1942, hurling the British back to El Alamein in Egypt, and was promoted to general-field marshal. Rommel's early successes in the Desert were due partly to superior equipment, but largely to a superb intelligence service and the speed and audacity with which he manœuvred his armour, throwing the Allies off balance and winning their grudging admiration. He was overwhelmingly defeated at El Alamein in November 1942 by the greatly augmented forces under General Montgomery, and from then on was continually on the retreat. Rommel was withdrawn from Africa on Mussolini's initiative, but Hitler rewarded him with the Knight's Cross with diamonds.

Rommel possessed a remarkable ability to exploit opportunities, and had no fear of using unorthodox methods. After evacuating Tunisia and being recalled, he held defence posts in Italy and the Balkans. After a thorough study of the German defence system in the West, he proposed to Hitler a fundamental alteration to von Rundstedt's anti-invasion scheme for northern France. He was given command of the two armies holding the most important section of the invasion coast. After the reorganization of February 1944 Rommel was given the primary responsibility for destroying the invading forces, and his proposals were bold and unorthodox. Because of his standing with Hitler he was able to act to a considerable extent on his own initiative, despite criticism from more conservative military leaders, and without opposition from Rundstedt, who became a mere figurehead.

Rommel was fully alive to the significance of the growth of Allied air power, and realized that the invasion had to be stopped at the Atlantic Wall. 'The high-water line,' he declared, 'must be the main fighting line . . . we must stop the enemy in the water, not only delaying him but destroying all his equipment while it is still afloat.'

He devised a radical and complicated scheme for protecting the coastline with every sort of under-water obstacle, and made plans to have all available manpower at the Atlantic Wall on the first day of the invasion. During the spring of 1944 Rommel, with his profound grasp of the situation, transformed the German defence by his untiring enthusiasm. Admiral Ruge said of him: 'Rommel brought a new impulse to the preparation. He fundamentally altered the underlying idea, thus changing the atmosphere of despondency and vague hope to one of hard work and clear plans.' Though given to sudden inspirations in the field, Rommel proved in these preparations that he could also be painstaking and thorough. He commanded Group B in France during the Allied invasion in June and July 1944, but was caught in an air raid during the Allied breakthrough at St-Lô. His staff car was machine-gunned, and Rommel, severely wounded, was forced to return home to recover. Becoming increasingly disillusioned with Hitler's egocentric conduct of the war, and refusal to face the facts of the invasion, Rommel gave cautious support to the 1944 plot to remove Hitler. Originally in favour of arrest rather than assassination—'To kill Hitler,' he said, 'would only make him a martyr'—in June he opted for swift action. Had the July assassination plot against Hitler succeeded Rommel would have been given a leading position in the new régime; as it was, his part in the plot was uncovered, and he had to choose between facing trial (which would unquestionably have ended in his execution and reprisals against his family) and taking his own life. He died by poison after a visit from Nazi officers, but whether in fact he committed suicide is still not certain. He was given a state funeral.

Rommel was an outstanding, daring, and well-liked commander, who had distinguished himself as far back as World War I, in which he won the Pour le Mérite, Germany's highest decoration. Between the wars he served as an infantry regimental officer and instructor.

ROOSEVELT, Franklin Delano, b. 1882. American statesman, President of the U.S.A. for most of the war, chiefly responsible for making his country 'the arsenal of democracy'. Even before the war he had stated his opposition to the aggressive aims of the Axis powers, which he saw as a hazard to his own country as well as to Europe.

In March 1941 the U.S. Congress passed the Lend-Lease Act. This was sponsored by Roosevelt and it gave the President power to supply war material to those nations whose defence was vital to the defence of the U.S.A. This Act virtually allowed the U.S.A. to provide unrestricted aid to the Allies, who were recognized as fighting battles in which the U.S.A. had an essential interest.

In August 1941 Roosevelt and Churchilll met at sea off Argentia, Newfoundland. This meeting led to the framing of the Atlantic Charter—a declaration of the broad war aims of the U.S.A. and the Allies who, the Charter declared, had no desire to enlarge their territories; countenanced frontier changes only in accordance with the freely expressed wishes of the population concerned; wanted all peoples to decide their own form of government; and wished to work together for peace.

By the time that the bombing of Pearl Harbor, on 7 December 1941, brought the U.S.A. into the war, significant preparations had already been started. At Roosevelt's urging, Congress had passed the first Selective Service Act, under the provisions of which basic military training had already been given to a million men. Plans were well advanced for the strengthening of the air force and navy; indeed, under Roosevelt's direction the U.S.A. developed the largest and most powerful navy the world had ever seen. A colossal air force was built, and an army recruited which, by the end of the war in Europe, totalled 7,700,000 effectives. Hundreds of training and conditioning centres were organized for the forces and, despite his severe physical handicap (the aftermath of an attack of poliomyelitis), Roosevelt travelled to many parts of the nation, helping to boost morale. In the course of the war more than 14 million people were drafted into the various military services. On the industrial front Roosevelt demanded a quota of war machinery that seemed fantastic at the time; but, in fact, almost all of it was delivered.

In January 1943 Roosevelt flew to North Africa for conferences at Casablanca with Churchill and the American and British commanders in that area. They resolved, among other things, that there should be no negotiated peace with any of the Axis powers. Both he and Churchill were committed to demanding an unconditional surrender.

In May 1943 Churchill flew to Washington to address Congress, where he pledged Britain to fight to the end in the war against Japan. In August Churchill and Roosevelt met yet again, this time in Quebec; there the invasion of the European mainland and the problem of China were discussed, and military decisions were taken. The setting up of S.E.A.C. was agreed, with Lord Louis Mountbatten as Supreme Allied Commander.

Roosevelt and Churchill had hoped that Russia would now join the Alliance, but Russia's chair remained unoccupied. But by October 1943 preparations had been made for a three-power conference of foreign ministers. This was duly convened in Moscow, and the subjects discussed included measures to shorten the war, military co-operation between the three countries, and the continuation of this collaboration after the war in order to maintain the peace.

In November 1943 Roosevelt flew to Cairo to confer with Churchill and Chiang Kai-shek. The three of them decided on the course of future military operations against Japan. From there Roosevelt and Churchill travelled to Teheran (28 November–1 December 1943) to discuss with Stalin the military operations against Germany. Roosevelt met Churchill again at the Second Quebec Conference in September 1944.

In February 1945 the leaders of the 'Big Three' Allied nations, Roosevelt, Churchill, and Stalin, met at Yalta in the Crimea. There the so-called 'Yalta Declaration' was signed. It dealt with the final stages of the war and the Allies' plans for the peace that would follow.

Roosevelt died suddenly on 12 April 1945, just before the war in Europe was officially declared over, and before the nuclear bombing of Hiroshima and Nagasaki, which together with the Russian declaration of war against Japan brought about the end of the war in the East. Roosevelt had proved himself an energetic, far-sighted, and inspiring war leader, and his loss was keenly felt by all the Allied nations.

ROSENBERG, Alfred, b. 1893. German writer and politician, the 'philosopher' of National Socialism. He was for some time editor of the official Nazi newspaper *Völkischer Beobachter*. Rosenberg was a leading Nazi racial theorist and, until 1941, was officially in charge of the education of party members. He also had responsibility for propaganda in foreign countries.

Rosenberg succeeded in bringing the Norwegian Fascist, Vidkun Quisling, to a meeting with Hitler in December 1939. He dreamed of 'converting Scandinavia to the idea of a Nordic community which would embrace all the Nordic peoples under the natural leadership of Germany'. When France had been defeated he was further responsible for collecting and sending to Germany valuable works of art of all kinds.

In 1941, at Hitler's request, Rosenberg produced a plan for the German administration of European Russia. In this he recommended the partition of the area into four *Reichskommissariaten*. He was subsequently made Minister for the Occupied Eastern Territories, but his authority was completely superseded by the powers held by Himmler and Goering. Against such opposition he carried no weight at all; indeed Rosenberg showed himself consistently to be vacillating and incompetent as an organizer, and he was apparently given responsibility by Hitler partly because there was no danger of his becoming a rival.

Rosenberg's main contribution was as the leading ideologist of National Socialism. He built up in his writings a theory and a justification for the meanderings of the Führer's distorted fantasies. The theories expounded in Rosenberg's main work, *The Myth of the Twentieth Century*, greatly influenced Hitler's thinking. In *The Myth*, a pseudo-scientific work, Rosenberg claimed that the Germans represented a pure Nordic race whose destiny was to rule Europe. He reserved his most vitriolic attacks for the real enemies of Germany—Jews, Russian Tartars, the Latin peoples, and the teachings of Christianity (especially those of the Roman Catholic Church).

Rosenberg never held a dominant administrative position in the Nazi hierarchy, but by his writings he had a large share of the responsibility for atrocities against slave labour forces and for the murder of several million Jews and other people. He was condemned to death by the International War Crimes Tribunal at Nuremberg in 1945.

RUNDSTEDT, Gerd von, b. 1875. German general, C.-in-C. in the West during the Allied 'Second Front' invasion of the European mainland. He was looked upon as the most offensive-minded of the generals, and was one of the last representatives of the Old Guard. He commanded Army Group South in Poland in 1939, and Army Group A in the Battle of France in 1940.

When the British were forced to the evacuation at Dunkirk, German armoured formations were ordered to stop and even, in some places, to pull back. This startling decision, which enabled 338,000 British and Allied troops to be transported safely to England, was long thought to have been taken solely by Hitler. But it was probably due also to Rundstedt's insistence that his troops were exhausted and needed time to recover, the extent of the French collapse not having been fully gauged.

In the German invasion of Russia in June 1941 Rundstedt was in command of Army Group South (one of three Army Groups taking part) whose aim was a thrust to the Caucasus. He was relieved of his command towards the end of November 1941 at his own request, after Hitler had refused permission for a tactical withdrawal to the River Mius.

He was made C.-in-C. on the Western front in 1942 and was responsible for preparations guarding against a possible Allied invasion. At the time of the invasion of 6 June 1944 he was in command of the whole Atlantic Wall from the Low Countries to the Bay of Biscay, and from Marseilles along the southern French shore, with 60 divisions. Twenty divisions were concentrated in the Calais-Boulogne area, largely as a result of Allied deceptive measures regarding the landing points. The Panzer divisions, which could have

done so much damage during the early days of the invasion, were dispersed over a wide area and were unable to make their full contribution for some time.

On 17 June 1944 Rundstedt, with General Rommel, met Hitler near Soissons and urged him, in view of the critical situation, to allow the 7th Army to withdraw towards the Seine and fight a defensive battle from there. But Hitler refused, and in early July Rundstedt was replaced in the overall command by Kluge. Two months later, however, he was reinstated, replacing Model, the successor to Kluge (17 August), and, in the West, he presided over the final withdrawals. On 16 December the famous 'Rundstedt offensive' was launched by the Germans in the Ardennes. Rundstedt, in fact, took little part in its planning and execution, and had no great confidence in it. The Allied forces were concentrated for attacks in the north and south, while the centre (the Ardennes sector) was relatively weak. Rundstedt assembled two Panzer armies, the 5th and 6th, plus the 7th and 15th Armies, with the aim of breaking through the Ardennes to the River Meuse, and eventually seizing the port of Antwerp, thus destroying the life-line of the northern armies, and cutting off General Montgomery's 21st Army Group. When the attack began the 5th Panzer army soon penetrated deeply towards the Meuse, creating a serious 'bulge' in the Allied line which virtually cut the American 12th Army Group in two. Both Panzer armies then swung north; there was fierce fighting at Marche, and later at Bastogne. For a time the Allies were in real difficulties. But the Germans were diminished in strength and had nothing in reserve; the Allies' counter-measures inexorably took effect. The Allies brought in heavy bombers to attack railways, and to prevent food and ammunition from reaching the Germans. By the end of January 1945 the Germans had been pushed back behind their frontiers, having sustained a loss of about 120,000 men. This was the final German offensive of the war. Rundstedt was captured by the Americans in 1945.

S

SALAZAR, Antonio, b. 1889. Autocratic ruler of Portugal, responsible for the country's policy of neutrality during the war. He saw his main task, despite the stupendous upheaval in Europe, as one of converting Portugal into a corporate and prosperous state, and he concentrated on domestic, especially financial, reform, avoiding foreign entanglements except when absolutely necessary. Salazar was able, to some extent, to increase his nation's international prestige by strengthening its ties with Brazil, Spain, the U.K., and the U.S.A., while a concordat of 1940 established a new *modus vivendi* with the Vatican.

Traditionally Portugal was Britain's ancient ally; but when war broke out it seemed clear that Salazar was not prepared to commit Portugal in any way and, in fact, he succeeded in avoiding involvement throughout. In August 1941, however, he asked for American protection when a German invasion seemed imminent, and looked to the Azores as a place of retreat.

In 1943, when the Allied situation was evidently improving, Salazar relaxed his impartiality sufficiently to permit the U.K. and the U.S.A. to use the Azores as a naval and air base. This was very important for the Allied war effort, because the islands allowed the Allies to close the gap in mid Atlantic in their war at sea. But apart from this aid Salazar kept his country consistently neutral.

SANSOM, Odette, b. 1912. One of the most famous agents of the British S.O.E., which helped to organize resistance in enemy-occupied countries. In November 1942 she landed by felucca on the French Riviera, where she became involved with the activities of 'Spindle', Peter Churchill's organization in Vichy France. She proved so useful as a courier that Churchill persuaded London to let her remain with 'Spindle', although she was to have worked with a new circuit based at Auxerre. In early 1943 internal dissentions and increased German activity led Churchill to move his group to Annecy. This did not save them, however, from the consequences of the break-up of 'Carte', an organization which had close connections with 'Spindle'. They were penetrated by Sergeant Bleicher ('Colonel Henri') of the Abwehr, who pretended to be an Allied sympathiser, and both Odette Sansom and Peter Churchill were arrested. Following an agreed plan, she pretended that she was married to Churchill and that he had only come to France on her insistence. By so doing she drew attention away from Churchill's real role in France. The Gestapo was determined to discover the whereabouts of the group's wireless operator, Adolphe Rabinovitch, and of another important British agent, Francis Cammaerts. Although subjected to the most brutal torture—her back was seared with a red-hot iron and her toe-nails were pulled out—she revealed nothing. She was sent to Ravensbrück concentration camp, where the Germans, under the impression that she was Winston Churchill's niece by marriage, singled her out for special treatment. In the last days of the war, Sühren, the camp commandant, drove her to the American lines. He believed she had influence which could protect him.

Born in Amiens and named Odette Brailly, she spent most of her childhood in Normandy. In 1931 she married Roy Sansom, an Englishman and the son of an old friend of the family, and she moved to England a year later. She was decorated with the G.C. for her work in the war.

SCHACHT, Hjalmar, b. 1877. German financier, President of the Reichsbank until 1939 and Minister without Portfolio until January 1943. He was dismissed for writing a letter to Goering in which he protested against the military call-up of 15-year-olds and repeated his view that the economy of Germany could not support a lengthy war. Even while he was minister he had no public duties, having been dismissed from the Reichsbank because of his opposition to certain aspects of the Nazi régime.

Schacht's anti-war views were known to his American contacts—in March 1940 he saw Sumner Welles, the U.S. Under-Secretary of State, who was visiting Germany. In 1940 and again in 1941 he offered to go to the U.S.A. to see if he could not engender there a more favourable attitude towards Germany.

He had been involved with the anti-Hitler conspirators since the 1938 plot, but he was never fully trusted because of his own Nazi background. He was arrested after the failure of the assassination attempt on Hitler in July 1944. He was taken to Ravensbrück concentration camp and later questioned in Berlin, but no evidence connecting him with the plotters could be produced. He spent two months in Flossenburg extermination camp, but was finally released by the Americans at Niedernorf, in April 1945. He was subsequently put on trial for war crimes at Nuremberg and acquitted.

SCHELLENBERG, Walter, b. 1911. German Intelligence chief who became head of the unified secret services after the arrest of Admiral Canaris in 1944 and the abolition of the Abwehr as a separate organization. Schellenberg was a lawyer by training, a graduate of the University of Bonn, and he joined the S.S. shortly after the Nazis came to power in 1933. He managed to obtain a post in the S.D. (the Intelligence and security service), where his education and his active and businesslike mentality attracted the attention of Heydrich, the head of the S.D. From then, until the fall of the Nazis in 1945, Schellenberg was involved in the unending series of plots and counter-plots —most of them trivial, some of them farcical, and some of them monstrous— that characterized the régime. Though by nature kind and appreciative of the civilities of life, he revelled in the subterfuges, ciphers, threats, probings, whispers, and lies of the Nazi secret world. Most of the leading figures of the Third Reich were known to him—including Hitler, Ribbentrop, Himmler, and Heydrich—and he observed them clearly and analytically, while still paying tribute to the power that they represented. Towards the end of World War II his was the guiding hand in Himmler's abortive attempts to surrender the German armies to the Western Allies, while continuing the fight against Russia.

SCOBIE, Ronald, b. 1893. British general who, after commands in Africa and Malta, commanded the Allied troops in Greece during the attempted Communist take-over following the German defeat. In October 1941 Scobie became G.O.C. 6th Division (later 70th Division) and in the same month his troops were landed in Tobruk to replace the outgoing besieged Australian garrison. In November they took part in the great winter offensive, whose objective was the reconquest of Cyrenaica—an offensive which saw the largest concentration of armoured vehicles so far employed in the Western Desert. The operation was conducted under Cunningham's command, and Scobie's task was to defend Tobruk and to make sorties for specific objectives.

He was appointed G.O.C. Malta in 1942, a time of crisis during which the safety of Malta was of prime importance because of its use as a base from which to attack German supply convoys going to Libya. In 1943 he became Chief of Staff, Middle East Command, and in 1944 he was made G.O.C. Greece. The Germans had hung on in Greece longer than had been expected, and it was not until 12 October that they withdrew from Athens. On 14 October a British force of about 5,000 men under Scobie moved into the capital, but it became clear that the former Resistance groups were now Communist controlled and were likely to try to seize power and establish a Communist régime. In early December the issue between Greek and Greek hardened and Scobie found himself involved in civil war and street fighting. He was given personal instructions by Churchill: 'We have to hold and dominate Athens. It would be a great thing for you to succeed in this without bloodshed if possible but also with bloodshed if necessary.' Churchill and Eden in fact went to Greece over Christmas. The combined political and military action produced, by 11 January 1945, a truce with the Communists. Constitutional authority in Greece was maintained—from the point of view of the Western countries, a vital necessity in the prevailing political situation.

SCOONES, Sir Geoffry, b. 1893. British general who took part in some of the fiercest fighting against the Japanese in Burma. From 1939 to 1941 he was on the General Staff at Allied H.Q., India, and was subsequently Director of Military

Operations and Intelligence. On 29 July
1942 he became commander of the 4th
Corps, which was stationed on the Imphal
plain in Assam, near the Burmese frontier.
Little fighting took place at first, except
for an offensive at Tiddim during the
monsoon of 1943, but there were considerable problems of organization to be
dealt with. Meanwhile S.E.A.C. was in
process of being formed: the 4th Corps
held the central part of the northern
front, under Stilwell.

The Supreme Allied Commander's
November 1943 plan had included the
advance of the 4th Corps across the
Chindwin, but in January 1944 the situation changed, with signs of a great Japanese offensive on the central front. By late
February Scoones had decided that the
best counter-offensive measure would be
to withdraw his forces to a strategically
strong position on the vast Imphal plain,
thereby extending Japanese communications. He then intended to destroy the
enemy by counter-attacking. His plans
were approved by General Slim, who was
now in overall command of operations
and who later praised Scoones for his
foresight and his steadiness in a crisis.
The Japanese attack by the 15th Army
under Mutaguchi began on 8 March, and
the withdrawal was duly accomplished by
5 April; the critical stages in the battles
of Imphal and Kohima took place during
that month. The Imphal–Kohima road
was open by 23 June after further fierce
fighting, and the first decisive battle of
the Burma campaign was won. Scoones
was ordered to co-operate in the new
British autumn offensive in Burma, but
on 7 December 1944 he was appointed
G.O.C. Central Command.

SENUSSI (Sayed Muhammad Idris el
Senussi), b. 1890. Arab statesman, leader
of the Muslim brotherhood of the Senussi.
The brotherhood worked against the
Italians and for the independence of
Libya, and consequently El Senussi
aided the British during the campaign in
North Africa. Since 1923, when Mussolini's rise to power had changed the character of the Italian occupation of Libya,
he had lived in exile in Cairo. In October
1939 Tripolitanian and Cyrenaican leaders
met, and entrusted their joint leadership

to El Senussi. In June 1940 Italy entered
the war; El Senussi then approved the
organizing of an Arab force under British
command for the liberation of Libya. The
resolutions of August 1940 (which proclaimed a Senussi Amirate over Cyrenaica
and Tripolitania and gave support to the
British) were approved by all the Cyren-
aicans, although the Tripolitanians were
divided. Throughout the war El Senussi
tried to obtain from the British a guarantee
that there would be post-war independence
for Libya under a Senussi government; he
did not succeed in obtaining this.

Libya had become the battle-ground of
North Africa: by February 1941 it was
occupied by the British; by June 1942 it
was lost to Rommel; and it was not completely liberated until February 1943. At
first El Senussi refused to return to Libya
while it was still under military occupation.
But he eventually made a triumphal visit
to Cyrenaica in July 1944.

SEROV, Ivan, b. 1908. Russian general,
commander of the secret police and one
of the more sinister figures on the Allied
side. When the Russians occupied the
Baltic States in 1939–40 he was responsible for the 'Sovietization' of the area,
the elimination of 'politically undesirable
elements'. He planned and supervised the
mass deportations of people suspected of
anti-Soviet sentiment.

Later he was Commissar for Internal
Affairs in the Ukraine, working under
Nikita Khrushchev who was the party
chief there. He was therefore in charge of
the N.K.V.D. (secret police) organs in
the Ukraine. Serov was primarily responsible for the campaign of terror and for
the deportations in the newly annexed
western Ukraine, northern Bukovina, and
southern Bessarabia: the total number of
those removed from the Ukraine to the
east was about 3½ million people. While
this movement to the east was taking
place the N.K.V.D. carried out mass
arrests and executions. Many prisoners
who languished in gaol with sentences of
more than 3 years were shot. In some
cities the N.K.V.D. was said to have
burned prisons with prisoners in them.
In 1941 Serov became Deputy Commissar
for State Security, serving under Beria,
and in 1943–4 he organized the mass

deportations of those suspected of disloyalty to the Soviet government (such as the Kalmyks and Crimean Tatars) to Siberia.

In 1945 he became Deputy Supreme Commander of the Soviet forces in Germany and head of *Smersh* (Russian abbreviation for 'Death to Spies'), and as such was responsible for all security measures there. He was awarded the Order of Lenin in 1940 and 1945, and the Order of Suvarov Class I in 1944.

SEYSS-INQUART, Arthur von, b. 1892. Austrian Nazi, Reich Commissioner in the German-occupied Netherlands. From October 1939 he had been Deputy Governor-General in the Polish General Government—over areas of Poland annexed neither by Germany nor by Russia. His policy was: 'We demand everything that is of use to the Reich and suppress everything that may harm the Reich.'

In May 1940 he became Commissioner in the Netherlands, and held the post until the end of the war. In it he followed the same principles as in Poland: the Dutch economy was made subservient to the Reich economy and prices went up while standards of living fell. Works of art to the value of about 40 million Reichsmarks were confiscated. On 21 March 1941, provoked by the growing Dutch Resistance, a decree was passed which gave him authority to mete out summary justice: serious offenders were shot. On 28 May 1941 he imposed collective fines on all Dutch cities where Resistance elements were suspected to exist. In 1943 he seized textiles and consumer goods for the German population. In addition he sent 5 million Dutchmen as workers to the Reich. Of the Jews he wrote: 'The Führer has declared that the role of the Jews in Europe has come to an end, and therefore it has come to an end.' He deported 117,000 of the 140,000 Dutch Jews.

Seyss-Inquart was arrested by the Canadians in May 1945 and, still loyal to Hitler, put on trial at Nuremberg. He was found guilty of war crimes and was executed.

SHAWCROSS, Hartley, b. 1902. British lawyer, U.K. Chief Prosecutor at the

Nuremberg war crime trials.

Appointed a King's Counsel in 1939, he became Chairman of the Enemy Aliens Tribunal. From 1941 onwards he held, among other posts, those of Deputy Regional Commissioner for the South Eastern Region and Regional Commissioner for the North Western Region. In the 1945 Labour government he became Attorney General, and it was in this capacity that he acted at the International Military Tribunal at Nuremberg. The trial, which began in November 1945, lasted almost ten months. Shawcross's task was to prove that the defendants, the chief surviving leaders of Nazi Germany, had conspired with one another to plan and to wage a war of aggression in breach of the treaty obligations by which Germany, like other states, had sought to make such wars impossible. The defendants included both individual German military, political, and economic leaders and also such organizations as the S.S., the S.A., and the German High Command. Shawcross's brief extended to proving that the German navy and army were in themselves criminal organizations, but the tribunal did not accept this contention. Most of the individuals accused, as well as the S.S. and the Gestapo, were found guilty. Shawcross's measured advocacy, his calm and deliberate phrases, accented the strangeness and, frequently, the horror of the story being unfolded in the court-room in a way that could never have been achieved by dramatic or flamboyant oratory.

SHINWELL, Emanuel, b. 1884. British politician, a noted parliamentarian, who throughout the war years maintained his stand of refusing to allow expediency to triumph silently over principle. He sat in the House of Commons as Labour M.P. for the Seaham division of Durham. He had been offered a position in Churchill's government, but he refused it in order to be able to carry out another function, more congenial to his political convictions, as critic of government policies and administration, with special concern for all aspects of war-time production.

Shinwell sat on the front bench with his fellow critic, Lord Winterton, where both men acted as leaders of an undeclared

Opposition; they were fleetingly dubbed 'Arsenic' and 'Old Lace', nicknames prompted by a currently popular play. They maintained a constant pressure on the government with their vigilant criticism; Shinwell, particularly, being noted for his well-informed and biting speeches. In the latter years of the war Shinwell was chairman of the committee that drafted the Labour party's election manifesto 'Let Us Face the Future'.

SHIRACH, Baldur von, b. 1907. Leader of the Hitler Youth since 1931, in August 1940 he was appointed Gauleiter and Defence Commissioner of Vienna, a post he held for the remainder of the war.

During the war years Shirach was implicated in the forcible removal of thousands of children and young people from the occupied eastern territories to Germany, and also in the deportation of 60,000 Jews from Vienna to eastern Europe for extermination. He claimed at his trial that he had not known of the Jewish massacres until late 1944; he had believed that the transported Jews were held in camps or were resettled. In his last telephone conversation with Hitler in April 1945 he asked that Vienna should be declared an open city for the sake of the war wounded. Shirach left Vienna before the Russians took it, and went to the Tyrol, where he worked as an interpreter for the Americans under the name of Richard Falk. But in June 1945 he wrote a letter to the U.S. authorities surrendering himself. During the Nuremberg war crimes trials he admitted: 'It is my guilt that I have trained youth for a man who became a murderer a million times over.' He was sentenced to 20 years' imprisonment for crimes against humanity.

Shirach's wife called him an 'idealistic ostrich who could never face the truth about himself or others'. This capacity for self-deception made it possible for him to remain to some extent unaware of the horrors of the Nazi Reich.

SHIRER, William, b. 1904. American journalist and commentator. At the beginning of the war he was representative of the Columbia Broadcasting System in Berlin. He stayed there during the invasions of Poland, Denmark, Norway, the Netherlands, Belgium, Luxembourg, and France. But in December 1940 he decided that increasing censorship no longer enabled him to give a true picture of events.

He entered France in June 1940 as one of the 12 foreign correspondents accredited to the German army. He achieved a scoop when the Franco-German armistice was signed at Compiègne on 22 June; having heard the proceedings over a German sound-track, he broadcast the news several hours before other correspondents knew of it. He was in Berlin during the autumn bombing offensive and once met 'Lord Haw-Haw' (William Joyce) in an air-raid shelter.

When he returned to the U.S.A. in December 1940 he received an award from the Headliners Club for general excellence in radio reporting. In 1941 he published a best-seller, *Berlin Diary*, which gave a day-to-day account of living in pre-war and war-time Germany. In the autumn of 1944 he revisited Paris and went to the American front. In May 1945 he covered the United Nations Conference at San Francisco, returning to Europe in October for the Nuremberg trials. Shirer's great talent as a journalist was his ability to give straightforward yet evocative descriptions of men and events.

SIKORSKI, Wladyslaw, b. 1881. Polish general and statesman, Premier of the Polish government-in-exile and C.-in-C. of the Free Polish forces. When Poland was invaded by Germany and Russia in 1939 Sikorski was refused a command by the military régime in Warsaw. Smigly-Rydz, Pilsudski's successor, had inherited Pilsudski's distrust of Sikorski.

Making his way to Paris, Sikorski took command of a force raised from the Polish miners in France. When Poland collapsed he was appointed Premier of the provisional Polish government in Paris, and C.-in-C. of its forces. By spring 1940 the Polish army had been reconstituted in France and numbered 100,000 men. But then France also fell to the Germans, and the Polish government-in-exile moved to London. Zealous to foster every patriotic impulse among his forces and the underground movement in Poland alike, he infused them with his own determination.

After Germany's attack on Russia in 1941 he signed a Polish-Soviet declaration of collaboration, ending the state of war between the two countries and repudiating the Soviet-German partition of Poland which had been agreed in 1939. In these negotiations his intention was to allow General Anders to organize a Polish army in Russia, made up of the P.O.W.s taken in 1939 and the thousands of Polish nationals who had been deported. The need for officers focused attention on the fate of 14,500 Poles, including 8,000 officers, who had been held by the Russians in three camps near Smolensk since 1939, and of whom nothing had been heard since April 1940. There was friction and suspicion between the Polish and Soviet governments; and, in April 1943, Sikorski informed Churchill of evidence that the Russians had murdered the Poles and buried them in the forests near Katyn. On 4 July 1943 Sikorski was killed in an air crash at Gibraltar.

SILLITOE, Percy, b. 1888. British police officer who had the unusual task of organizing his police command into what was virtually a supporting force for the vast armies preparing to invade the European mainland.

In March 1943 he became Chief Constable of Kent, responsible for welding the nine police forces of the county into one in order to meet the immediate requirements of the Allied invasion forces then gathering in S.E. England. In August 1943 the first big pre-invasion test took place, and Sillitoe visited every police station in the county to give the watchword 'The convoys MUST go through'. Every road and bridge was surveyed so that when any was bombed alternative routes could be quickly adopted; often the police had to clear streets of traffic while invasion barges and other heavy equipment were escorted through. In June 1944 the Germans began to use the V-1 weapons, flying bombs; and the V-2-range rockets followed. When it was decided to put every available A.A. gun in Britain on the Kent coast, this vast move was completed in 4 days, followed by a huge procession of barrage balloons.

Sillitoe always believed that police work needed fresh ideas and that 'almost any-

one can stay too long in a job'. He carried out his reforms with courage and understanding. Concerned for his men's welfare, he did much to improve the status of the police. He had a commanding presence and it used to be said that he made a fine entrance—invariably one minute late.

SIMOVIĆ, Dušan, b. 1882. Yugoslav general and political leader, and Serbian nationalist. In 1939 he was Chief of the Army General Staff, and in the following year Chief of the Air Force Staff. From December 1940 his office at Zemun became a centre of underground resistance to German penetration into the Balkans and to the inertia of the Yugoslav government.

In February 1941 Hitler, seeking the right to move military equipment across Yugoslavia, pressed for her adherence to the Tripartite Pact. Simović warned the Regent, Prince Paul, that Serbia would not accept capitulation to Hitler's demands, and that the dynasty was at stake. On 25 March the Yugoslav government signed the Axis pact secretly in Vienna, and two days later Simović proclaimed an adroit and bloodless *coup d'état*. Overnight the conspirators had seized key points in Belgrade, and they installed the young Peter II effectively on the throne amid general excitement.

Churchill, now trying to form a Balkan front with Turkey and Yugoslavia, immediately sent General Dill to negotiate an agreement with Simović. But Dill found that Simović, 'a leader, and able, but in no sense a dictator', was preoccupied with administrative concerns and questions of law and order. Simović was determined to fight Hitler, but he wanted to avoid provoking Germany until he had gained enough time to prepare. Therefore, apparently oblivious to the threatening danger, he agreed only to staff talks with Dill without obligation on either side. On 4 April Churchill appealed directly to Simović, and then, on 6 April, Hitler invaded Yugoslavia and bombed Belgrade.

Yugoslav armed resistance collapsed after 14 days, and Simović fled to Greece with King Peter. He became Premier of the government-in-exile in London, but resigned in 1942. Early in 1945 King Peter named him as a member of the proposed Regency Council, but Tito opposed the nomination. Nevertheless Simović returned to Yugoslavia in May, to live there in his retirement.

SINCLAIR, Sir Archibald, b. 1890. Scottish Liberal politician, leader of the Liberal party, and Secretary of State for Air in the Churchill administration. In the early years of the war, before the R.A.F. resources had been built up and supplemented by American strength, the major question was how to use the small force of bombers in the most effective way. Sinclair was adamant that the most telling use of air strength would be all-out attacks on the heart of Germany's oil and industrial centres in order to cripple her war effort. But, clearly, air strength was also needed to support the war at sea (which Churchill always held to be crucial to the outcome of the war) and to co-operate with the army. Resources being limited, clashes of opinion inevitably arose about such policy. In 1940 Sinclair stated his position: 'We regard the destruction of Germany's oil sources as the foundation of our major strategy which aims at the reduction of the German war potential, and we shall continue to attack oil stocks in Germany on all possible occasions.' In the event, the drawbacks to this were the poor results obtained from night attacks, and, by the spring of 1942, when Sinclair reasserted his view to Portal, the Chief of Air Staff, saying that the resumption of the offensive 'might be the moment for switching a substantial part of our bomber effort on to oil', his views were decidedly unpopular. Figures showed that precision bombing of oil had not been as successful as Sinclair and others had hoped, and General Brooke, the C.I.G.S., recorded in April 1942 that Churchill backed him up in an argument with Sinclair about army support from the air: 'Churchill rubbed into Sinclair the necessity for devoting more love and affection to those air forces destined for army requirements.'

America's entry into the war in 1941 inevitably brought major changes of aim and policy in air planning. Sinclair held his ministerial position for the duration of the war and was responsible for a number of decisions concerning air

strength and strategy. His task was not an easy one. At one point he expressed his worry that carelessly worded announcements of the R.A.F.'s targets might alienate Church leaders, whose condemnation of the bombing offensive might have a disturbing effect on the morale of the crews of Bomber Command.

SKORZENY, Otto, b. 1908. German soldier, a dashing and resourceful exponent of irregular warfare. When war broke out Skorzeny tried to join the Luftwaffe, but was rejected at the age of 31 as being too old. In February 1940 he left his native Vienna to join the Adolf Hitler S.S. Regiment in Berlin; it was there that, noting the automatic and predictable reactions of well-disciplined troops, the idea was born on which his later career was based—that of turning the training of a well-drilled enemy to the enemy's disadvantage and thus causing confusion.

Skorzeny saw service in France, the Netherlands, and Russia, but in December 1942 was invalided home. Considered unfit for active service, he was given a desk job. But without notice he suddenly found himself entrusted with the task of setting up a school of warfare on 'Commando' lines—Hitler had demanded the formation of a Commando unit and the General Staff passed the job on to the seeming nonentity Skorzeny, hoping, it is said, by this means to sabotage the plan.

Skorzeny began by studying British Commando methods and found the British attempt to kidnap Rommel particularly instructive, as an example of the importance of removing the 'brains' of the enemy. His first missions (in the Middle East and Russia) failed, mainly because the High Command refused to release the necessary supplies. The capriciousness of the political leaders, who at the last moment changed their minds about the objectives, did not help, either. Towards the end of July 1943 Hitler entrusted him with the mission for which he is best known—the rescue of Mussolini, a captive of the new Italian government who were trying to negotiate an armistice with the Allies. Skorzeny finally located him at the isolated Hotel Campo Imperatore, which was situated in a small mountain resort in the Abruzzi in central Italy. On 12

September Skorzeny landed with 90 soldiers in gliders, and thanks to the speed and obvious determination of this small force the garrison of 250 surrendered within a few minutes; Mussolini was removed in a light aircraft. As a result of this spectacular feat Skorzeny was given 4,000 more troops. He was later involved in plans to kidnap Pétain and Tito, but these plans were never put into operation.

In the autumn of 1944, when it became known that Horthy, the Regent of Hungary, was putting out feelers in the hopes of negotiating an armistice with the Russians, Skorzeny was called in once again. Skorzeny managed to kidnap the instigator of the negotiations, the Regent's son Nicholas Horthy, and had him flown to Berlin. Horthy was forced to revoke his instructions and to resign.

One of Skorzeny's most effective actions was 'Operation Grief', an offshoot of the Rundstedt offensive in the Ardennes in December 1944. He disguised a number of German soldiers as Americans and put them behind the American lines. The idea was that they should seize the Meuse bridges and cause chaos among the enemy. After some of the infiltrators had been captured spy-fever gripped the Allied ranks and it even led to the isolation of General Eisenhower, for security reasons, at a critical point in the campaign.

Skorzeny was tried at Nuremberg as a war criminal, but was eventually acquitted. His release hinged largely on the evidence of a British officer who testified that Skorzeny and his men had done nothing that their Allied counterparts had not attempted or carried out.

SLESSOR, Sir John, b. 1897. British air marshal who, as commander of Coastal Command, 1943–4, played a major part in the defeat of the U-Boats. When war broke out he was Director of Plans at the Air Ministry, and early in 1941 he went on a special mission to the U.S.A. with selected officers of the other two Services to meet their American equivalents. The most important result of these discussions —which led to similar conferences later— was agreement on the overall strategic concept of the war should both America and Japan become involved: that the Allies should concentrate on knocking out

Germany and that Japan should be contained until Hitler was beaten.

Slessor became A.O.C. No. 5 Bomber Group and in 1942 Assistant Chief of the Air Staff; this post was a new one and he was in charge of policy, attending the major Allied conferences. In January 1943 he accompanied the Chief of the Air Staff to the Casablanca Conference, at which one of the decisions taken was that the defeat of the U-Boats must have first priority. In the following month he became A.O.C.-in-C. Coastal Command. Fired with the offensive spirit, he set about using his shore-based aircraft against U-Boats in the Bay of Biscay on their route to the Atlantic from French bases. Under his control the air weapon became an equal partner with the navy in the struggle. Rockets fired from aircraft inflicted great damage, and the early summer of 1943 saw the decisive phase in ending the U-Boats menace—a vital step towards the Allied invasion of the mainland of Europe.

From January 1944 Slessor was C.-in-C. of R.A.F. forces in the Mediterranean and also Deputy C.-in-C. Allied Air Forces in that area. He played a significant part in the Riviera landings of August 1944.

SLIM, Sir William, b. 1891. British general who gained renown for restoring the morale of the British and Indian troops in Burma and leading the 14th Army to victory over the Japanese. In 1945 he became C.-in-C. of the Allied land forces in S.E. Asia.

In 1940 Slim commanded an infantry brigade of the noted 5th Indian Division in N.E. Africa which fought its way into Eritrea. He was wounded but recovered in time to lead the 10th Indian Division in Iraq in 1941. On 8 June of that year, when the British and Free French forces entered Vichy-held Syria, Slim's division was suddenly transferred from the Iraq to the Syrian command, and invaded from the east. After that campaign ended, Slim was put in charge of the British force that entered Iran on 25 August from Iraq to enforce Allied demands for the expulsion of hundreds of German agents then in the country. 'By this time I was becoming accustomed to invasions,' wrote Slim. 'This was the fifth frontier I had crossed in the past year.' Slim's 10th Indian

Division routed their opponents in Iran and made the first contact with Russian troops in Teheran.

In 1942 Slim was sent to Burma in command of the 1st Corps. After Rangoon fell to the Japanese in March 1942 it was he who was responsible for the orderly retreat from Burma 900 miles back into India. The march was undertaken in the most difficult conditions, when the men of the Burma divisions were at their lowest ebb. That morale was maintained and that the formations remained disciplined bodies of troops was largely due to Slim. They reached Imphal in mid May.

In December 1943, during the Allied counter-attack launched in Burma against the Japanese, Slim was given command of the 14th Army. February 1944 marked the turning point of the Burma campaign, when the British decisively defeated the Japanese in the Arakan. This was the first time that a British force had thwarted a major Japanese attack, and the 14th Army followed this up by routing the enemy and driving him out of positions that had been prepared for months, and that the Japanese fanatically held to the death. Thus the myth of Japanese invincibility (for which Slim never had any sympathy) was finally crushed. The 14th Army went on, under Slim's command, to dislodge the Japanese at Imphal and Kohima in a campaign of two months' heavy fighting. Gradually the Japanese were driven back the way they had come. By March 1945 Mandalay was in British hands.

Following the clear-cut British victory in the battle of central Burma, the 14th Army still had to battle nearly 400 miles to Rangoon. With the monsoon on its way there was a very real danger that transport would not hold out, or alternatively that it might get bogged down in the deep mud. An officer under Slim's command testified to his leadership thus: 'I don't think anyone really doubted that we would make it when Bill Slim told us we could and we'd got to.' But the 14th Army that triumphantly reached Rangoon in early May 1945 found that the Japanese had gone. 'The population in thousands welcomed our men with a relief and joy they made no attempt to restrain,' wrote Slim. 'We were back.'

During World War I Slim had served in Gallipoli, France, and Mesopotamia. He had transferred to the Gurkha Rifles on being granted a regular commission in 1920.

He was an admired, trusted, and well-liked commander, and his army achieved the greatest land victory over the Japanese of any troops in the war.

SMIGLY-RYDZ, Edward, b. 1886. Polish statesman and general. Designated by Pilsudski in 1935 as his successor, Smigly-Rydz was the virtual ruler of Poland when the Germans invaded in 1939.

It was he, as Marshal and Inspector-General of the Polish forces, who directed the fight against the aggressors. Arguing that 'with the Germans we may lose our freedom, with the Russians we should lose our soul', he refused to admit Russian troops to Polish territory, even when the Germans were obviously about to attack. Fearing to be accused of provocation by mobilizing in good time, and with anachronistic faith in the power of their cavalry, the Poles were unprepared for the German 'Blitzkrieg'. The government stood its ground, and the army fought hard to defend the country's long frontiers against forces twice its size. But the Panzer divisions raced forward at a speed which upset all calculations.

After a fortnight Smigly-Rydz suggested falling back to the south-east corner of Poland, to hold it as a bridgehead from which the whole country might ultimately be reconquered with French and British help. But three days later the Russians invaded across the eastern frontier. Smigly-Rydz fled to Romania with the Polish government, and was there interned. The Free Polish government in Paris criticized his conduct of the campaign, and dismissed him from his post as C.-in-C. In 1941 he escaped to Poland and took an active part in underground activities. He is said to have been killed by the Germans in 1943.

His real name was Rydz, to which he had added the alias of Smigly ('lightning') whilst organizing the Polish Legion during World War I. He was an accomplished painter.

SMITH, Walter Bedell, b. 1895. American general, one of the most determined and diplomatic planners and administrators of the war. In 1939 he was called to Washington to become Assistant Secretary, and later Secretary, to the War Department General Staff. In February 1942 he emerged as a major military figure when, on the recommendation of General Marshall, he became Secretary of the Joint Chiefs of Staff and the first U.S. Secretary of the Combined Chiefs of Staff, whose function was to co-ordinate the military efforts of Britain and America. Like his British opposite number he had a straightforward manner and strong opinions combined with a respect for higher authority. In their hands the Combined Chiefs of Staff organization functioned with unexpected smoothness.

In September 1942 Bedell Smith went to Britain as General Eisenhower's Chief of Staff. The two men worked closely together over the later part of the North Africa campaign and in the invasion of Normandy. Bedell Smith had to perform many duties outside the normal scope of a staff officer. It was he who conducted negotiations about the possibilities of an armistice with Italian envoys in Lisbon and with General Castellano in Sicily. Also it was he who, with the German General Jodl, signed the instrument of Germany's unconditional surrender on 7 May 1945.

Bedell Smith had worked his way up from the ranks, and his lack of a West Point military training was a handicap in his early career. But he made up for this by his own intensive study and his later work at the U.S. Army's senior training school (the Army War College in Washington), from which he graduated in 1937. General Eisenhower described his Chief of Staff as a godsend: a master of detail with clear comprehension of main issues. Bedell Smith also had many war-time dealings with Churchill, who admired his tenacity and intellectual ability and added to his American nickname of 'Beetle' that of 'the American Bulldog'.

SMUTS, Jan Christiaan, b. 1870. South African soldier and statesman who was chiefly responsible for South Africa's involvement in the Allied war effort. For a decade befoie the war the two main South African parties had been fused; Hertzog,

leader of the Nationalist party, was Prime Minister, and Smuts, leader of the United party, was deputy. When the Germans invaded Poland in 1939 the two men were sharply divided on the issue of neutrality. The far-sighted Smuts, alive to the dangers of Hitler's acquisitive policy, argued against neutrality, and won a difficult debate in Parliament on this issue. He became Prime Minister at the head of a party that was pledged to oppose Germany.

From 1940 onwards he was commander of the Union defence forces and supervised South Africa's war effort, which was impressive, despite active opposition at home. South African troops were prominent in the Ethiopian, North African, and Italian campaigns, and the country had a significant place in Allied war production.

Smuts, as C.-in-C. (as well as Prime Minister) visited South African and other troops in the North African and Ethiopian theatres of war. He was a confidant of Churchill and was involved in several major decisions regarding strategy and command. In October 1940 Smuts paid an 8-day visit to the East African front, going first to Khartoum for a conference with Anthony Eden. Later he was largely responsible for the decision to wage a vigorous campaign against the Axis powers in East Africa.

At Cairo, where he met Churchill in August 1942, he joined General Brooke in persuading Churchill that Montgomery was the right choice as commander of the 8th Army. Churchill had the highest regard for Smuts's opinion and Brooke remarked of him in his diary: 'Smuts I look upon as one of the biggest of nature's gentlemen that I have ever seen. A wonderful, clear grasp of all things, coupled with most exceptional charm. Interested in all matters and gifted with the most marvellous judgment.'

Smuts visited the U.K. 4 times during the war and attended several meetings of the War Cabinet. In 1945 he went to the San Francisco Conference and played a major role in drafting the Charter of the United Nations. In 1946 he attended the peace conference at Versailles—the only person present who had also attended the previous Versailles Conference. When

177

Smuts was made a British field marshal, he accepted this tribute with characteristic modesty: 'I trust my friends and those who have known me as General Smuts for the last forty years will not hesitate to use my old title . . . I am too old now to change names.'

SOMERVILLE, Sir James, b. 1882. British admiral whose ships destroyed units of the French fleet in Oran harbour in order to prevent their falling into German hands. In 1940 he was given command of Force H in the Mediterranean, based on Gibraltar, and in July of that year it fell to him to discharge what Churchill called 'one of the most disagreeable and difficult tasks that a British admiral has ever been faced with': he had to threaten force against the French naval vessels harboured at Oran and Mersel-Kebir unless they were sailed to a place out of reach of the Axis. Somerville was confident that his former colleague Admiral Gensoul would stand by the French undertaking to let no vessel pass to the enemy, and was strongly opposed to using force. But, when the French refused to accept the British terms, he was obliged to obey the orders from London and fire on the French ships; 1,297 French lives were lost. According to the British official naval historian, the three flag officers involved, including Somerville, viewed the government's orders with something approaching horror and they all believed that given time for negotiation a peaceful settlement could have been found.

In 1941 Somerville shelled Genoa, and played a decisive role with Force H in sinking the battleship *Bismarck*, the pride of the German navy. His ships gave distinguished service in escorting supplies to Malta, and in covering the hazardous operation 'Tiger'—a convoy of tanks transported through the Mediterranean to General Wavell in the Western Desert.

From 1942 to 1944 he was C.-in-C. of the new Eastern fleet based on Ceylon, but he relied on a secret base at Addu Atoll in the Maldive Islands until the clear superiority of the Japanese fleet rendered expedient a temporary withdrawal to Kilindini on the Kenya coast. From there, to forestall the Japanese, he successfully

attacked Diego Suarez in Madagascar. Somerville was present at the Washington Conference in 1943, and became head of the British naval delegation in Washington in August 1944.

SØNSTEBY, Gunnar, b. 1918. Outstanding member of the Norwegian Resistance movement. When war broke out he was studying economics at Oslo University, and working part time as an accountant. Exempt from military duty for reasons of health, he joined the Norwegian Resistance at its inception.

In 1943 he was summoned to England for training by the S.O.E., returning to Norway as a member of the 'Kompani Linge', and became the leader of its Oslo group. These young men were chiefly occupied with sabotage, and their targets included the Gestapo H.Q. in Oslo, a store of aeroplane spares, a Luftwaffe establishment, and an armament works. They also helped to blow up sulphuric acid containers at a chemical works, a pyrites mine, and factories of a sulphur company.

In May 1944 they effectively obstructed German attempts at organized labour conscription—first by attacking the Norske Folk insurance company's punched-card machine (used for conscription records), then by demolishing the Labour Office where an index of conscripts was kept. The Germans then tried withholding ration-books from men who failed to produce conscription cards, so Sønsteby's group held up a lorry containing 75,000 new ration-books, and distributed them to almost all the men threatened by conscription.

In 1945 the group attacked the administrative building of the Norwegian railway company. But the peak of their achievements came a few days before Germany surrendered, when they captured the records of Quisling's Department of Justice and the Nazi-controlled police, thus acquiring the necessary evidence to prosecute traitors and war criminals after the war ended. The head of the Norwegian sector of the S.O.E. said of Sønsteby that he was 'in all probability the most efficient and most productive secret agent in Norway'. He worked under many disguises and aliases: *No. 24, Kjaken, Broch,*

Erling Fjeld. He later wrote a book
Report from No. 24.

SORGE, Richard, b. 1895. German journalist and spy for Russia, possibly the
most successful secret agent of the war.
His main sphere of action from 1933
until his arrest in 1941 was in Japan,
where the astounding feats of his spy
ring literally helped to change the course
of the war. He had been made field commander of Soviet military spies in the Far
East as early as 1929, and had set up a
China Unit with its H.Q. in Shanghai
whose object was to collect information
about the Chinese Nationalist forces. In
1933, after a successful stay in China,
during which he gained valuable practical
experience, Sorge was sent to Japan,
whose growing links with Germany were
causing alarm in Russia.
Here he proceeded to organize the first
major foreign spy ring in Japan's history.
It was to operate undetected for a period
of 8 years. His 'cover' job was in Tokyo
as senior German journalist for the influential *Frankfurter Zeitung*, virtually the
one German paper that was still independent
of the Nazis. This, together with his deep
knowledge and understanding of Japanese
culture and political and economic affairs,
quickly provided him with access to the
highest diplomatic circles. The four other
members of the inner ring, hand-picked
by Sorge for their ability, soon acquired
a similar status. A Japanese journalist
and expert on Chinese affairs, Hozumi
Ozaki, became the confidant of the Prime
Minister, Prince Konoye, and was entrusted with the most confidential information. Sorge himself had great influence
with the German ambassador Major-
General Ott, who even allowed him to
draft reports to Berlin. Contacts between
members of the ring were wisely kept to a
minimum, and many of them were unknown to one another until after their
arrest. During his years in Japan Sorge
kept up his pose as a loyal Nazi and was
even asked by Berlin to become the Führer
of all the Nazis in Japan—an offer he
declined. Sorge's main duties were: to
discover whether Japan intended to attack
the Soviet Union; to report on changes
in the strength and disposition of the
Japanese armed forces; to report on the

Japanese army's role in political affairs
and indicate the inferences that could be
deduced from its state of preparedness;
to trace the development of Japanese
heavy industries; to watch the progress
of German-Japanese relations; to discover
Japan's policy towards China and Manchuria and her relations with the U.K.
and the U.S.A. who, so Russia believed,
would support any Japanese advance into
Siberia. The information gathered by the
ring was sent to Moscow, either by micro-
films carried to Shanghai or Hong Kong,
and delivered there to Soviet Union
couriers, or by radio.
It was not until a radio message was
intercepted in 1938 that the Japanese had
the first inkling that a spy ring was operating in their midst. Sorge provided his
masters with advance information about the
negotiations between Germany and Japan
that led to the Anti-Comintern Pact of
1936, and later about the talks that culminated in a military alliance in 1940. In
May 1941, five weeks before the invasion
of Russia, Sorge reported that the 170
German divisions which were massed on
the Russian borders would invade on 20
June. He was able to assure Russia that
Japan herself had no intention of attacking and, just before his arrest, sent details
about the impending attack on Pearl
Harbor. During the early stages of the
Pacific war the Allies learned that the
Soviet Union had the most reliable information about the Japanese order of battle.
This was probably based largely on information that Sorge and his colleagues had
transmitted during the winter of 1940–1.
Sorge was arrested in October 1941, and
was hanged three years later.

SPAAK, Paul-Henri, b. 1899. Foreign
Minister of Belgium at the time of the
German invasion, and an unrelenting
opponent of the occupying enemy. After
the U.K. and France declared war on
Germany Spaak, realizing Belgium's
vulnerability, believed that the country
should remain neutral and rejected overtures from the Allies, who were seeking
to send troops into Belgium in an attempt
to forestall Germany. When Germany
invaded on 10 May 1940 Spaak called on
Britain and France to fulfil their treaty
guarantees. King Leopold took immediate

control of the Belgian army. As the Germans advanced, and the position became more obviously hopeless, Spaak and his Premier, Hubert Pierlot, were appalled at the King's evident intention to remain in Belgium come what may. In the strongest terms they urged him to continue the struggle alongside the Allies in France. They parted from him at Wynendaele on 25 May and were taken to England via Dunkirk. Three days later Leopold capitulated, and public feeling ran high against the Belgian refugees and soldiers in France. In their interest, and to restore Belgium's reputation, Pierlot and Spaak went to Paris and there issued a statement accusing Leopold of a defeatist surrender and of treating with the enemy. Later Spaak recognized both charges to be unfounded. After France fell Pierlot and Spaak fled to Spain, and ultimately to London, where they exercised the functions of a Belgian government until they returned to liberated Brussels in September 1944.

Spaak played a prominent part in promoting the Benelux customs agreement of 1944, and in the birth of the United Nations at San Francisco in June 1945. Although he was in exile in London during the war, England remained a strange country to him, and he found the British a source of unending, and frequently amused, wonder.

SPAATZ, Carl, b. 1891. American general, C.-in-C. of the U.S. air forces bombing Germany. He later exercised a similar command in the Pacific. Himself an outstanding pilot, he welded his forces into a devastatingly powerful weapon. In January 1942 he was appointed chief of the Air Force Combat Command. In the following March he was made commanding general of the 8th Air Force, and in July 1942 he was transferred to the European theatre of operations, based in the U.K. There were difficult problems of inter-Allied organization to cope with, but Spaatz was extremely successful in establishing a close co-operation with the R.A.F. In February 1943, after the Allied landings in North Africa, he was given command of the N.W. Africa Air Force. This Allied air force played a large part in the Tunisian and Sicilian campaigns and in the invasion of Italy. Spaatz was

given his major appointment as commanding general of the U.S. Strategic Air Forces in January 1944. His command included the 8th Air Force in the U.K. and the 15th Air Force in Italy, operating under the direct control of the Joint Chiefs of Staff in Washington. During the next few months American bombers made daylight raids on industrial targets in German and German-held territory. Special emphasis was laid on the destruction of synthetic fuel plants and crude oil refineries. When Eisenhower, the Allied Supreme Commander for the 'Second Front' invasion of the European mainland, took over operational command of the strategic air forces in March 1944, the destruction of railway communication networks became the main objective of both American and British bombers. The Allied bombing attacks reached the peak of their intensity just before D-Day, 6 June: as many as 1,200 U.S. bombers with heavy fighter escorts were being used in a single day, and by D-Day the Americans had dropped 1,550,000 tons of bombs on German-held territory. The bombers played a decisive role in the subsequent campaign until the surrender of Germany.

Spaatz was appointed to the H.Q. of the Army Air Forces on 11 March 1945. In July he was detailed to command the U.S. Strategic Air Forces in the Pacific: the 8th and 20th Air Forces based on Okinawa and the Marianas. He had also to direct the activities of the fleets of heavy bombers which were operating against the Japanese mainland. The planes that dropped the atomic bombs on Hiroshima and Nagasaki were under his command. Perhaps of all the air force leaders of the war Spaatz could with most justification be said to have had command of the air.

SPEER, Albert, b. 1905. German architect and administrator, one of the few gifted and rational members of the National Socialist hierarchy. He designed a number of the grandiose monuments of the Nazi régime, including Hitler's Chancellery in Berlin and the stadium at Nuremberg. In 1942 he succeeded Fritz Todt (who was killed in an air crash in that year) as minister for armaments and munitions and inspector-general of roads, water, and power, and in 1943 he was also given responsibility for the direction of the war economy. In these posts Speer was extremely successful; that Germany was able to maintain a high level of industrial production despite the Allied air onslaught was partly due to his talents in planning and administration.

In 1944 Speer became convinced that Germany had lost the war and should try to obtain acceptable peace terms from the Allies. He told Hitler of the conclusion he had reached, and, strangely, the Führer (who was exacting savage revenge on the enemies—real and supposed—by whom he thought himself surrounded) took no action against him. Speer had long been one of Hitler's particular favourites, one of the few people with whom he could discuss his own artistic yearnings. When, in the last stages of the war, Hitler ordered the German armies to leave destruction behind them as they retreated, Speer countermanded his instructions.

After the war Speer was put on trial at Nuremberg as a war criminal, chiefly because he had been head of the Todt Organization, which used conscripted labour for construction work; part of the Todt work force was slave labour from concentration camps and other sources. He was sentenced to imprisonment for 20 years.

SPEIDEL, Hans, b. 1898. German general, a staff officer of outstanding capability and one of the most assiduous workers for engineering an armistice with the Western Allies. He was Chief of Staff to the military commander of occupied France from 1940 to 1942, and in 1944 he became Chief of Staff to General Rommel, then commanding the German forces north of the Loire. He thus played a conspicuous part in the fighting in northern France after D-Day.

Speidel was in touch with the leaders of the conspiracy to overthrow Hitler, but was not actually involved in the plot. In May 1944 he arranged a meeting with Rommel and Stülpnagel to consider how the war in the West could be ended and the Nazi régime abolished. He was not able to get Rundstedt's approval for a plan to achieve an armistice without

Hitler's consent, but he did secure Rommel's conditional support for a *coup d'état* in which Hitler would not be assassinated but brought to trial. Speidel attended other conferences and a plan, based on an immediate armistice with the Allies (who, it was assumed, would join an anti-Nazi government in fighting Bolshevik Russia), was drawn up. However, the Allied landings in Normandy forced the conspirators to change course, and a new plan was produced which led on 20 July to the last attempt to assassinate Hitler. Speidel, almost alone among the army conspirators in the West, survived to describe what happened.

Later, refusing to carry out Hitler's order to destroy Paris before the advancing Allies, he was arrested and imprisoned. Under incessant interrogation he refused to give anything away. After seven months in custody he escaped into hiding until the Allies finally set him free.

A brilliant general staff officer, he was a man of high education and culture.

SPRUANCE, Raymond, b. 1886. American admiral who was one of the most successful naval commanders of the Pacific war. Forces under his leadership caused immense damage to the Japanese at relatively low cost. Spruance had a major part in working out the circular battle formation which helped to make the American carrier groups the most powerful fighting fleets in naval history. He won praise for his imperturbability in action.

Shortly before the U.S.A. entered the war he was placed in command of a cruiser division of the Pacific Fleet at Midway; this formed part of the force sent in June 1942 to stop a Japanese attempt to invade Midway Island. After the fleets had engaged, the force commander's flagship, the carrier USS *Yorktown*, was put out of action (and later sunk by a Japanese submarine) and Spruance took charge of the battle operations. The Battle of Midway, which is considered to be among the decisive victories of history and was the turning point of the Pacific war, showed Spruance's extraordinary capabilities. Fleet Admiral Chester Nimitz, C.-in-C. of the Pacific Fleet, made him his Chief of Staff and, in this position, Spruance planned many campaigns.

In November 1943 Spruance returned to sea in charge of the naval forces involved in the assault on Tarawa in the Gilbert Islands. Three months later, as commander of the Central Pacific Fleet, he directed the successful attacks against the Marshall Islands, and an aerial attack on the great Japanese naval base at Truk in the Carolines in what he called 'a partial settlement' for Pearl Harbor. On 19–20 June Mitscher's Task Force 58, going into action under Spruance's orders, won an overwhelming victory in the Battle of the Philippine Sea, virtually putting an end to the Japanese carrier force which sought to disrupt the American invasion of the Mariana Islands.

In February 1945 Spruance led the 5th Fleet (formerly the Central Pacific Fleet) in the first carrier strike on Tokyo and directed the naval side of the assault on Iwo Jima. He was planning the naval phase of American landings in Japan when the war ended. By many authorities he was rated the finest American naval combat commander of the war, and among the great fighting admirals of history.

'STAINLESS STEPHEN' (Clifford Baynes), b. 1891. British comedian, one of the real troupers of the traditional music-hall world who, in addition to other war work, did a six months' tour to the Middle East and India, ending up with the 14th Army in Burma in 1943–4. Basil Dean in *The Theatre at War* described how 'Stainless Stephen' mysteriously disappeared shortly after his arrival in Calcutta and was eventually located among the front-line troops on the Chindwin River, giving hourly turns to the men, almost in their foxholes. The exploit remained in the memory of many who fought in Burma, and they continued to show their nostalgic appreciation in riotous welcomes at no fewer than 10 Burma Star Reunions at the Albert Hall. 'Stainless Stephen' was also a regular turn at Service rallies in Glasgow and Edinburgh.

'Stainless Stephen' was a soldier, 1914–1919, and first broadcast in 1924. He was a regular performer with the B.B.C. and became highly successful in the leading variety theatres. His stage name was taken

from Sheffield, his home town. 'Stainless Stephen's' original and comical diction and essentially British humour, with scripts always written by himself, endeared him to a very wide audience over a long period.

STALIN, Joseph, b. 1879. Russian dictator. As virtually the supreme ruler of his country, Stalin directed Russia's part in the war with skill, determination, and ruthlessness, fighting not only for Russia's survival but for her pre-eminence in the post-war world. Faced with the apparent choice of an unwelcome anti-Hitler coalition with the West or an alliance with Hitler, Stalin in the pre-war years had at first preferred to consolidate the anti-Hitler coalition. Between 1935 and 1939 the communist parties of various countries established 'popular fronts' to help Russia to find bourgeois democratic allies opposed to Hitler. But the notorious non-aggression pact of August 1939 between Russia and Germany came as a complete reversal of this policy; Hitler and Stalin agreed to share their areas of influence in Eastern Europe. Hailed by Stalin as an instrument of peace, the true significance of the pact was revealed in September when Stalio's Red Army proceeded to occupy eastern Poland after that country's defeat by Germany. A further pointer to Stalin's imperialistic ambitions came in November, with the unprovoked Soviet attack on Finland. Much later, when Churchill accused Stalin of double-crossing the U.K. in 1939, just as the move towards agreement between Russia and Britain seemed to be progressing smoothly, Stalin claimed that he was convinced that Britain had been bluffing—because she was obviously so unprepared for war. Moreover, he said, since Germany would inevitably attack Russia ultimately, by occupying a stretch of Poland betVeen Russia and Germany, Russia had longer to prepare for the German invasion.

The attack by Germany on Russia came in June 1941 and, in spite of warnings, caught Stalin unawares, as he later publicly admitted. He had already assumed supreme power as Chairman of the Council of Ministers on 6 May in anticipation of dangers ahead, but he was still hoping to postpone the inevitable clash with Germany. A Defence Committee was hastily formed, with Stalin as a prominent member. Churchill, despite previously cool relations with Russia, promptly allied the U.K. with Russia's struggle against Nazism, and pledged Britain to provide the utmost material assistance. Stalin soon showed himself to be a demanding and querulous ally; within a month of Russia's position having changed from that of a bristling non-belligerent to that of a friend in need, Stalin sent Churchill the first of a long series of messages urging the prompt creation of a 'Second Front' in France to relieve the pressure on Russia. This issue was to become Stalin's main controversy with Churchill during 1942 and 1943, though as Allied power increased his demands became less dictatorial. For as early as September 1941 Stalin's 'request' sounded more like a demand: 'The Germans believe that the threat from the West is a bluff and are moving all their forces to the East without fear,' he complained, adding that it was British failure to act in France which had allowed Hitler to capture half the Ukraine and sweep up to Leningrad. This was obviously untrue: the defeats in the Ukraine were partly due to Russia's unpreparedness but even more to superior German generalship. As Churchill said to the British ambassador in Moscow: 'Nothing that we could do or could have done would affect the struggle on the Eastern front.'

Although Stalin assumed overall responsibility for the major military decisions of his government, he nevertheless allowed his generals plenty of tactical, and sometimes even strategic, freedom. After the early chaos, his overall strategy became discernible. It was to retreat without wasting any more energy than strictly necessary, to build up power, and make his opponent diffuse his troops and dilute his power—only then could Russia begin to take the initiative. In July 1941 he made the historic appeal to the Soviet people to 'scorch the earth' occupied by the invaders: 'Conditions in occupied areas must be made intolerable for the enemy and all his accomplices They must be hunted and exterminated at every step, and all their aims frustrated.

... In the event of any retreat of the Red Army ... we must not leave ... even one pound of grain or one gallon of petrol to the enemy. All useful materials which cannot be carried with us must be absolutely destroyed.' This drastic policy was carried out to the letter in the first months of war, during the crushing German successes in the Ukraine and their subsequent advances. The Germans reached Kiev in September 1941 to discover that it had been methodically destroyed.

Stalin acted (apparently) with extraordinary courage and coolness even in the most alarming conditions; he refused to leave the Kremlin when Hitler's armies were at the gates of Moscow and the Soviet government was evacuated. The last-minute evacuation of industrial plant and millions of industrial workers from areas likely to be occupied, which Stalin insisted on, was largely responsible for Russia's recovery from the first blows of the war and for its ability to build up an enormous army. On the political side Stalin emphasized Russia's patriotism and traditions—even those that at other times might have seemed anathema to the doctrinaire Party man. He described the struggle as 'The Great Fatherland War' and was eloquent in his praise of the national heroes of Mother Russia. He reinstated the Orthodox Church as a great Russian institution and disbanded the Communist International. These measures were carefully designed to boost morale at home and to appease Russia's critics abroad. He succeeded in both these aims, and the picture of Russia as a threatened homeland rather than as a hotbed of revolution helped to smooth relationships with the U.S.A. and the U.K.

It was, perhaps, in his foreign policy that Stalin showed his genius. His dictatorial and somewhat unbending attitude to the Western Allies helped him in the hour of need, and he was to prove himself a difficult and devious ally. At the first meeting with Churchill in Moscow, in August 1942, Stalin began by accusing the Western powers of being 'too much afraid of fighting the Germans' because they had not established the 'Second Front' that Stalin demanded. The meeting ended on a more amicable note, with Stalin slightly placated by Churchill's revelation of the plans for the landings in N.W. Africa. His communications afterwards, though persisting in demands for a 'Second Front', became less hostile. General Brooke, who met Stalin at the Moscow meeting, made this assessment of him: 'I was much impressed by his astuteness and crafty cleverness. . . . He is an outstanding man . . . but not an attractive one. He has got an unpleasantly cold, crafty, cruel face and whenever I look at him I can imagine him sending off people to their doom without even turning a hair. On the other hand there is no doubt that he has a quick brain and a real grasp of the essentials of war.' Ian Jacob also commented on Stalin's calculating and cruel nature, adding acidly: 'I should say that to make friends with Stalin would be equivalent to making friends with a python.'

The significance of this 'crafty' dictator's influence on Allied strategy was only fully realized much later. Stalin's continued demands for the Allies to strike across the Channel jolted many politicians in the West into believing that if something were not done soon Stalin might quite happily make a separate peace with Hitler in the East. This gnawing fear was of extreme significance, for the Western Allies' need to secure Russia's absolute co-operation put Stalin in a powerful position. The apparent success of the Teheran Conference of November–December 1943, at which Stalin promised Russian support for 'Overlord' and for the war against Japan, together with Roosevelt's enthusiasm for the outcome of his own diplomacy, helped to conceal from the Western Allies Stalin's real objective. While the Western Allies were bending every effort simply to winning the war, Stalin's political strategy took account of long-term objectives. He wanted the Western Allies to concentrate on Western Europe and the western Mediterranean because he wished to keep Anglo-American forces out of those Balkan countries that he intended to 'liberate'. The Teheran Conference established Allied military strategy for 1944, but, vastly more important, it gave Russia a pre-eminent position politically in post-war Eastern Europe by diverting the agreed

strategy from the chosen area of Soviet operations.

Stalin's adroit haggling at the Yalta Conference of 1945 and his subsequent high-handed behaviour in Eastern Europe consolidated Russia's position. Nowhere was Stalin's ruthlessness more clearly demonstrated than in Poland. In flagrant violation of the Yalta Agreement that the provisional Polish government should be accepted but reorganized on a more democratic basis, Stalin authorized the Polish government to take over the administration of the disputed German territory, imposing Poland's western frontier at the rivers Oder and Neisse, the line which Britain and America had always rejected. Churchill and Truman were faced with a *fait accompli* when they met Stalin at Potsdam in July to discuss the post-war settlement of Europe; and though on paper the western frontier had still not been decided, the Poles remained in occupation of the doubtful territories. The Red army willingly helped them to drive out most of the 7 million Germans remaining in the area. Stalin had taken the matter into his own hands, with a cynical disregard for his promise; and the Polish experience was repeated in other countries of Eastern Europe where 'liberation' by the Red army was the prelude to reorganization as Soviet satellites at the mercy of Communist minorities. The climax of Stalin's career came in 1945; as generalissimo and unchallenged leader he was submerged in adulation and the centre of a mythology that assumed absurd proportions towards the end of his life.

STARK, Harold, b. 1880. American admiral. In 1939 President Roosevelt appointed him Chief of Naval Operations. For nearly 3 years, as professional head of the naval establishment, Stark was in charge of the immense naval expansion programme and the operations of more than 1,000 vessels of the U.S. fleet, plus its fast-growing air arm. In the summer of 1941, before the U.S.A. entered the war, he established naval patrols in the Atlantic to prevent attacks by German submarines and surface ships on American merchant and naval shipping. Convoys were organized to protect cargo vessels carrying supplies to American oversea bases and

the U.K. Towards the end of 1941 the
U.S. fleet was put on a war footing as
tension between the U.S.A. and Japan
increased. When Japan bombed the U.S.
Pacific Fleet at Pearl Harbor in December
the rest of the U.S. navy was ready for
action.

In March 1942 Stark was transferred
to London as commander of U.S. naval
forces operating in European waters, a
post which involved not only administrative and logistical command of U.S. ships
and bases, but also considerable diplomacy. He also served as naval adviser to
the U.S. Embassy in London and, as such,
represented the U.S. navy at all conferences concerning naval operations in
Europe. He attended the Washington
Conference of May 1943, when Operation 'Overlord' was planned. By July
bases and accommodation in Great
Britain for the U.S. navy had been provided, and Stark's directive, 'Get to know
your opposite number' was so well
carried out, as the American forces in
Europe built up, that co-operation between
the various Allied naval forces was effected
without any major misunderstandings or
disagreements.

STAUFFENBERG, Claus von, b. 1907.
German staff officer, a Swabian aristocrat,
who was a leading figure in the plot to
assassinate Hitler. In the early stages of
the war Stauffenberg had distinguished
himself in the organization department
of the Army High Command. Later he
transferred to the Afrika Korps; he was
badly wounded, and lost an eye and his
right hand. Posted back to the General
Staff in Berlin his talents and standing won
him a position as Chief of Staff to General
Olbricht, deputy commander of the Home
Army. He therefore had access to a great
amount of secret information on all
military and political operations of the
German army, and was also influential in
building up the Reserve Army.

Stauffenberg's determination to remove
Hitler did not develop only with the prospect of defeat. A devout Catholic and a
man of a deep moral convictions, he
believed that Hitler was 'evil incarnate'
and should be destroyed for Germany's
sake. He was no Nazi and Schlabrendorff
later said of him that 'his calm courage,

his circumspection, clarity of mind, tenacity and persistence, as well as his professional knowledge and ability, made him
a natural "general manager" of the
Resistance'.

In 1943 plans were laid for the first
attempt at assassination. Also, with the
help of General Olbricht, Home Army
units were to seize control of the major
cities. The first attempt was planned for
March. It came to nothing because at the
last minute the conference which Hitler
was to have attended was cancelled. There
were no more opportunities that winter.
Stauffenberg concentrated on building up
an organization capable of taking over the
government once Hitler had been removed.
By June 1944 he had worked out plans
for the transfer of power and had had the
necessary network ready for action.

In June 1944 General Fromm, the
commander of the Home Army, appointed
Stauffenberg his Chief of Staff. In this
post Stauffenberg had official reasons for
attending Hitler's staff conferences whenever Home Army matters were on the
agenda. As he was alone among the inner
circle of conspirators in having access to
Hitler without being searched, Stauffenberg
suggested himself as the assassin. The other
conspirators did not favour this idea: he
had drawn up the 'Valkyrie' plans, and
should be available to take charge in
Berlin and direct the seizure of power.
(Officially the 'Valkyrie' plans were a
guard against civil disturbance in Germany;
only the conspirators knew their real
purpose.) It was agreed that Stauffenberg
should carry a bomb into a conference in
his briefcase, leave the meeting on some
pretext before the device exploded, and
make his way to Berlin at once, while all
radio communications were to be put out
of action by an accomplice as soon as
Hitler was dead.

By July the conspirators knew they must
act quickly and before the Allied forces
in Normandy could win a decisive victory;
otherwise the Western powers might not
be amenable to the idea of a compromise
peace. On 11 July Stauffenberg represented
Fromm at a conference at Berchtesgaden.
The bomb was in his briefcase, but neither
Himmler nor Goering was present at the
meeting, and it had been planned to kill
them as well as Hitler himself—several

of the highest army officers had agreed to go along with the plot only on this condition—so Stauffenberg did not use the bomb. Another attempt on 16 July also miscarried.

Stauffenberg determined that at the next opportunity, come what may, he would explode the bomb if Hitler were there. On 20 July he attended a meeting at Hitler's H.Q. near Rastenburg in East Prussia. The venue had been changed from a well-protected bomb-proof shelter (inside which a bomb would have exploded with maximum effect) to a wooden building. Neither Himmler nor Goering was present, but Stauffenberg set the bomb, was duly called away to the telephone, and left for Berlin unchallenged. But it so happened that one of the officers present had slightly moved the briefcase, and when the bomb exploded it was farther from Hitler than Stauffenberg had intended; also one of the table supports sheltered the Führer. Hitler was wounded, but not critically; 4 officers were killed. Moreover Stauffenberg's confederate at Hitler's H.Q., who was to contact the conspirators in Berlin as soon as the bomb exploded and then to sabotage the communications centre at H.Q., failed to do so. Hitler was therefore able to learn what was going on in Berlin. He quickly discovered that the attempt on his life was not an isolated incident but part of a well-directed plot. But the members of the conspiracy did not succeed in consolidating their position. Goebbels, in Berlin, was able to act against them and, after a period of confusion, Fromm had them arrested. Stauffenberg, with others including Olbricht, was taken down to the courtyard of the War Ministry (where the conspirators had their H.Q.) and shot out of hand in the light of a lorry's headlamps. In the moments before the shots were fired he shouted, 'Long live our sacred Germany!'

STETTINIUS, Edward, b. 1900. American industrialist and statesman who succeeded Cordell Hull as U.S. Secretary of State at the end of 1944. He was brought into public service by President Roosevelt at the outbreak of the war in Europe to become chairman of the War Resources Board. Its task was to make a survey of the raw materials which would be needed

if the U.S. were to become involved in the war. In May 1940 the President appointed him a member of the National Defense Advisory Commission, with responsibility for industrial materials. To take up this post Stettinius resigned the chairmanship of the U.S. Steel Corporation and other business commitments. In January 1941 he became chairman of the priorities board and director of the priorities division in the newly created Office of Production Management. His function was to conserve necessary raw materials for defence industries. Eight months later Roosevelt appointed him Lend-Lease administrator. He took up this appointment with enthusiasm, and in 1943 published *Lendlease: Weapon for Victory*. He was also appointed a member of the Canadian-American Joint Defense Production Committee and, from December 1941, was a member of the U.S. Board of Economic Warfare.

Stettinius succeeded Sumner Welles as Under-Secretary of State in October 1943 and went to London in April 1944 for talks on American-British differences in policy regarding Poland, Italy, and France. He later organized and directed preparations for the Dumbarton Oaks Conference in August–October 1944. As American representative at this conference he collaborated with delegates from the U.K., Russia, and China in drafting proposals for a world organization—the United Nations. He succeeded Cordell Hull as Secretary of State on 1 December 1944. In this capacity he went with Roosevelt to the Yalta Conference in February 1945. The decision was made to call the conference in San Francisco that set up the U.N. in June 1945, and Stettinius was appointed U.S. delegate.

After a short visit to Moscow he next headed the U.S. delegation at the conference of American republics on the problems of war and peace. He helped to draft the Act of Chapultepec which proposed a system of mutual defence for the western hemisphere. President Truman asked him to continue as Secretary of State and serve as chairman of the U.S. delegation to the United Nations. Truman later accepted his resignation as Secretary of State and appointed him permanent U.S. representative to the United Nations.

STILWELL, Joseph, b. 1883. American general who commanded Chinese and American troops in the China-Burma-India theatre (1942–4). After serving in Combat Intelligence during World War I he made China and the Chinese a special study, and had 13 years' service as a soldier in China in the inter-war years. His ability to come to terms with circumstances out of the ordinary and his undoubted military gifts impressed General Marshall, and in 1941 the U.S. War Department, fearing that China might be forced to a separate peace with Japan, ordered Stilwell to improve the fighting efficiency of the Chinese army and appointed him to command the U.S. Army forces in China, Burma, and India.

In 1942 he became Chief of Staff to Chiang Kai-shek. He fought unsuccessfully against the Japanese to preserve the Chinese supply line through Burma, the Burma Road. Forced to retreat to India, he built up his forces for the eventual counter-attack. In 1944, when the Japanese overran the U.S. air bases in eastern China, the Americans proposed that Stilwell be given command of all Chinese forces, but Chiang Kai-shek and the local advisers forced his recall in November 1944. In June 1945 he became commander of the U.S. 10th Army in the Pacific.

Known to all as 'Vinegar Joe', Stilwell, with his rather myopic look, often gave the impression of general distrust of the world and those in it whom he had to meet. He was very much a 'character' and a subject of interest and amusement to the Allied forces in S.E. Asia. Though Stilwell frequently expressed a particular distaste for the British, General Slim, commanding the 14th Army, found that he could be relied upon in co-operation and that when he said he would do a thing he did it. Close associates said he was two people in his behaviour—one with an audience and another without. It pleased him to be known as a 'tough guy', but he had genuine qualities of determination and single-mindedness and a military panache that were valuable. He has been accused of misuse of some of his best troops, such as 'Merrill's Marauders', but he had few first-class troops at his command and he had to operate in exceptionally difficult circumstances. In Slim's opinion he was not a great soldier, but he was a remarkable leader in the field.

STIMSON, Henry, b. 1867. American statesman, Secretary of War from June 1940 to the end of the conflict. When he took up office, at the age of 73, he immediately collected around him a team of civilian administrators—Patterson, McCloy, Lovett, and Bundy—who were to serve him faithfully throughout the war. Initially the main concern was to prepare the U.S.A. for a possible struggle. Stimson supported the Compulsory Service Act of September 1940, and was a firm advocate of Lend-Lease. He was concerned at the lack of naval help being given to Britain in the Atlantic and sought the repeal of the Neutrality Act, which would thus allow the arming of merchant shipping.

After Pearl Harbor he was convinced of the necessity and practicability of an early Allied invasion of N.W. Europe. He argued the point with Churchill on a visit to London in July 1943, and was relieved when the Quebec Conference in August 1943 confirmed the priority of 'Overlord'. His basic conviction about post-war policy was that the economy of a defeated country should not be destroyed—hence his opposition to the Morgenthau Plan.

Perhaps his most significant contribution to the war effort was the support he gave to scientific research. Early in 1942 he set up an organization to advise the Joint Chiefs of Staff on scientific issues. From 1941 he was concerned about the problems of nuclear fission. Between 1943 and 1945, when the atom bomb was in the making, he was directly responsible for the entire project. On 25 April the new President, Harry S. Truman, was informed that the bomb was ready and could be used. Stimson resigned in September 1945, soon after the Japanese surrender.

STIRLING, David, b. 1915. British Commando leader, the founder of the S.A.S. An officer of the Scots Guards, he transferred to a Commando unit in 1940, and went to the Middle East with 'Layforce' in 1941. In July he presented plans to Generals Ritchie and Auchinleck for a special force to make raids on aircraft behind enemy lines. He was authorized to raise a force consisting of 60 men and 6 officers. These he trained at Karbit in the Canal Zone. Their first offensive by parachute was a disaster, and Stirling decided to use the Long Range Desert Group to transport his men to their objectives. In December, operating from Jalo, S.A.S. units destroyed 90 aircraft in 2 weeks, and Stirling was given permission to recruit more men. Their successes continued, and in 1942 the S.A.S. was made a regiment and Stirling a lieutenant-colonel.

By this time the six-foot-six colonel was a legend in the Desert, and was known in the German press as 'the Phantom Major'. On 10 January 1943, while on a training exercise, he was captured by German soldiers specially brought in to track down the S.A.S. But by then S.A.S. units had destroyed 250 aircraft, hi-jacked lorries, mined roads, derailed trains, and made themselves such a general nuisance to the Axis forces that Rommel could say of Stirling's capture: 'Thus the British lost the very able and adaptable commander of the desert group which had caused us more damage than any other British unit of equal strength.'

After some time at an Italian prison camp at Gavi, from which he escaped four times, he was sent to the German security prison camp at Colditz Castle for the remainder of the war.

STOPFORD, Sir Montagu, b. 1892. British general, commander of the corps that raised the siege of Kohima, in Assam, and reopened the road to Imphal. The Imphal battle was the greatest jungle battle of the war.

Stopford went to Burma in November 1943 to take over command of 33rd Indian Corps. When, early in 1944, the Japanese crossed the Chindwin and advanced on Manipur, Lord Louis Mountbatten ordered Stopford's corps to move to Assam to counter the threat to the Bengal–Assam railway. This move, right across India, was effected with great speed. The drive of the Japanese forces' southern flank up from Tiddim was not successful; but farther north the Japanese straddled the Imphal–Kohima road, thus cutting all Imphal's land communications and seriously threatening the supply route to northern

Burma. The British and Indian garrison at Kohima, outnumbered by more than four to one, and under a deadly barrage from the heights above the town, held out until it was relieved by 33rd Corps, which advanced from Dimapur. Despite the monsoon 33rd Corps then pressed on, covering 52 miles in 7 days, and linked up with troops of 4th Corps who were fighting their way north from Imphal. Thus the siege of Imphal was raised, and 33rd Corps then pursued the Japanese into central Burma. It took part in the battles of Mandalay and Meikteila, and eventually reached Prome. In one of the fiercest and most exhausting operations of the war, Stopford pressed his troops hard; but he also drove himself hard and was greatly admired and trusted as a commander.

STREICHER, Julius, b. 1885. German journalist and politician, the chief propagandist of the campaign of hate against the Jews. Until 1943 he edited *Der Stürmer*, a journal which he had founded in 1923 and in whose columns no anti-Semitic diatribe was too absurd, scurrilous, or obscene for publication. *Der Stürmer* had a semi-official standing, and copies of each issue were displayed throughout the Reich in special show-cases in public places.

A man of gross appearance and extreme coarseness of speech and manner, Streicher was one of Hitler's earliest supporters and took part in the Beer Hall Putsch in 1923. He was the initiator of the Nazi rallies at Nuremberg, and promoted the Nuremberg Decrees against the Jews in 1935. Until 1940 he was Gauleiter of Franconia. After the war Streicher was tried at Nuremberg as a war criminal and was sentenced to death and executed.

STRYDONCK DE BURKEL, Victor van, b. 1876. Belgian general, C.-in-C. of the Free Belgian forces. He commanded the First Military Area from September 1939 until Belgium fell in May 1940. He then went to England and became C.-in-C. of the Belgian forces there. In September 1944 he returned to liberated Belgium at the head of the Belgian Military Mission to S.H.A.E.F., and later he became chairman of the Belgian ex-Servicemen's association.

A modest man without political ambitions, and widely respected, he was loyal to King Leopold and to the Belgian government-in-exile in London, and he never lost faith in the outcome of the war. He had been honoured after a charge at Burkel in 1918, and permitted to add 'de Burkel' to his name.

STÜLPNAGEL, Karl von, b. 1886. German general, military governor of France, a leading member of the July 1944 plot to assassinate Hitler. He had voiced opposition to the Nazis as early as 1938. In 1939 he was Quartermaster General, and became Deputy Chief of Staff. His arguments against Hitler's projected Western offensive went unheeded, and he helped to plan an army *coup d'état* for 5 November. The plot collapsed through the last-minute defection of Field Marshal von Brauchitsch.

In 1940 and again in 1941 Stülpnagel and his collaborators sought support at high army level. In 1941 he was on the Eastern front and commanded an army in the encirclement of Kiev. In 1942 he was transferred to occupied France. In May 1944 he planned, with Rommel and Speidel, to conclude an armistice without Hitler's consent; but Rundstedt, C.-in-C. West, refused to co-operate. In July Rundstedt was replaced by Kluge, who agreed to support a *coup d'état* if Hitler were assassinated.

By then Stauffenberg and Tresckow, in Berlin, were planning their last desperate attempt at assassination, which took place on 20 July; meanwhile preparations for the military coup in France had been completed under Stülpnagel. On receiving the 'Valkyrie' signal that Hitler was dead, he had all Nazi officials in Paris arrested, and called on Kluge to lead the revolt in the West. But Kluge had learned that Hitler was still alive, revoked Stülpnagel's instructions and suspended him. Summoned before Keitel, Stülpnagel tried to shoot himself while on the journey to Berlin but, being found still alive, was nursed back to health, put on trial, and hanged.

Said to have been a cultured and high-minded man, Stülpnagel was the only German commander in the West who was wholeheartedly committed to carrying out unhesitatingly the prearranged plans upon the death of Hitler. Nevertheless he had not carried out his duties as military governor of France without some degree of ruthlessness; one of his observations was: 'The better known the hostages to be shot, the greater will be the deterrent effect.'

SZABO, Violette, b. 1918. Resistance fighter. She was a gay, intelligent, half-French girl from Brixton, in London, who joined the A.T.S. soon after the war began, but was brought in by the S.O.E. when her knowledge of French became known. When she had finished her training as an agent in 1944 she was selected to join a Resistance network in France operating at Rouen and Le Havre. But the circuit was broken before she was sent to it, and many of its members were captured. In April Violette and another agent were parachuted into France. She went to Rouen to reconnoitre, and they both returned to England on 30 April to report.

On the night of 6 June 1944 a team of four people including Violette was dropped in the Limoges area to take charge of a *Maquis* group whose S.O.E. instructor had been posted elsewhere for D-Day. Two days later Violette and 'Anastasie' (the leader of the local *Maquis*) were ambushed by a unit of *Das Reich* Panzer Division, which was moving from Toulouse to reinforce the German army in Normandy. Violette hurt her ankle and was left, at her own request, in a wood in a cornfield. She was a crack shot, and held off a large force of Germans for two hours until she ran out of ammunition. Then she was finally captured and taken to Limoges prison, and from there to Paris. She refused to talk, and was sent with two other captured S.O.E. agents, Denise Bloch and Lilian Rolfe, to Ravensbrück on 8 August. Violette's cheerfulness sustained her companions through the next few months' ordeal. They were shot on 26 January 1945.

T

TEDDER, Sir Arthur, b. 1890. British air marshal, General Eisenhower's deputy in the invasion of N.W. Europe. In 1939 he was Director-General of Research and Development at the Air Ministry. Then he moved to the Middle East; first as Deputy, and then, in 1941, as A.O.C.-in-C. He found there a diminished air force and, while awaiting reinforcements by sea, established a mobile repair organization which salvaged damaged aircraft and returned them fit for battle. Meanwhile he reserved his limited resources for vital objectives, and declined to dissipate them in lesser enterprises. As the Luftwaffe built up its strength in Libya he and Air Vice Marshal Coningham together set out to win control of the air, pounding the enemy airfields and supplies, and forcing enemy planes into battle. Tedder believed this to be the principal role of the air force, giving it priority over the support of land or sea operations. Effective air mastery was achieved by the Allies in the Mediterranean in time for Montgomery's offensive at El Alamein, and Tedder's system of pattern bombing, to clear a path through tank defences (the 'Tedder carpet'), contributed to the brilliant advance through to Tunisia.

Following the Casablanca Conference in January 1943 Tedder was appointed Allied Air Commander in the Mediterranean. Responsible for Allied air operations in Tunisia, Sicily, and Italy, he worked closely with Eisenhower's staff, aiming at the complete integration of air, land, and sea operations. This harmonious partnership led Churchill to propose Tedder's appointment as Eisenhower's Deputy Supreme Commander of the Allied Expeditionary Force which was to stage the invasion of N.W. Europe, with responsibility for Allied air operations in western Europe. Prior to the Allied invasion he advocated the strategic bombing of French and Belgian railways—a controversial step which Eisenhower approved as essential to isolate the battlefield. On 9 May 1945, on Eisenhower's behalf, he signed the instrument of surrender.

A desk commander by choice and training, who refused to glamorize himself,

Tedder was a specialist in strategy. He refused to bid for popularity, and Eisenhower called him 'one of the few great military leaders of our time'.

TERAUCHI, Count Juichi, b. 1879. Japanese general and supreme commander of the Japanese Forces of the Southern Region. He had been War Minister in Koki Hirota's government in 1935. In early 1942 he was commanding the Japanese troops in the Indo-China-Malaya area and was instructed to provide labour for the building of a 250-mile railway line through Thailand to Burma. It was estimated that such a project would normally take 5 years, but Terauchi was ordered to complete it in 18 months. General Tojo, the Japanese Prime Minister, agreed that Allied P.O.W.s should be used, and nearly 50,000 were brought from camps all over S.E. Asia. Conditions were indescribable. Almost a third of the men died on the work. The building of the Siam railway became one of the horror stories of history.

From May 1944 Terauchi had his H.Q. in Manila in the Philippines until the Japanese were driven out by the Americans early in 1945. In early 1945, when General Slim's 14th Army was racing, against the monsoon, to Rangoon, Terauchi ordered General Kimuru to hold southern Burma at all costs and if possible Rangoon too. But this city fell to the 14th Army in May. On 14 August Japan submitted in unconditional surrender, but it was not until September that Mountbatten's forces reoccupied Singapore. On 12 September Mountbatten accepted the surrender of 690,000 Japanese remaining in S.E. Asia. One principal actor was missing from this ceremony—Terauchi had suffered a stroke. In Saigon a few months later Mountbatten accepted from Terauchi his ceremonial sword, forged in 1292; later Mountbatten presented the sword to King George VI.

THOMAS. *See* YEO-THOMAS, F. F.

TIMOSHENKO, Semyon, b. 1895. Russian marshal, a skilled and inventive commander who carried much of the burden of Russia's defence during 1941 and 1942 before the German advance was finally turned.

Following an exciting career in the Imperial army during World War I, and a rapid promotion in the Red army (helped by the friendship of Stalin), Timoshenko was a general by 1939. For his successful command in the Russo-Finnish campaign of 1940 he was given the position of Commissar of Defence, which he held until Germany's declaration of war on Russia, when he was given command of the central sector of the front. Taking advantage of the bitter winter, he fought a clever and stubborn delaying action, which although it failed at any point to achieve the offensive, prevented the Germans from getting to Moscow at that point of the campaign—a failure which they never retrieved.

In September 1941 he was transferred to the southern sector, where he failed to stop the German advance into the Crimea and on Stalingrad, notwithstanding his energetic attempts to seize the initiative. Before the Battle of Stalingrad Timoshenko (under fire for his failures to date) was removed to the quieter north-western front. From here he was finally shifted to a staff position at Stalin's H.Q., where he spent the rest of the war.

TITO (Josip Broz), b. 1892. Yugoslav Communist party chief, national hero, and leader of the Resistance group known as the Partisans, who played a major role in freeing Yugoslavia of the Axis occupation forces. Tito, who had become the Secretary-General of the Yugoslav Communist party in 1937, did not actively fight the Germans and their allies until they attacked the Soviet Union in the summer of 1941. At that point Comintern appeals prompted him to organize and lead an armed rising against the Germans. He took field command of the Partisan guerrillas in August 1941, after having worked for a time in Belgrade to rally and form his troops. His immediate efforts were amazingly successful, and he cleared the Germans out of much of Serbia by mid September. However, his energies were diverted from the enemy when he tried and failed to reach an accommodation with the leader of the other important Resistance group, the Četniks. Draža Mihajlović, the Yugoslav army officer who led the Četniks, was anti-Communist as

well as anti-Fascist. In the struggle between the two men to gain control of the Resistance movement open clashes occurred. This dissension allowed the Germans to move in again and, by December 1941, most of Serbia was once more under Axis control.

Tito led his weakened forces into the mountains of eastern Bosnia, where he formed the First Proletarian Brigade. After several further retreats Tito's forces recovered and fought their way northward, taking Bihać on the Croatian border in November 1942. Tito and the Partisans established the Anti-Fascist National Liberation Committee, basically a political organization, with the aim of unifying all religious and ethnic groups against the occupiers. In January 1943 the Germans launched another offensive. With the co-operation of Montenegrins, Četniks, and Italians, they got Tito into a trap. He escaped encirclement only by a dramatic flight across the Neretva River. In the following May Tito narrowly escaped capture again, this time in the Maglić mountains.

The Partisans enjoyed a temporary military respite with the surrender of Italian forces in September 1943. But immediately after, a German onslaught, Operation 'Thunderbolt', pushed them back into the Bosnian mountains. 'Thunderbolt' lasted until February 1944, during which time the Germans took Dalmatia and its offshore islands, except for Vis.

Meanwhile Tito had finally won British support. This came after a visit from Brigadier Fitzroy Maclean, who parachuted into Bosnia in the summer of 1943. The Partisans started to get the material aid that enabled them to keep fighting. By the time of the Teheran Conference at the end of November 1943 Tito had convened the Jajce Conference and had become Marshal of Yugoslavia. He was also self-appointed Prime Minister and Minister of Defence. After the Teheran Conference Anglo-American assistance flowed in for the Partisans, and by May 1944 Tito had the total support of the Allies. In the same month a German parachute attack on Partisan H.Q. at Drvar nearly killed Tito. He took refuge on the island of Vis.

In August 1944 Tito paid a secret visit to Moscow and met Stalin for the first time. Shortly after he went to Italy to confer with Churchill and General Wilson, the Allied C.-in-C. in the Mediterranean. Churchill persuaded Yugoslavia's exiled king, Peter, to recognize Tito. The British Prime Minister also oversaw the signing of an agreement for post-war co-operation by Tito and the royalist Prime Minister Ivan Šubašić. Tito reaffirmed this agreement at a later meeting with Churchill, but would not countenance the restoration of the king. Returning to his H.Q. on Vis, Tito stepped up the campaign against the Germans By the end of August 1944 the Partisans had the Germans in retreat. Tito continued to supervise the final moves of the Yugoslav liberation campaign from Vis. Two months later he led a victorious Partisan force into Belgrade, accompanied by Soviet troops under Marshal Tolbukhin. In March 1945 Tito set up a provisional government with himself as Prime Minister and Šubašić as Foreign Minister. His position was recognized by the U.K., the U.S.A., and the Soviet Union at the Yalta Conference of February 1945.

Tito's qualities of leadership and personal courage won the admiration even of his enemies. Himmler said about him: 'Though he is our enemy, I wish we had a dozen Titos in Germany, men who can lead and who have such determination and good nerves that if they were eternally encircled they would never give in . . .' Tito's quality as a leader can be measured not only by his victory over the Axis powers, but also his success in unifying Yugoslavia.

TIZARD, Sir Henry, b. 1885. British scientist who made important contributions to the development of defence against air attack.

From 1933 he had been chairman of the Aeronautical Research Committee and had played a pioneering part in the development of operational radar. He was also a member of other committees concerned with problems of air warfare. In the first months of the war he acted as scientific adviser to the Chief of Air Staff. However, in June 1940 he resigned from most of his wide responsibilities as a government adviser (retaining only his membership of the Aeronautical Research Committee) because he considered that his position had become ambiguous since the

formation of the Churchill administration: Sir Archibald Sinclair, the new air minister, was taking advice on scientific matters from Professor Lindemann (Lord Cherwell), Churchill's adviser. Tizard and Lindemann did not always see eye to eye.

Tizard, however, was able to play a part that in the event was of even greater importance in the prosecution of the war. He led a group of scientists and Service officers to the U.S.A. as an initial step in Anglo-American scientific co-operation for war purposes—in particular in the field of invention. Among the matters discussed (and the information disclosed to the Americans) was the extremely successful work of British scientists on radar.

After his return to the U.K. Tizard became adviser to the Minister of Aircraft Production (at first Lord Beaverbrook) and, from June 1941, represented the Ministry on the Air Council. In 1942 he was elected president of Magdalen College, Oxford (his old college), but he continued to give advice to Service chiefs on a variety of matters. In 1943 he spent 3 months in Australia at the invitation of the Australian government, advising on scientific aspects of the defence of that country and helping to co-ordinate military research in Australia and the U.K. In 1944, with the end of the war in sight, he agreed to act as chairman of a committee established by the chiefs of staff to study the implications, in defence terms, of the development of new kinds of weapons.

Tizard's importance as a scientific adviser to the government of the U.K. was overshadowed by that of Lord Cherwell, largely because Cherwell enjoyed Churchill's patronage. Nevertheless Tizard had tremendous influence and, consequently, great significance in any assessment of the war effort. Like Cherwell he helped at a commanding level to determine the implications of technological advances and consequently to shape policy.

TODT, Fritz, b. 1891. German engineer. One of the earliest members of the Nazi party, he was responsible for building the *Autobahnen* (motor highways) and the West Wall, known to the Allies as the *Siegfried Line*. He was allowed to dispose of an army of his own workers (the Todt

Organization) specially created to complete the Wall in the shortest possible time.

In 1939 work proceeded at an accelerated rate, the Todt Organization combining with construction firms, several army divisions, and virtually the entire Reich labour service. Hitler made a final inspection with Field Marshal Keitel just before war began, and later the Wall was extended eastwards from Basle to Lake Constance. He also built the *Felsennest* (Hitler's H.Q. near Aachen), which was a bunker installation blasted out of a wooded mountain top, and he was responsible for a second H.Q. in the Black Forest. He was made a major-general in recognition of his work. From 1940 to 1942 he organized the construction of a chain of submarine bases along the northern coast of France. In the Moscow offensive the Todt Organization undertook massive works on communications; miles of Russian railways were reconstructed and altered to the standard German gauge, and depots were established behind the Moscow front.

Todt became minister for armaments and munitions in 1940, and inspector-general of roads, water, and power in 1941. He was killed in 1942 when his plane crashed at take-off near Rastenburg, and was succeeded in most of his responsibilities by Albert Speer.

TOGURI D'AQUINO, Iva Ikuko. *See* 'TOKYO ROSE'.

TOJO, Hideki, b. 1884. Japanese general and politician, the leader of the militarists, and the man who, as Premier, led Japan into the war in 1941. In 1940 Tojo became War Minister in Prince Konoye's government and, expecting Britain's early defeat, pressed for a Tripartite Pact of mutual assistance with Germany and Italy; this was duly concluded in September.

He was leader of the army faction which favoured military expansion southwards rather than a premature war with Russia. Believing that Japan could achieve a quick victory in the south, he was impatient with those who wanted the 'China Incident' concluded before any further adventures were undertaken. In 1941 Tojo's group commissioned Unit 82 to ascertain whether a 'march on the Southern Road' was feasible. The unit found the enemy weak, suggested plans for a short, sharp war and directed large-scale amphibious manœuvres in southern China. To placate the militarists temporarily, Konoye agreed in July to the occupation of bases in southern Indo-China by agreement with Vichy France. The economic sanctions by the U.S.A. and the U.K. which followed led to increasing demands for war; but Konoye sought a settlement with the U.S.A. over the question of oil supplies. A fierce struggle ensued and, on 14 October, Konoye resigned. Correctly believing that Tojo had the army's confidence, the Emperor appointed him Premier. But he was an authoritarian (nicknamed 'Razor') and his government was in fact a military dictatorship. Negotiations were continued, but in a new, threatening atmosphere, and the American fleet at Pearl Harbor was attacked on 7 December. Under his direction Japanese forces throughout S.E. Asia and the Pacific carried all before them. Dedicated to the establishment of a 'New Order in Asia', Tojo set up puppet governments in the conquered territories. The period of unalloyed success, however, was short, and when events began to go badly for Japan Tojo was blamed for his optimism and inefficiency. After the fall of Saipan, in the Marianas (which was within bombing range of Japan), on 9 July 1944, he and his Cabinet resigned.

After the war Tojo was one of seven Japanese leaders condemned to be hanged. He had tried but failed to kill himself. He was convicted of bearing the 'major responsibility for Japan's criminal attacks on her neighbours' and of failing to enforce the laws of war with regard to prisoners and internees, whose 'barbarous treatment' was 'well known' to him.

'TOKYO ROSE' (Iva Ikuko Toguri D'Aquino), b. 1916. Propaganda broadcaster on Tokyo Radio. An American citizen of Japanese parentage, she broadcast messages designed to undermine the morale of the American and other Allied armed forces. Her seductive tones earned her the nickname of 'Tokyo Rose', coined by troops in the South Pacific. Her usual performance consisted of popular tunes interspersed with lines of sexy chatter and references to 'the girl back home drinking with some fellow who's rolling in easy money' calculated to demoralize her listeners. In fact she often caused them some amusement as, for example, when she referred to the Marines on Guadalcanal as 'summer insects which have dropped into the fire by themselves'. After the completion on schedule of the first phase of the Japanese plan of conquest 'Tokyo Rose, your friendliest enemy' broadcast the news to the troops in her celebrated silken voice: 'Why don't you go home? It's all over in Burma. . . . Wouldn't a nice thick steak taste good right now?' After the war she was indicted for treason by a grand jury at San Francisco. The prosecution did not ask for the death penalty, and she was sentenced to 10 years' imprisonment and a fine of $10,000.

TOVEY, Sir John, b. 1885. British admiral who directed many of the measures taken to protect Allied convoys of merchant ships carrying vital war supplies. From 1940 to 1943 he was C.-in-C. Home Fleet, based on Scapa Flow, which had been rendered safe from submarine attack. In May 1941 there took place the operation for which his name will be chiefly remembered—the chase and sinking by the Royal Navy of the new German battleship *Bismarck*, the most heavily armoured ship afloat; she was on a sortie in the Atlantic and threatening no fewer than 11 British convoys. 'You are the pride of the navy,' Hitler had said when visiting her earlier that month, and Churchill called her eventual destruction 'a naval episode of the highest consequence'.

Thereafter Tovey's chief concern was to keep watch on the northern passages, helping to get the convoys through to Murmansk. For better effect he moved his main concentration to Iceland. From there he was engaged in operations against the battleship *Tirpitz*, which was operating from Norway. Tovey was critical of the Admiralty's instruction that his prime object must be to protect the convoys, not to destroy the enemy. In his view, to sink the *Tirpitz* was 'of incomparably greater importance to the conduct of the war than the safety of any convoy'. In March 1943 it was partly on Tovey's advice that the risky Arctic convoys were temporarily

suspended. Shortly afterwards he struck his flag, and in July he became C.-in-C. Nore. In 1945 he was responsible for the safety of the convoys to Antwerp, which were assembled in the Thames and sailed from there.

Tovey's outspoken views on naval strategy were not always appreciated in London, but his conspicuous courage and fair-mindedness inspired confidence throughout the forces which he commanded.

TOWNSEND, Peter, b. 1914. British fighter pilot who destroyed at least 11 enemy aircraft, including the first German bomber to be shot down on English soil. He received three awards (D.S.O., D.F.C. and Bar), and each citation mentioned his outstanding leadership and determination.

In the early part of the war he was with 43 Squadron, first patrolling the northeast coast, and then affording fighter protection to Scapa Flow. In May 1940 he was given command of 85 Squadron. In July, whilst patrolling the North Sea, he was shot down; he was picked up by a mine-sweeper and had returned to flying with his squadron by the afternoon. During the Battle of Britain his squadron was in the front line, based on Croydon. Shot down over Kent with a severe foot injury, he was nevertheless back flying within three weeks. By this time his squadron had suffered heavy casualties and had been withdrawn to the Midlands. In 1941, now a wing-commander, he relinquished this command. In February 1944 he was appointed Air Equerry to King George VI.

TRESCKOW, Henning von, b. 1901. German general, one of the leaders of the July 1944 plot to overthrow Hitler. While Chief of Staff to Field Marshal von Bock and to his successor von Kluge, Tresckow became the leader of an anti-Hitler group amongst the army officers fighting on the Eastern front.

The original aim was a military *coup d'état* in which Hitler would be arrested and brought to trial. But having failed to achieve active support at high army level the conspirators decided late in 1942 that assassination was the only solution. Tresckow, anxious to end the war before the collapse of the Eastern front, grew impatient with leaders of the plot in Berlin who hoped to take Hitler alive, and began to plan assassination independently. On 13 March 1943, assisted by his A.D.C., Fabian von Schlabrendorff, Tresckow made his own attempt by enticing Hitler to Smolensk and smuggling a time-bomb into the returning aircraft. But it failed to go off. Altogether some half-dozen attempts were made during 1943, with Tresckow playing a leading part in formulating the plans for the *coup* which would follow Hitler's death.

From October 1943 Claus von Stauffenberg became the driving force of the conspiracy, and the two men became close friends. The Allied invasion of Normandy injected a new consideration into the situation. Tresckow, by this time Chief of Staff of the 2nd Army on the crumbling Russian front, was asked for advice and gave the reply: 'The attempt must succeed *coûte que coûte*. If it fails, we must act in Berlin. It is now no longer a question of practical results, but of showing to the world and to history that the Resistance movement risked the last throw.'

After Stauffenberg's disastrous attempt on 20 July 1944 Tresckow committed suicide. A Prussian conservative, he preserved an individual outlook and disliked exaggerated emphasis on military qualities and customs. After World War I, and before rejoining the army in 1924, he had had considerable success as a stockbroker. By his associates he was considered a man of exceptional integrity and kindness.

TRUMAN, Harry S., b. 1884. American statesman, elected Vice-President in 1944, who became President of the U.S. after the death of Roosevelt in April 1945. The state of Missouri had re-elected Truman to the Senate in 1940. The work that brought him into the limelight in the early years of the war was his chairmanship of the Senate Special Committee to investigate the National Defense Program.

Truman was responsible for the formation of the committee, which exposed a number of irregularities in the allocation of defence contracts. This, together with its criticisms of parts of the proposed programme, saved the nation billions of dollars. He had advocated the setting up of such a committee in March 1941 because

he had been alarmed by allegations of extravagance and partiality in the construction of Fort Leonard Wood in his own state, Missouri. The White House and the War Department were at first opposed to the idea of the Senate committee. Such a body was obviously vulnerable to manipulation by unscrupulous politicians with axes to grind. But General Marshall, the Chief of Staff, came out strongly in its favour, and the committee was eventually given the go-ahead. Truman, as chairman, soon showed his sense of responsibility and tact. His sympathetic attitude created an atmosphere in which the committee found itself helping to shield the War Department from public criticism; abuses and deficiencies were corrected unobtrusively before they could cause any scandal. The committee, indeed, soon became a valuable asset. Truman had many confidential meetings with Roosevelt, Marshall, and Henry Stimson, the Secretary of War. Several of these contacts developed into close friendships, and as such were to be of incalculable value to him later when he was suddenly thrust into the presidency. Truman's record stood him in good stead for the vice-presidency in 1944, and he was duly elected under Roosevelt in November of that year. On 12 April 1945 Roosevelt died, and Truman immediately became President.

Truman had not been a member of Roosevelt's inner circle and at first he tended to rely for help and advice on Roosevelt appointees. Generally speaking, Truman firmly upheld Roosevelt's policies, but as his confidence increased he steadily substituted his own departmental advisers for the Roosevelt Cabinet members. Only three of the original Cabinet remained at the end of 1945. Truman ordered the continuation of preparations for the San Francisco Conference which was to be convened in April in order to establish the United Nations. Not long afterwards he came up against Stalin's arbitrary behaviour over Poland, in blatant disregard of the Yalta Agreement. Polish underground leaders, who had been invited to Moscow for talks with a pledge of safe conduct, were arrested in Poland by the Russians. Truman, still clinging to the Roosevelt illusion of Russo-American co-operation, sent Harry Hopkins on a special mission to Moscow in the hope that the Polish issue could be resolved. This was the first occasion on which Truman had experienced Stalin's obstinacy and ruthlessness, and the mission proved fruitless. As the 'hot war' approached its end, it became increasingly clear that the 'cold war' was just beginning. Truman adopted the policy of containment of Russia. In July 1945 he went to the Potsdam Conference in Berlin, and there met Stalin and Churchill. The war leaders discussed the campaign against Japan and turned their attention to a number of post-war problems. It was at the conference that the Russian leader presented the Allies with a *fait accompli* regarding Poland's western frontier. On his way home from Potsdam Truman announced the dropping of the first atomic bomb on Japan. He had authorized the bombing of Hiroshima on 6 August 1945, because he was convinced that it would end the war and so ultimately save possibly millions of lives. On 14 August the war against Japan was over.

This 'everyday American' who described himself as 'the hired man of 150,000,000 people' went on to lead his nation for seven years, at a time when old power blocs were crumbling and important new alignments began to emerge. His forthright manner and dogged adherence to aspects of policies which he considered vital created some enemies; but he won the esteem and approbation of millions for his courage and unswerving dedication in the face of the most intractable challenges.

TUCK, Robert Stanford-, b. 1916. One of the greatest British fighter pilots of the war. He first saw action in May 1940 as a flight commander with 92 Fighter Squadron over Dunkirk. On that occasion he was heard to whoop with glee over the radio as he led his section into the middle of a large formation of Me. 109s. The squadron destroyed 11 of the enemy for the loss of 1 Spitfire, which crash-landed on the beach, and Tuck was credited with one 'kill'. That same afternoon, while on a second patrol over the same area, he shot down 2 Messerschmitt 110s. He followed up with a couple of Dornier 17s the next day and another the following morning, making a total of 6 in 3 days. After this

feat he wrote to his parents that he found being a fighter pilot 'the most fascinating occupation in the world'. In September 1940 he led 265 Squadron to the defence of London, and by the end of 1941, when the Battle of Britain had been won and Fighter Command was able to go over to the offensive, he was a wing-commander holding the D.S.O., the D.F.C. and two bars, and officially credited with 29 'kills'. The next year Tuck was out on a low-level patrol over France when a German shell blew most of the engine out of his Spitfire, and he landed in the middle of the anti-aircraft battery which had shot him down. On his way down, however, he had returned fire and disposed of one gun crew. One of his shells went right up the barrel of the gun, splitting it open, and the Germans were so amused by his marksmanship that they did not immediately avenge their dead comrades. A gunner clapped him on the back, shouting in appreciation: 'Good shot, Englander.' Tuck later escaped from a German prison camp into Russia, and turned up in Italy in the spring of 1945. His war-time career thus ended as dramatically as it began and, indeed, along with Bader, Tuck came to symbolize the heroism of the fighter pilot of World War II.

TWINING, Nathan, F., b. 1897. American air general who commanded the U.S. 13th Air Force in the South Pacific, one of the most powerful air formations in the war. Twining was Chief of Staff to the commander in the South Pacific from 1942 to 1943, in which year he was assigned to the 13th Air Force. In this position he was responsible for the air offensive against the Japanese on Guadalcanal and elsewhere. His success was outstanding, and his experience was then availed of in the European theatre when he was sent to Italy in 1944 to command the U.S. 15th Air Force, based there, in the strategic bombing of Germany and eastern Europe. He then returned to the Pacific to direct a force of B-29s in the assault on Japan. Twining had a reputation as a tough and uncompromising leader, had a formidable grasp of the technicalities of strategic bombing, and employed his forces with imagination and the ability to exploit promising situations.

U

UDET, Ernst, b. 1896. German air force general. As Director-General of Equipment for the Luftwaffe, he took over much of the power of the Inspector-General, Milch. He had been one of Germany's leading aces in World War I—credited with shooting down 62 enemy planes—and later had achieved a reputation as a stunt flier. Although he had a talent for design, he gave prime importance to speed and manœuvrability, and was inexpert in long-range bombing and transport problems. The Luftwaffe largely owed to him its concentration on single-engined fighters. In 1937 he had personally flown the Messerschmitt 109, destined to play so large a part in the Battle of Britain. His own bias, together with the German concept of the Luftwaffe as a mainly tactical force, committed Germany to the dive-bomber and to light and medium bombers during the early part of the war. The development of the Junkers 87 had derived from his purchase of two dive-bombers while on a visit to the U.S.A.

When Hess sought his help to get the chance to fly (Hitler had forbidden Nazi leaders to pilot their own planes in war time) Udet dared not agree without Hitler's written permission. Hess went instead to Messerschmitt.

Udet was cosmopolitan in outlook, something of a dilettante, a wit and a 'good fellow' disinclined to machinations. After a serious quarrel with Goering, an old friend of his from their days in the Richthofen squadron in World War I, he committed suicide in November 1941. His death was officially described as an accident while testing a new air weapon.

UMBERTO, Prince, b. 1904. Crown Prince of Italy, and after the capture of Rome by the Allies in 1944, Regent for his father, King Victor Emmanuel III. Umberto commanded the Italian armies that invaded France in 1940, but would have achieved little without the aid of German armour. In Italy he was generally regarded as being implicitly loyal to the Fascist régime, and was rumoured as a possible successor to Mussolini. Germany—always conscious of friendly elements in Italy and anxious to ensure that pro-German sentiments were fostered—was encouraged by Mussolini to establish warm relations with Umberto. But as time went on the Nazis felt less certain of the Crown Prince's real attitude, and found his response ambivalent and enigmatic. However, in February 1943 the German Foreign Minister, Ribbentrop, visited Victor Emmanuel for the express purpose of conferring an honour upon Umberto. In July 1943 Mussolini was deposed and in September the Italian forces surrendered. The royal family moved to southern Italy where the King carried on the government with the support of the Allies and with Marshal Badoglio as Premier.

The day after Rome was liberated, on 4 June 1944, the King transferred his powers to Umberto as Regent and Lieutenant-General of the Realm, although he did not abdicate until 1946. Churchill met Umberto in August 1944 (by which time he was commanding the Italian forces on the Allied front) and was impressed by 'his powerful and engaging personality, his grasp of the whole situation, military and political'. Churchill hoped that Umberto would play his part in building up a constitutional monarchy in a free and united Italy. This never came about.

URQUHART, Robert, b. 1901. British general who commanded the 1st Airborne Division in the heroic action at Arnhem, in the Netherlands, in 1944. Urquhart had been in North Africa as a general staff officer with the 51st Highland Division from 1942 to 1943, and he commanded 231 Malta Brigade in Sicily and Italy.

The action at Arnhem was the most critical part of a daring operation which aimed to seize 9 bridges in the Netherlands by airborne landings, thus enabling the Allies to drive straight through to the Zuider Zee and the Ruhr. Had the whole project succeeded the Netherlands, and perhaps all Western Europe, could have been spared another winter at war. Urquhart's assignment, the capture of the bridge at Arnhem, involved even more dangers than were known at the time. The first of his men landed successfully north of the Rhine and a small force quickly reached the north end of the bridge. Another group landed next day, but unforeseen opposition barred their way to the bridge, and bad weather prevented the arrival of reinforcements, food, and ammunition. For a week Urquhart and his men endured violent assaults in their encircled positions, and every effort of ground and airborne forces to link up with them proved vain. Finally, General Montgomery ordered the survivors to withdraw; only about 2,400 of the original 10,000 men were brought back safely across the Rhine.

V

VIAN, Sir Philip, b. 1894. British naval officer who achieved renown in February 1940 when, in H.M.S. *Cossack* and commanding a destroyer flotilla, he boarded the German prison ship *Altmark* in a Norwegian fiord and liberated 299 British prisoners. At this time he was a captain. In May of the same year he led the evacuation of Namsos aboard H.M.S. *Alfridi* which was sunk, fighting to the end. His quality was shown again in May 1941 when he commanded the 4th Flotilla in operations against the *Bismarck*, and his initiative significantly helped in delivering the enemy to the destroying force.

Two months later (by this time an admiral) Vian successfully raided Spitzbergen. He commanded a squadron in the first Battle of Sirte in December 1941, and tribute was paid to his 'determined and spirited leadership' while covering convoys headed for Malta. His flagship H.M.S. *Naiad* was sunk off North Africa in March 1942. In the second Battle of Sirte he again showed 'decisive leadership', handling his force with such skill and determination that the far stronger enemy was effectively repelled.

In the invasion of Sicily in July 1943 he was in command of an assault force from the H.Q. ship H.M.S. *Hilary*. At Salerno he commanded a squadron of aircraft-carriers and then a cruiser force, landing troops brought from Tripoli. In June 1944 he was naval commander of the Eastern (British) Task Force for 'Neptune' (code-name for the cross-Channel part of the 'Second Front' invasion of the European mainland); and on D-Day he watched the operations from the cruiser H.M.S. *Scylla*, and controlled the night surface patrols.

In late 1944 Vian was given command of the Eastern fleet's aircraft-carrier squadron, based on Trincomalee, Ceylon, and directed attacks on oil refineries in Sumatra. Shortly afterwards he joined the British Pacific fleet in Australia, newly created to operate with the U.S. forces in the final struggle against Japan, and took part in the assault on Okinawa.

Although he had no great administrative talent, Vian was an ideal war-time leader at sea. He was perhaps the most dashing British naval leader of the war.

VICTOR EMMANUEL III, b. 1869. King of Italy throughout the course of the war, he disapproved of Italy's participation in the war on Germany's side, and threw in his lot with the Allies after Mussolini's deposition. However, his long association with the Fascist régime made his continuance on the throne unacceptable to the new Italian government.

Having allowed himself to become the figure-head and supporter of the Fascist régime, Victor Emmanuel had reluctantly accepted the Rome-Berlin Axis. But he had himself led Italy into World War I on the Allies' side, and he now strongly opposed her entry into war in support of Germany. He sent the Duke of Aosta and the then Crown Prince Umberto to try to dissuade Mussolini. But the reply was a threat to depose the royal house 'unless they stopped interfering in matters which were Mussolini's concern alone'. The threat closed the subject: Mussolini declared war on 10 June 1940, and the King withdrew from politics for the time being.

By 1943 the Allies were in Tripoli, supplies were short, and there were murmurs against the Duce. Gradually the King himself became involved. After the Allied landings in Sicily in July the Fascist Grand Council forced Mussolini's resignation, and called on the King to give the country a lead. Victor Emmanuel formally authorized Mussolini's arrest, having made arrangements to ensure his protection. Then he took command of the armed forces and appointed Marshal Badoglio as Premier. He escaped from German-controlled Rome in September, just before the armistice with the Allies, and carried on the royal government from southern Italy with Allied support. He stood by Badoglio, promised help for the Allies, and urged the declaration of war by Italy on Germany. But the survival of the monarchy, which had opened the door to Mussolini in 1922, caused friction in the government. In the end the King promised to cede his powers to his son Umberto as soon as Rome was liberated. On 5 June 1944 he signed the operative decree declaring Umberto Regent and effectively ending his public life, although he did not abdicate until 9 May 1946.

Victor Emmanuel was a very small man; he was a noted coin collector and he spoke good English. He was shrewd and determined, but intrigue was alien to his nature. Mussolini despised and made use of him, but counted on his support to the end. Bidding Mussolini farewell before his arrest the king said: 'At this moment you are the most hated man in the country. I am your only remaining friend.' Victor Emmanuel showed physical courage, when, as a youth tried to assassinate him in 1941, he calmly turned to his companion in the carriage and said: 'That boy is a poor shot, isn't he?'

VLASOV, Andrei, b. 1900. Russian general, a commander of some talent, who, after being taken prisoner, fought with the Germans against his former comrades. He belonged to a Great Russian peasant family and rose, through party membership, and after service as military adviser to Chiang Kai-shek between 1938 and 1939, to become one of the most energetic of the Red army commanders. He distinguished himself in the defence of Kiev and Moscow, but in 1942 was taken prisoner by the Germans.

Willing to be used against his former associates, he was at first employed in making propaganda speeches. Then, in November 1944, Himmler authorized him to form an anti-Stalinist 'Committee for the Liberation of the Peoples of Russia', recruited from Soviet P.O.W.s and civilian deportees in Germany. He was given command of a special force to fight on the already collapsing Eastern front. In fact Vlasov's troops did little but cause some anxiety to the German General Heinrich, who feared they might desert.

Vlasov surrendered to the Americans in May 1945. He was handed over to the Russian authorities and was executed.

VOROSHILOV, Kliment, b. 1881. Russian marshal who commanded the northern armies during the German advance on Leningrad. In 1939 he was People's Commissar of Defence, and in this capacity he received the Anglo-French military mission which arrived in Moscow on 11 August. The ensuing negotiations

were markedly unenthusiastic on the Russian side, and Voroshilov insisted that Poland could not be defended against Nazi aggression unless she allowed Soviet troops to enter her territory. France and Britain were not prepared to remonstrate with Poland or to negotiate seriously with Russia on this point. Then Ribbentrop arrived in Moscow, and the Soviet-German Non-Aggression Pact (which included an agreement on the partition of Poland) was signed on 24 August 1939.

On 8 May 1940, after Russian troops had fought in Poland and Finland, the Red army was reorganized and Voroshilov ceased to be Commissar of Defence. He became Deputy Premier and Chairman of the Defence Committee. Germany attacked Russia on 22 June 1941. On 3 July Stalin appointed a State Defence Committee consisting of himself, Voroshilov, Molotov, Malenkov, and Beria. This committee was responsible not only for the military conduct of the war but also for the rapid mobilization of the country's resources. The front was divided into three major sectors each under a separate command. Voroshilov became commander of the northern sector, which included the Baltic and northern fleets. But although he had made his name as a fighter in the civil war he was unable to stem the swift German advance on Leningrad: the city was virtually surrounded by the end of August and subjected to heavy bombardment. Voroshilov is said to have panicked and, believing all was lost, gone to the front determined to die by a German bullet. Stalin sent Marshal Zhukov to take over the defence of the city on 11 September, and Voroshilov was set to training new armies. In December 1941 he was appointed commander of Soviet forces, Far East. But his career as an active military leader was over.

When Churchill visited Moscow in August 1942 Voroshilov acted as military spokesman in talks with Generals Brooke and Wavell. The British put forward a plan to establish an Anglo-American air force in Transcaucasia to assist the Russians. But the offer was finally refused by the Russians in May 1943. Voroshilov accompanied Stalin and Molotov to the 'Big Three' meeting at Teheran in November. When Churchill presented Stalin with a sword specially commissioned by King George VI to commemorate the defence of Stalingrad, Stalin accepted it ceremoniously and handed it to Voroshilov, who promptly dropped it. Late in the war he signed the armistice with Hungary on behalf of the Allies.

Voroshilov was a popular figure in Russia. But his most marked talents were those of a diplomat rather than of a military commander.

VYSHINSKY, Andrei, b. 1883. Russian lawyer, politician, and diplomat, Molotov's deputy Foreign Minister from 1940. He antagonized Molotov by gaining Stalin's confidence and by reporting to him directly, over Molotov's head.

A Menshevik in his early career, Vyshinsky had moved left when he saw that the Bolshevik régime had come to stay. He tried to compensate for his past by toadying to Stalin, and by willingly undertaking risky operations which called for particular shamelessness. In June 1940, when the Soviet government was spreading its tentacles into eastern Europe, it was Vyshinsky who went to Latvia, after the President's deportation to Russia, to nominate a provisional government to

manage new elections. In August 1944 it was Vyshinsky who, on behalf of his government, denied the use of Russian airfields to British and American planes supporting the Warsaw Rising. In February 1945 it was Vyshinsky who bullied King Michael of Romania into dissolving Radescu's all-party government and setting up the Groza administration.

From 1943 to 1945 Vyshinsky was Soviet representative on the Allied Mediterranean Commission. He was present at the Yalta Conference in February 1945. A prolific writer and speaker on Soviet law, he was the leading exponent of Stalinism in legal theory and practice, and postulated that confession by the accused was adequate proof of guilt. He was reported to have had a violent temperament, but a Polish representative in Moscow said of him: 'In a way, Vyshinsky was the perfect diplomat. He was capable of telling an obvious untruth to your face; you knew that it was a lie, and he knew that you knew it was a lie; but he stubbornly adhered to it. No other diplomat was able to do this with such nonchalance.' In the 1930s Vyshinsky had become notorious outside Russia as the public prosecutor in the treason trials.

W

WAINWRIGHT, Jonathan, b. 1883.
American general who gained fame for
an epic fight in the face of overwhelming
odds. After General MacArthur was
ordered to leave the Philippines to make his
base in Australia in March 1942, Wainwright remained to conduct the vain fight
of the American and Filipino forces on the
Bataan Peninsula and Corregidor. The
position was hopeless from the start, but
Wainwright continued the struggle for
longer than seemed possible. He was
forced to surrender in May 1942, was
held prisoner for 3 years by the Japanese,
and was subjected to many outrages.

He was released from a prison camp in
Manchuria in 1945 and was present at the
surrender of the Japanese delegates on
board the USS *Missouri* in Tokyo Bay.
On his return to the U.S.A. he was
promoted and received the Congressional
Medal of Honor. He was then given
command of the 4th Army.

Wainwright was a cavalry officer and
served in the Philippines in 1909–10.
During World War I he served on the
staff of the 82nd Division in France. He
described his experiences as a P.O.W.
vividly in his autobiography *General
Wainwright's Story*.

WAKE, Nancy, b. 1916. Resistance fighter.
She was an Australian journalist and in
November 1939 had married Henri Fiocca,
a French businessman. She worked as an
ambulance driver until France fell, and
then went to Marseilles. Subsequently,
with the encouragement of her husband,
she became involved in Resistance escape
organizations under the alias of 'Lucienne
Carlier'. She came under suspicion and
left for Spain. In Toulouse she was
arrested and beaten by the Vichy police,
but was later released and in June 1943
she arrived in England.

She then joined the S.O.E. to be trained
for work as a British agent in occupied
territory. She was parachuted into the
Auvergne in February 1944 and after some
initial difficulties made contact with the
Maquis, assuming the role of 'Madame
Andrée'. Her access to money, arms, and
wireless communication gave her a commanding place in local Resistance operations. The exploits of the *Maquis* with
which she was connected included the
sabotage of prearranged targets on D-Day,
engagement in a battle with 22,000 S.S.
troops on 20 June, in which the *Maquis*
inflicted heavy casualties, and the destruction of the German H.Q. at Montluçon.
The Allied landings in the south of France
took place on 14 August 1944 and Nancy
Wake entered Vichy with the *Maquis* on
30 August. There she was informed of her
husband's death in 1943 at the hands of
the Gestapo.

She was a brave and spirited woman
with a lively sense of humour, and was
awarded medals for gallantry by Great
Britain, France, and the United States.

WALKER, Frederic, b. 1896. British naval
officer, described by Churchill as 'our
most outstanding U-Boat killer'. When
war broke out Walker was the commander
in charge of the experimental department
at H.M.S. *Osprey*, the anti-submarine
base at Portland. At the beginning of 1940
he joined the staff of Admiral Ramsay at
Dover, with overall responsibility for
anti-submarine defences. In October 1941
he joined the sloop H.M.S. *Stork* as
senior officer, 36th Group. This was the
beginning of his active anti-U-Boat career.
Between December 1941 and June 1942
Walker and his group destroyed 7 U-Boats.
He was promoted captain and, after a
brief spell commanding the escort base
at Liverpool, returned to sea in H.M.S.
Starling, as senior officer of the famous 2nd
Escort Group. Between April and August
1943 he made 6 trips, many in the Bay of
Biscay, and played an important part in
the engagements which were to put the
German U-Boats on the defensive. Later in
the year he was on patrol in the Atlantic as
part of the counter-measures to Doenitz's
new U-Boat offensive there. Other
operations that followed in quick succession included the escort of an American
ship to Russia and operations in the
English Channel in readiness for D-Day.
Walker died on 9 July 1944, and was
buried at sea.

He was an obstinate, blunt man who
had had some difficulties with his superiors
in peace time. In war he came into his
own, and his decisiveness and inventive-

ness in action earned him respect and
affection.

WALLIS, Barnes, b. 1887. British aeronautical engineer, designer of bombs used
in aerial warfare, and, in particular, inventor
of the 'bouncing bomb'. Immediately
after Dunkirk in June 1940 Wallis, realizing that aerial bombing would be the only
means of attack available to Britain for a
considerable time, devoted himself to the
perfection of a giant weapon. He devised
the 'Grand Slam' and the 'Tall Boy',
but it took three years for the Air Ministry
to see the possibilities of these monster
bombs. In March 1945 Bomber Command
dropped on Bielefeld viaduct Wallis's
first 'Grand Slam', weighing 10 tons.

On 16 May 1943 Wing Commander
Guy Gibson led the R.A.F. attack which
destroyed the Möhne and Eder dams
supplying the Ruhr industries. Wallis had
invented a 'bouncing bomb' for this
operation after long research. The bomb,
delivered from a height of only 60 feet,
'bounced' on water to its target at the
base of the dam. It was one of the most
ingenious inventions of the war, and was
startlingly successful.

Wallis had been a designer for Vickers
before World War I, and after a time in
the Royal Naval Air Service returned to
Vickers as chief designer of the airship
department. In the 1920s he was responsible for the design and construction of
the airship R.100.

WATSON-WATT, Robert, b. 1892. British
engineer and inventor, a pioneer in the
development of radar. In 1935 he had
suggested that an aircraft might be
detected by the echo set up when it
passed through radio waves, and this
was demonstrated by experiments
sponsored by the Air Ministry in 1935.
By early 1936 the apparatus was giving
the height and distance of approaching
planes, and Watson-Watt evolved a
method of determining also the bearing,
so that before long aircraft 75 miles
away were being accurately monitored.

By an early stage in the war the east
coast of Great Britain was provided with
a radio screen consisting of a chain of
stations from the Orkneys to the Isle of
Wight. New devices, with which Watson-

Watt was closely associated, were developed by military, university, and industrial teams. These included a system for
improving the accuracy of anti-aircraft
gun range finding; an air interception
system to enable fighters to locate enemy
aircraft at night with the help of ground
control; air- and sea-borne radar to
detect U-Boats; systems for assisting
bombers to find targets; identification
devices for shipping and aircraft; and other
measures to counter German technological
developments.

He was closely concerned with the
research stations first at Orfordness, then
at Bawdsey, and finally at Malvern. In
late 1939 and early 1940 he made several
visits to France to help with radar development, and he advised the U.S.A. after
Pearl Harbor on radar defence.

Watson-Watt was a blunt and outspoken
man, and a worker of tremendous energy.
Tedder included him among the 'three
saviours of Britain', and there is little
doubt that the Battle of Britain was won
nearly as much on the screens of the radar
stations as in the air.

WAVELL, Sir Archibald (Viscount
Wavell), b. 1883. British general (field
marshal 1943); he was one of the most
respected commanders of the war, but
more than once had to direct affairs in
situations where success was virtually
impossible to attain. Wavell became
C.-in-C. Middle East in July 1939. His
main task, until Italy entered the war in
July 1940, was to complete the arrangements for the defence of the Middle East
and North Africa, particularly those
relating to supply. His forces were considerably smaller than those of the Italians,
even including reinforcements from India
and the Dominions. On 13 September 1940
the Italian 10th Army advanced into Egypt
and were 60 miles inside the border by 18
September. On 9 December Wavell's
Western Desert Force (consisting of 7th
Armoured Division and 4th Indian
Division) began to drive them back. Sidi
Barrani was taken on 11 December, by
4 January the Italians had been driven out
of Egypt, and on 22 January they surrendered Tobruk. On 14 December 4th
Indian Division had been ordered to
East Africa and had been replaced by 6th

Australian Division. The 7th Armoured Division now moved rapidly to Bedafomm and 6th Australian Division to Benghazi, which it captured on 6 February. By now the British were effectively in control of Cyrenaica, and the Italian 10th Army had been destroyed: some 130,000 prisoners had been taken. At this point Wavell was instructed to send some of his troops to Greece: the Greek government, whose forces had held their own against the Italians, had asked for British help in the face of a German threat of invasion. The first units of the British force, under the command of General Maitland Wilson, left North Africa for Greece on 5 April, the day before the Germans invaded Greece. The Germans swiftly overran the country, and the British troops were withdrawn. The Greek debacle was followed by a similar disaster in Crete. Meanwhile the German Afrika Korps, under General Rommel, had established itself in Tripoli and begun to fight its way eastwards. After a series of brilliant actions the Axis forces were by 11 April on the Egyptian border. Wavell, despite a crippling lack of resources, had to fight on three fronts: Iraq, Syria, and the Western Desert. On 2 July Churchill made him C.-in-C. India, replacing him by General Auchinleck, the then holder of the Indian appointment.

When Japan entered the war in December 1941 Wavell was nominated Supreme Commander, S.W. Pacific, during the swift Japanese advance and the resultant loss of Singapore and Burma. The german front was judged the more important, and Wavell had to make do with little support on the Burmese front.

In June 1943 Wavell became Viceroy of India in succession to the Marquess of Linlithgow. The first concern of his incumbency was the swift relief of the Bengal famine. He was deeply involved in the difficult political situation of the time.

Despite his apparent failures in the face of great odds, Wavell is generally agreed to have been a brilliant general. General Rommel carried a translation of Wavell's book *Generals and Generalship* with him throughout his Western Desert campaign. A sportsman and anthologist (*Other Men's Flowers*), he was a man of many talents and, in spite of his taciturnity,

much loved by those who served under him.

WEDEMEYER, Albert, b. 1897. American general who succeeded General Stilwell as commander of U.S. troops in the China-Burma-India theatre. From 1941 to 1945 Wedemeyer served in the War Plans Division of the General Staff. In August 1943 the Allies created a new command, S.E.A.C., for operations based on India and Ceylon against Japan. This was a completely integrated H.Q., inter-Service and inter-Allied. Lord Louis Mountbatten was made supreme commander; for his Deputy Chief of Staff he chose the experienced Wedemeyer.

The original plans for seaborne attack on the territories occupied by Japan were quickly changed—by strategic circumstances and the needs of the European theatre—to a slogging land and air battle; in the early stages of planning the various offensives Wedemeyer represented the supreme commander at decision-making conferences in the U.S.A. and he strongly contested alternative plans advanced by General Stilwell, the commander of American forces in China. At the end of 1944 he took over from Stilwell, who had become *persona non grata* with Chiang Kai-shek.

A handsome and impressive figure, with much experience of the world, Wedemeyer was a convinced and active anti-communist. Early in his career he had seen service in China, the Philippines, and Europe. He graduated from the General Staff in 1936, and then spent two years at the War College in Berlin.

WEIZMANN, Chaim, b. 1874. Scientist and Zionist leader. During the war he held an appointment as chemical adviser to the British Ministry of Supply, but his energies were primarily directed to furthering the Zionist cause. From the outset he pressed for the formation of a Jewish Brigade to fight against the Germans. After an interview with Churchill in September 1941 success in this project seemed likely. But despite Weizmann's efforts nothing significant developed until 1944, when Jewish Commandos were used in Europe.

In early 1940, and again in 1941, Weiz-

mann went to the U.S.A. to confer with
Zionist leaders: he met Roosevelt for the
first time in February 1940. In February
1942 a further trip to the U.S.A. on a
scientific mission was cancelled because
Weizmann's son Michael, an R.A.F. pilot,
was reported missing. However, he spent
just over a year in America between 1942
and 1943, devoting himself to the task of
winning support for Zionism among leading political figures and in the State
Department. But he also had to deal with
strife within the Zionist movement itself:
Ben-Gurion, the Palestine leader, was
challenging Weizmann's autocratic
methods of leadership.

In October 1943 Weizmann saw Attlee
and Churchill, receiving assurances of
their commitment to the Jewish cause.
He was summoned by Churchill in early
November 1944 to discuss the partition
of Palestine. But on 5 November Lord
Moyne was assassinated in Cairo by
members of an extremist Zionist organization known as the Stern gang; anti-
Zionist feeling in Britain hardened.

In mid November Weizmann visited
Palestine and was given an overwhelming
reception by the Jewish community. In
the following March he returned to London for a glaucoma operation. A month
later the war with Germany was over.
Weizmann continued to work for a Zionist
settlement in Palestine, and pressed for
increased Jewish immigration from Europe.
He was disappointed by what seemed to
be a retreat from past promises by Churchill in June 1945, and also by the anti-
Zionist Bevin's appointment as Foreign
Secretary in the post-war Labour government.

Weizmann had been active in politics
since his early youth, and had been in
large measure responsible for the Balfour
Declaration. By the time of the war his
gifts for diplomacy were still outstanding,
but he was growing old. He impressed
many people by his deep personal commitment to an idealistic form of Zionism,
and by his persistence in trying to realize
his vision.

WERRA, Franz von, b. 1914. German
fighter pilot who gained celebrity because
of his escape from captivity in Canada.
He was shot down over Kent in September

1940 and interned in a camp in the Lake
District. Within ten days of arriving
there Werra had devised a plan for escape
and he disappeared for three days and
nights. Police and troops were called in
to take part in the search and he was
eventually recaptured and given 3 weeks
in 'the cooler'. He was then transferred
to another camp near the village of Swan-
wick but managed to escape again by
tunnelling under the camp fences.

Impersonating a Dutch pilot in the
R.A.F. who had crash-landed, he demanded to be taken to the nearest R.A.F.
camp, where he was later caught in the
act of stealing a Hurricane plane. After
this second attempt he was shipped to
Canada, where he escaped once more and
made his way by rowing boat to the
U.S.A. Fearing, however, that the
Americans might send him back to Canada,
he fled to Mexico and thence home to
Germany.

His escape had consequences out of all
proportion to its significance as an
individual feat of daring. The information he gave was made into a booklet
which became the Luftwaffe's standard
guide to aircrew and P.O.W. security.
Until Werra's escape German propaganda
—alleging that Nazi prisoners were ill
treated—had played right into the hands
of British interrogators, but his report
gave the lie to the stories of British
brutality.

After a period as an adviser on P.O.W.
camp security he was posted to the
Russian front with No. 53 Fighter Squadron. Although he had been well up with
the other German fighter aces before his
capture his 'count' was now relatively
low and he was therefore credited with 8
more victories—for propaganda purposes
—during the 3 months he spent in Russia.
In October 1941 he was posted to coastal
defence duties in Holland. A few weeks
later, whilst on patrol, his engine developed
a fault and his aircraft dropped into the
sea. The court of inquiry into the loss of
the aircraft said that the accident was due
to engine failure or the pilot's carelessness.

WEYGAND, Maxime, b. 1867. French
general, Supreme Allied Commander at
the time of the fall of France. In August
1939 Weygand was nominated C.-in-C. of

French forces in the Eastern Mediterranean
in the event of mobilization. As the
Germans outflanked the Maginot Line
and stormed into France, Weygand was
summoned from Beirut on 19 May 1940
to assume command of the French armies,
replacing General Gamelin. He also became Supreme Allied Commander. But the
position had by then become hopeless.
On 28 May the evacuation of the B.E.F.
from Dunkirk began; it was completed
on 4 June. The Germans wheeled southwards on 5 June and Weygand ordered
his armies to hold the Somme–Aisne line
at all costs. By 12 June he had come to
the conclusion that the only way to save
his country was to persuade the government to ask for an armistice. The new
Pétain government signed an armistice
on 22 June, and Weygand became
Minister of National Defence.

On 6 September he was made Delegate
General of the Vichy government in
French Africa and took over command of
the land and air forces in that area. He
interpreted the armistice terms in the
narrowest possible way, and never wavered
in his support for the Allies. His 12-
month mission involved extremely complex personal decisions concerning his
relations with Vichy, the British and
United States governments, the Axis
Powers, and de Gaulle. On 18 November
1941 the Vichy government, under heavy
German pressure, dismissed him. He
continued to live in retirement in France
until 12 November 1942 when he was
arrested by the Gestapo and removed to
Germany as a hostage for General Giraud.
Released eventually by Allied forces, he
was again arrested in France on 10 May
1945 and accused of collaboration with the
Germans. He was acquitted in 1948.
Weygand, a man of honour, always acted
strictly on principle in the difficult situations that he had to face.

'WHITE RABBIT'. *See* YEO-THOMAS,
F. F.

WHITTLE, Frank, b. 1907. British aeronautical engineer and air force officer, a
pioneer of jet propulsion. He pursued
single-mindedly his idea for jet-propelled
aircraft. The frustrations that this involved

arose largely because he was dependent
on government policy and support.
Whittle had patented in 1930 basic
designs for a turbojet engine. His company, Power Jets, was engaged on the
development of engine prototypes, and
had Air Ministry backing. In 1940 a high-
level report listed the jet engine among
projects of first priority, and this report
produced more support. But a satisfactory
method of helping Whittle's work was
never really achieved. The Air Ministry
and the Ministry of Aircraft Production at
first gave contracts for the manufacture of
engines to the British Thompson Houston
and Rover companies: these contracts
led to trouble with Power Jets, especially
over patents. By the end of 1941 Power
Jets was given some freedom to manufacture for itself, and became associated
with Rolls-Royce. But in April 1944
Power Jets was nationalized, and became
Power Jets (Research and Development)
Ltd. It was later to become the National
Gas Turbine Establishment.

Although plans were made for the production of jet-powered planes in Britain
in 1940, technical problems developed
between 1941 and 1942 connected with
surging, reliability, and performance of
rotary components, and combustion. These
problems led to modifications in design.
The first flights with Whittle's engine took
place in May 1941. By 1943 flight testing
was possible. The 'Meteor I' aeroplane
was operational in early 1944, and the
production of 'Meteor III's' and
'Vampires' was in progress by the end of
that year. Priority was given to their
production until the summer of 1945,
when the war ended.

The first jet aircraft constructed and
flown were German and Italian. Their
engine designs derived from the designs
that Whittle had patented in the 1930s.

WILHELMINA, Queen of the Netherlands,
b. 1880. On 13 May 1940 she embarked
on a British ship at the Hook, 4 days
after the German army had invaded the
neutral Netherlands. Her ministers joined
her in London soon afterwards, and she
issued a proclamation announcing the
transference of the government of the
Netherlands to the U.K. Throughout the
war she attended to the affairs of govern-

ment, broadcast on special occasions to
the occupied Netherlands, and concerned
herself with the welfare of the Dutch in
England, particularly the 'Engeland-
vaarders'—men and women who had
escaped from occupied territory to join
the forces of the Allies.

In January 1942 the Dutch suffered a
further blow when the Japanese began an
offensive against the Dutch East Indies.
The islands were quickly overrun. Not
until September 1944 did the tide turn
for the Netherlands. In that month the
Allied armies in N.W. Europe reached
the Dutch frontier. By October the three
provinces of Zeeland, Limburg, and North
Brabant had been liberated. At the beginning of 1945 the government-in-exile
resigned, and a provisional government of
very similar composition was formed by the
Queen; this ministry remained in office
until liberation was completed. Queen
Wilhelmina visited the liberated provinces
as a guest of the authorities in March and
returned to her country as Queen on 2
May, 6 days before VE-Day. A woman
of strong religious faith, she revealed in
her autobiography that she was sustained
during the sufferings of the war by her
belief in divine guidance.

WILLKIE, Wendell, b. 1892. American
lawyer and industrialist, an internationalist
and, on occasion, the eyes and ears of
President Roosevelt in the President's
dealings with foreign statesmen. Willkie
was the Republican nominee in the 1940
U.S. presidential elections. He was a surprise candidate, a public utilities expert
who had become well known as a champion
of the rights of the individual against the
New Deal. He did unexpectedly well, and
after his defeat in 1940 visited the U.K.
privately in January 1941, where he met
the King and the Prime Minister, to whom
he brought a letter from Roosevelt. He
went back home to take part in the debate
on Lend-Lease, which he strongly supported. The Bill was passed in March.
During 1941 he was in close touch with
Roosevelt, and in August 1942 he left on
a 31,000-mile world trip as presidential
envoy, going to the Near East, Russia,
and China: in each country he visited the
front lines and met world leaders including
Stalin, Chiang Kai-shek, and de Gaulle.

He returned in mid October, convinced that
Germany would not defeat Russia. He
believed that the post-war world should
become a commonwealth of free nations,
and his internationalism was expressed
in a best-selling book *One World*, which
was published in 1943. In July 1943 he
indicated that he would run for President,
but withdrew in April 1944 after a defeat
in the primaries in isolationist Wisconsin.
He died in October 1944.

Willkie, an unorthodox Republican,
earned the deep respect of Roosevelt. His
internationalist ideas, which challenged a
whole tradition of American isolationism,
prepared the ground for the creation of
the United Nations after the war.

WILMOT, Chester, b. 1911. Australian
journalist who was celebrated for his vivid
front-line reports. In 1940 he became war
correspondent for the Australian Broadcasting Commission, and spent the next
two years in the Middle East—in Syria
and Libya, where he was caught up in the
siege of Tobruk—and New Guinea. In
1944 Wilmot became a war correspondent
for the B.B.C. In this capacity he accompanied the 6th Airborne Division into
Normandy on D-Day, and closely followed
the whole campaign from Normandy to the
Baltic. He sent back first-hand reports of
many operations, especially on the British
and Canadian fronts. He was also present
at the Nuremberg trials of war criminals.

Wilmot was an outstanding broadcaster, a
man of immense energy and concentration.
His unconcern for danger when in pursuit
of a story was matched only by his insistence on authenticity. Once when he was
asked to procure recordings of German
mortar bombs ('Moaning Minnies') he
assembled his recording apparatus in the
thick of an attack, with bombs bursting
so close that the needle was blown off the
disc. The troops were fond of him because
of his reputation for trying to see a situation from the soldiers' viewpoint before
reporting on it.

WILSON, Sir Henry Maitland, b. 1881.
British general (field marshal 1944),
known as 'Jumbo' because of his supposed
elephant-like appearance, who directed
the ill-starred campaign in Greece in 1941,
and who later became Supreme Allied

Commander in the Mediterranean. At the beginning of the war he was G.O.C.-in-C. (in command of the British troops) in Egypt and responsible for its defence under General Wavell's overall Middle East Command. He contributed greatly to the early successes of 1940–1, when the Italians were driven out of Cyrenaica. Although General O'Connor held executive command, Wilson did much of the operational planning and directing during the first stages.

In March 1941 he commanded the British force in Greece, though he had little say in the planning of the campaign. His skilful withdrawals undoubtedly minimized losses. Almost at once Wilson had to face a revolt in Iraq, which he successfully put down. In June and July he captured Syria from the Vichy French. His tact, combined with his hearty, direct manner did much to pacify these politically stormy areas. In 1941 he commanded in the Palestinian, Transjordanian, and Syrian areas. He was G.O.C. the 9th Army, and C.-in-C. Persia-Iraq Command from 1942 to March 1943. Despite his strong, forceful character and a skilled tactical sense he was passed over for the 8th Army command in 1941. But in February 1943 he succeeded Alexander as C.-in-C. Middle East—a command that then included the 8th Army among its forces. In January 1944 Wilson succeeded Eisenhower as Supreme Allied Commander in the Mediterranean. He was concerned there with broad administrative questions of policy and strategy rather than executive command (General Alexander directed the Italian battle). He maintained excellent relations between U.S. and British forces. In November he succeeded Sir John Dill as Head of the British Joint Staff Mission in Washington, and attended the Yalta and Potsdam conferences.

'Jumbo' Wilson was a tall, lumbering man, but his bluff appearance belied his judgment and tact. His military reputation was one of the few which escaped Churchill's criticism.

WINANT, John, b. 1889. American diplomat, U.S. ambassador in London throughout most of the war. A man of understanding, elegance, and charm, he became an extremely popular figure in Great Britain, and was pre-eminently successful in explaining the U.K. in the U.S.A. and the U.S.A. in the U.K. Roosevelt appointed him ambassador to the U.K. in January 1941, and he took up his appointment in February. He succeeded Joseph Kennedy. From the outset he greatly eased the path of Anglo-American relations. He travelled widely, made information about the U.S.A. available to the British people, and encouraged broadcasting from London to the U.S.A. Most American contact with Britain was channelled through the U.S. Embassy, which dealt directly with every British ministry.

In May 1941 Winant visited the U.S.A., returning with promises of American support in the event of an Anglo-Russian alliance. He was with Churchill when news of the Japanese attack on Pearl Harbor was heard over the wireless. He again went to the U.S.A. in February 1942 and in the spring of 1943, and he was responsible for Mrs Roosevelt's visit to the U.K. in October 1942. He attended the 1943 Casablanca and Teheran conferences, and travelled to Malta with Churchill. In 1943, also, he was made American representative on the European Advisory Commission, and he was American representative at the first meeting of the United Nations. He remained ambassador in London well into the Truman administration.

Winant was a shy and sensitive man and his deep devotion to the Anglo-American alliance made him one of America's most successful ambassadors in London. He formed close personal relationships with Churchill and many other British leaders.

WINGATE, Orde, b. 1903. British soldier, a pioneer of novel forms of guerrilla warfare. He achieved fame when his 'Chindit' force operated successfully behind the Japanese lines in Burma.

Wingate arrived in Cairo in October 1940, seconded from an anti-aircraft unit at the request of General Wavell, C.-in-C. Middle East. He was sent to Khartoum to organize assistance for the Ethiopian nationalists, led by the exiled Emperor Haile Selassie, who were in revolt against the Italian occupation. Between January and late May 1941 he was leader of a guerrilla force, 'Gideon Force', which by a series of stratagems managed to secure the evacuation of a number of Italian forts, taking many prisoners. In May the Emperor entered Addis Ababa, which had been taken by a British army from the south on 6 April.

When he returned to Cairo Wingate found the army preoccupied with defeats in North Africa and Greece; he fell ill and attempted suicide. After convalescence in the U.K. he was called by Wavell, by then C.-in-C. India, to help in stemming the advance of the Japanese in Burma. In May 1942 he went to Burma and inspected the terrain before the British retreat. He then put forward proposals for the formation and training of guerrilla forces known as 'long-range penetration groups' for service behind the enemy lines. His plan exploited two novel features of modern war: the possibility of air-drop supplies, and long-range communication by wireless. In February 1943, 8 groups of 'Chindits' (named after *Chinthe*, the dragon-like stone guardian at the entrance to Burmese temples), trained by Wingate in central India, crossed the River Chindwin. Until June, when the survivors returned, the Japanese were harassed, railway lines were cut, the Irrawaddy was crossed and re-crossed, and the feasibility of this type of operation was thoroughly demonstrated. One Chindit commented: 'Compared to what he put us through in training, the operation was a piece of cake.' These exploits captured the imagination of the British public and raised morale in India. The publicity brought him to the notice of Churchill, who took Wingate with him to the Anglo-American meeting at Quebec in August 1943.

Wingate returned to India with authority to direct a large-scale long-range offensive against the Japanese in Burma. He was under the overall command of Lord Louis Mountbatten, the Supreme Commander, S.E. Asia. But Wingate had to face much opposition from men on the spot. In February 1944 his three brigades crossed into Burma, two of them by air. The Japanese began a major offensive against India on 5 March. Chindit activity played a notable part in the failure of the Japanese operation, which was halted by 20 April, paving the way for the British reconquest of Burma. Wingate was killed in an air crash in Assam on 24 March.

He was an unusual man of deep religious conviction. He believed himself to be the instrument of a higher power. This deep-seated belief in his vocation as a soldier made him a successful innovator and leader, but a difficult subordinate. Churchill said of him: 'He was a man of genius who might well have become also a man of destiny.'

WITZLEBEN, Erwin von, b. 1881. German general involved, with an ever-widening circle of conspirators, in a number of plots against Hitler. All these plots failed to achieve their purpose: originally to capture Hitler and put him on trial, but later to kill him. The reasons for their failure are debatable, but among them were consistent bad luck and recurrent failures of nerve and leadership. The outbreak of the war in September 1939 gave the conspirators more scope but, since Witzleben was no longer serving in Berlin, it became difficult to concentrate sufficient support in the capital.

Witzleben became C.-in-C. West in May 1941. In July, after the fall of France, he was made a field marshal. An attempt against Hitler was planned for the summer of 1942: Witzleben went into hospital for an operation in March, and while he was there Hitler dismissed him, leaving the conspirators with no trustworthy senior serving general. By early 1943 the mood of the country had changed and the time seemed ripe for success. An attempt took place on 20 July 1944, when Stauffenberg placed a bomb in the conference room in Hitler's H.Q. at Rastenburg. The bomb exploded but failed to kill Hitler; it was some time before the assembled conspirators in Berlin knew of this failure, but they had, in any case, not acted with sufficient speed and certainty to grasp control of the governmental machinery. Witzleben was among the scores of conspirators arrested. He was put on trial, found guilty, and hanged in circumstances of great brutality in August 1944.

WOLFF, Karl, b. 1900. German S.S. general, best known for his negotiations with the Allies over the surrender of the German army in Italy. Wolff was Himmler's Chief of Staff before the war, and acted as his liaison officer with Hitler's

H.Q. until 1943. He was a man of some charm and was intimate with Himmler, who called him 'Wolfchen'. He had experience of Italian affairs dating back to the 1930s, and he accompanied Hitler to Rome in 1940.

On 8 September 1943, when Italy surrendered, he was appointed military governor of North Italy. When Mussolini returned to Italy on 27 September, Wolff accompanied him and helped to re-establish the skeleton Fascist régime under German control. His duties, apart from liaison with Mussolini, were to organize the departure of Italian recruits for training in Germany and to contain the Partisans.

Wolff's peace initiative began with a meeting between his representative and a representative of Allen Dulles of the OSS. An anti-Fascist prisoner was released as a token of good faith, and Wolff subsequently made two visits to Switzerland for talks. But the negotiations were interrupted when he was summoned to Berlin, where he met Hitler on 18 April 1945. Also there was some American hesitancy following the death of Roosevelt. The formal documents of surrender were signed on 29 April. Wolff at first arrested the commander of the German forces in Italy, who declined to accept the idea of surrender; however, agreement was finally reached to effect the surrender on 2 May. Wolff's success during March and April, when the situation was complex and plot-ridden, was to keep his negotiations secret while maintaining relations with both Mussolini and the Partisans.

WOOD, Sir Henry, b. 1869. British conductor, who endeavoured through the medium of the Promenade Concerts or 'Proms' to increase the number of people who could appreciate orchestral music. Originally an organist, he had a long and distinguished career as a conductor, and his connection with the Queen's Hall in London started in 1895. After the destruction of this famous concert hall by enemy action he transferred to the Albert Hall, where he continued his concerts of classical music. To those who lived through the era the Proms will always be associated with Sir Henry Wood and especially with his determination that even under war conditions civilized music should be made

available to his countrymen. He died in August 1944.

WOOD, Sir Kingsley, b. 1881. British politician, Secretary of State for Air from May 1938, who by March 1940 had at least doubled R.A.F. fighting strength. In April he became Lord Privy Seal. In May he advised the friend he admired, Neville Chamberlain, to resign. Under Churchill he was Chancellor of the Exchequer.

In 1940 he made the innovation that income tax should thereafter be deducted at source, compulsorily. Under the influence of eminent economists, including J. M. Keynes, the Budget soon became a tool of the war economy, and there was a price control policy. In 1941 Wood increased standard income tax to the high rate of 10s. in the pound, and reduced tax exemptions. By these means he increased the number of tax-payers by two million, but made compensation by granting credits to be claimed after the war. This, in effect, introduced compulsory saving. By his controls Wood managed to contain the increase in the cost of living at 30 per cent above that of 1939; much of the credit was his. Kingsley Wood died in September 1943, on the day he planned to announce his 'Pay As You Earn' income tax scheme. He was brisk but friendly, was business-like, and would listen to advice. People enjoyed working for him. The government valued his skill at parrying criticism, and his firmness once his mind was made up.

WOOLTON, Lord (Frederick Marquis), b. 1883. War-time Minister of Food, a successful businessman who applied business methods to the huge task of feeding a nation at war. He had served from September 1939 as director-general at the Ministry of Supply, concerned with supplies to the Forces. In April 1940 Chamberlain asked him if he would accept the post of Minister of Food. Even though this meant abandoning considerable business interests Woolton agreed. He made his war-time reputation in this office. Occasionally Woolton's methods meant by-passing orthodox Whitehall procedure. Once he managed to anger the Chancellor, Kingsley Wood, over a wheat purchase. Later Wood said to him: 'You are the only minister who ever comes to me to apologize for saving money.'

Woolton took pains to explain his policies to the public, and to ration only goods of which he could guarantee supply. His department's motto was: 'We not only cope, we care.' He instituted mobile canteens, and he gave press conferences and chatty radio talks to explain such necessary complications as his 'points' rationing system, or to encourage people not to waste food. He was particularly anxious to feed the nation scientifically, and to provide extra milk, oranges, and vitamins for expectant mothers and children; also, he tried to ensure proper hospital diets. In consequence he received photographs of healthy children inscribed: 'One of Lord Woolton's babies.'

In November 1943 Churchill made him Minister of Reconstruction with a seat in the War Cabinet. His new department dealt with the provision of food, housing, and work. It was particularly involved with planning for the post-war years, and it did some preliminary work towards a National Health Service.

Woolton's name became a household word. It was very largely due to his work that food rationing, which could so easily have been a source of serious resentment and discord, was accepted stoically and cheerfully.

Y

YAMAMOTO, Isoroku, b. 1884. Japanese admiral and naval C.-in-C. The man who devised the plan for the attack on the U.S. Pacific Fleet at Pearl Harbor, he became a national hero in Japan after his death in 1943. Before the war Yamamoto had been instrumental in building up the Japanese air force and navy, which he equipped with aircraft carriers. He was personally opposed to war with the U.S.A. and he was in some danger of assassination by extremists because of his political views.

In 1940 Yamamoto conceived the idea of the Pearl Harbor attack as a means of giving Japan control in the Pacific, by crippling the American fleet at one blow. Japan decided on war in December 1941 and Yamamoto won approval for his plan despite strong naval opposition. The air torpedo attack, by 360 aircraft from a position 300 miles from Pearl Harbor, was launched on 7 December, and the Americans were taken completely by surprise: 8 battleships, 11 other naval vessels, and nearly 200 planes were put out of action. However, the oil tankers were not bombed, and there were no aircraft carriers at Pearl Harbor. The success at Pearl Harbor was followed by a further success in March 1942 at the Battle of the Java Sea, when Allied hopes of creating a naval front in the Dutch East Indies against the Japanese collapsed.

Yamamoto was now set on a new policy. He argued that, since American resources were so much greater than the Japanese, Japan's aim should be to inflict maximum damage in minimum time: the objective should be the destruction of the American fleet and the seizure of Hawaii, which was defended by the base on Midway. Before this plan went into effect the Battle of the Coral Sea took place on 7 May. The losses on each side were small, but the myth of Japanese invulnerability had been dispelled. The Midway plan went ahead, though Japanese morale was low, and fully trained pilots were scarce. By this time, too, the Americans had cracked the Japanese code. They knew of the attack and were prepared to defend Midway. Hostilities began on 4 June 1942. By 6 June Yamamoto, who had taken over

command, ordered a retreat. The Japanese were heavily defeated: they lost twice as many aeroplanes and ten times as many men as the Americans, while four carriers were destroyed for only one American loss. Midway was one of the decisive naval battles of history.

Later in June Yamamoto ordered the occupation of Guadalcanal in the southern Solomons, where the Japanese began to build an airfield. But an American task force landed there in August. For 5 months a protracted battle was fought for the island. It ended on 7 February 1943 when the Japanese finally withdrew. Losses had been heavy on both sides, but the Americans had the advantage, for example in their radar defences.

On 17 April 1943 the Americans picked up a radio signal which gave details of a flight which Yamamoto intended to make the following day. Fighters were ordered to intercept him, and his plane was shot down with no survivors. He was given a state funeral.

Yamamoto was an intelligent, well-informed sailor with considerable experience of the West—especially the U.S.A., where he had studied at Harvard and served as a naval attaché. Pearl Harbor had been an undoubted short-term success, but strategists have since questioned whether it could have had any long-term effectiveness. Certainly Yamamoto made a mistake in repeating the same pattern at the battle of Midway. He was convinced, however, that in the long run Japan must lose the war, and that quickly won successes would enable her to obtain the best terms from the U.S.A.

YAMASHITA, Tomoyuki, b. 1885. Japanese general, known as 'the Tiger of the Philippines'. In late 1940 he was made Inspector General of the Japanese air force by the War Minister, General Tojo, and was appointed to head a military mission to Germany. In December 1940 he saw Hitler and Mussolini; his report concluded that it would be unwise to declare war on the U.S. and Britain: the air force should be improved and the army mechanized before engaging in war. His report did not please Tojo.

In December 1941, when Japan attacked the American Pacific Fleet at Pearl Harbor, he was commanding the 25th Army and under orders to invade Malaya and capture Singapore. On 7 December the 25th Army landed in Thailand and began the invasion of Malaya. Although this had been expected, no decisive action was taken against the invading forces, and Yamashita succeeded in bluffing the Allies into believing that his army was better equipped and of greater strength than in truth it was. Speed and surprise were the two main factors leading to the success of his invasion and the capture of Singapore, which was surrendered unconditionally by the British G.O.C., General Percival, on 15 February 1942. Here leaflets dropped over the city contained a message from Yamashita advising immediate surrender of the British forces and promising to treat the defenders as soldiers-in-arms. In Churchill's words the defeat was 'the greatest disaster to British arms which our history records'.

Tojo had become Premier in October 1941, and he seems to have feared that the War Ministry might have to go to Yamashita. He had Yamashita posted to command the 1st Army Group in Manchuria. In July 1944, when the Tojo government fell, the new government recalled Yamashita to become supreme commander in the Philippines, where the Japanese were being heavily pressed by the resurgent Americans under MacArthur. In October Yamashita arrived on the island of Luzon, and planned to fight the major battle there. However, he was overruled by the War Ministry and ordered not to surrender the island of Leyte. In October the Americans landed there in strength, and by Christmas all resistance was over. The Japanese forces had been considerably weakened in this action, and in January 1945, when the Americans invaded Luzon, Yamashita withdrew to the hills, leaving Manila an open city. It was defended against his orders; some of the heaviest fighting and atrocities of the war occurred during the battle for Manila. Despite lack of supplies, Yamashita still fought on until 2 September, when he surrendered after hearing of Japan's capitulation. He was put on trial for war crimes on 29 October, condemned to death, and executed on 27 February 1946.

Yamashita was a formidable general of the old school, with a deep personal devotion to the Emperor. Unlike many high-ranking Japanese officers he did not engage in politics, nor did he use power to further his own ends. He claimed that he would have prevented the atrocities that took place under his command had circumstances permitted.

YEO-THOMAS, Forest Frederick, b. 1902. An agent of the British S.O.E. whose sobriquets were, amongst others, the 'White Rabbit' and 'Shelley'. Bilingual in French and English and an ardent Gaullist, he was three times parachuted into France to work with the French Resistance. In 1939 he had enlisted in the R.A.F., becoming a sergeant-interpreter with the Advanced Air Striking Force. Later he was commissioned. Early in 1943 he was dropped by parachute into France for liaison with the various underground organizations and to get the movements in the northern zone of France to accept central direction for their military activity. He was forced to return to France later that year following the arrest of the leading Gaullist, Jean Moulin, and the subsequent disintegration of the fabric of command in the *Maquis*. His mission was not only to attempt to restore Gaullist control in the face of communist counterclaims, but also to get some idea of the *Maquis*'s requirements in the way of armaments and supplies. His task proved hazardous and he was all but captured six times before his eventual return to England. A particularly remarkable incident was his journey from Lyons to Paris, during which he found himself forced to sustain a conversation with Barbié, the head of the Lyons Gestapo. In February 1944 he made his third visit to France, to attempt to rescue his friend Pierre Brossolette from Rennes prison. He was betrayed by an arrested subordinate, and captured by German security officers on the steps of Passy Métro station. He was subjected to the most appalling tortures in an attempt to force him to reveal information useful to the Germans. Despite such barbarities as being immersed head downwards in ice-cold water whilst his legs and arms were chained, he revealed nothing. After a series of bold attempts to escape from various French prisons, he was transferred to Buchenwald con-

centration camp, where he assumed the
identity of a Frenchman named Chouquet
who died of typhus on the day before an
order for Yeo-Thomas's execution arrived.
In April 1945 he finally succeeded in
escaping to the Allied lines.

Yeo-Thomas was educated in France
and in England. Although under age, he

served in the latter part of World War I,
and subsequently fought with the Poles
against the Russians during 1919 and 1920.
He was captured by the Bolsheviks but
escaped the night before he was due to be
shot. Between the wars he worked in Paris,
from 1932 as a director of the fashion house
of Molyneux. He was awarded the G.C.

Z

ZEITZLER, Kurt von, b. 1895. German general; a brilliant staff officer and an expert in mobile warfare, he was appointed to exacting posts while still a relatively junior commander. He served as a corps Chief of Staff in the Polish and French campaigns of 1940 and then, in 1941, as Chief of Staff of the 1st Panzer Group (later 1st Panzer Army) in Russia. He succeeded Halder as Chief of the Army General Staff in September 1942.

Zeitzler was to some extent a 'yes-man', and had all the qualifications for the post of Hitler's assistant: he simply required of every staff officer that he should 'believe in the Führer and his methods of command'. But his faith in Hitler quickly began to wane.

In the autumn of 1942 the Germans were overstretched in Russia, and it was becoming apparent that the Russians could encircle them at Stalingrad. Hitler persistently refused Zeitzler's request that Paulus's 6th Army should be allowed to withdraw and, in January 1943, to capitulate. After the inevitable surrender of the 6th Army, however, Zeitzler was able to persuade Hitler to agree to strategic withdrawals at Moscow and Leningrad. In the spring of 1943 Zeitzler planned operation 'Citadel', a German offensive at Kursk; but this did not take place until July—too late for success. Then in spring 1944 came the Crimean disaster. By now Zeitzler was ill and disillusioned. In July 1944, after the German collapse on the Upper Dnieper, Zeitzler resigned his appointment on grounds of ill-health. Hitler had him dismissed from the army without the customary right to wear uniform. Zeitzler had an attractive personality and, for a time, a talent for dealing with Hitler. It was remarked of him by a diplomatic observer that 'this new Chief of Staff is not in the old Prussian tradition'. But in the end he proved as intractable to the Führer as officers who were in that tradition.

ZHUKOV, Georgi, b. 1896. Russian general, probably the most powerful Russian commander of the war. He had already made his name in 1939 by destroying the Japanese 6th Army in Mongolia, Japan's heaviest defeat before the war.

On 3 February 1941, Red Army Day, he wrote an article in *Pravda* about the new professionalism of the army. In fact the Red army still had much obsolete equipment, and the production of new weapons and tanks was slow. It was particularly short of motorized transport. Very few soldiers were experienced in warfare, and there was a lack of specialized troops, notably of tank crews.

Germany attacked Russia on 22 June 1941, with striking initial success. On 19 July Stalin took over the command of the Commissariat of Defence, at the same time becoming C.-in-C. of the army. Zhukov became director of the High Command of the army and, in August 1942, Deputy Commissar for Defence. He played an important part in the overall strategy of the war and was personally involved in the defence of Leningrad and Moscow, the battles of Stalingrad and Kursk, the campaign in the Ukraine which led to the liberation of Belorussia, and, finally, the Russian capture of Berlin. Here he signed the document formally concluding the war, on 8 May 1945, and afterwards became head of the Russian military administration.

As a field commander Zhukov was forceful and imaginative. He served with distinction at the unsuccessful defence of Smolensk in August 1941, and on 11 September he replaced Voroshilov in command of the northern sector and became responsible for the defence of Leningrad. He was called from there to Moscow, and on 10 October was appointed C.-in-C. of the whole Russian western front. He held this front against two German autumn offensives, and on 6 December 1941 a Russian counter-offensive was launched. The entire German front was pushed back, but by February operations were at a standstill. The next great battle was for Stalingrad. In mid November 1942 the counter-offensive, partly planned by Zhukov, began; the Russian armies broke through from the north-west and the south of Stalingrad, meeting on the River Don, and effectively encircling General Paulus's 6th Army. Although General von Manstein's forces were only 25 miles west of Stalingrad, no attempt was made to link up the two German armies, and Paulus surrendered on 31 January 1943. In July 1943 Zhukov prepared to counter the Kursk offensive. The Germans were heavily defeated in the biggest tank battle of the war, and Hitler abandoned the operation.

In June 1944 four Soviet armies, including those on the Belorussian front under Zhukov, broke through the German Brobruisk–Mogilev–Vitebsk line. By September Zhukov was just outside Warsaw; but he did not offer support to the Polish insurgents who were engaged in a desperate battle with the Germans (ultimately being beaten into surrender) and the Russian forces did not take the city until January 1945. On 16 April Zhukov launched the final offensive of the Oder, and Berlin capitulated on 2 May after a battle lasting for a week—during which time Zhukov is supposed to have kept himself awake by sipping cognac.

Zhukov, a brilliant general, was also a remarkable personality and proud of his exploits. He was a good-natured extrovert, whose friendship with General Eisenhower was frowned upon by Stalin.

ZUCKERMAN, Solly, b. 1904. British scientist who acted as adviser to various military organizations, including Combined Operations H.Q. His unique contributions to the British war effort began with his study of the effect of bomb explosions on the human body. Zuckerman was at the time a lecturer in the Department of Human Anatomy at Oxford, and his research was undertaken at the request of the Ministry of Home Security. He showed that bomb casualties were due chiefly to the indirect effects of blast, and

his conclusions influenced in a major way not only plans for defence against enemy air attack but also those for the Allied bombing offensive.

Towards the end of 1942—by which time the importance of utilizing scientific knowledge and methodology in war planning had been recognized by most war leaders, civil and military—Zuckerman went to Cairo to carry out a study of British bombing operations in North Africa, with the purpose of improving techniques and assessing the potentialities of aerial bombing. His conclusions and recommendations were given operational effect in the planned bombing of Pantelleria in May and June 1943 (resulting virtually in the 'capture' of the island by bombardment) and in the aerial onslaught on communications in Italy that preceded the Allied invasion of Sicily. This latter attack demonstrated that a railway network could be methodically disrupted by a scientific choice of targets and proper timing.

In 1943 Zuckerman, as scientific adviser on planning to the Allied Expeditionary Air Forces, was asked to make recommendations that could have a vitally important effect on the success or failure of the projected invasion of Europe. When the troops eventually landed, the Germans would depend heavily on the railways for transporting reinforcements to the battle areas. The Allies hoped to put the railways out of action by bombing. Zuckerman produced a plan for doing so by concentrating on the destruction of control centres and repair and maintenance services and installations. In the event this plan was effective and immensely hampered the Germans during the critical phase of the Allied build-up.